{ ONE SHOW INTERACTIVE/ volume III }

advertising's best
interactive and new media

COLUMBIA COLLEGE CHICAGO
LIBRARY
600 S. MICHIGAN AVENUE
CHICAGO, IL 60605

{A PRESENTATION OF/ the one club for art & copy }

PRESIDENT	Bob Barrie
EXECUTIVE DIRECTOR	Mary Warlick
INTERACTIVE DIRECTOR	Kevin Swanepoel
EDITOR	Kevin Swanepoel
CONTRIBUTING EDITOR	Diane Deely
CD-ROM PROGRAMMERS	Alan Alston
DESIGN AND LAYOUT	Kevin Swanepoel Diane Deely
PUBLISHER & DISTRIBUTOR	Rotovision S.A.
SALES OFICE	Sheridan House 112-116a Western Road Hove, East Sussex, BN3 1DD United Kingdom
TELEPHONE	+44 (0) 1273-72-7268
FAX	+44 (0) 1273-72-7269
IN ASSOCIATION WITH	The One Club for Art & Copy 32 East 21st Street, New York, NY 10010
TELEPHONE	(212) 979-1900
FAX	(212) 979-5006
EMAIL	orders@oneclub.com
WEB SITE	www.oneclub.com
COPYRIGHT © 2000	A collection by The One Club for Art & Copy, Inc. All rights reserved. No part of this book or CD ROM may be reproduced in any way by any means whatsoever without express permission in writing from the owners.
FIRST PRINTING	ISBN 2-88046-459-5
PRODUCTION & SEPARATION	Provision, Singapore
TELEPHONE	(65) 334-7720
FAX	(65) 334-7721

{2000 ANNUAL/ contents}

IV	The One Club for Art & Copy
V	One Show Interactive Director
VI	Judging Criteria
VII	One Show Interactive Judges
VIII	About the Judges

GOLD SILVER BRONZE AWARDS

2	Banners
10	Beyond the Banner
12	Promotional Advertising
30	Corporate Image - B2C
48	Corporate Image - B2B
64	e-Commerce
70	Integrated Branding
78	Broadband
88	Self-Promotion
102	Non-Profit Organizations
112	College Competition

MERIT AWARDS

116	Banners
146	Beyond the Banner
163	Promotional Advertising
183	Corporate Image - B2C
209	Corporate Image - B2B
219	e-Commerce
223	Integrated Branding
229	Broadband
236	Self-Promotion
250	Non-Profit Organizations
254	College Competition
256	Corporate Profiles
274	Index

{THE ONE CLUB/ for art & copy}

The One Club for Art & Copy, based in New York City, was founded in 1975 and is a non-profit organization designed to maintain the highest standards of creativity in advertising. Its 1,000 members include many of advertising's most respected art directors and copywriters, as well as students of advertising.

As part of its mission to promote high standards of creative excellence, The One Club produces the advertising industry's most prestigious awards program, The One Show. Judged by a panel of the advertising industry's elite creative directors, this annual event acknowledges excellence in art direction and copywriting in a variety of categories, including television, radio, newspapers, magazines, billboards and public service announcements. The coveted One Show "Gold Pencils" are regarded as the zenith of achievement in the advertising world.

The One Club regularly produces a variety of events and programs that encourage aspiring advertising types to hone their craft.

These programs include:

- "Gold on Gold" lectures (award-winning industry professionals discuss the creative process)
- Portfolio reviews
- The One Show College Competition
- Creative workshops
- *one. a magazine* — a quarterly publication by and for advertising creatives
- One Club gallery exhibitions
- The One Show annual, the indispensable hardcover reference showcasing the best advertising worldwide
- One Show Interactive annual, the first book of its kind, highlighting the best new media advertising

In 1995, The One Club established an education department, dedicated to fostering the creative talents of advertising students nationwide. The department administers scholarships to outstanding students in advertising programs at a select number of colleges and advertising schools throughout the country.

In 1998, The One Club launched One Show Interactive, the first award show dedicated exclusively to advertising in new media. With the One Show Interactive awards, The One Club extended its mission of recognizing creative excellence to the new media field.

In addition to producing One Show Interactive, The One Club has supported the new media community through a series of exhibitions focusing on new techniques and highlighting creativity in online advertising. "Web Sites at an Exhibition" in 1997 and "New Media at an Exhibition" in 1998 attracted audiences from both traditional advertising sectors and the new media community.

{THE ONE CLUB/ interactive director}

With the One Show Interactive now in its third year, things are really beginning to happen. The days are long gone when movement across the screen represented an interactive breakthrough, or when online advertising was limited to the banner. The internet has established itself as an important new medium, and in the last couple of years the advertising industry has finally embraced it. Working on interactive accounts has become a vibrant alternative for top creatives, opening up avenues where they can reinvent their careers and break new ground. On the other side of the fence, traditional brick and mortar companies have realized the necessity of using the internet as part of their complete marketing strategy.

The result of all this is the kind of environment where creative boundaries are always being challenged. And in more ways than one, the keyword is interaction: traditional agencies now need to think across all mediums, and new media agencies must incorporate established advertising concepts, so that neither are left out in the cold. As the winners in this year's show prove, it's the integration of the old and the new that provides us with truly exciting work.

Kevin Swanepoel
Interactive Director
Editor

{JUDGING CRITERIA/
awarding excellence in new media}

THE OBJECTIVE — To award pencils for new media that excels in all areas—concept, graphic design, architecture and technology. The primary focus must be on meeting an advertising objective.

CONCEPT — Relating to the creativity of the idea/mission behind the interactive advertising and the innovative application of technology toward its end.

GRAPHIC DESIGN — When judging the graphic qualities of the work, all aspects related to visual presentation, such as the color, type design and page layout, were considered.

COPY — Effective writing which generates interest and conveys information is crucial to the success of online advertising.

INFORMATION ARCHITECTURE — Each entry was judged on its ease of navigation and the degree to which the work's structure, links and interaction effectively achieved its purpose—did the site, banner or digital piece lead the viewer to the most important aspects of the site?

INNOVATION — One Show Interactive acknowledges designers and programmers who creatively use cutting-edge technology to achieve an advertising or branding objective rather than merely to produce really "cool stuff" for technology's sake.

{ ONE SHOW INTERACTIVE/ judges }

ALAN ALSTON
radarboy studios, Cape Town

PETER ARNDT
FCB Worldwide, New York

TOM BEEBY
Modem Media. Poppe Tyson, Wesport

MATT BERNINGER
Icon Nicholson, New York

KIM CARTER
EURO RSCG/DSW Partners, Salt Lake City

KEVIN CHIU
R/GA Interactive, New York

MATT CUMMING
EURO RSCG Partnership, Sydney

HILLMAN CURTIS
hillmancurtis.com, New York

KEVIN DREW DAVIS
Wieden + Kennedy, New York

BERNIE DECHANT
Sapient, San Francisco

MATT FREEMAN
DDB Digital, New York

DAVID GLAZE
Genex Interactive, Los Angeles

SABINE GRAMMERSDORF
OlgilvyInteractive, New York

JAMES HILTON
AKQA, London

MATT JONES
Sapient, London

DARRELL KANIPE
Martin Interactive, Richmond

RICHARD MELLOR
Hyperinteractive, London

SVEN MENTEL
Elephant Seven, Hamburg

CLEMENT MOK
Sapient, San Francisco

CHRIS NEEDHAM
AGENCY.COM, New York

PJ PEREIRA
AgêncinaClick, São Paulo

ANETTE SCHOLZ
Scholz & Volkmer, Wiesbaden

PETER SEIDLER
Razorfish, New York

JANIS NAKANO SPIVACK
Organic, San Francisco

KOTARO SUGIYAMA
Dentsu, Tokyo

TOM SUITER
marchFIRST, San Francisco

PACO VIÑOLY
Lot21 Interactive Advertising Group, San Francisco

MICHAEL VOLKMER
Scholz & Volkmer, Wiesbaden

CHRIS WORTH
OgilvyInteractive, Paris

{ONE SHOW INTERACTIVE/ judges}

ALAN ALSTON
Head Scientist
radarboy studios, Cape Town

Alan was one of the founding members of Armadillo Interactive and instrumental in the company's eventual growth into OgilvyInteractive, South Africa. Moving from an initial focus on broadband multimedia and CD-ROM development, he still focuses on multimedia, but with the narrowband realities of the web added to the mix.

He recently joined radarboy studios—a poineer in scaleable vector graphics and narrowband communications devices.

He has worked with such clients as Volkswagon, Audi, SAB, NIB, and IOL, and has been the recipient of local and international awards.

Alan is also founder of e-vent, a web-based entertainment portal.

PETER ARNDT
Associate Creative Director
Interactive, FCB Worldwide, New York

Peter's passions are brand building, interactivity, and music. Currently at FCB Worldwide, Peter has built and co-leads a group focusing on interactive brand advertising with clients like Jeep, Chrysler, Padron Cigars, Warner Bros., Comedy Central, ShopVac, Coleman, and Little Caesars.

Peter graduated from CCS in Detroit with a B.F.A. in Graphic Communications majoring in Art Direction. He's worked at various other ad agencies, including Campbell-Ewald and McCann-Erickson. Peter also writes and produces music in his own studio as an outlet for his more abstract ideas.

TOM BEEBY
VP/Creative Director
Modem Media. Poppe Tyson, Wesport

Tom is responsible for Modem Media. Poppe Tyson's IBM and JC Penney creative product. From ensuring adherence to established brand equities and web standards, to providing and implementing a creative vision and monitoring strategic accuracy, Tom plays a crucial role in the development of these initiatives globally.

Tom ensures that all of the work produced for these clients stays true to the vision of establishing long-term customer relationships through the employment of MeBusiness practices.

Tom joined the agency from Bastoni Barnes, where he wrote print, radio and direct mail campaigns for Seagram's, Tag Heuer, Dunn & Bradstreet, GE, Exxon and Mercedes.

MATT BERNINGER
Creative Director
Icon Nicholson, New York

An accomplished art and creative director, Matt coaches designers in visual identity development for interactive environments. He supervises art production, graphics development, and design guidelines on projects for clients such as Thomas Register, Reader's Digest, and Mashantucket Pequot Museum. Matt's unique strength lies in his ability to match target-audience demographics with a user interface that best supports the client's brand identity.

He recently served as art director in Icon Nicholson's relaunch of The Metropolitan Museum of Art web site and online store (www.metmuseum.org).

Matt graduated from the University of Cincinnati, College of Design, Art, Architecture and Planning.

{ ONE SHOW INTERACTIVE/ judges }

KIM CARTER
Creative Director Interactive
EURO RSCG/DSW Partners, Salt Lake City

Kim has directed and produced groundbreaking work for Iomega and Intel and the Intel "Web Outfitter" Service Site.

His online and offline work for a variety of accounts has garnered awards in a broad spectrum of categories including identity, packaging, collateral, advertising and web.

Some of the many honors Kim has received include awards from Communication Arts, the Clios, Addys, The One Show, and the New York Art Directors Club.

KEVIN CHIU
Senior Art Director
R/GA Interactive, New York

Kevin serves as the creative lead for R/GA's IBM account, and has lead the development and design of over 30 IBM web sites and wireless applications including IBM.com. Prior to joining R/GA, Kevin was associate creative director at Nicholson NY, where he worked on a variety of interactive projects for Sony, IBM, Motorola, General Electric, and the Manshantucket Pequot Museum. During his first tenure with IBM, Kevin pioneered the first rich media banners that in 1997 won IBM its first interactive Gold Pencil and a Clio nomination.

In addition to five Gold Pencils, two Clios, and a Cannes Gold Cyber Lion, Kevin won "Best of Show" at the 1999 One Show Interactive Awards for his game "Snowcraft." Kevin has served on the jury panel of the One Show Interactive and the London Advertising Awards.

MATT CUMMING
Executive Creative Director/Partner
EURO RSCG Partnership, Sydney

Matt spent a few years in the music video industry working as a stylist and art director before starting a career in advertising as an art director for Saatchi & Saatchi and EURO RSCG in Sydney. He worked with clients such as Toyota, British Airways and Philips.

In 1996, he established the interactive department for EURO RSCG Sydney. In 1998 it was named Interactive Agency of the Year by local industry trade magazines *B&T* and *Adnews*, and again in 1999 by *Adnews*.

Matt has served as a judge for The London International Advertising Awards, the Cannes Cyber Lions, and Australia's A.W.A.R.D.

Matt's awards include a 1998 Yahoo!/*Adnews* Internet best online ad award, as well as awards from the One Show Interactive and Ad-Tech.

HILLMAN CURTIS
Principal
hillmancurtis.com, New York

Hillman's innovative use of motion graphic design has garnered him the Communication Arts Award of Excellence, a One Show Gold Pencil, New Media Invision Bronze, the South by Southwest Conference's "Best Use of Design" and "Best of Show," and a *How* magazine Top 10 Web Site.

His work is also featured in major design magazines and books. Hillman has appeared as a speaker at design conferences worldwide. His company's current client roster includes Intel, Iomega, 3com, Hewlett-Packard, OgilvyOne, DSW, SonicNet, Macromedia, Capitol Records, Lycos, WebTV and Sun. His book, *Designing Flash Motion Graphics*, was published February 2000.

Hillman also acts as a strategic advisor to Razorfish.

{ONE SHOW INTERACTIVE/ judges}

KEVIN DREW DAVIS
Interactive Creative Director
Wieden + Kennedy, New York

Kevin joined Wieden + Kennedy, Portland, in early 1997, charged with integrating interactive capabilities within the agency's global network.

To date, he has produced interactive work for Nike, Calvin Klein's cKone, Microsoft, ESPN, HypoVereinsbank, Audi, AltaVista and Suretrade, and has received numerous awards for Wieden + Kennedy's online work.

Prior to Wieden + Kennedy, Kevin worked for GSD&M and The Richards Group in Texas, and eventually became one of the founders of BlueMarble ACG in New York.

He is now focusing on the interactive efforts for Wieden's rapidly expanding New York office.

BERNIE DECHANT
Creative Director
Sapient, San Francisco

Bernie co-founded Adjacency in 1995, where, as art director, he helped lead a multidisciplinary team to strategize, design, and develop web presences for Apple Computer, Caterpillar, Esprit, Land Rover, Nordstrom, Patagonia, Specialized, Tag Heuer, Williams Sonoma and Virgin Entertainment. His team and their work have been recognized by *Graphis*, *Critique*, and *Print*, as well as by the Clio Awards and The One Club.

In 1999, Sapient acquired Adjacency. Since then Bernie has led Sapient's San Francisco creative group, continuing to produce high-quality work including the award-winning redesign of Adobe.com.

MATT FREEMAN
Co-Chief Creative Officer/Managing Partner
DDB Digital, New York

Matt runs DDB Digital's creative network and drives the operations and growth of the agency.

Previously, Matt was executive creative director of Modem Media. Poppe Tyson. Matt has worked on many national and global brands such as Johnson & Johnson, Hasbro, IBM, Dean Witter, Kodak, Valvoline, Chase, Minolta and the Fluid Milk Processors Association.

Matt's work has won numerous awards from such competitions and events as the Art Directors Club, Cannes, New York Festivals, CEBA, FSC, Ad-Tech, the International ANDY Awards, and The One Show, and he has served as a judge for the Clio Awards, the ANDY's and the Hatch Awards. Matt has also been recognized by publications including *The Wall Street Journal*, *CNNfn*, *CNBC*, *AdAge*, *Adweek*, *Forrester Research*, *ID* and *Creativity*.

DAVID GLAZE
Creative Director
Genex Interactive, Los Angeles

David brings more than 15 years of advertising and graphic design experience to Genex.

David's work has won recognition from design competitions including the Communication Arts annuals, One Show Interactive, and the International Automotive Advertising Awards. He also frequently serves as a judge for interactive competitions and speaks at industry events.

His experience in graphic design includes many years at The Designory in Long Beach, California developing projects for major automotive manufacturers. As an art director, he worked at Saatchi & Saatchi in Los Angeles and Benton & Bowles in New York. He earned a B.F.A. in Graphic Design from the University of Michigan School of Art.

{ ONE SHOW INTERACTIVE/ judges }

SABINE GRAMMERSDORF
Associate Creative Director
OgilvyInteractive, New York

As associate creative director, Sabine develops creative strategies, technical solutions, and and works to maintain the integrity of the project's concept.

Before joining OgilvyInteractive Sabine was an art director at Elephant Seven Multimedia GmbH.

Sabine has received distictions in publications such as the Art Directors Club annual and German Multimedia annual.

She has also won numerous awards, including a London International Advertising Award and a One Show Interactive Gold Pencil.

JAMES HILTON
Executive Creative Director
AKQA, London

James oversees and guides the award-winning creative team at AKQA, which is the UK's largest independent new media agency.

AKQA's clients include Microsoft, BMW, Orange, Sainsbury's, Nike, Sega, Carlsberg, Nestle and Land Rover.

MATT JONES
Creative Director
Sapient, London

Matt has five years experience in building web sites from concept to delivery for some of the biggest brand names.

He has been involved in the birth of large news and information sites in the UK, including the BAFTA award-winning BBC News Online.

At Sapient, Matt is responsible for guiding the concept development, design, and information architecture process to create user-centered, effective e-commerce and e-business solutions for start-ups and established brands.

Through teaching and competition/theory work, Matt is exploring how digital design through new platforms such as wireless internet access is permeating and affecting architecture and the environment.

DARRELL KANIPE
Senior Writer
Martin Interactive, Richmond

Darrell is a 1993 graduate of the University of North Carolina at Chapel Hill School of Journalism, where he learned to write about himself in the third person.

After three meeting-filled years in general advertising, he turned his focus to the brave new frontier of the world wide web. Over the last four years, Darrell has mastered the art of the comma chain while successfully leading award-winning, integrated programs of positioning, branding, corporate identity, direct response, and new media for clients as diverse as Coca-Cola, Saab, Finlandia Vodka, Gerber, Seiko, Kellogg and Marriott.

{ONE SHOW INTERACTIVE/ judges}

RICHARD MELLOR
Creative Director
Hyperinteractive, London

Ranked as one of the most successful creative directors in new media, Richard continues to garner new media accolades. This includes an EPICA Gold, Marketing Design Award, a D&AD Silver, a Eurobest Gold, several London International Advertising Awards and (of course) a One Show Interactive Gold Pencil. His regular television appearances include the highly rated "Chips with Everything" for Sky Digital, which is part of its dedicated computer channel programming.

Having served as an elected director on the board of D&AD, he remains steadfast and passionate towards encouraging and promoting the next generation of new media creative talent.

Richard is also a founding member of the Dante Academy, the New Media Creative Directors Forum, and the Internet Design Excellence Association (www.the-idea.com).

SVEN MENTEL
Creative Director
Elephant Seven, Hamburg

Sven trained as an advertising executive at a small ad agency in Berlin. He moved to Hamburg in 1992 to work for Germany's Springer & Jacoby as a print producer. Two years later he changed his profession and became a copywriter in the multimedia department of S&J.

Sven and his team have won awards at several international festivals including The One Show, New York Festivals, Emma Awards, London International Advertising Awards, New Media Invision and ADC Germany. He worked on accounts such as Mercedes-Benz, McKinsey, Seat, BfG Bank, Amnesty International, and BMW Financial Services. Sven also lectures on interactive media at several advertising schools.

CLEMENT MOK
Chief Creative Officer
Sapient, San Francisco

Clement was the founder of Studio Archetype, now part of Sapient, and two other successful software companies: CMCD and NetObjects. CMCD is the publisher of the award-winning Visual Symbol Library, a collection of royalty-free digital photographs and spot animations. NetObjects is an internet software company, which was cited by *Fortune* magazine as one of the top 25 coolest technology companies in 1996.

Prior to forming his own agency, Clement spent five years as a creative director at Apple Computer. Currently, Clement is on the Board of Trustees at Art Center College of Design and AIGA.

CHRIS NEEDHAM
Vice President of Creative Services
AGENCY.COM, New York

A graduate of Yale University, Chris has been an AGENCY.COM creative director since 1996. He has directed accounts as varied as MetLife, British Airways, GTE, Claris and Nancy Friday. In 1998 he was promoted to senior creative director with management responsibilities for the Texaco, Kmart, and British Airways accounts.

In June 1999, he became vice president for the department, where he oversees creative development across all accounts in the New York office.

Chris has written a book on the Unabomber, edited film scripts for Spike Lee, and conceived and produced a successful online soap opera.

{ ONE SHOW INTERACTIVE/ *judges* }

PJ PEREIRA
Chief Creative Officer and Co-Founder
AgênciaClick, São Paulo

PJ Pereira was the creative director of the interactive division of DM9DDB for four years, where he won more awards than any other new media creative in Brazil. With DM9DDB his team has won such awards as two gold Cyber Lions and awards from One Show Interactive and The New York Film Festivals. His work was included on the list of the top 30 most creative interactive agencies in the world by *Advertising Age International*.

In December of 1999, PJ co-founded AgênciaClick, which has become one of the largest new media agencies in the country. Accounts include General Motors, iG, aJato Broadband, Fox Movies and Lucky Strike. PJ has also served as a judge for the Cannes Lions, and is a member of the board of the Adtech Latin America.

ANETTE SCHOLZ
Co-Founder
Scholz & Volkmer, Wiesbaden

From 1989 to '94 Anette studied at the University of Wiesbaden. In 1994 she founded, together with Michael Volkmer multimedia agency Scholz & Volkmer.

With General Motors as its first client, Scholz & Volkmer focused on CD-ROM titles for the automobile industry. Soon the company started to develop training software and marketing CD-ROMs for Daimler Chrysler. Today the agency provides a range of multimedia services for customers such as Hewlett-Packard, Liebherr, and Agfa. Scholz & Volkmer has won more than 30 international awards over the last five years. In 1998 and '99 the company was chosen as the second most creative multimedia agency in Germany. Anette also lectures at the University of Hamburg.

PETER SEIDLER
Chief Creative Officer
Razorfish, New York

Peter has provided the creative direction for such clients as The Warner Music Group, Guardian Insurance, Sotheby's International Realty, Carnegie Hall, Banker's Trust, Elektra Entertainment, FAO Schwartz, NBC, PriceWaterhouse and Viacom.

Peter's contributions have been recognized by such publications as *New York Magazine*, which named him one of "10 New Yorkers Who Make a Difference."

Peter speaks regularly at design conferences and internet industry events, and is an adjunct professor at New York University's Interactive Telecommunications Program. Peter also judges prestigious advertising awards events such as Communication Arts, the Clios, and the One Show Interactive.

An active member of the New York New Media Association and the Association of Graphic Designers, Peter holds a B.A. in philosophy from NYU, and an M.F.A. in conceptual art from California Institute of the Arts, and has followed this with post-graduate work at the Whitney Museum's Independent Study Program. Peter's conceptual art projects are in New York's Museum of Modern Art.

JANIS NAKANO SPIVACK
Chief Creative Officer
Organic, San Francisco

Janis draws on 15 years experience in traditional advertising and interactive communications to direct the creative vision and strategy for Organic.

Over the course of her career, Janis has built online commerce and entertainment environments, developed content for numerous interactive platforms, including interactive television, cable modems, and CD-ROMs.

Janis has created award-winning traditional advertising campaigns for broadcast, print, and outdoor.

Before joining Organic, Janis worked as an interactive creative consultant for a variety of clients, including Nike, Turner New Media, LivingBooks, daVinci Time & Space, and her own online service, goFISH!.

{ ONE SHOW INTERACTIVE/ judges }

KOTARO SUGIYAMA
Senior Creative Director
Dentsu, Tokyo

Kotaro received a degree in Economics from St. Paul's University, Tokyo. After graduation, he joined Dentsu's Creative Department. Kotaro then founded a division that integrated interactive communications into the company. He now oversees the creative quality of the agency's online ad work. His work www.willing-to-try.com has won an INVISION Award, and a London International Advertising Award.

Kotaro has twice been part of the Cannes International Advertising Film Festival Cyber Jury. He has also been a judge in the cyber categories of the London International Advertising Awards, One Show Interactive, and The Clios. Kotaro has also been featured in the British industry magazine *Campaign*.

TOM SUITER
Chief Creative Officer
marchFIRST, San Francisco

Tom has been instrumental in directing a number of identity and web development programs for such clients as United Airlines, Apple, Pixar, and Norwegian Cruise Lines. Before founding CKS Partners in 1991, Tom was creative director for Landor Associates' corporate identity practice. While at Landor, Tom directed major identity programs for such companies as GE, Japan Airlines, World Wildlife Fund, Hyatt Hotels, and Mercedes-Benz Signature Service.

Before joining Landor, Tom served as creative director and creative services director for Apple Computer. His team was also responsible for the international introduction of the Macintosh and Apple II product. Tom attended Art Center College of Design. He currently sits on the national board of AIGA.

PACO VIÑOLY
Creative Director
Lot21 Interactive Advertising Group,
San Francisco

Paco Viñoly has led the design department of Lot21 since its inception in February 1998. The agency recently won recognition from the IAB as its 1999 Agency of the Year. Paco has worked on interactive campaigns for many high-visibility clients, such as BankAmerica, KBKids, Palm VII and New Line Cinema.

Paco has led pioneering efforts in broadband networks, as well as new technology implementation. His work has been recognized by both national and international organizations.

Prior to Lot21, Paco served as associate director of admissions at the Art Center College of Design. Prior to this, Paco gained valuable online experience working for IBM on its internet efforts. Paco also sits on the creative review panel for Microscope.

MICHAEL VOLKMER
Co-Founder
Scholz & Volkmer, Wiesbaden

After an education in photography and some working experience as a cameraman, Michael studied visual arts at the University of Wiesbaden. Together with Anette Scholz he founded the multimedia agency Scholz & Volkmer in 1994.

With General Motors as its first client, Scholz & Volkmer focused on CD ROM-titles for the automobile industry. Very soon the company started to develop training-software and marketing CD-ROMs for Daimler Chrysler. Today the agency provides a full range of multimedia services for customers like Hewlett Packard, Liebherr and Agfa.

Scholz & Volkmer has won more than 30 international awards over the last five years. In 1998 and '99 the company was chosen as the second most creative multimedia agency in Germany. Michael also lectures at the University of Darmstadt.

{ ONE SHOW INTERACTIVE/ judges }

CHRIS WORTH
Interactive Creative Director
OgilvyInteractive, Paris

Chris Worth is an interactive creative director with experience at several agencies including Ogilvy in Singapore and Paris, where a series of essays on advertising and the web gained an audience of 200,000. His own web site about technology and media, chrisworth.com, gets over 30,000 visitors a month.

A past winner of WPP's Atticus Award, he's now CEO of web start-up 10KC.com, a teamwork application company for ad agency networks. He can be contacted at chris@chrisworth.com.

The Pawn Emporium — We buy and sell gold, silver and bronze. Our specialty: precious metal pencils. Large selection to choose from. Huge inventory. Fast transactions. No hassles. Confidential. Satisfaction guaranteed.

gold, silver and bronze
pencil winners

{BANNERS/ single}

Gold

AGENCY	FCB Worldwide/Southfield
CLIENT	Little Caesars Enterprise, Inc.
ART DIRECTORS	Geoffrey Gates, Peter Arndt
WRITER	Dan Sicko
DIGITAL ARTIST	Geoffrey Gates
PRODUCER	Kathleen Starr
MULTIMEDIA	DragonFly Studios
PROGRAMMER	DragonFly Studios
CREATIVE DIRECTORS	Husam Ajluni, John Gregory, Peter Arndt
URL	www.webspot.com/littlecaesars/banners/makingdough.html
ID	00 0001 N

making dough — On the way to "Making Dough"

My partner, Peter Arndt, came up with the idea for "Making Dough" in a gestalt (God bless you!) one night. It was near the end of the production of the Little Caesars "Nibbles" WebSpot®, while we were all dreaming up banner ideas to help promote it. As usual, everyone was hungry. And the pizza delivery guy was a half hour late.

virtual pizza — Luckily, Peter dabbles in Director, so he cropped off Little Caesar's arm, tossed a lump of pizza dough into the flat scanner — and voila! In virtually no time, Peter had pounded out his first virtual pizza. We all salivated over it. Where was that pizza delivery guy, by the way?

From there, artist Geoff Gates and writer Dan Sicko added cheese, Pepperoni, and more cheese. Finally, Gil Clough and John Round at Dragonfly — with help from FCB producer, Kathy Starr — folded in their own brand of sauce and delivered the pizza banner in its finished form.

mere pixels — Though mere pixels, it was nevertheless much tastier than what the delivery guy finally brought that night.

{BANNERS/ single}

	Gold
AGENCY	Freestyle Interactive/San Francisco
CLIENT	Sonic Net
PRODUCER	Kim Askew
PROGRAMMERS	Keith Neal, Steve Von Worley
CREATIVE DIRECTOR	Mike Yapp
URL	www.freestyleinteractive.com/clients/sonicnet/guitar
ID	00 0002 N

virtual guitar   Jammin' in a banner. Sonic Net, the leading online source for music reviews and news, wanted more brand awareness. With a 5-chord, play it in a banner guitar, Freestyle gave it to them in spades. Viewers actually play the virtual guitar in the banner, picking individual strings or strumming chords with full audio. For the musically challenged, the guitar can even play itself

{BANNERS/ single}

AGENCY	Silver
	FCB Worldwide/Southfield
CLIENT	Comedy Central
ART DIRECTOR	Anne Bourseleth
WRITER	Dan Sicko
DIGITAL ARTIST	Freestyle Interactive
PRODUCERS	Kathleen Starr, Shawn Vine
MULTIMEDIA	DragonFly Studios
PROGRAMMER	Freestyle Interactive
CREATIVE DIRECTORS	Husam Ajluni, John Gregory, Peter Arndt
URL	www.webspot.com/pages/cheesy_poofs
ID	00 0003 N

the call came — In mid-October of 1999, our team had just finished producing two WebSpots and banners for Comedy Central's "The Man Show," and were about to celebrate with some beer when the call came to quickly come up with a campaign of standard and "rich media" banners to help promote their hit "South Park" during November sweeps. (Whew!)

get creative — We immediately sent out for more beer and set about to "get creative."

special thanks to those in the trenches — Within a couple of days, we were sober again and in the midst of producing five "rich media" pieces and the first slew in a slurry of standard banner ads. I can't be more specific, because everything was a blur. And, therefore, still is a blur. Our whole team had a hand in the creative energy that produced "Cheesy Poofs," along with all the others. Special thanks to those in the trenches, including my partner, ACD Peter Arndt, and (alphabetically) Sam Ajluni, Anne Bourseleth, Dan Sicko, Melissa Gessner, Scott Lange, AE Rod Rakic, producer Kathy Starr, and coordinator Shawn Vine. Without you, we never could have pulled it all off. Or returned all the bottles.

{BANNERS/ single}

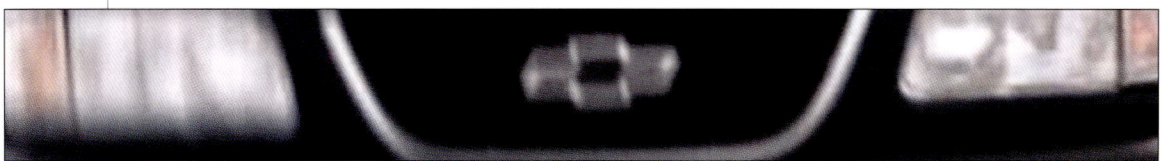

Bronze

AGENCY	Agenciaclick/São Paulo
CLIENT	General Motors of Brazil
ART DIRECTOR	Edwin Veelo
WRITER	PJ Pereira
DIGITAL ARTIST	Edwin Veelo
PRODUCER	Jean Boechat
MULTIMEDIA	Marcelo Siqueira
PROGRAMMER	Vitor Bonate
CREATIVE DIRECTOR	PJ Pereira
URL	www.agenciaclick.com.br/awards/shaking
ID	00 0004 N

user experience You must use your imagination to understand this banner. It is typically an interactive piece, based on the user experience, not art direction or copy (well it doesn't have copy anyway...). It's just the front of a GM pick-up bouncing up and down. But if you mouse over it, the banner will switch to the internal panel of the car and your entire browser window will shake.

{BANNERS/ campaign}

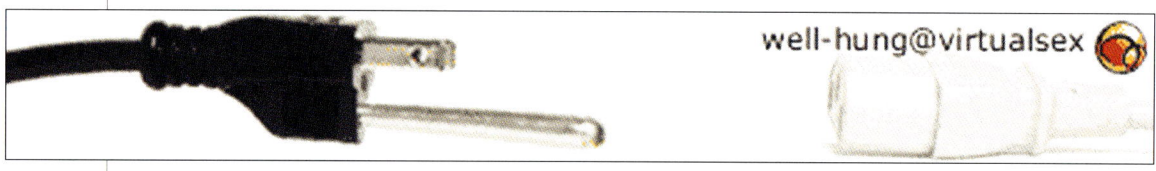

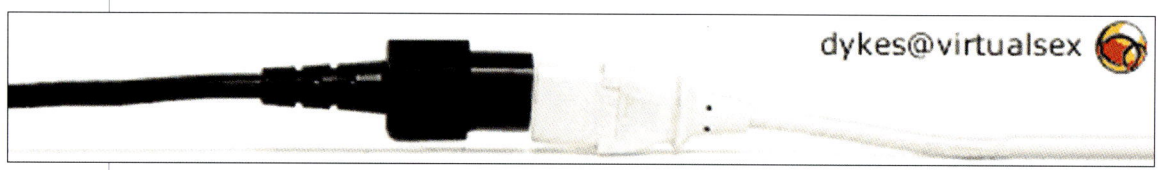

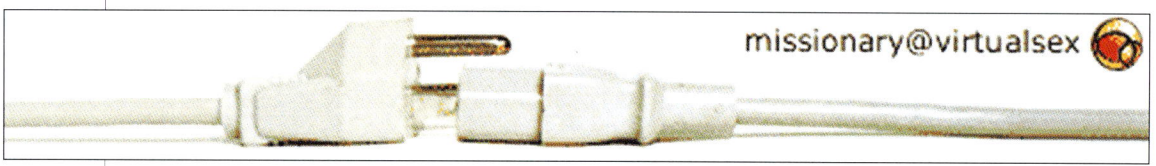

Gold

AGENCY DM9 DDB Publicidade/São Paulo
CLIENT Uol-Universo Online
ART DIRECTOR Andrea Evora Cals
WRITER PJ Pereira
PRODUCER Zeno Millet
URL www.dm9.com.br/festival/uol/big.html
ID 00 0005 N

without appearing offensive or vulgar

UOL, one of the largest Brazilian portals, has entrusted us with the task of advertising, internally, their virtual-sex chat section. The question was, how to do that without appearing offensive or vulgar, and how to turn that task into a challenge to our creativity? The idea sprang up from the names we (in Brazil) call objects we use in our daily work to connect the electric and electronic appliances to a power source: male (the plug) and female (the socket outlet). Nothing more appropriate than using them "in person" and showing how much sensuality and personality a simple power cable can have. Actually, the target was stirring the imagination of the user, who readily identifies sexual situations familiar to all of us. Because of its subtle humor, the trick creates instant empathy with the viewer. We used hardly any technological gimmicks at all. Instead, we created only an animated gif. Its simplicity and easy-to-grasp understanding of a subject we are all well-acquainted with and enjoy made this campaign a great success.

{BANNERS/ campaign}

	Silver
AGENCY	Euro RSCG Partnership/North Sydney
CLIENT	Orange
ART DIRECTOR	Scott Ex Rogers
WRITER	Scott Mortimer
PROGRAMMER	Shmuel Bonkowski
CREATIVE DIRECTOR	Scott Ex Rodgers
URL	http://203.30.131.55/oneshow/banners/orange.htm
ID	00 0006 N

very tightly integrated

"Orange" was launched in Australia in one week on television, press, poster, and internet. The internet component of that campaign seen here, is very tightly integrated with the mainstream work. Simplicity is a major part of the Orange message, so simplicity is key for all executions. The campaign used three colors: black, white, and orange, which translated beautifully to the banners.

interaction with the images

Black and white allowed us to use a lot of movement in very small file sizes, and movement brought the images to life. We wished we could get the images to move in the press and poster work as well. User-activated sound was introduced to the phase II banners, providing more interaction with the images. This launch was perhaps a bit unusual in that it is a pure branding campaign on the internet, not designed to drive clicks to the web site but to reinforce the launch message across various media.

{BANNERS/ campaign}

	Bronze	signs of drug use	The signs of drug use aren't always obvious.
AGENCY	Martin Interactive/Richmond		That's why it's easy for a parent to overlook behavior changes and mood swings; they simply mark it off as growing pains. With that in mind, we decided that this banner campaign should be rather unassuming itself. It shouldn't use the latest technology, which could eliminate parts of our audience and overpower the message. But it should offer a simplified, interactive view of warped innocence. The result is what you see in this annual.
CLIENT	Drug Free America		
ART DIRECTOR	Robbie Wagner		
WRITER	Darrell Kanipe		
DIGITAL ARTIST	Robbie Wagner		
PRODUCERS	Darrell Kanipe, Shelly Norman		
MULTIMEDIA	Jackie Pittmen		
PROGRAMMER	Robbie Wagner		
CREATIVE DIRECTOR	David Parish		
URL	www.martininteractive.com		
	ID 00 0007 N		

{BANNERS/ campaign}

Little Jack Horner sat in the corner smoking some crack to get high.

Little Miss Muffet sat on a tuffet, a dirty needle in her vein.

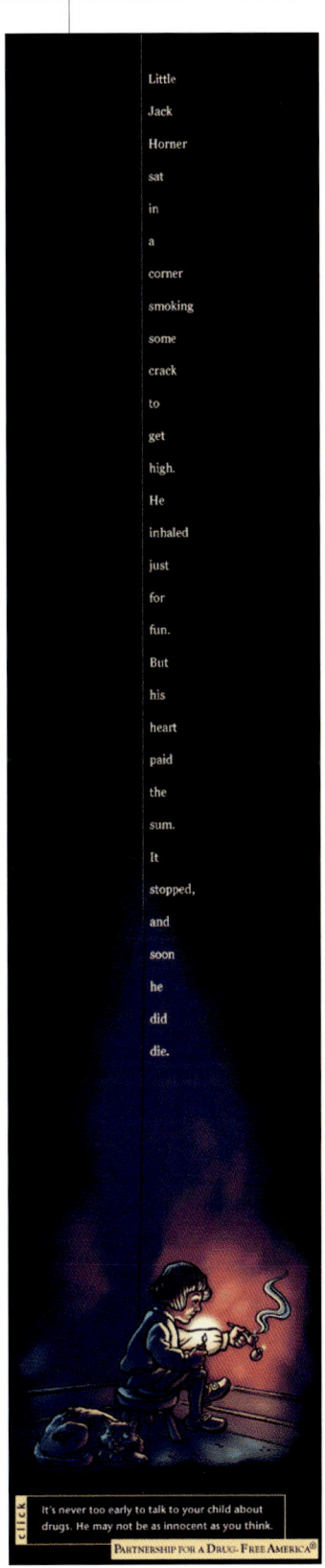

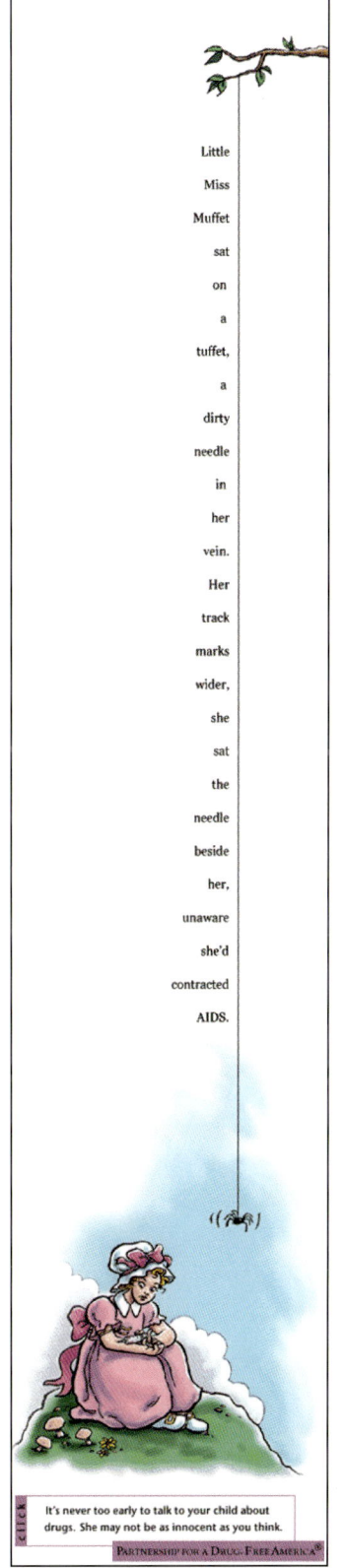

{BEYOND/ the banner}

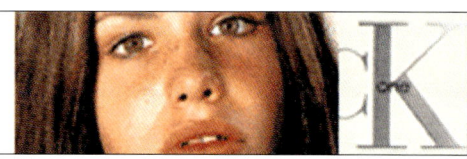

Gold

AGENCY	Wieden + Kennedy/New York
CLIENT	Calvin Klein
ART DIRECTORS	Kevin Drew Davis, Michael Prieve
WRITERS	Brant Mau, Stacy Wall
DIGITAL ARTIST	Michael Delhaut
PHOTOGRAPHER	Richard Burbridge
PRODUCERS	Katie Raye, Elaine Thomas
PROGRAMMER	Michael Macrone
URL	www.wk.com/online/ckone/award.htm
USERNAME	online
PASSWORD	7fot92
ID	00 0008 N

encouraging the viewer — Because this campaign was e-mail-based, it didn't have a corresponding URL or web site to visit. The print and television were tagged with the e-mail address of the character represented, encouraging the viewer to write and begin an e-mail relationship with the character. When we began to plan online media, the challenge was figuring out exactly what would appear if/when someone clicked.

navigation between characters — When the banner was clicked, a series of pop-up windows appeared — one containing a photo of the character with a corresponding sound file of it speaking, another displaying one of its e-mails, and a third being used as a navigation between characters.

{BEYOND/ the banner}

	Silver
AGENCY	*OgilvyInteractive/New York*
CLIENT	*IBM*
ART DIRECTOR	*Juan Gallardo*
WRITER	*David Levy*
DIGITAL ARTIST	*Rachel Heapps*
PRODUCERS	*Jude Raymond Fish, Angie Ahn, Heavy Industry*
CREATIVE DIRECTOR	*Audrey Fleisher*
URL	*http://199.229.12.135/awards2000/ ibm_grammy.html*
ID	00 0009 N

the strategy

The strategy of the IBM "e-culture" campaign was to profile a range of companies who've benefited from their internet partnerships with IBM. By using rich media, we hoped to seduce a banner-weary audience with both playful interactivity and state-of-the-art production values, blending animation, voice, and music in ways that make "media convergence" more than a mere catchphrase.

fun and intrigue

The interactive banners work, one hopes, by offering a bit of fun and intrigue before the serious sell: For the Grammy Awards, it's a chorus of vocalists, activated by rollovers. Once the user clicks through to the pop-up interstitial, the story is told in the client's voice, accompanying a Flash animation of the backstage buzz and glamour of the Grammy Awards. Viewers are reminded that grammy.com "is an IBM e-business" and are gently bombarded with the curvaceous "e" logo — in the hope that it becomes as recognizable a symbol for the internet generation as the stolid blue "IBM" was for their fathers and mothers.

{PROMOTIONAL ADVERTISING/ web sites}

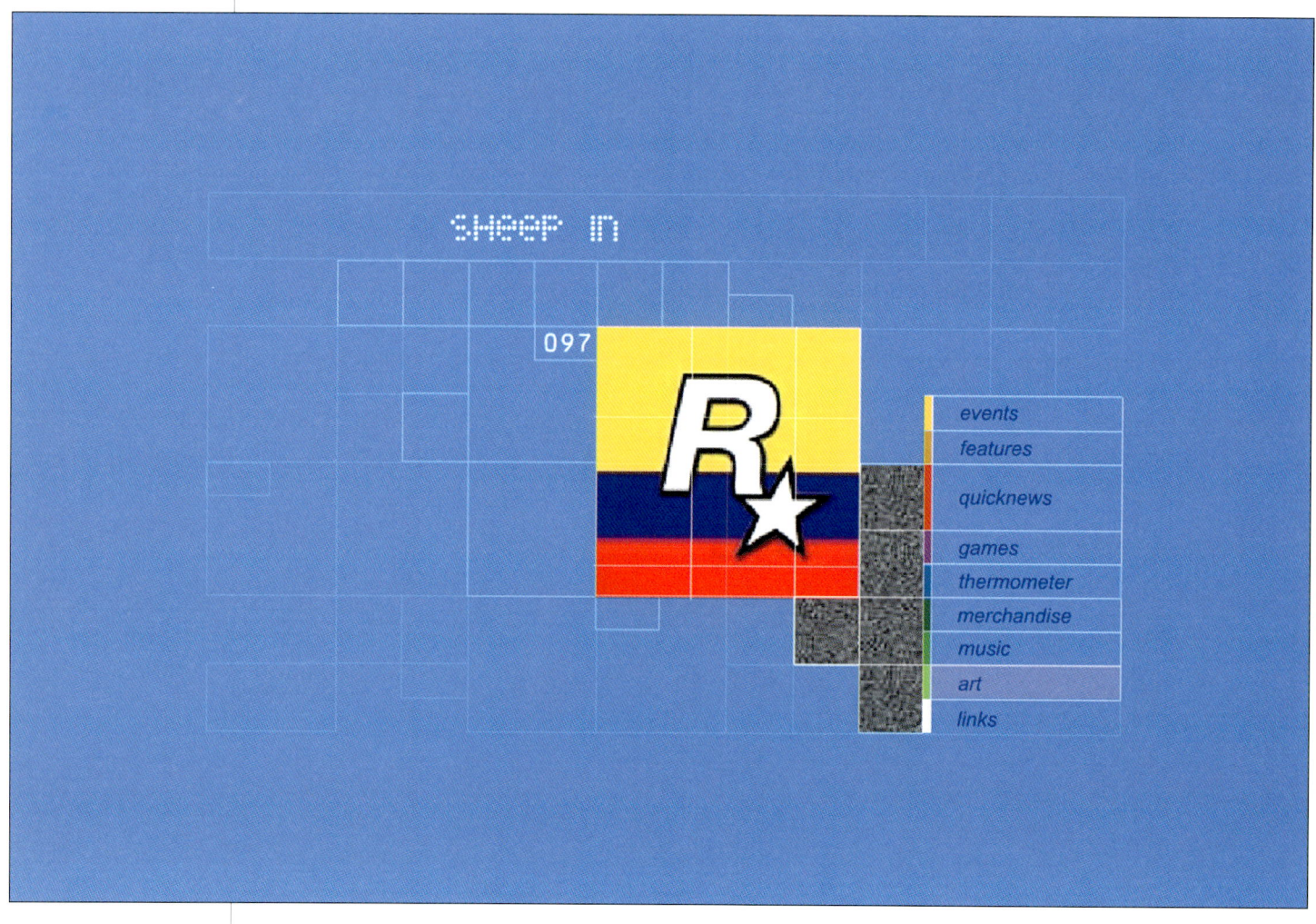

Silver
AGENCY Oyster Partners/London
CLIENT Rockstar Games
ART DIRECTOR James Chaytor
WRITER Dan Houser
CREATIVE DIRECTOR Hugo Manassei
DIGITAL ARTIST Jake Portman
URL www.rockstargames.com
ID 00 0010 N

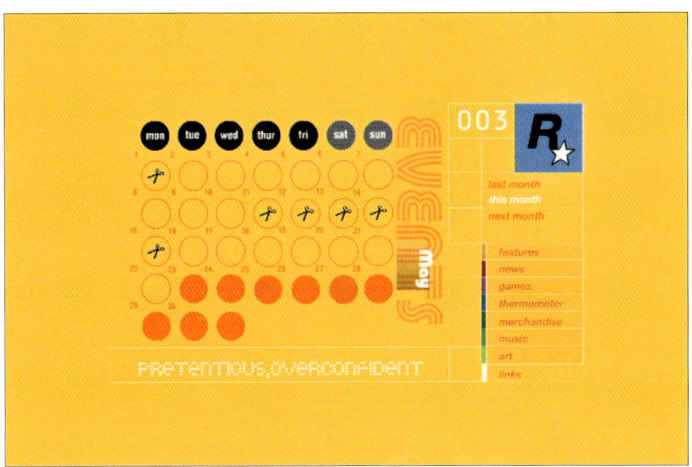

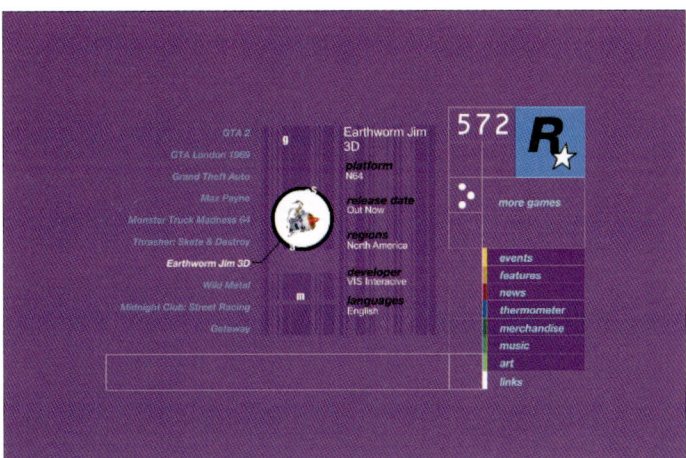

Rockstar brand values
: http://www.rockstargames.com reflects Rockstar brand values, which emphasize gaming as one element among wider social choices for the young urban professionals who are Rockstar's target audience.

dynamic and immersive atmosphere
: Designed entirely in Flash and Flash Generator to create a dynamic and immersive atmosphere, this site's retro-futuristic design reflects the eclectic Rockstar aesthetic and casts a knowing, technological look back at the '80's as the era of such cult figures as Don Simpson, The Who, and "Hart to Hart."

truly visionary
: Julian Marsh, Account Manager at Oyster Partners, describes Rockstar as "truly visionary in that the creative process was not constrained by technical limitations. Paradoxically this creative freedom was occasionally quite limiting, as the designers would conceptualize something incredible and then we would run into technical problems trying to shoe-horn the creative visualization into Flash Generator to get the required functionality, whilst not compromising the project creatively. However, it became worth it, as we realized the potential of fusing genuinely interesting and innovative interfaces with the mass of content supplied by the client. We felt that a new dawn had arrived, one in which interesting experiences could be created out of current evolving content on a mass scale."

{PROMOTIONAL ADVERTISING/ web sites}

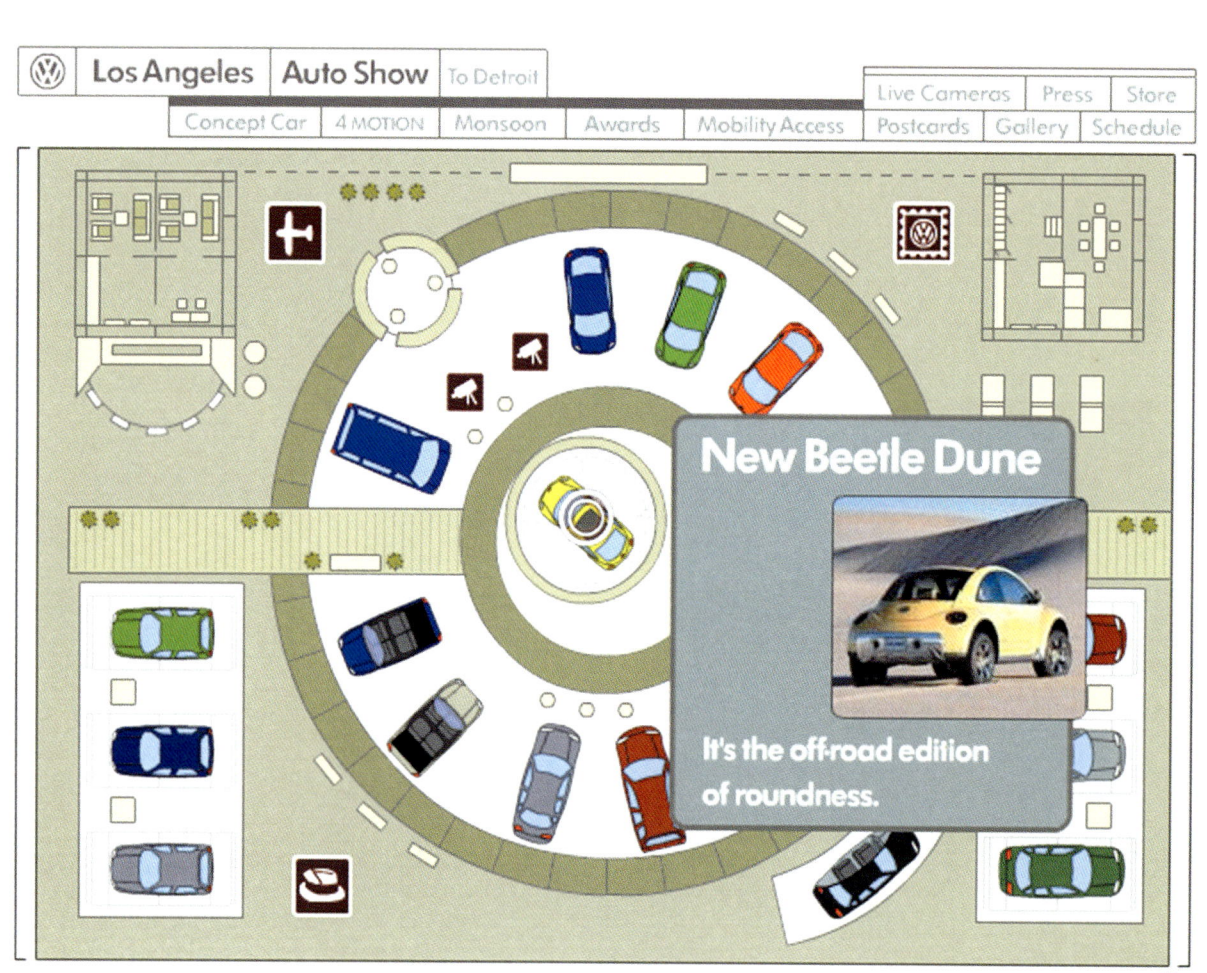

	Silver
AGENCY	Arnold Communications/Boston
CLIENT	Volkswagen of America, Inc.
ART DIRECTORS	Robert Hodgin, Natalie Acoca
WRITERS	Paisley Schade, Tim Brunelle
DIGITAL ARTISTS	Kate Jensen, Robert Hodgin, Natalie Acoca, Mark Kraus, Marc Van Norden
PHOTOGRAPHER	Bill Cash
PRODUCERS	Jon Groves, Chris Jensen
MULTIMEDIA	Robert Hodgin, Peter DuCharme
PROGRAMMER	Jon Groves
CREATIVE DIRECTORS	Ron Lawner, Alan Pafenbach, Bill Whelan, Tim Brunelle
URL	www.vw.com/autoshow
ID	00 0011 N

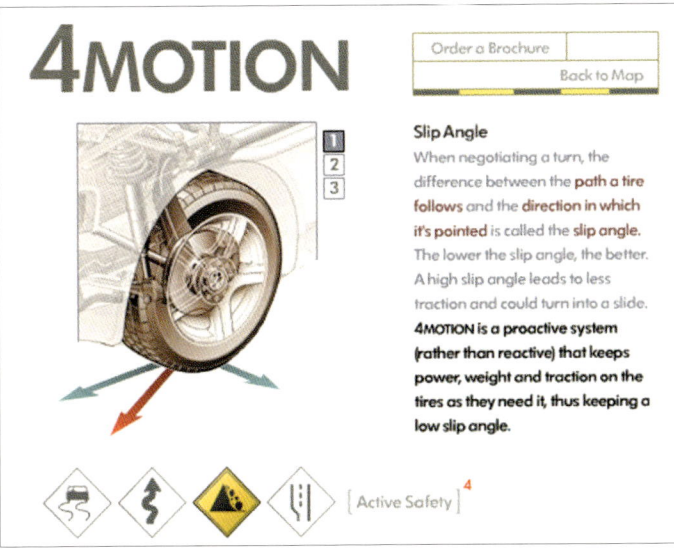

like a circus   Have you ever walked through the Detroit or Los Angeles auto shows? They're kind of like a circus. Noisy. Distracting. There's too much to look at.

dynamic and multifaceted   We felt vw.com/autoshow had to mirror that experience. It had to be as dynamic and multi-faceted as these two shows are in person. But we also had the opportunity to show stuff you couldn't see in the auditoriums. The look is adopted from blueprints of the actual floorplans. Pop-up windows for each of the topics offer quick, scintillating feedback. (Of course, if you wanted to dig deep--if you were the press, for instance--you could.) It was about the volume of things.

The only problem with doing this site was the go-live date: January 5th. The production artists and developers had a lousy Christmas and New Year vacation.

{PROMOTIONAL ADVERTISING/ web sites}

Bronze

AGENCY | Scholz & Volkmer/Wiesbaden
CLIENT | USM U. Schaerer Söhne AG
ART DIRECTOR | Peter Reichard
WRITER | Mareike Schmiedt
PROGRAMMER | Manfred Kraft
URL | www.eleven22.com
ID 00 0012 N

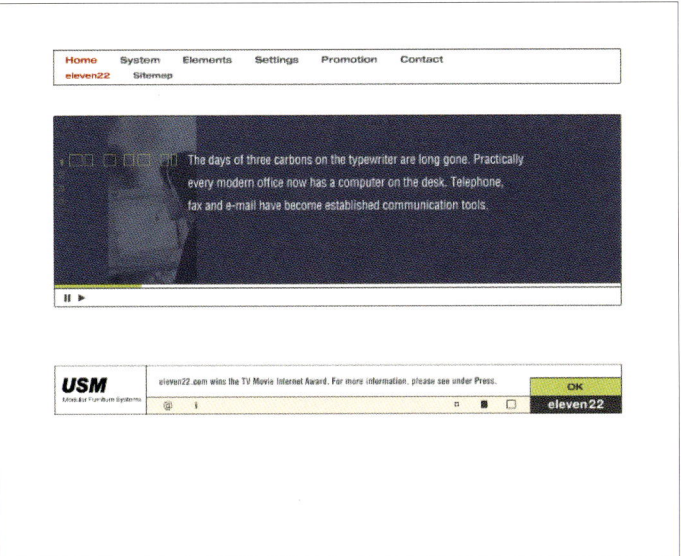

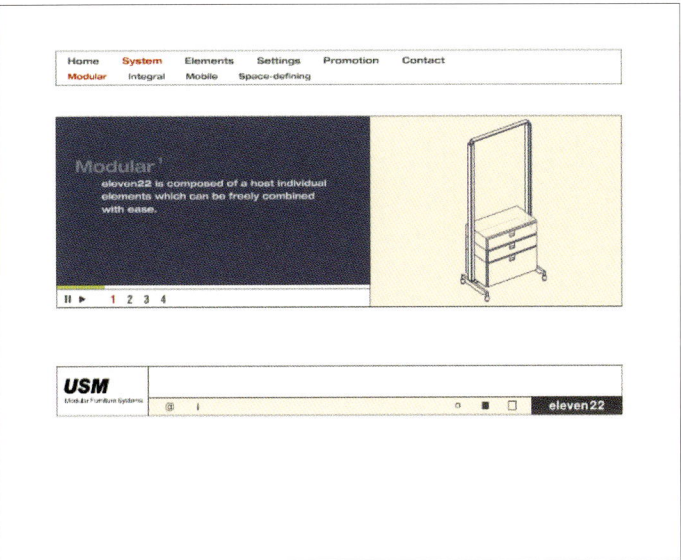

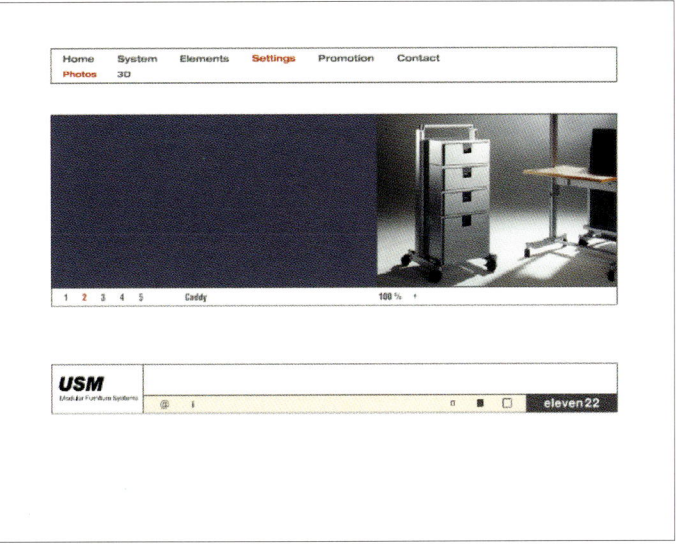

comprehensive — The web site http://www.eleven22.com presents the office system "eleven22" of the Swiss furniture manufacturer USM U. Schaerer Söhne AG. Numerous interactive illustrations, Flash animations, and text convey a comprehensive picture of the properties of the office furniture systems.

the focus - 3D — In launching its new product "eleven22," USM for the first time uses only the web site and CD-ROM as its media. There is no print information at all (e.g., a leaflet or a catalogue). Potential buyers are sent to the web site, where they can find detailed information about the office system. As the sole means of communication, the web site carries an interactive introduction of the individual product components, the combinations of colors and materials, as well as the configuration possibilities. The focus of this execution lies in 3D presentations and animations.

simple and functional — From the design point of view, the web site follows the simple and functional aspects of the furniture.

{PROMOTIONAL ADVERTISING/ CD-ROM}

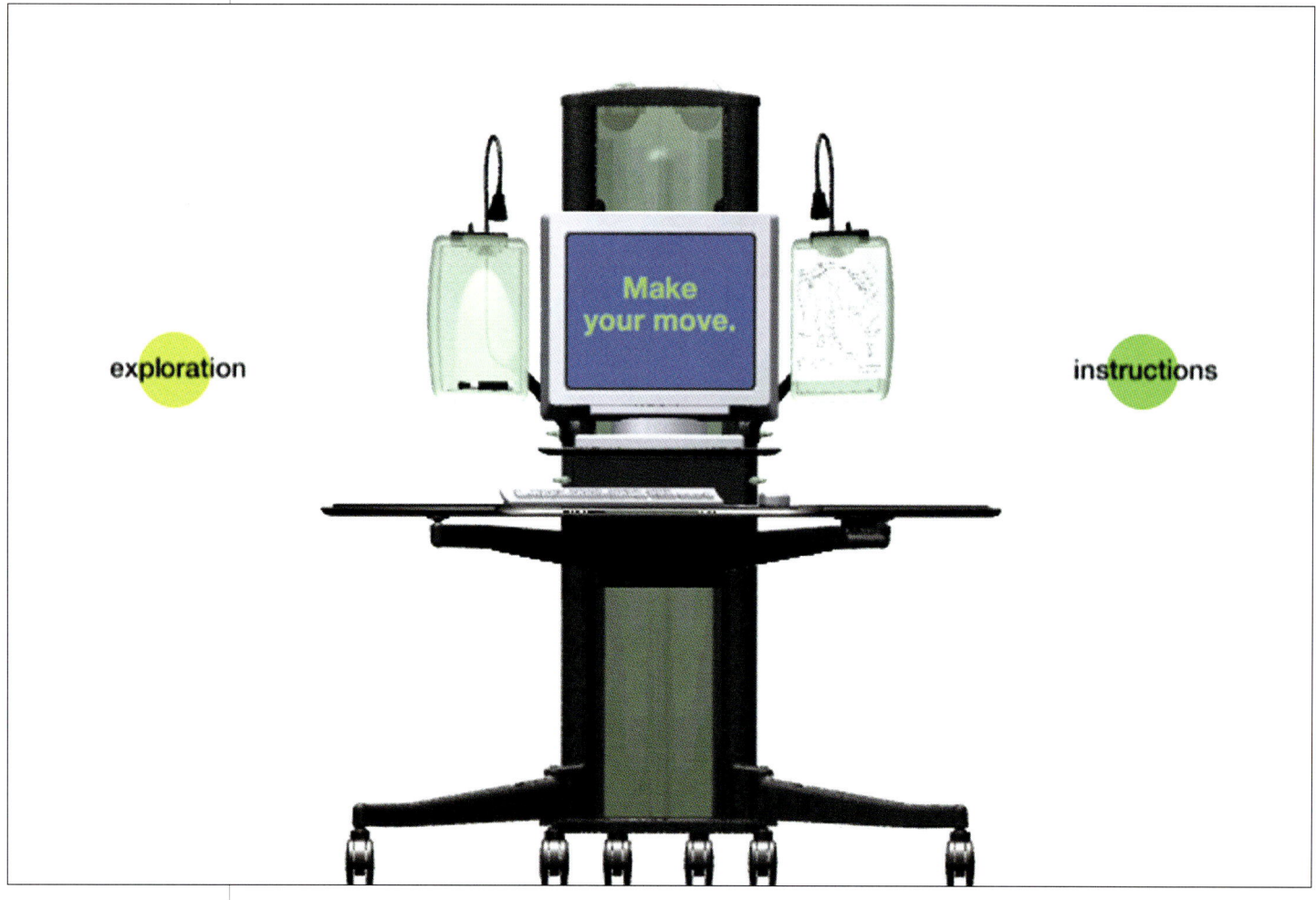

Gold
- **AGENCY** Genex/Los Angeles
- **CLIENT** Herman Miller
- **ART DIRECTOR** Chip McCarthy
- **WRITER** R. Elliot
- **DIGITAL ARTISTS** Amanda Dulkinys, Wilson Yin
- **PRODUCERS** Karen Helweg, Ray Odell
- **MULTIMEDIA** Stephen Brand
- **PROGRAMMER** Brendan Murphy
- **CREATIVE DIRECTOR** David Glaze
- **ID** 00 0013 N

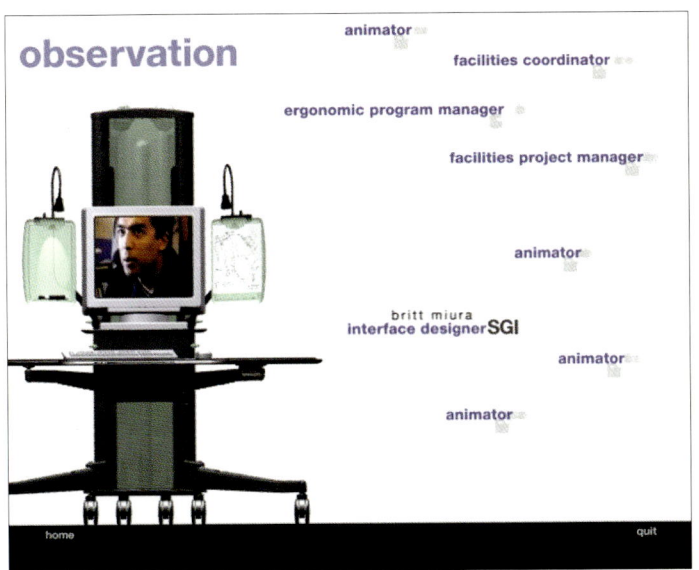

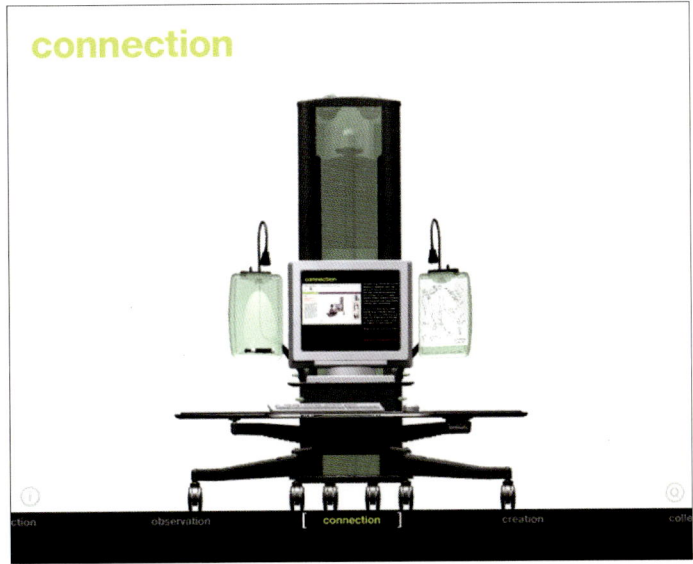

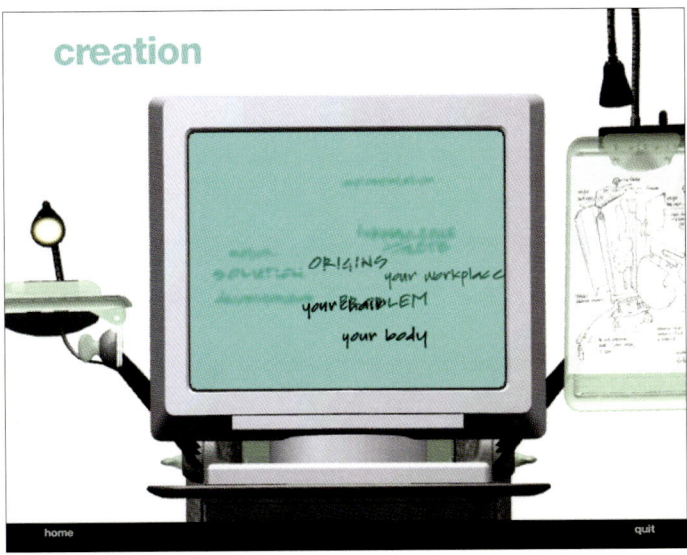

dynamic movement and versatility — Genex was asked to demonstrate the dynamic movement and versatility of Herman Miller's new Levity Collection of computer furniture. Levity was, at the time, so new that there wasn't any product available to show or shoot. It has more moving parts than the high-end Swiss Army knife. And it's backed by intensive research and design methodology.

furniture lust — So the Genex team was left wondering how to create "furniture lust" for a brand new product that didn't quite yet exist.

intelligence, quality, and innovation — The answer was to create a CD-ROM that could be mailed to prospective Levity candidates. We designed it to reflect the traits of the Herman Miller brand: intelligence, quality, and innovation. To mimic the fun of interacting with the furniture, and to model all the furniture in 3D, using the pieces themselves as the main navigation, we added as much groovy animation as possible and pressed the equivalent of the "send" button. It's worked out well.

Thanks to a great client and a great team. Our money says the Levity Collection furniture will soon be held in higher regard than the highly coveted Aeron chairs.

{PROMOTIONAL ADVERTISING/ CD-ROM}

Silver

AGENCY	RAW Interactive/New York
CLIENT	American Express, commissioned by Strategic
ART DIRECTORS	Terje Vist, Matthew Chun
WRITERS	Bob Egan, Kathy Probe
DIGITAL ARTISTS	Randy Belluardo, Eliseo Garcia
MULTIMEDIA	Mark Barasch, Steve Fein
PROGRAMMER	Jose Rodriguez
CREATIVE DIRECTORS	Alexis Rodriguez, Bill Goldstein
ID	00 0014 N

web savvy audience   We designed the Blue CD-ROM to appeal to a computer and web savvy audience. The introductory animation is a QuickTime movie that was assembled in After Effects, using 3D-rendered wire frames and other images edited either in Photoshop or Illustrator.

brilliant   Our main interface features brilliant, randomly flashing light bursts emanating from the outer edge of a moon-like sphere, accompanied by ambient and electronic music. 2001 meets a Rave party.

flaring-of-light effect   The flaring-of-light effect was achieved through manipulating a loop of video images we created using a Sony digital TRV-900 and flashlights in a dark room. We also captured images of light emanating from scanners scanning. Other interfaces incorporated video collages, rotating wire frames, type manipulation, and the layering of different colors and images.

The images were edited in Photoshop or Illustrator, and the animations, plus some movements, were created or edited through After Effects. All other media were then imported, assembled and programmed in Director for the final product.

a rectangular-shaped CD   In keeping with the credit card theme, we elected to use a rectangular-shaped CD card. Special compression and advanced programming techniques were required for the media-rich product to fit on the compact-sized CD-ROM.

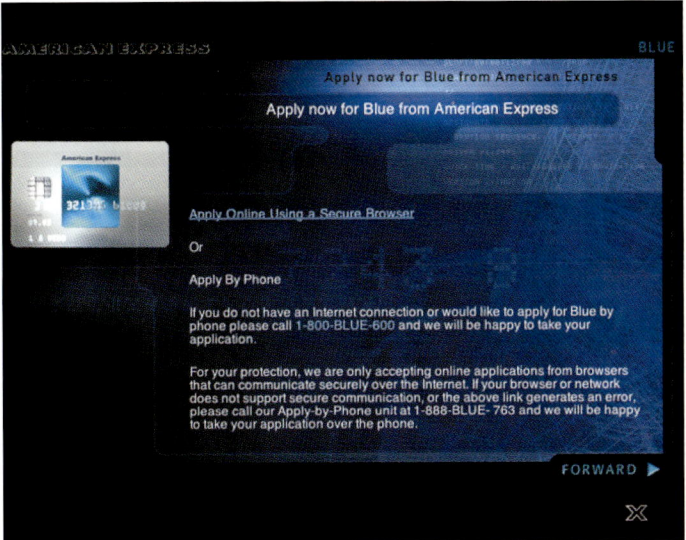

{PROMOTIONAL ADVERTISING/ CD-ROM}

```
The best creative works all
have one thing in common.
```

Bronze

AGENCY	tinderbox interactive/Capeto
CLIENT	The Association of Marketers
ART DIRECTORS	Andries Odendaal, Clint Bryce
DIGITAL ARTIST	Andries Odendaal
PRODUCER	Christia Burger
MULTIMEDIA	Paul Tooze
PROGRAMMER	Paul Tooze
CREATIVE DIRECTOR	Clint Bryce
ID	00 0015 N

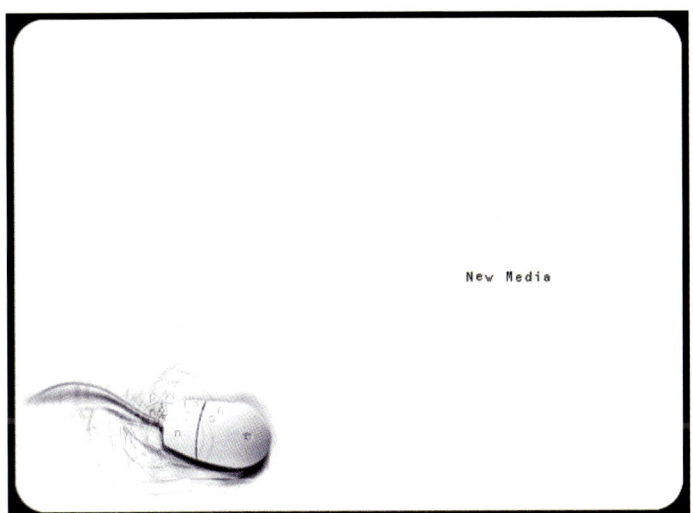

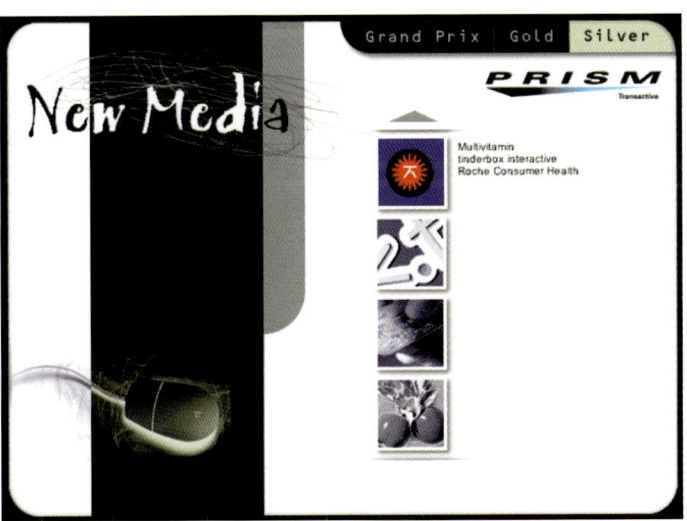

they're all here	The creations that won Grand Prix, Gold and Silver awards in the International, TV, Radio, Cinema and New Media categories for the prestigious South African Loerie awards held every year at Sun City;
	The tension with creating a CD-Rom of this nature (showcasing the brilliant ideas of the nations best advertising agencies) is that it's important to realize that the primary goal of the CD-Rom is to bring life to the adverts themselves, and not fall into the trap of trying to get too clever with your interface design so much so that it gets in the way.
trouble already	That said, this is one of those rare products in which we were the client. Trouble already. And each year we challenge ourselves to think out of the box in order to bring to the screen an interface and menu choice systems that have not previously been experienced.
challenged for a new concept	We took our cue from the desks of all creative teams when challenged to find a new concept. They are all faced with a blank piece of paper and only through exploration are discoveries made— something we knew our audience would be familiar with. Our interpretation of this was to introduce a blank screen with one simple line of copy which then fades to reveal only a few scribbles. With some dexterous lingo code (thanks Paul!) numerous ASCII characters meander the screen in a sort of digital brownian-movement. Only when the viewer positions the cursor over one of the conceptual scribbles do the characters snap to life and scurry to reveal, in unison, the particular menu choice. Of course, once the cursor shifts elsewhere, the ASCII characters resume their random calling over the blank sheet.
	The remaining architecture pays homage to the numerous adverts and web sites that were awarded accolades.
we had, in fact, cracked it	How did we come up with the idea? The tried and trusted corner pub which was more than pleased to serve the dry red helped. And the rummage through the scribbles and notes the morning after revealed that we had, in fact, cracked it.
	But you should experience it for yourself. Afterall, it did earn us a One Show pencil.

{PROMOTIONAL ADVERTISING/ other digital media}

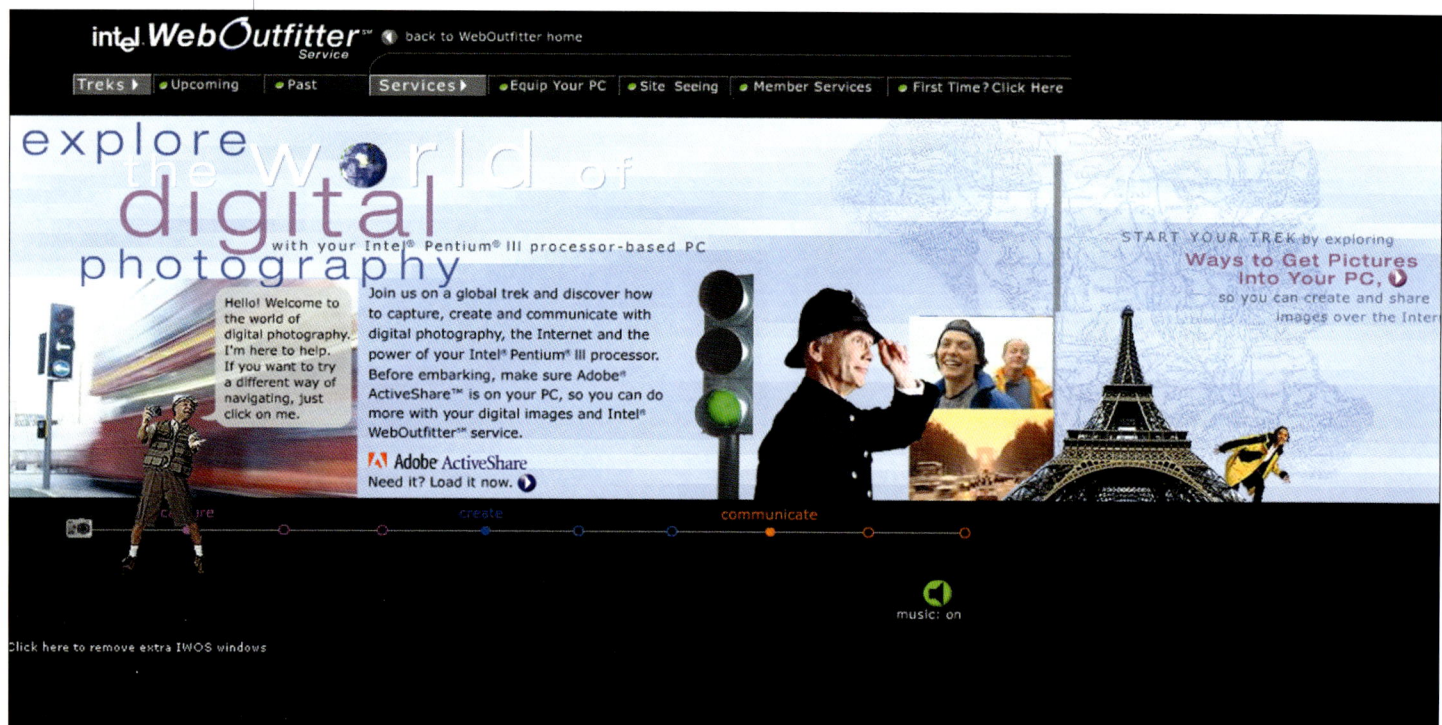

Gold

AGENCY	EURO RSCG DSW Partners/Salt Lake City
CLIENT	Intel
ART DIRECTORS	Dung Hoang, Steve Newman, Kimball Carter
WRITERS	Jennifer Ward, Eric Young
DIGITAL ARTIST	Damian Burns
PHOTOGRAPHER	Michael Schoenfeld
PRODUCERS	Michael Aaron, Wayman Hearn
PROGRAMMER	Tim Watrous
CREATIVE DIRECTORS	Kimball Carter, Steve Newman
URL	http://awards.dsw.com/sites/trek3/index.htm
ID	00 0016 N

encouraging the viewer

The Intel® WebOutfitters™ service was created for a very elite audience:

People who own a PC with an Intel® Pentium® III processor. It was built to showcase tools, content, and capabilities only available to this (then small) group of users. In addition, the site needed to deliver brilliant motion graphics never before seen on slower computers.

inspires users

To accomplish these goals, we pushed Macromedia® Flash further than we had ever pushed it, creating a massive horizontal scroll that encouraged people to learn about digital photography literally by picking up a camera and starting to explore. The site highlights a slew of affiliates and tools associated with digital photography and, of course, inspires users with many visually rich (and processor-intensive) photographs.

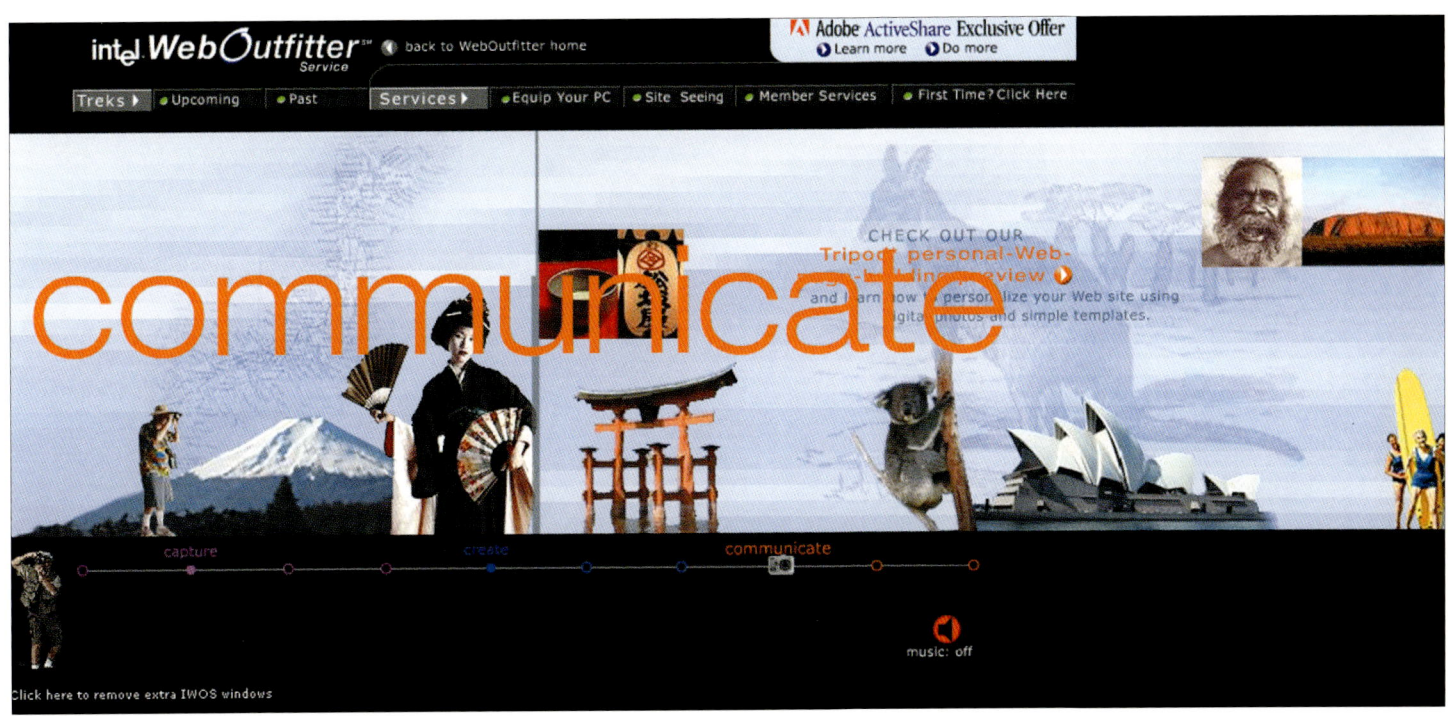

{PROMOTIONAL ADVERTISING/ other digital media}

	Silver
AGENCY	EURO RSCG DSW Partners/Salt Lake City
CLIENT	Iomega
ART DIRECTORS	Jared Allen, Scott Eggers
WRITERS	Joe Totten, Tony Hirsch
DIGITAL ARTISTS	Steve Warner, Dennis Millard, Brent Evans
PHOTOGRAPHER	Paul Wakefield
PRODUCER	John Blodgett
MULTIMEDIA	Hillman Curtis
PROGRAMMER	Mac Baker
CREATIVE DIRECTORS	Stephen Thompson, Eric Bute
URL	http://awards.dsw.com/sites/iomega/Y2K_Trailers/train_composite.html
USERNAME	oneshow
PASSWORD	DSW
ID	00 0017 N

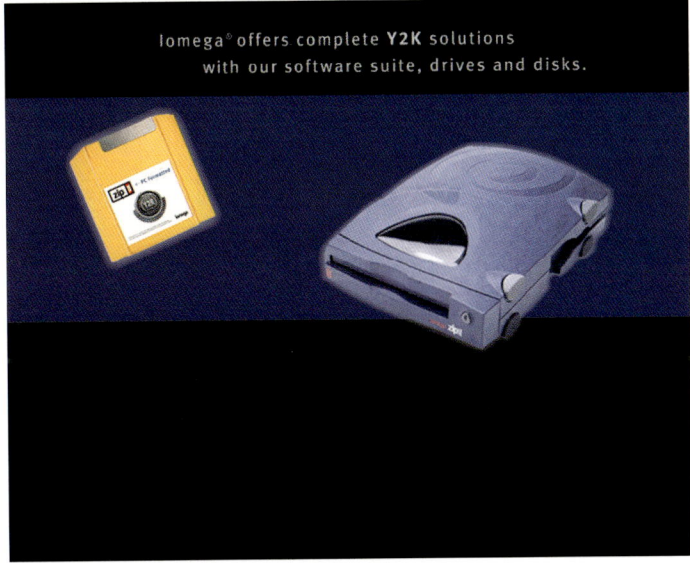

Y2K is old news

By the time you're reading this, Y2K is old news.

But it was very much top of mind when this site was created. Iomega wanted people to prepare for the potential disaster by utilizing Iomega® storage products and some clever software solutions; hence, an Iomega Y2K site with the theme of "taking your information safely from this millennium into the next."

we used motion and sound to increase the drama

The site itself was very informative and helpful, but, well, rather flat. We needed an emotional way to introduce this extremely volatile issue. That's where these Macromedia® Flash trailers came in. Building upon the imagery from our integrated campaign, we compared Y2K to the looming disaster of a giant wave, a speeding train, and a herd of stampeding bulls. We used motion and sound to increase the drama, a brief flicker, then a blank screen to remind people what could happen if they didn't prepare.

Of course, as we all know now, Y2K was the disaster that didn't happen.

{PROMOTIONAL ADVERTISING/ other digital media}

	Bronze
AGENCY	EURO RSCG DSW Partners/Salt Lake City
CLIENT	Iomega
ART DIRECTORS	Jared Allen, Scott Eggers
WRITERS	Joe Totten, Tony Hirsch
DIGITAL ARTISTS	Steve Warner, Dennis Millard, Brent Evans
PHOTOGRAPHER	Paul Wakefield
PRODUCER	John Blodgett
MULTIMEDIA	Hillman Curtis
PROGRAMMER	Mac Baker
CREATIVE DIRECTORS	Stephen Thompson, Eric Bute
URL	http://awards.dsw.com/sites/iomega/Y2K_Trailers/wave_composite.html
USERNAME	oneshow
PASSWORD	DSW
ID	00 0018 N

Y2K is old news

By the time you're reading this, Y2K is old news.

But it was very much top of mind when this site was created. Iomega wanted people to prepare for the potential disaster by utilizing Iomega® storage products and some clever software solutions; hence, an Iomega Y2K site with the theme of "taking your information safely from this millennium into the next."

we used motion and sound to increase the drama

The site itself was very informative and helpful, but, well, rather flat. We needed an emotional way to introduce this extremely volatile issue. That's where these Macromedia® Flash trailers came in. Building upon the imagery from our integrated campaign, we compared Y2K to the looming disaster of a giant wave, a speeding train, and a herd of stampeding bulls. We used motion and sound to increase the drama, a brief flicker, then a blank screen to remind people what could happen if they didn't prepare.

Of course, as we all know now, Y2K was the disaster that didn't happen.

{CORPORATE IMAGE - B2C/ web sites}

CONCAVE SCREAM

Gold

AGENCY	Ad Planet Kinetic Interactive/Singapore
CLIENT	Concave Scream
ART DIRECTOR	Sean Lam
WRITER	Sean Lam
DIGITAL ARTIST	Sean Lam
PHOTOGRAPHER	Claire Lim
PRODUCER	Sean Lam
PROGRAMMER	Sean Lam
CREATIVE DIRECTOR	Sean Lam

ID 00 0019 N

unobtrusive navigation

This fully Flashed site was designed for indie band Concave Scream.

Predominantly black and white with unobtrusive navigation, it aims to project the band's philosophy of "no frills" and their belief in allowing music to speak for itself.

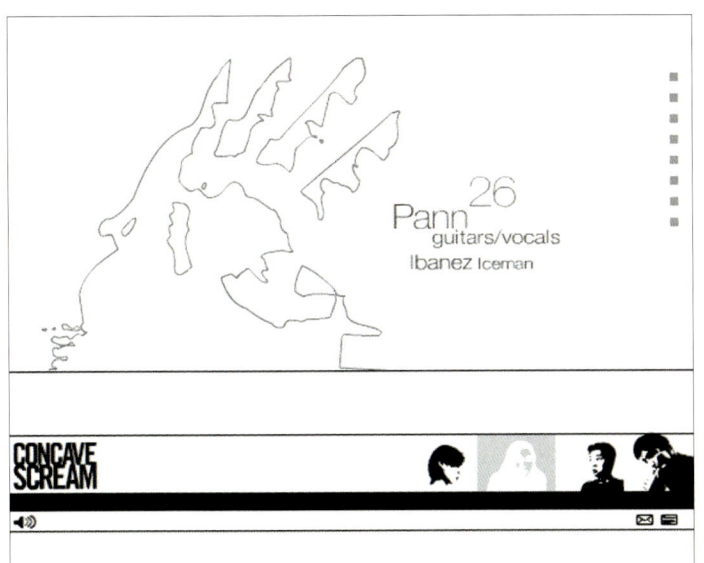

{CORPORATE IMAGE - B2C/ web sites}

	Gold
AGENCY	Deepend London/London
CLIENT	Viaduct
ART DIRECTOR	Alex Griffin
WRITER	James Mair
DIGITAL ARTIST	Alex Griffin
PHOTOGRAPHER	Keith Parry
PRODUCER	Louise Holben
PROGRAMMER	Guillaume Baut-Menard
CREATIVE DIRECTOR	Simon Waterfall
URL	www.viaduct.co.uk
	ID *00 0020 N*

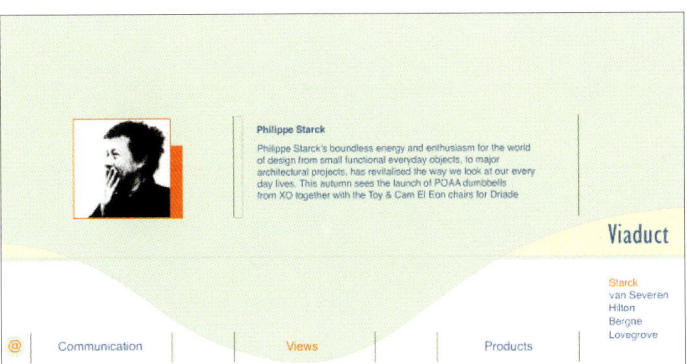

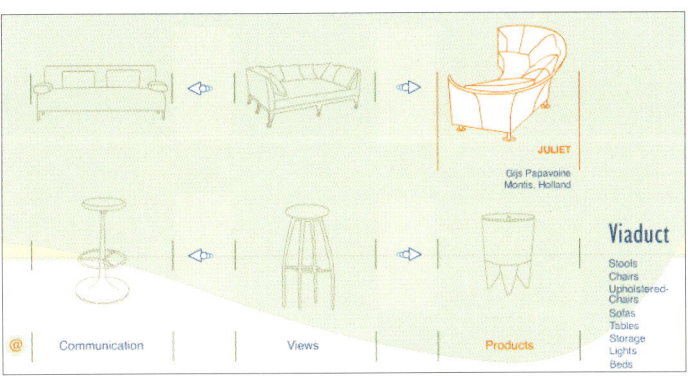

commitment to minimalist and contemporary style

Deepend was commissioned to create a site that would communicate Viaduct's values and reflect their commitment to minimalist and contemporary style.

www.viaduct.co.uk launched in September 1999. Housed within a dramatic 1930s industrial gallery space, Viaduct supplies an extensive range of furniture, compiled from the collections of leading contemporary European designers.

fluid and sophisticated

Says Alex Griffin, "During the research phase of the project, I visited Viaduct's showroom in London and was struck by the quality and light of the space, which really acts as a backdrop for these stunning pieces of furniture. I wanted to recreate that feeling and impact of visiting the showroom, while retaining its accessibility to the furniture. I think I achieved this through the green background shade, mimicking the industrial concrete floor in the showroom, a smooth, fluid and sophisticated environment to reflect the minimalist and contemporary style of the company, and sharp injections of form and color to represent intrinsic elements such as furniture and contributing designers."

{CORPORATE IMAGE - B2C/ web sites}

Silver

AGENCY | Resource/Columbus
CLIENT | Burton Snowboards
ART DIRECTORS | Garrick Reischman, Dan Coe
PRODUCER | Diane Meves
PROGRAMMERS | Andrew Bornand, Randy Hall
CREATIVE DIRECTORS | Dennis Bajec, Greg Vennerholm
URL | www.burton.com

ID 00 0021 N

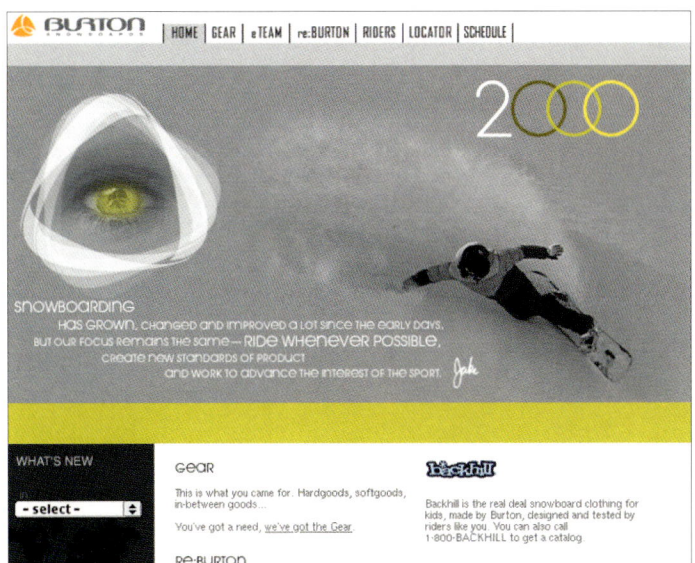

cutting edge, hip, and technologically savvy audience

The Burton 2000 site is designed to connect snowboard riders with one another, and to provide the latest information about Burton products and the sport of snowboarding itself. The site is completely redesigned every year to keep up with the expectations of its cutting edge, hip, and technologically savvy audience.

The current site includes a complete online catalog of Burton products, a Dealer Locator section, and the Pro Team section, where users can check up on their favorite riders. Enthusiasts can also join the e-team, an online community of riders who exchange information and share their love of the sport. Even those new to the sport can check out the "newbie" section to learn tips and techniques on how to get started!

it's a passion

If there is one word that can describe snowboarding — the sport, the community, the people who ride — it's passion. Best put in the words of Jake Burton, "Snowboarding has grown, changed, and improved a lot since the early days but our focus remains the same — ride whenever possible." This passion is a key element in the success of the Burton site. The designers on this site are snowboard enthusiasts themselves, so it's not too difficult to get into the mind of that target audience!

{CORPORATE IMAGE - B2C/ web sites}

Silver

AGENCY *Sapient/San Francisco*
CLIENT *Adobe*
ART DIRECTORS *Bernie DeChant, Dave Le*
PRODUCERS *Pascal, Jonathon Chiappa*
PROGRAMMERS *Pascal, Jonathon Troiano, Shawn Collins, Gene Lee, Marcus Hasselblad*
URL *www.adobe.com*
ID *00 0022 N*

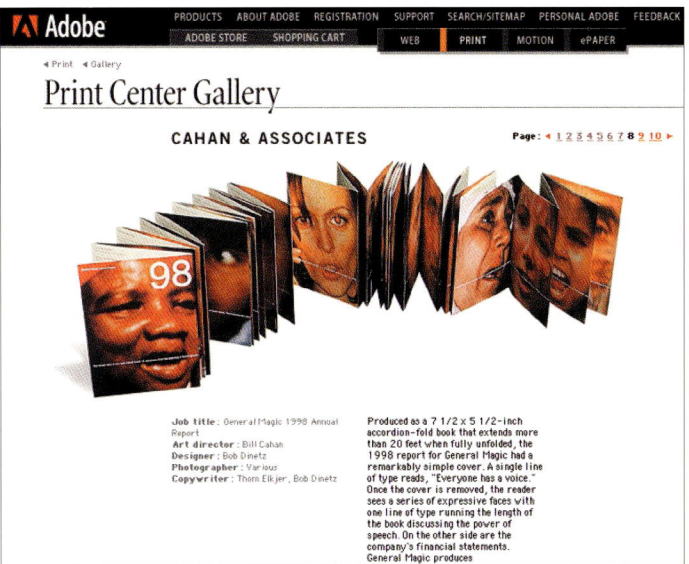

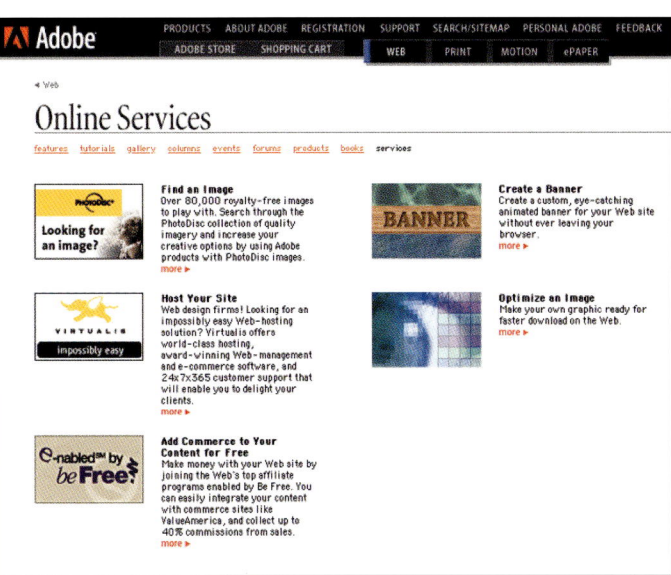

a dream project — Adobe.com was a dream project for many on our team.

inspire and inform users — The goal of the Adobe.com redesign was to create the ultimate destination site for creative professionals. We set out to create an easy-to-navigate site that would inspire and inform users, support existing customers, and facilitate sale of product. Our team streamlined the store's browsing and purchase processes, created a product library section with tutorials, tips, and techniques, and developed channels focused on the customers' areas of interest (PRINT, WEB, MOTION, ePAPER). These features all helped showcase Adobe's brand and establish it as a leader in internet technology and design.

collaboration and innovation — The inspiration and success of the site are the result of the tight collaboration, innovation and continual refinement from everyone on the team: strategists, information architects, designers, site developers, programmers, project managers, and the client.

Adobe.com was a dream project for many on our team, especially the designers and site developers who couldn't imagine a world without Photoshop and Illustrator.

{CORPORATE IMAGE - B2C/ web sites}

Bronze
AGENCY Ad Planet: Kinetic Interactive/Singapore
CLIENT Pestbusters
ART DIRECTORS Sean Lam, Benjy Choo
WRITER Michele Klyne
PRODUCERS Benjy Choo, Sean Lam
PROGRAMMERS Sean Lam, Benjy Choo
CREATIVE DIRECTORS Benjy Choo, Sean Lam
ID 00 0023 N

informative but entertaining

The challenge to the web site designers was to create a site both informative and entertaining, such that it shakes the perception that pest control is dull, boring, and distasteful. The web site had to reflect the client's leading position, it's superior technology and research developments, as well as the company's culture of fun.

{CORPORATE IMAGE - B2C/ web sites}

EXPRESS
THE SUMMER RUNWAY

Bronze

AGENCY	Resource/Columbus
CLIENT	Express
ART DIRECTOR	Elaine Murray
DIGITAL ARTIST	Jason Oleszczul
PROGRAMMERS	Joel Stanley, Mandar Mhaskar, Jeff Blankenberg, Jeff Jarry
CREATIVE DIRECTOR	Christopher Barcelona
URL	www.expressfashion.com
ID	00 0024 N

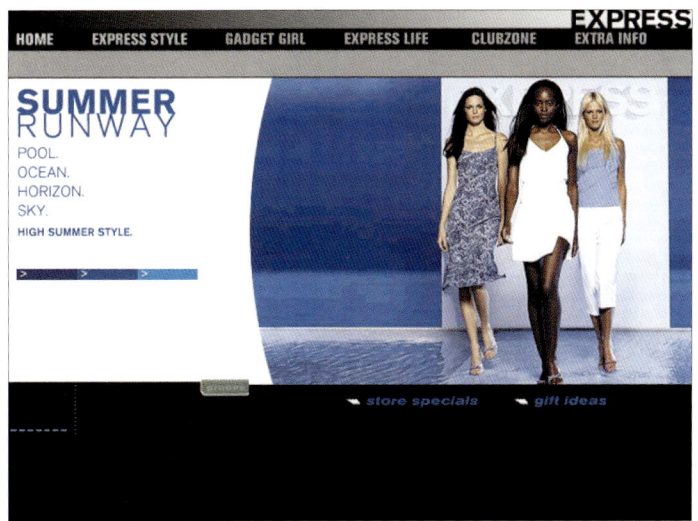

urban, sexy, and up-to-date

The Express site is aimed at young women just out of college who are looking for affordable but trendy clothing. The Express girl is modern, urban, sexy, and up-to-date on the latest fashion, technology, and music. Our objective was to target the Express customer beyond just fashion and include lifestyle.

gadget girl

We needed to get inside of her head — what does this Express girl want to know? Who does she want to be? What type of life does she want to live? After careful consideration and lots and lots of research, we came up with a slew of perfect solutions! Not only can visitors view recommended outfits and create their own, other sections create lifestyle-focused experiences. The site offers a section where visitors can listen to samples of the hottest tunes. The "Gadget Girl" highlights all of the latest technology: palm pilots, cell phones, and the best web sites to find all of their favorite items.

"getting into the head"

Visitors can access the Express little black book to find out all of the hippest places to go in New York and other cities, and much, much more. Let's just say we definitely found "getting into the head" of the young, urban, and hip Express girl quite a blast!

{CORPORATE IMAGE - B2C/ CD-ROM}

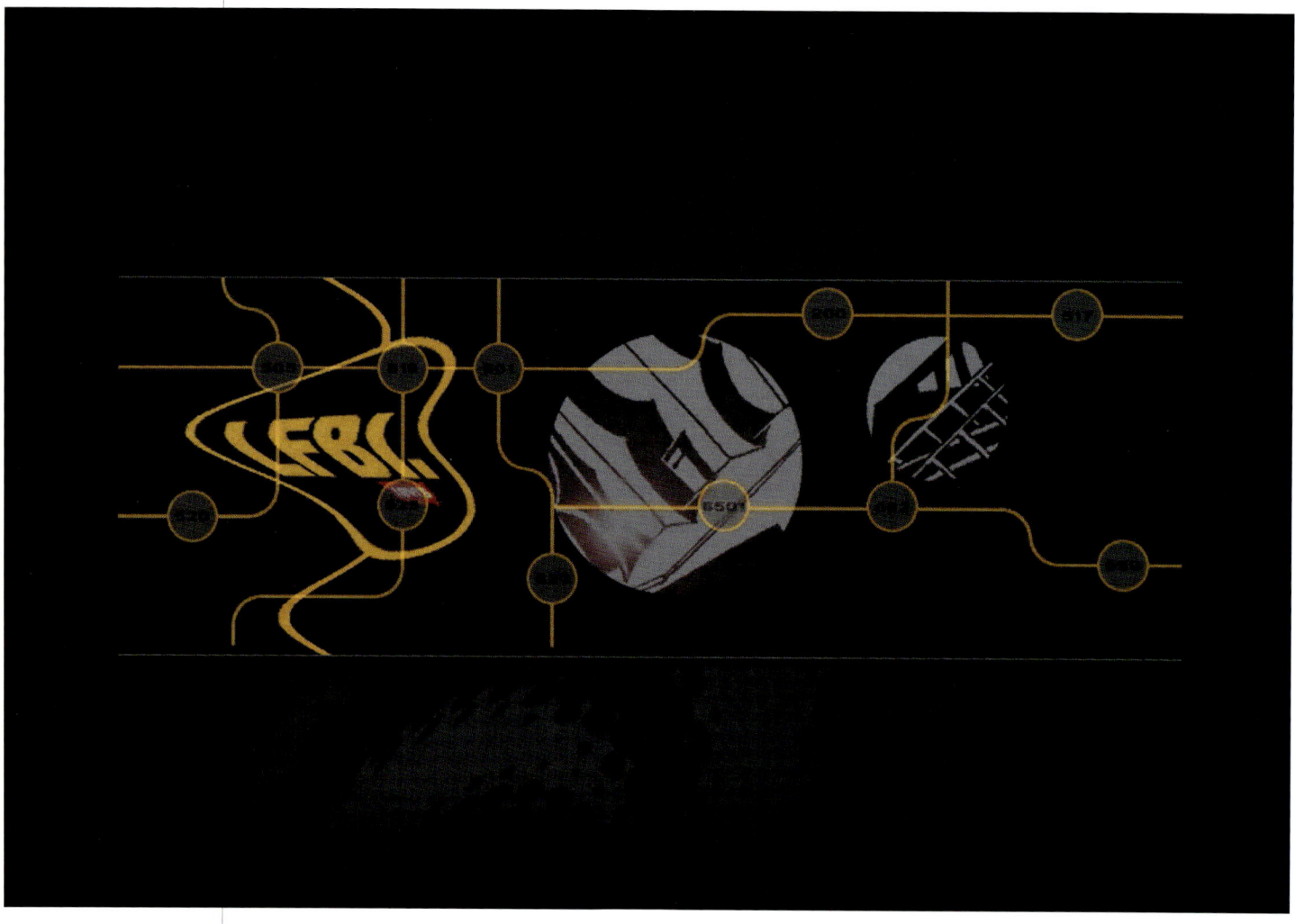

Silver
- **AGENCY** *Elephant Seven/Hamburg*
- **CLIENT** *Levi Strauss Germany*
- **ART DIRECTOR** *Nadim Habib*
- **WRITER** *Daniel Richau*
- **PRODUCERS** *Dirk Kedrowitsch, Nicole Reichert*
- **PROGRAMMERS** *Klemens Heinen, Andreas von Raven*
- **CREATIVE DIRECTORS** *Barbara Schmidt, Paul Apostolou*
- **ID** *00 0050 N*

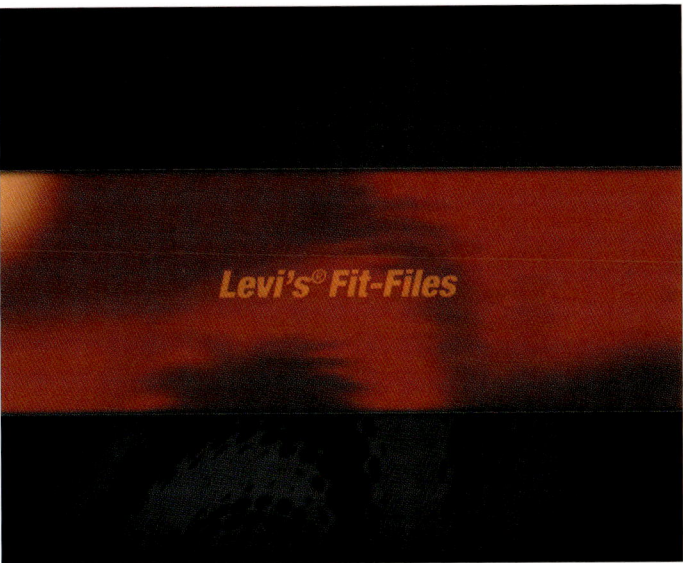

Levi's detective	The Levis Fit Files PC game is the main feature of a promotion for the whole Levi's range of products. You play the part of a Levi's detective in the service of the LFBI, the Levi's Fit Bureau International.
your mission:	Capture aliens that have surreptitiously mingled with ordinary people. How you find them: They wear low-quality copied jeans. On this quest, all kinds of different characters help you to collect clues. Each of these characters stands for a different Levi's fit.
a comprehensive marketing package	If you correctly identify the aliens, you are supplied a one-word solution that would have made you able to win a trip to London (if you would have sent it back during promotion time). The CD-ROM has been part of a comprehensive marketing package containing advertising media like flyers, posters, window stickers, signs for shelves, collection boxes (for solution cards), and mouse pads.

{CORPORATE IMAGE - B2C/ other digital media}

Silver

AGENCY *Deepend London/London*
CLIENT *Apple Computer*
ART DIRECTOR *Richard Schatzberger*
DIGITAL ARTIST *Richard Schatzberger*
PRODUCER *Tom Hostler*
PROGRAMMER *Richard Schatzberger*
URL *www.deepend.co.uk/awards/oneshow/lff.html*
ID *00 0025 N*

energy and passion
Richard Schatzberger, Art Director and interactive designer, was commissioned to promote London's Film Festival. Deepend's solution, harnessed the energy and passion of the Festival's varied program by presenting a daily pick of highlights, such as a specific trailer, short film or interview, titillating the viewer with previews of tomorrow's exclusive content.

fluid motion
Comments Richard Schatzberger, "The fusion of QuickTime and Flash was the perfect environment to design this channel. The design took on the fluid motion of the movie medium and incorporated the brand values of the festival itself. Bold coloration was used to give the channel a fun, exciting, and fast feel."

{CORPORATE IMAGE - B2C/ other digital media}

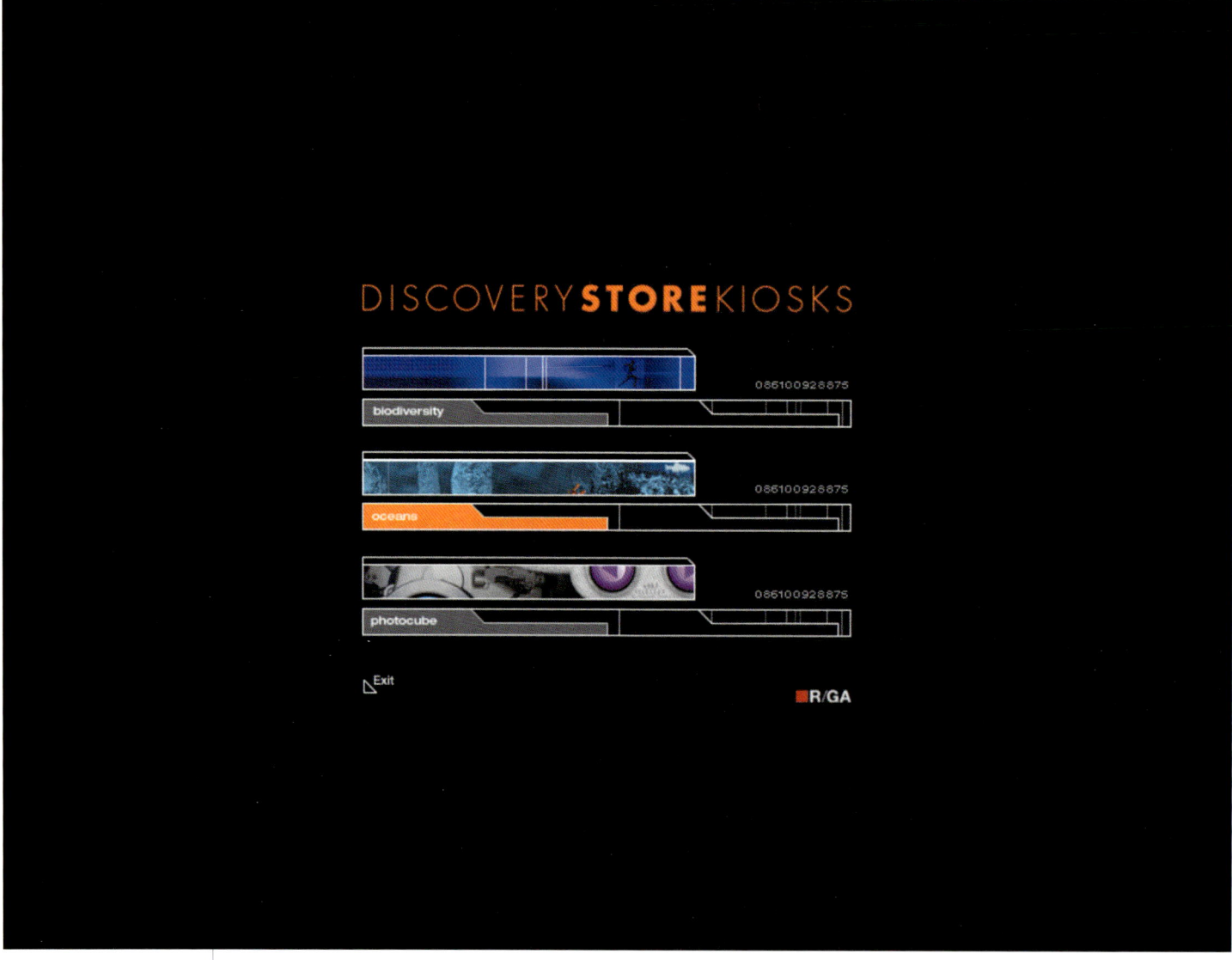

	Silver
AGENCY	R/GA/New York
CLIENT	Discovery Communications Inc.
ART DIRECTORS	Vincent Lacava, Lesli Karavil
PRODUCER	Scott Schneider
PROGRAMMER	John Jones
CREATIVE DIRECTOR	Frank Lantz
	ID 00 0026 N

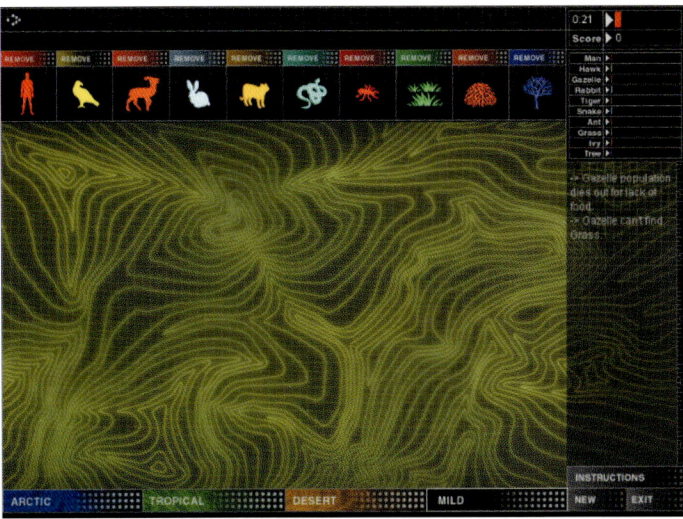

biodiversity — Biodiversity was the first and the most difficult kiosk. There were any number of times where our ambition to simulate biodiversity in 3 minutes or less—which had seemed quite reasonable at an earlier time—appeared to be completely absurd.

Working birth and death into the game was tricky and a problem that plagued us the longest. Up until the last 1/4 of development the game balance was still off; creatures kept dying out before giving birth, new creatures had to wait until they were born, and the whole system would come to a grinding halt.

As it turned out, the solution for the stagnant system was to allow creatures to displace other creatures the second they were born, rather than force them to queue for space in the ecosystem. As soon as we did that, it began to work just as we'd hoped.

shapeshifter — We were glad to work on this after Biodiversity, which had so many difficult design issues. Shapeshifter was conceived as a game where the player could see the world through the eyes of different sea creatures. Originally the plan was to have the viewpoint shift, scale to change, etc., but it became apparent that this would have been a very disorienting & awkward game experience.

photocube — Photocube was initially conceived as a sort of Jules Verne-esque time machine, complete with the clunkiness that formed the pre-computer-age vision of technology. When you look at the kiosk's interface you see metal, exposed wires, screws—details of construction that are all missing from today's ergonomic models. We wanted it to have the feel of a nickelodeon, with the charm encapsulated in the idea of peeking through a small space to see a set of moving pictures, yet add touches to bring it right up to par with modern kids' expectations of an interactive experience.

{CORPORATE IMAGE - B2B/ web sites}

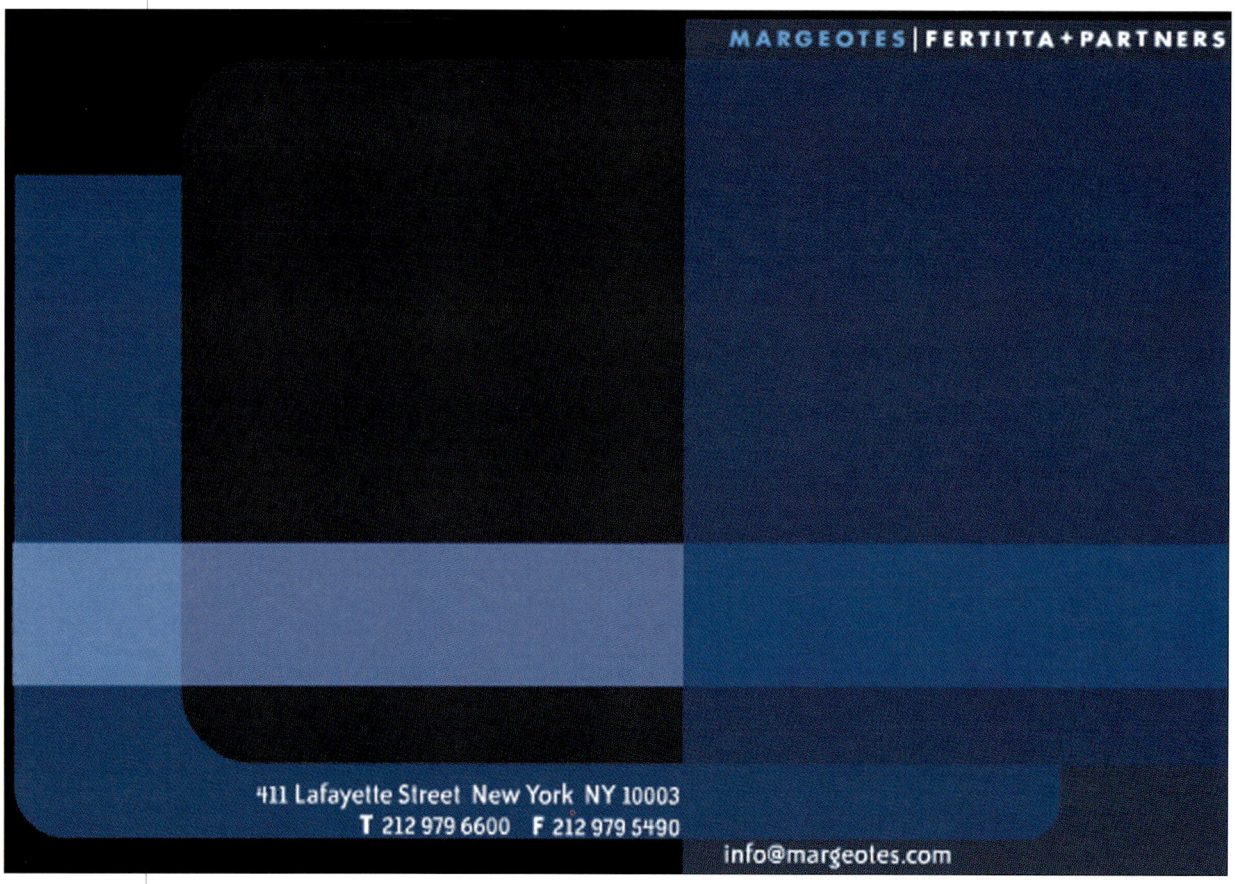

Gold

AGENCY Dennis Interactive/Margeotes Fertitta + Partners/New York
CLIENT Margeotes, Fertitta + Partners
ART DIRECTORS Justin Crawford, Ze Frank, Zoe Chan, Vivian Leung
WRITERS Alison Gragnano, Hal Williams
PHOTOGRAPHER Celeste Crosby
PRODUCER Mindy Roland
PROGRAMMERS Chris Phoenix, Sebastian Bylinski
CREATIVE DIRECTORS Greg Knoll, Alison Gragnano
URL www.margeotes.com
ID 00 0027 N

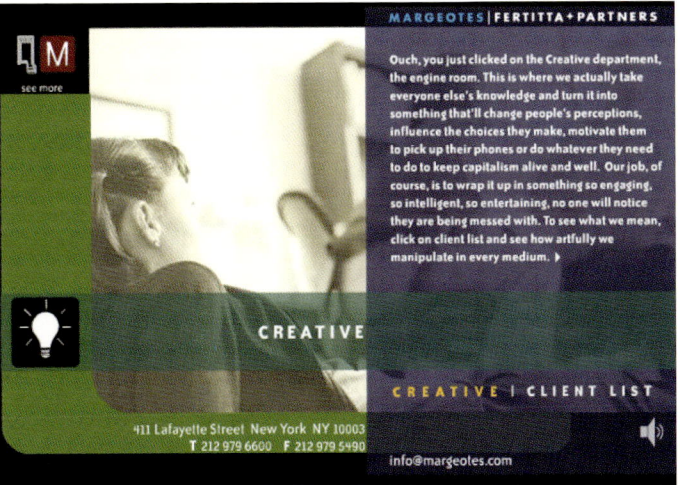

the challenge was to create a unique virtual experience

www.margeotes.com was a joint project effort between Dennis Interactive and Margeotes Interactive. The challenge was to create a unique virtual experience that provided users with information on the company and expressed the personality and culture of Margeotes Fertitta + Partners. It needed to be sophisticated, elegant, and fun, a site that people would enjoy interacting with.

users control their experience

We selected Flash as the best means for delivering compact rich media and achieving Margeotes' desired goals. It was decided the navigational system should be smooth and fluid and surprise the user with interesting transitional elements. The central idea behind the site was to use Margeotes' actual space as an interactive medium, where the user could learn about each department and service by interacting with the multi-layered, expanding, and contracting Margeotes "office." We took the virtual/actual space idea one step further by visually orienting the user with the office's Manhattan location.

The use of color, movement, and music, combined with a navigational scheme to give the users control over their experience with the choices they make, is what makes this online experience so effective.

{CORPORATE IMAGE - B2B/ web sites}

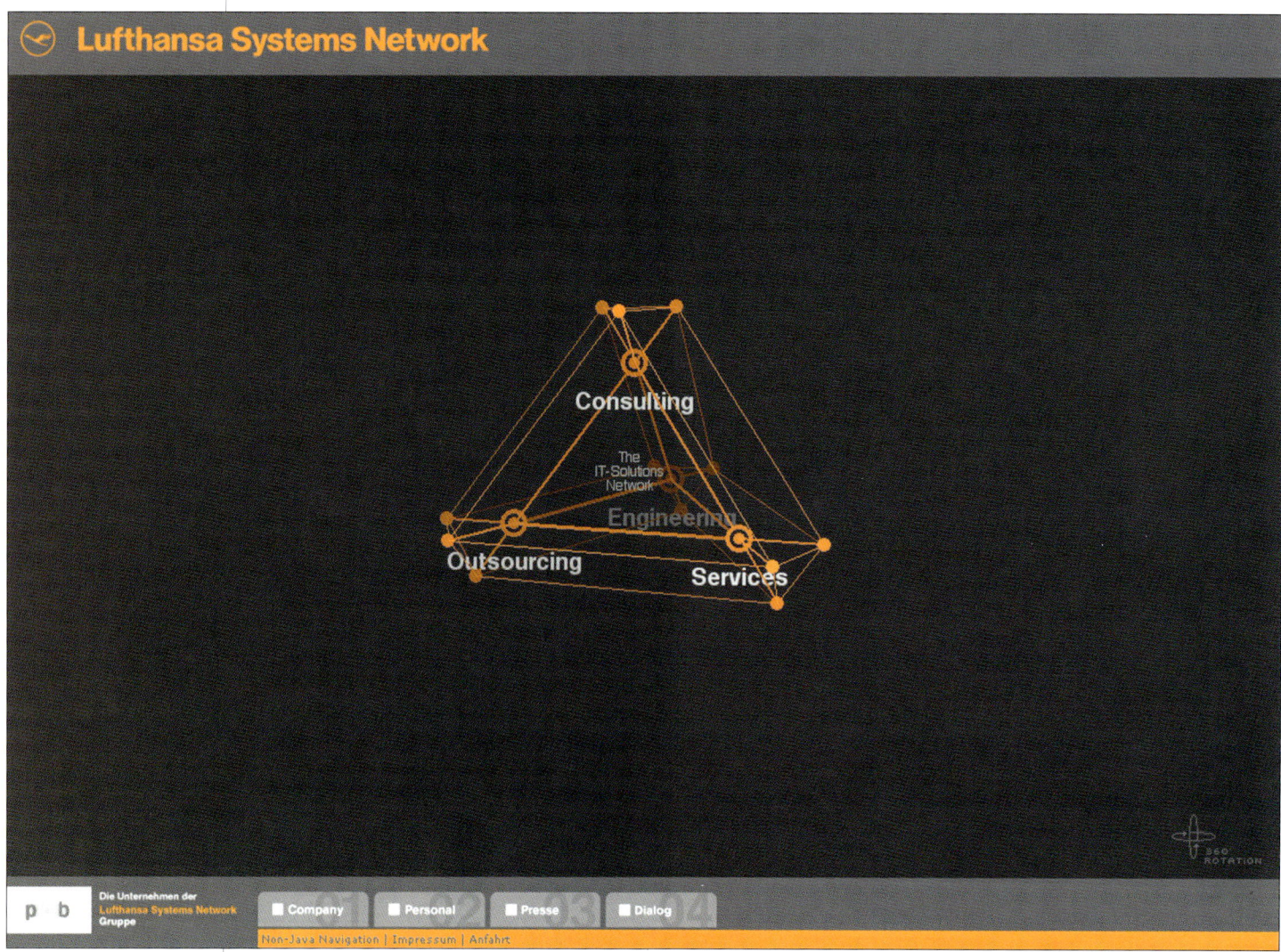

	Silver
AGENCY	Fork Unstable Media/Hamburg
CLIENT	Lufthansa Systems Network
DIGITAL ARTIST	Andrea Mittmann
PROGRAMMER	Jan-Michael Studt
CREATIVE DIRECTOR	Jeremy Abbett
URL	www.lhsysnet.com
	ID 00 0028 N

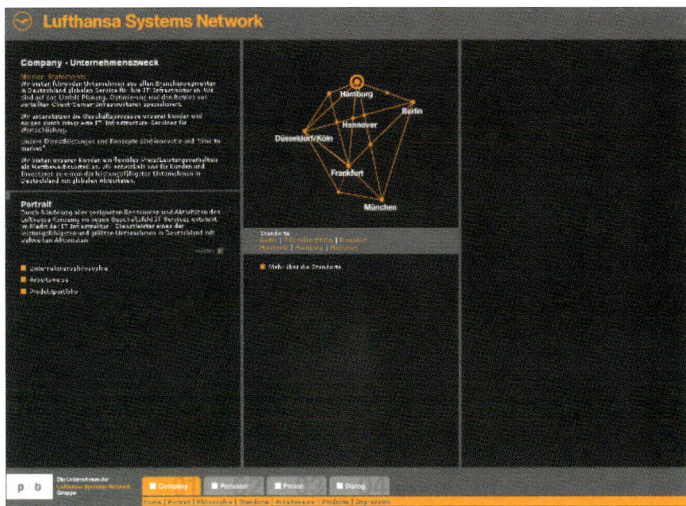

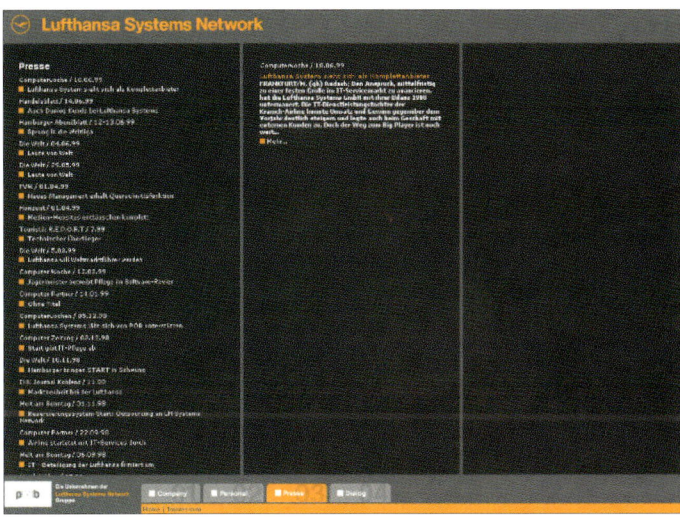

dynamic organizational structure

We wanted the site to be a visual impression of the dynamic organizational structure.

When we began designing the web site of the Lufthansa Systems Network, the IT branch of Germany's number one airline, we took it as a special challenge to visualize a vast network of interdisciplinary IT departments under one headquarters in Hamburg.

navigation is the leading key visual

Lufthansa Systems Network provides sophisticated Client-Server Infrastructure Services for clients around the world. Fork developed a 3-D Java-based navigation tool that succeeds in visualizing the sheer scope and intricacy of this vernetzung within a sitemap-structure that encourages browsing complex topics and services within a simple information hierarchy. As users narrow their focus around a particular theme, the Java navigation collapses into a narrow representation of immediately related links and simple HTML.

The site gives new clients and decision-makers a convincing visual impression of the dynamic organizational structure of the network where navigation is the leading key visual for describing Lufthansa Systems Network GmbH and learning more about it.

{CORPORATE IMAGE - B2B/ web sites}

Bronze
AGENCY | Renaissance Multimedia/New York
CLIENT | Renaissance Multimedia
ART DIRECTOR | Jenya Spektor
WRITER | Andrew Edwards
PHOTOGRAPHER | Ed Mullen
PRODUCER | Mailet Lopez
PROGRAMMER | Jenya Spektor
URL | www.vizyinteractive.com
ID 00 0029 N

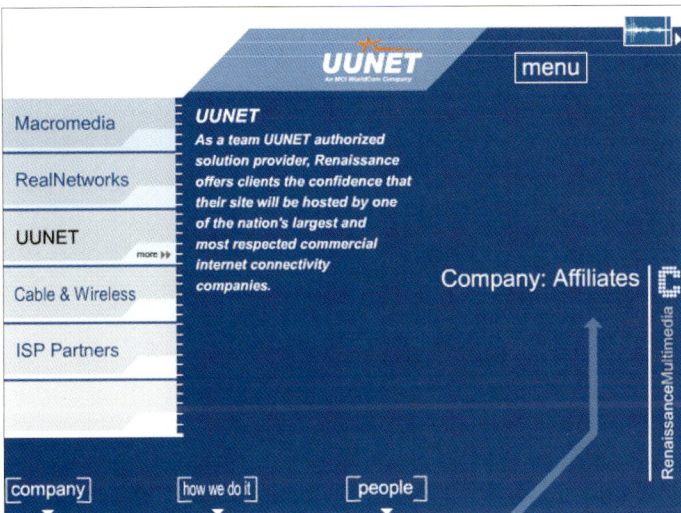

the history	Renaissance Multimedia (now Vizy Interactive) was founded in 1993 and today, with offices in New York, Boston and London, is one of the top 30 interactive agencies, providing end-to-end ebusiness solutions to our clients. In developing our web site we wanted to target prospective clients and showcase our best work; especially our ability to engage users with active content using Macromedia's Flash technology.
the situation	In developing the site, we wanted to show that we develop great on-line user experiences, using the best technology and design. We also wanted to show that our company is based on the capabilities of our staff. Designers, programmers, marketing specialists all worked together to create a collaborative success. The site was developed over the course of two months, using nearly equal parts technology, skill, spirited discussion, and pizza.
the Flash site	The result is a clean, straightforward expression of our collective outlook: which is, first to engage the users, then to inform them, then to lead them towards more interactivity with our company. A window into the likes and dislikes of our personnel encourages contact with us, and we believe this open attitude has helped us win new business.
the future	Our skilled designers, programmers and emarketers are busy on the next version of our Vizy Interactive site. We hope to see you here next year.

{CORPORATE IMAGE - B2B/ CD-ROM}

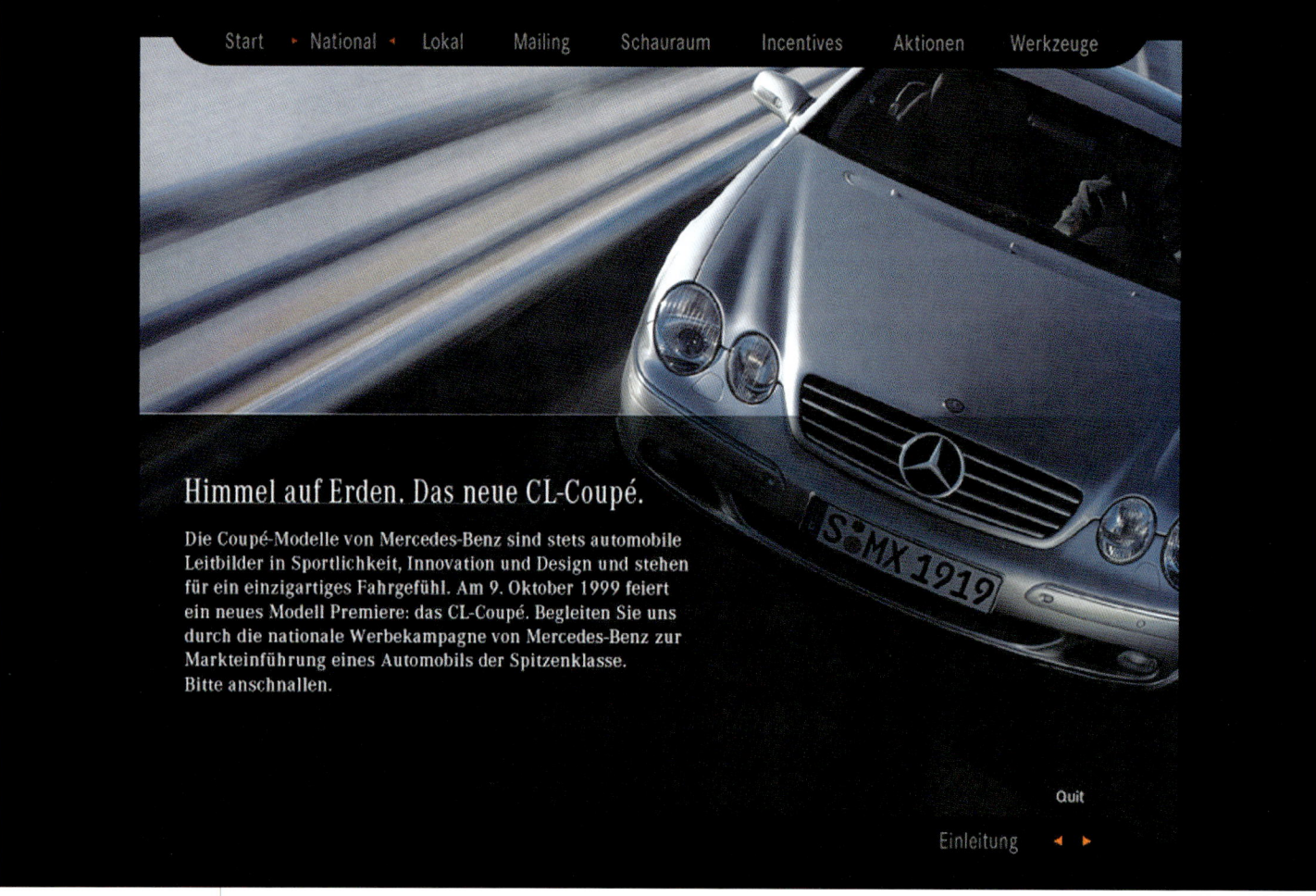

Gold
- **AGENCY** Elephant Seven/Hamburg
- **CLIENT** DaimlerChrysler AG, Stuttgart
- **ART DIRECTOR** Oliver Viets
- **WRITER** Nina Koerfers
- **PRODUCERS** Dirk Kedrowitsch, Marc Treichel
- **PROGRAMMER** Ralf-Ingo Koch
- **CREATIVE DIRECTORS** Barbara Schmidt, Paul Apostolou
- **ID** 00 0030 N

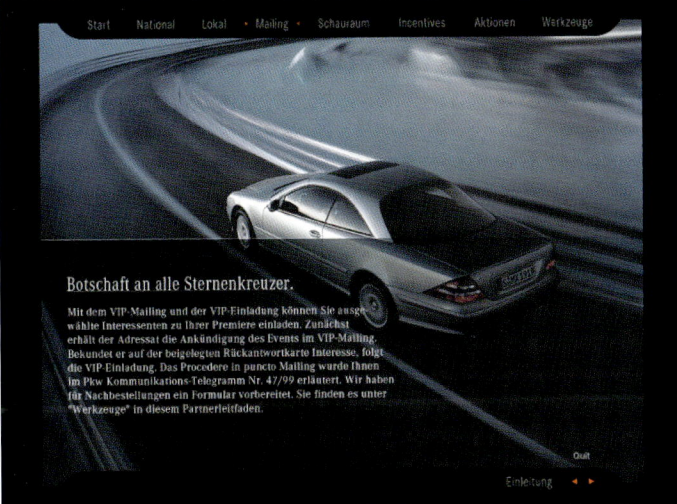

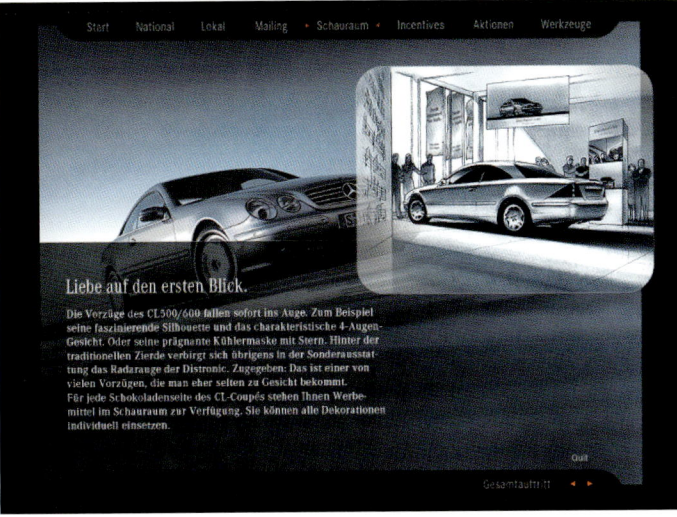

an internal communication tool	The Mercedes-Benz Partnerleitfaden on CD-ROM is an internal communication tool that informs about 800 Mercedes-Benz dealers in Germany of the marketing activities for the launch of new model ranges. The Partnerleitfaden for the brand-new CL coupe went out to the partners in July 1999.
why a CD-ROM	Why a CD-ROM and not a conventional printed catalogue? Simple. The electronic version has distinct advantages. Mercedes-Benz partners gain inspiration from examples of customer mailings that are available as data files. They can also choose from a wide selection of give-aways and request these immediately by order form.
presented as they are intended	Partners are, of course, also informed of Mercedes-Benz print, radio, TV, and outdoor advertising. The CD-ROM, however allowes films and radio commercials to be presented as they are intended: in sound and pictures.
special tools	Even the partners' own advertising activities have stepped up a gear: Special tools allow dealers to edit predesigned ad motifs on a PC. The print ad is then sent as a file for exposure or directly to the publishers.

This saves a lot of work in pre-press, as well as time and money.

{CORPORATE IMAGE - B2B/ CD-ROM}

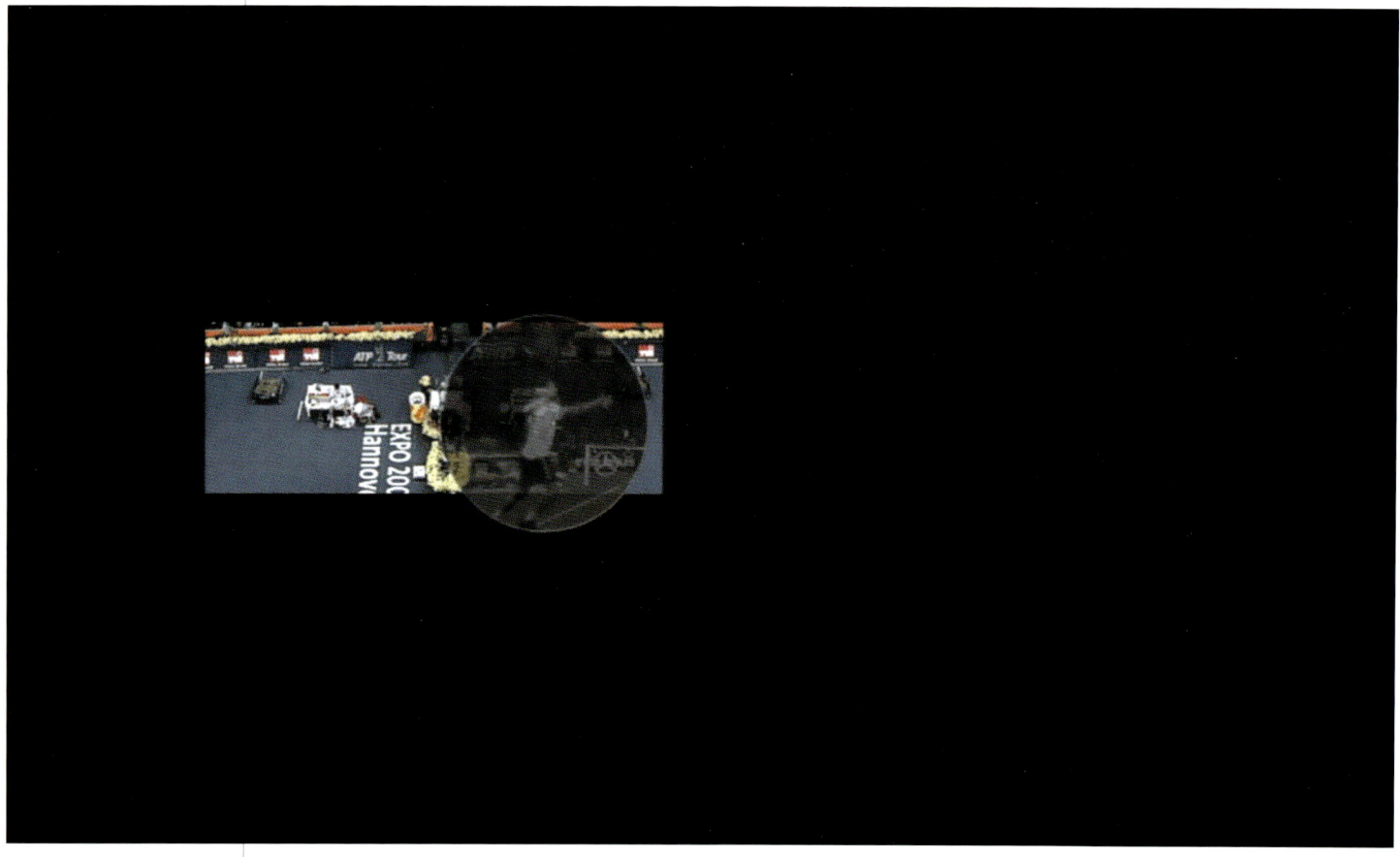

	Silver
AGENCY	Elephant Seven/Hamburg
CLIENT	Quba Werbeagentur, Thomas Querfurth
ART DIRECTORS	Andi Henkel, Michael Vogt
WRITER	Marcus Reisiger
PHOTOGRAPHERS	Andi Henkel, Florian Bruchhaeuser
PRODUCER	Heidi Hamann
MULTIMEDIA	Florian Bruchhaeuser
PROGRAMMER	Florian Bruchhaeuser
CREATIVE DIRECTORS	Barbara Schmidt, Paul Apostolou
ID	00 0031 N

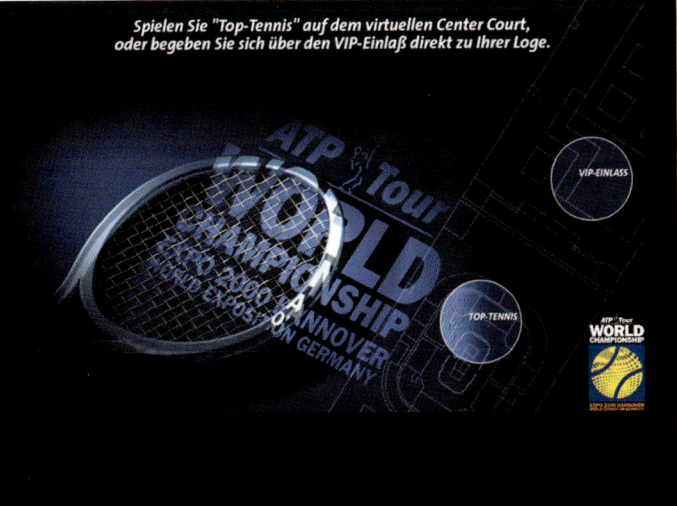

a virtual guided tour

The task of the ATP Tour World Championship CD-ROM: To show German managers and marketing heads how impressive Center Court VIP boxes at the ATP Tour World Championship in Hanover really are, and to encourage them to make reservations for this prestigious event. The CD-ROM is laid out like a virtual guided tour, taking you around the EXPO Tennis Dome, the biggest free-standing hall in Europe, while making use of 3-D animation, 360-degree panorama, Quicktime movies, sounds, visuals, and an interactive tennis game.

fluid and sophisticated

After a hostess welcomes the user at the entrance to the Center Court, one gets a VR-panorama to call up highlights of past games and victory ceremonies, and even go on a "test sit-down" in a VIP box, which provides outstanding views of Center Court action. Those who prefer sweating to sitting can pick up their own racquet and challenge any ATP tour member to a video-game tennis match. If you are not tough enough, find out why by reading the players' portraits. Or make an interactive interview with the reigning world champion, Alex Corretja. Or just dig into the "interactive buffet" as a foretaste of delicious things to come. Elephant Seven has developed this CD-ROM together with the Quba Advertising Agency.

{CORPORATE IMAGE - B2B/ CD-ROM}

CLICK LOGO TO BEGIN

Bronze
AGENCY *Biggs/Gilmore/Kalamazoo*
CLIENT *Michigan Fresh Vegetable Council*
ART DIRECTOR *Linda Foster*
WRITERS *Kathleen Widner, Beth Stuever*
DIGITAL ARTISTS *Jon Austin, Stan Capshaw*
PRODUCER *Sara Burhans*
PROGRAMMERS *Jon Austin, Jeff Yonkers*
CREATIVE DIRECTOR *Ernie Cox*
ID *00 0032 N*

| vegetables | Vegetables are good for you. Michigan vegetables are even better. |
| Michigan vegetables — just better | Vegetables grown in Michigan are fresh. They have their own identity. Michigan vegetables are more colorful than the other vegetables. The hue is brighter on Michigan-grown red peppers. Michigan spuds taste better than the ones grown out West. Michigan asparagus snaps louder when broken in half than the ones from out of state. Carrots grown in Michigan really do improve your vision. |

{CORPORATE IMAGE - B2B/ other digital media}

what is an IBM Business Partner?

click here to find out >>>

Silver

AGENCY	OgilvyInteractive/New York
CLIENT	IBM
ART DIRECTOR	Renee Rotkopf
WRITER	Jay Zasa
DIGITAL ARTISTS	Victor Velez, Jose Galvez
PHOTOGRAPHER	David Barry
PRODUCERS	Pat Dwyer, Jeremy Rosenberg, Leslie Albright, Heavy Industry
MULTIMEDIA	Malvika Mitchell
CREATIVE DIRECTOR	Audrey Fleisher
URL	http://199.229.12.135/awards2000/partnerworld/PWonline.html#
ID	00 0033 N

a bridge between print and the web

The IBM PartnerWorld campaign aims to encourage technology professionals to become IBM Business Partners.

This interactive module forms a conceptual bridge between the print component of the campaign, which focuses on individual business partners but provides few facts about the PartnerWorld program, and the PartnerWorld web site, which is informational but does not reflect the "partner as hero" theme of the campaign.

The piece introduces the partners, gives an overview of the benefits of forming a business partnership with IBM, and allows users to learn more about the individual business partners— including hearing sound clips taken from interviews with the partners.

{CORPORATE IMAGE - B2B/ other digital media}

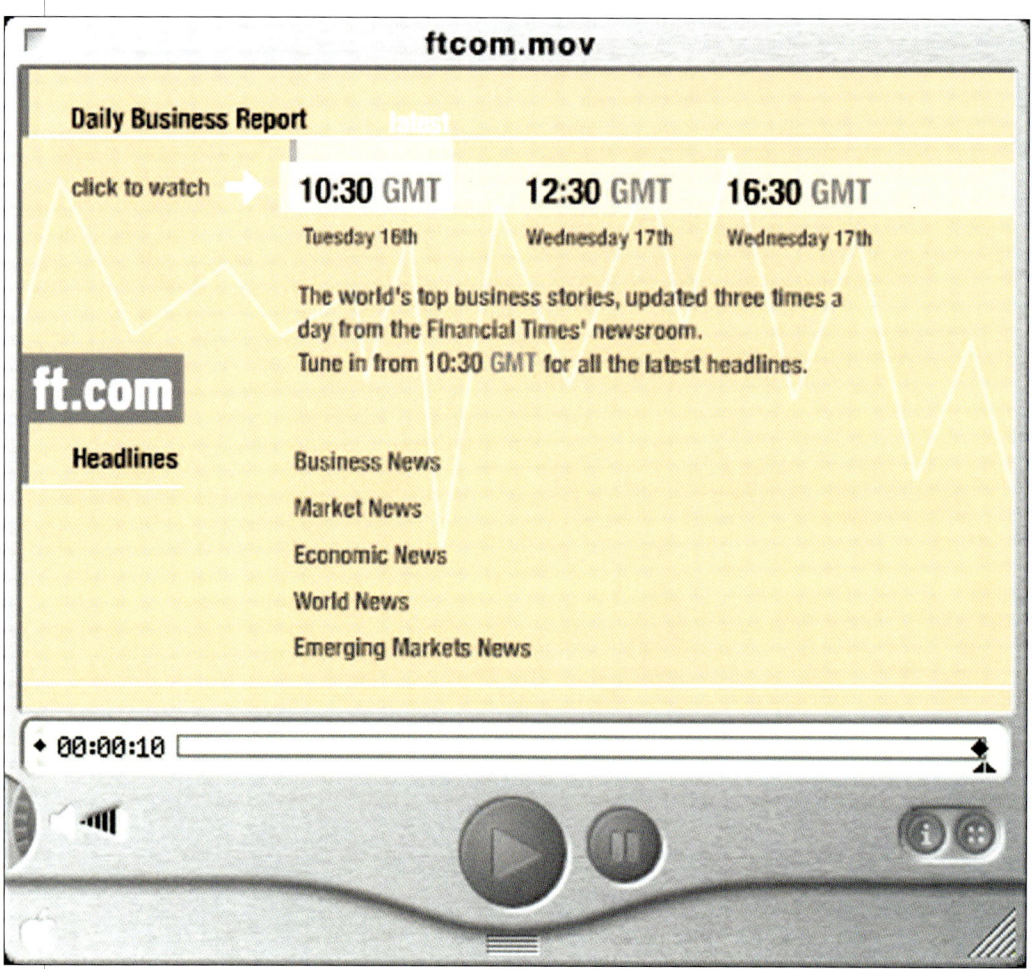

Bronze

AGENCY	Deepend London/London
CLIENT	FT.com
ART DIRECTOR	Nicky Gibson
PRODUCER	Tom Hostler
DIGITAL ARTIST	Nicky Gibson
PROGRAMMER	Nicky Gibson
URL	www.apple.com/quicktime/hotpicks/news/ftcom/

ID 00 0034 N

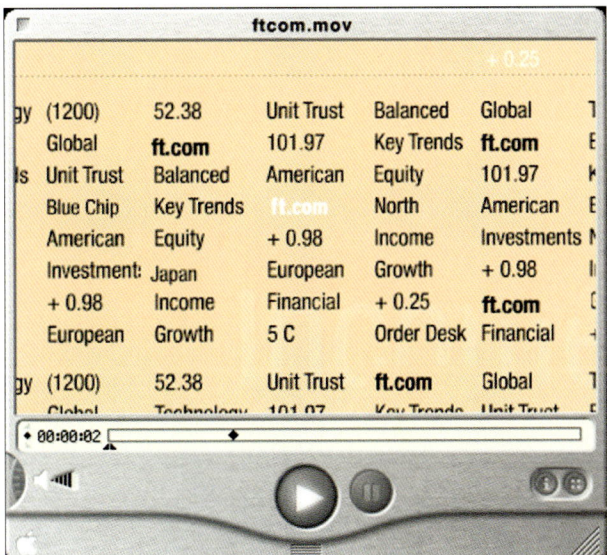

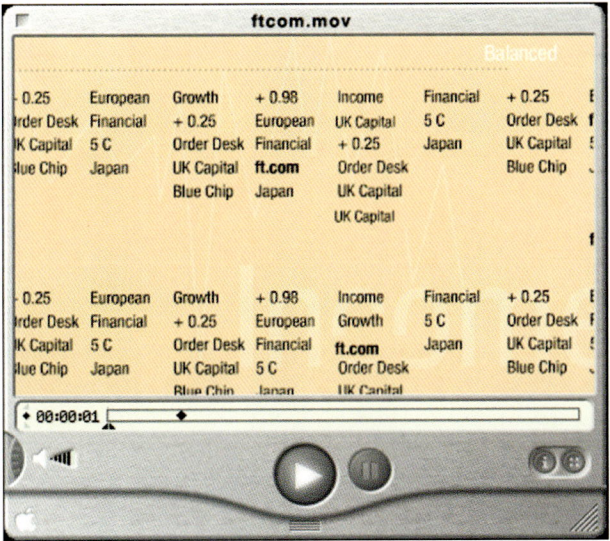

financial information resource

The introductory sequence of the FT.com's QuickTime channel was designed to enhance the FT brand by affirming it as a financial information resource. The rows and columns of financial information refer to stock market listings, while the ever-changing markets were represented by constant motion in the main interface area.

{E-COMMERCE/ web sites}

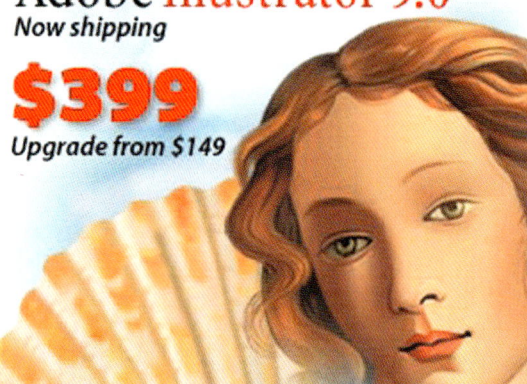

	Gold
AGENCY	Sapient/San Francisco
CLIENT	Adobe
ART DIRECTORS	Bernie DeChant, Dave Le
PRODUCERS	Pascal, Jonathon Chiappa
PROGRAMMERS	Pascal, Jonathon Troiano, Shawn Collins, Gene Lee, Marcus Hasselbald
URL	www.adobe.com/store/main.html
	ID 00 0035 N

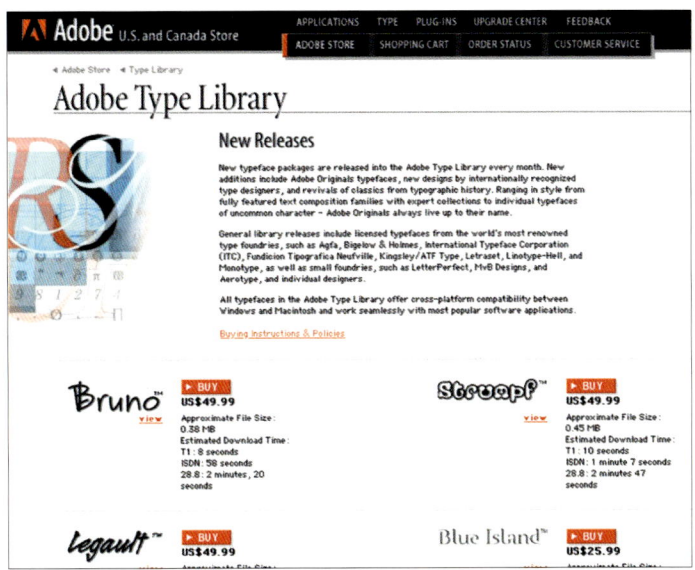

the Adobe.com redesign An integral part of the Adobe.com redesign, was to develop the Adobe Store to allow customers to find and purchase any of Adobe's products using a simple, easy-to-use one-stop shop.

return for inspiration Along with the product library, a comprehensive support section, and channels that showcase how Adobe's products are used in the real world, the site offers customers the information they need to learn about Adobe products, allows them to make purchases, gather support, and return for inspiration.

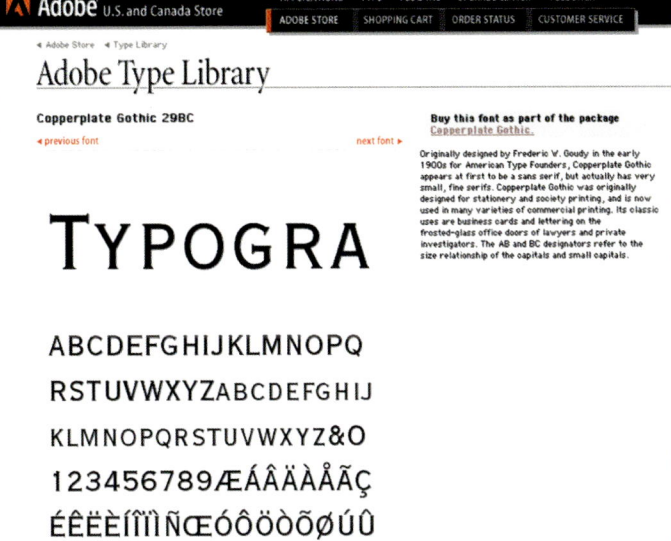

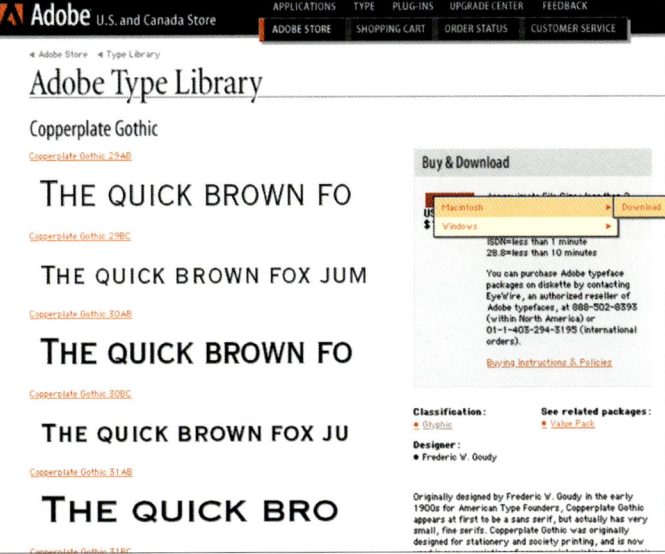

{E-COMMERCE/ web sites}

AGENCY	Silver Sapient/San Francisco
CLIENT	United Airlines
ART DIRECTOR	Philip Kim
WRITER	Dorothy Ivanovich
PROGRAMMERS	Jeremiah Wells, Al Forrestier, Isabel O'Meara, Alejo Jumat, Brian Slutz Roshan Shankur, Rangarajan Sudharsan, Dejan Vucinic, Suhail Ali, Andy Ocken
URL	www.Ual.com
	ID 00 0036 N

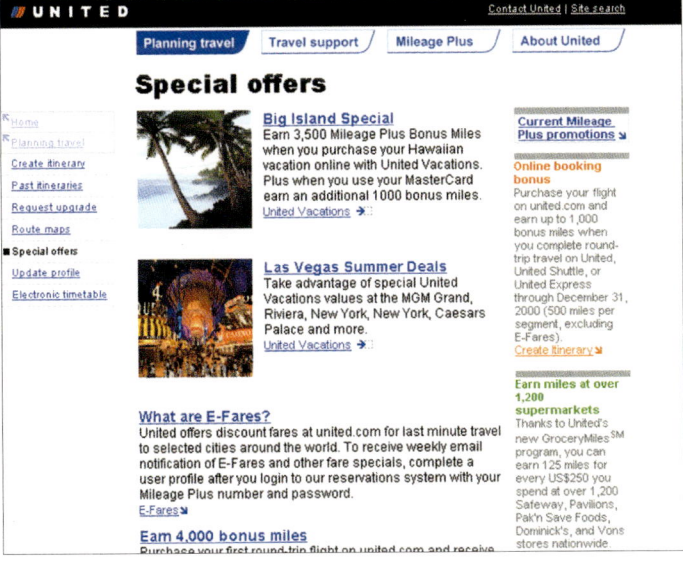

simple, hassle-free travel experience

Create a simple, hassle-free travel experience — this was the goal we set ourselves for United Airlines Online. Next challenge? How to make the site valuable enough for United's primary audience, frequent business travelers, to return to day after day. The solution was simple — we asked them. We staged rapid prototyping sessions with groups of key customers and asked them to "build" their ideal web site. The results were eye-opening, challenged all our preconceived notions about how these discerning users behave online and offline, and provided valuable insight into the tasks they were likely to perform.

the number one airline site

We used this data to drive the final design solution and align the customer needs with United's business goals, technology drivers, and the newly launched United brand identity. As a result, we differentiated United from its competitors and made it the number one airline site (Gomez Poll) for business flyers.

a design point of view

From a design point of view, United.com complements all the other visual touch points a customer will have with United, whether it is the cabin interior of their plane, the signage as they navigate a busy airport — or even the logo on a pack of sugar.

{E-COMMERCE/ other digital media}

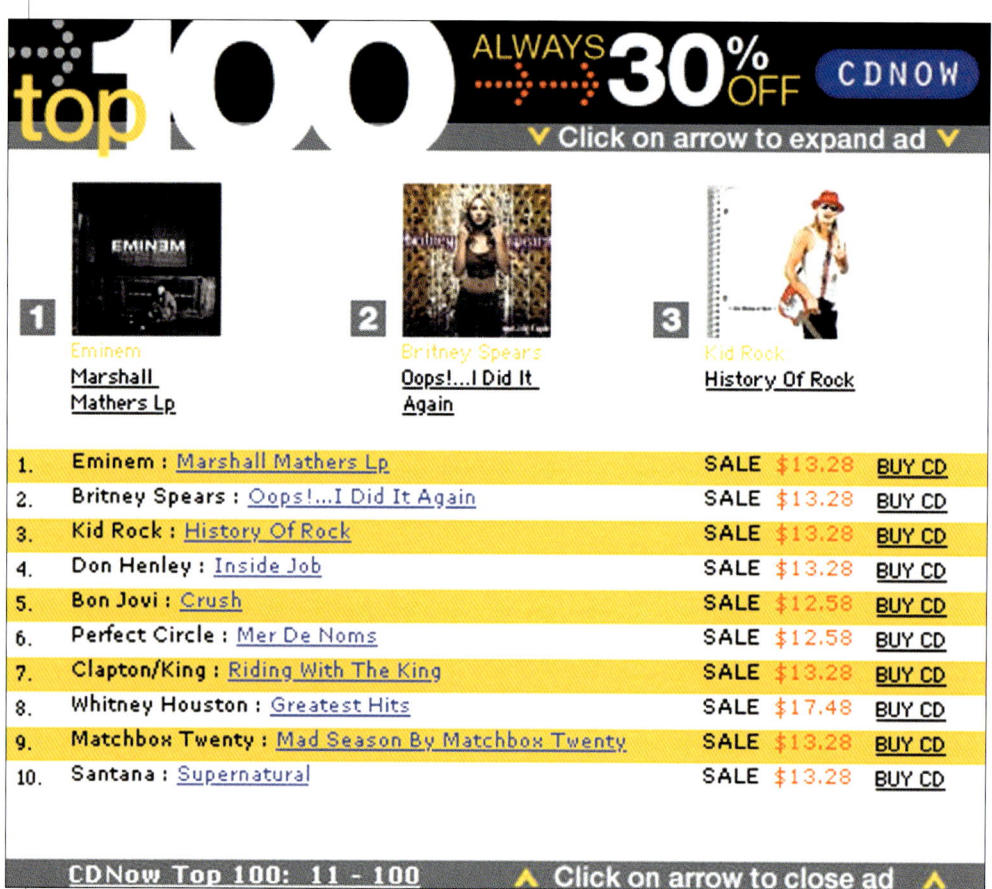

	Bronze
AGENCY	Organic/New York
CLIENT	CDNOW
ART DIRECTOR	John Pompa
WRITER	Dan Ligorner
DIGITAL ARTIST	John Pompa
PRODUCER	Christi Frum
PROGRAMMERS	Aimee Drayer, Sergio Jimenez
CREATIVE DIRECTORS	Stephen Tortorici, Monique Te Selle
URL	http://ads.organic.com/oneshow/cdnowexpando.html
ID	00 0037 N

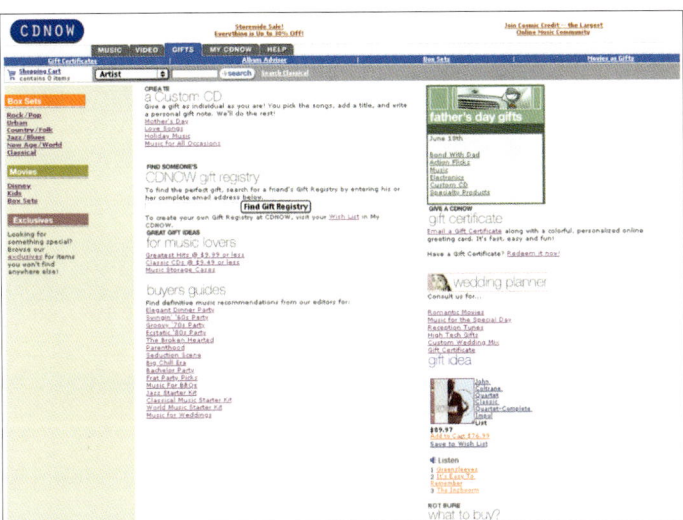

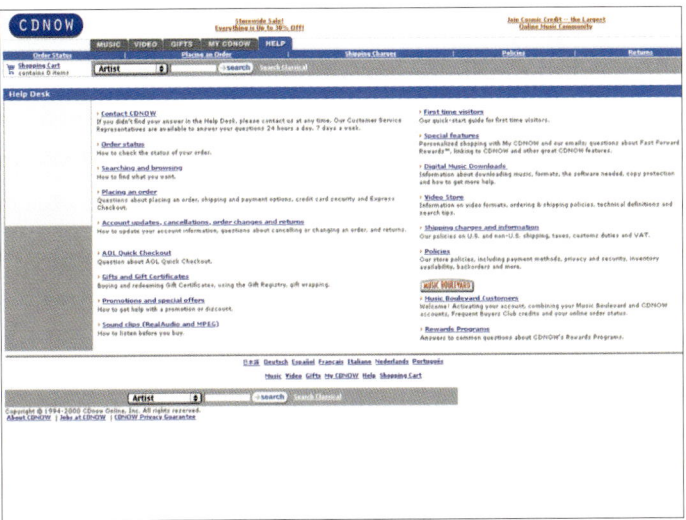

one of those unique ideas

Imagine consumers clicking on an ad that doesn't send them off into cyberspace. The "Expand-O" was one of those unique ideas developed by Organic's creative team to showcase the features and functionality of a smart web site right in the ad.

Conceived in technology and dedicated to the proposition that all ads can deliver more than a banner, the concept was simple: Click on an ad and it expands to a window that delivers dynamically updated content from the client's server, directly through the ad.

dynamically updated ad

CDNOW loved it. Organic built it. And the result is the CDNOW Top 100 Expand-O ad. But technology aside, the Expand-O demonstrates a smart way to leverage the CDNOW brand and bring its content forward, to deliver consumers CDNOW's real time "Top 100" sellers. More to CDNOW's point, this dynamically updated ad was a great solution for a client whose business is dependent upon delivering data-driven content.

{INTEGRATED BRANDING/ campaign}

Gold
AGENCY Arnold Communications/Boston
CLIENT Volkswagen of America, Inc.
ART DIRECTORS Bill Whelan, Robert Hodgin, Dower Phillips
WRITERS Tim Brunelle, Lance Jensen
DIGITAL ARTIST Robert Hodgin
PHOTOGRAPHER Bill Cash
PRODUCERS Bill Whelan, Jon Groves
MULTIMEDIA Robert Hodgin, Ben Neill, Peter DuCharme
PROGRAMMER Jon Groves
CREATIVE DIRECTORS Ron Lawner, Alan Pafenbach, Lance Jensen
URL www.turbonium.com
ID 00 0038 N

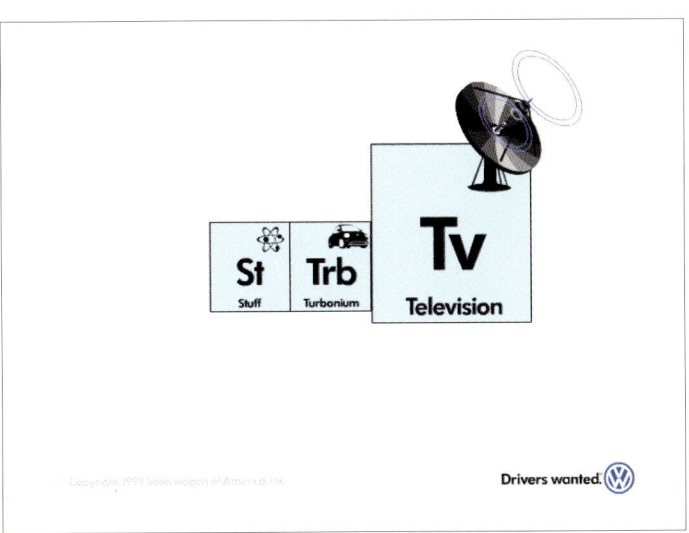

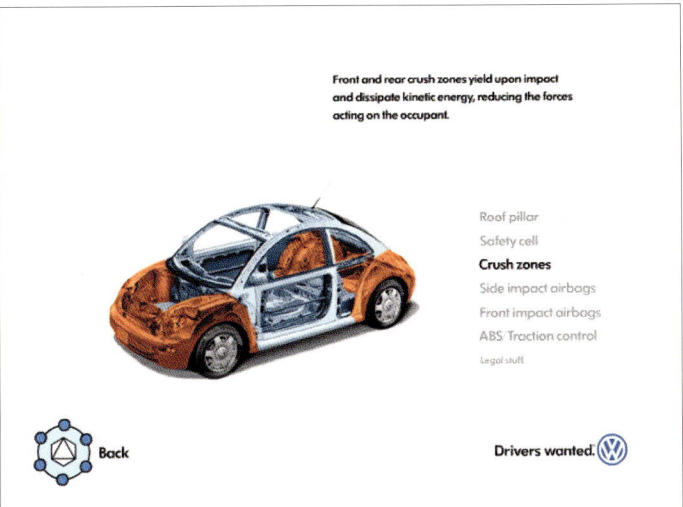

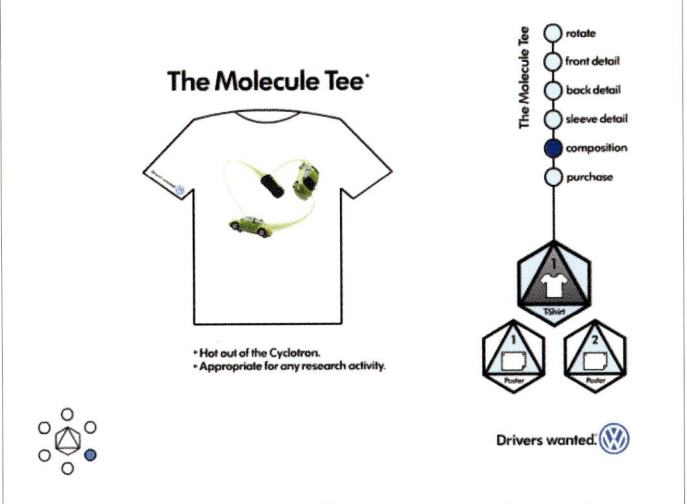

little blood was shed   It all happened really fast. We'd produced print and were in the midst of finishing TV for Volkswagen's Turbo Beetle. The work was based on this fictitious new element: "turbonium." Alan Pafenbach asked us to create a web site to enhance the concept--oh, and we had three weeks before the spot broke nationally. Surprisingly very little blood was shed.

the first time   Turbonium marked the first time an automotive advertiser integrated an idea across television and a web site. (Thanks to Tesa and Liz at VW for believing.)

best of show   Winning Best of Show is an amazing, huge honor that for some strange reason has yet to be followed by amazing, huge raises. Big shout-outs to the folks at Macromedia for developing Flash. And to Ben Neill and Pete DuCharme for music and sounds. Who knows, maybe right now is the real golden age of advertising.

Bill Whelan
Robert Hodgin
Jon Groves
Tim Brunelle
Dana Satterwhite
Will Uronis
Dower Phillips

{INTEGRATED BRANDING/ campaign}

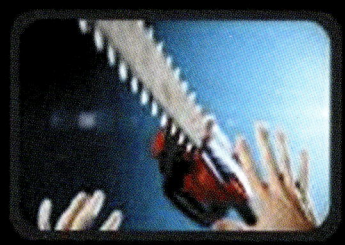  

Gold
AGENCY Wieden + Kennedy/Portland
CLIENT Nike
ART DIRECTORS Andy Fackrell, Robert Rasmussen
WRITERS Dylan Lee, Brian Ford
DIGITAL ARTIST One9ine
PRODUCERS Katie Raye, Jim Woolfrey, Elaine Thomas, Katie Shields
MULTIMEDIA One9ine
PROGRAMMER One9ine
CREATIVE DIRECTOR Steve Sandoz
URL www.wk.com/whatever/choose.html
ID 00 0039 N

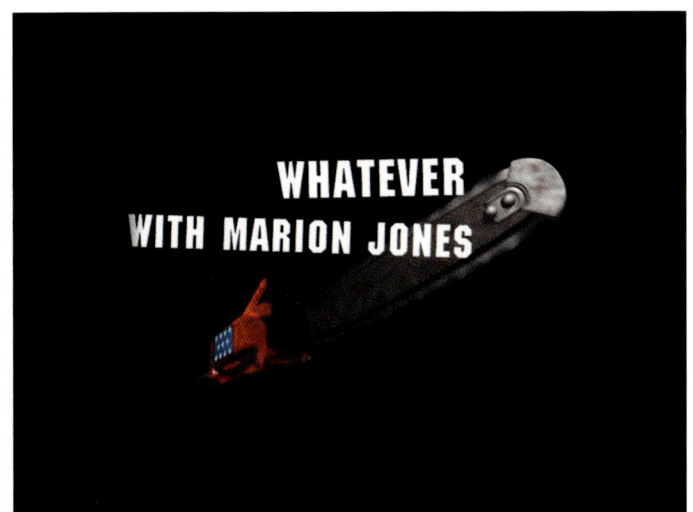

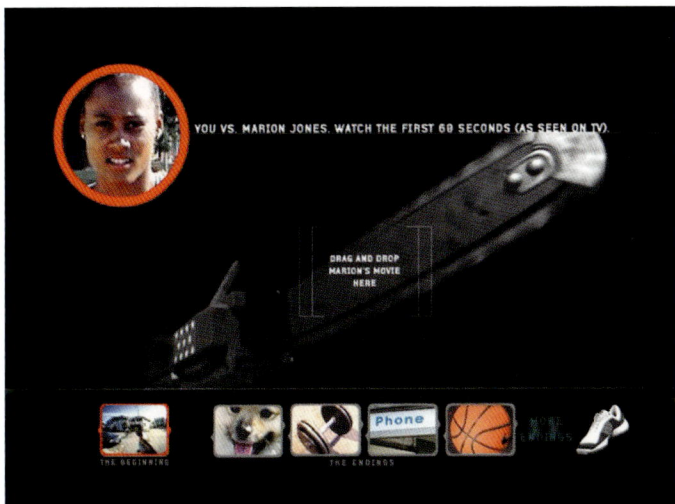

actual consumer e-mail

My family saw the "whatever" commercial on TV this evening and were really excited about logging on and selecting an ending. My grandson watched with bated anticipation. We chose the "dog" ending and when it finally finished loading, we all gathered around the computer to see our ending. We were totally shocked to see the man get his arm cut off and then throw it in the trash. My 6-year-old granddaughter almost threw up.

My wife and I have purchased Nike products since they were introduced and have really enjoyed the quality and superior craftsmanship with which they are made. We have spent a lot of money on Nike products for ourselves and our family, but if this is the best advertising our money can support, I can assure you that Reebok or some other shoe company will be glad to have our business. I am highly disappointed that you chose this route to take in advertising. Please change your policy so that it doesn't include graphic or crude humor.

Sincerely, Eddie W., Wedowee, Alabama

{INTEGRATED BRANDING/ campaign}

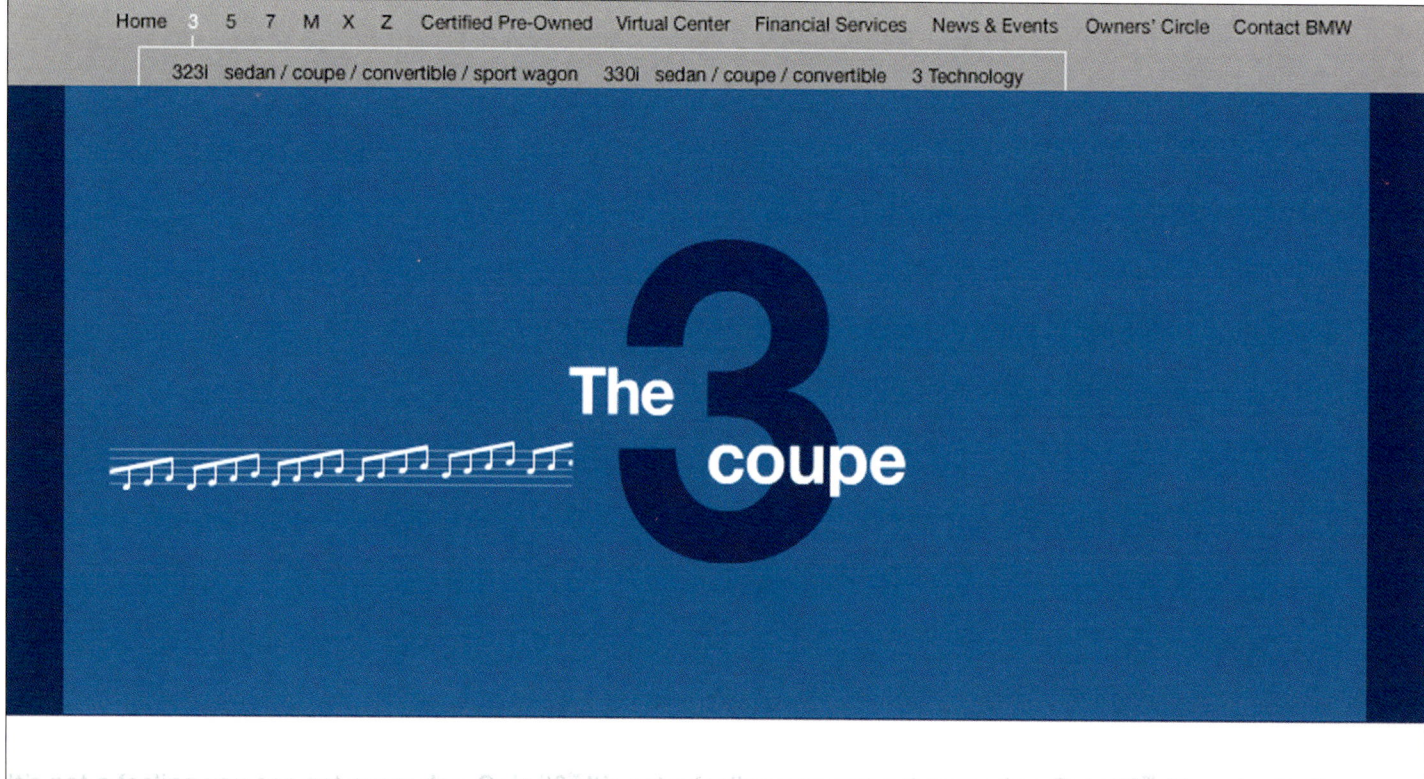

	Silver
AGENCY	Duffy Design/Minneapolis
CLIENT	BMW 3 Series Coupe
ART DIRECTOR	Kevin Flatt
WRITER	Chuck Carlson, Russ Stark
DIGITAL ARTISTS	Tracey Hogenson, Laurie Brown
PHOTOGRAPHERS	Mark LaFavor, Various
PRODUCER	Jennifer Bremer
MULTIMEDIA	Mark Sandau, Christian Erikson, Tom Kunder
PROGRAMMERS	Heather Duke, John Keller, Bob Carlson, Dave Thompson, Shelly Malmquist
URL	www.bmwusa.com/3coupe
ID	00 0040 N

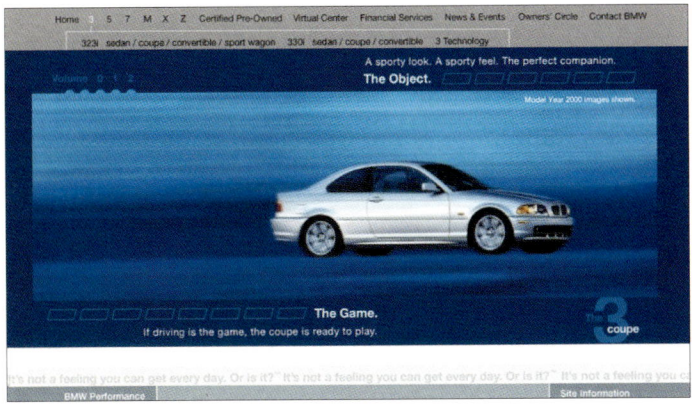

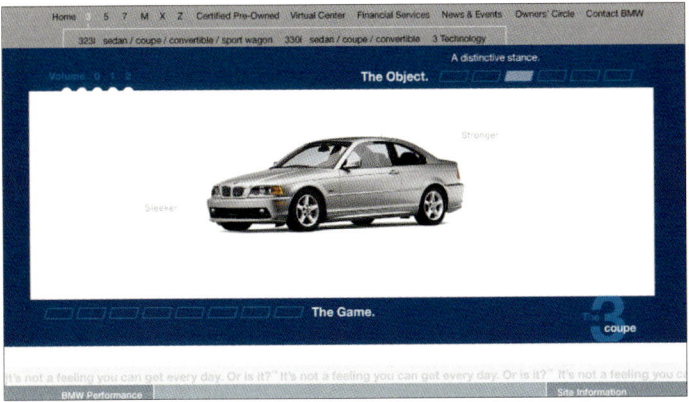

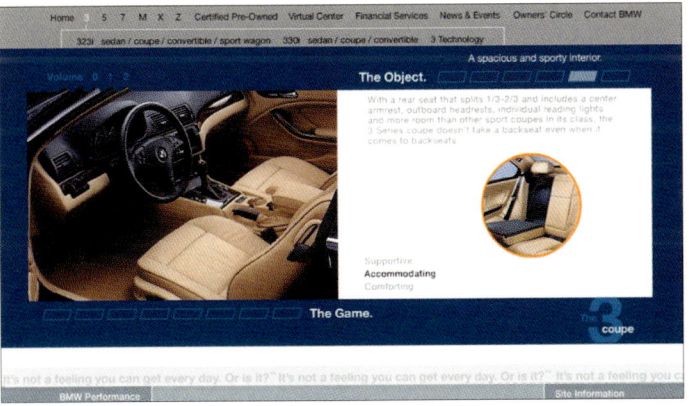

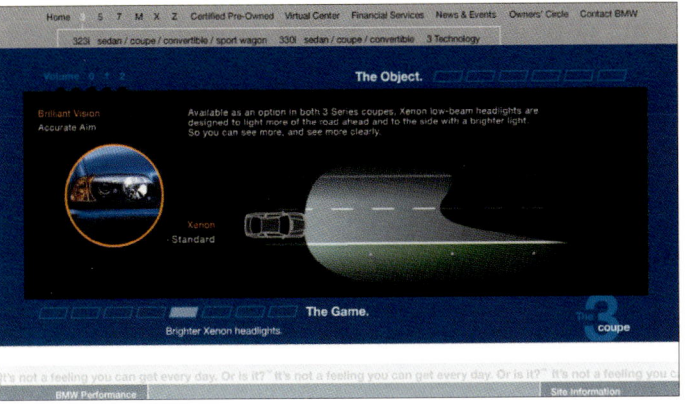

high-energy, engaging web experience

Our assignment for the interactive component of the BMW 3 Series Coupe integrated brand campaign was to create a high-energy, engaging web experience that showcased the performance and design attributes of the new coupe.

passionate drivers

It all happened rather quickly. We started with what we knew about the 3 Series Coupe audience – they are passionate drivers who want a car that gives back, one that becomes a partner in their driving experience. Accordingly, we wanted to involve site visitors in the process of discovering the details of the coupe online. We thought about which development software to use, opting for Macromedia Flash to maximize the motion, sound, and interaction potential of the web. With Flash in mind, we conceptualized the 3 Series Coupe experience to mirror the new coupe's sporty looks and aggressive performance, concentrating equally on the coupe's advanced technology and the emotional aspects of a driver and car relationship. We adapted music and graphics from the T.V. and print campaigns for optimal delivery on the web. Finally, when our 30-minute start-up meeting was over, we jetted out of the office to grab lunch, take a second look at the Creative Brief, and talk about the details.

{INTEGRATED BRANDING/ campaign}

Bronze
AGENCY Digitas/Boston
CLIENT American Express
ART DIRECTOR Holly McGrath
WRITER Kathy Probe
PRODUCER Jessica Pezzulo
PROGRAMMERS Genevieve Futrelle, Alec Simonson
CREATIVE DIRECTORS Bill Heard, Oonie Chase
URL http://home4.americanexpress.com/blue/splash.asp
ID 00 0041 N

{BROADBAND/ web sites}

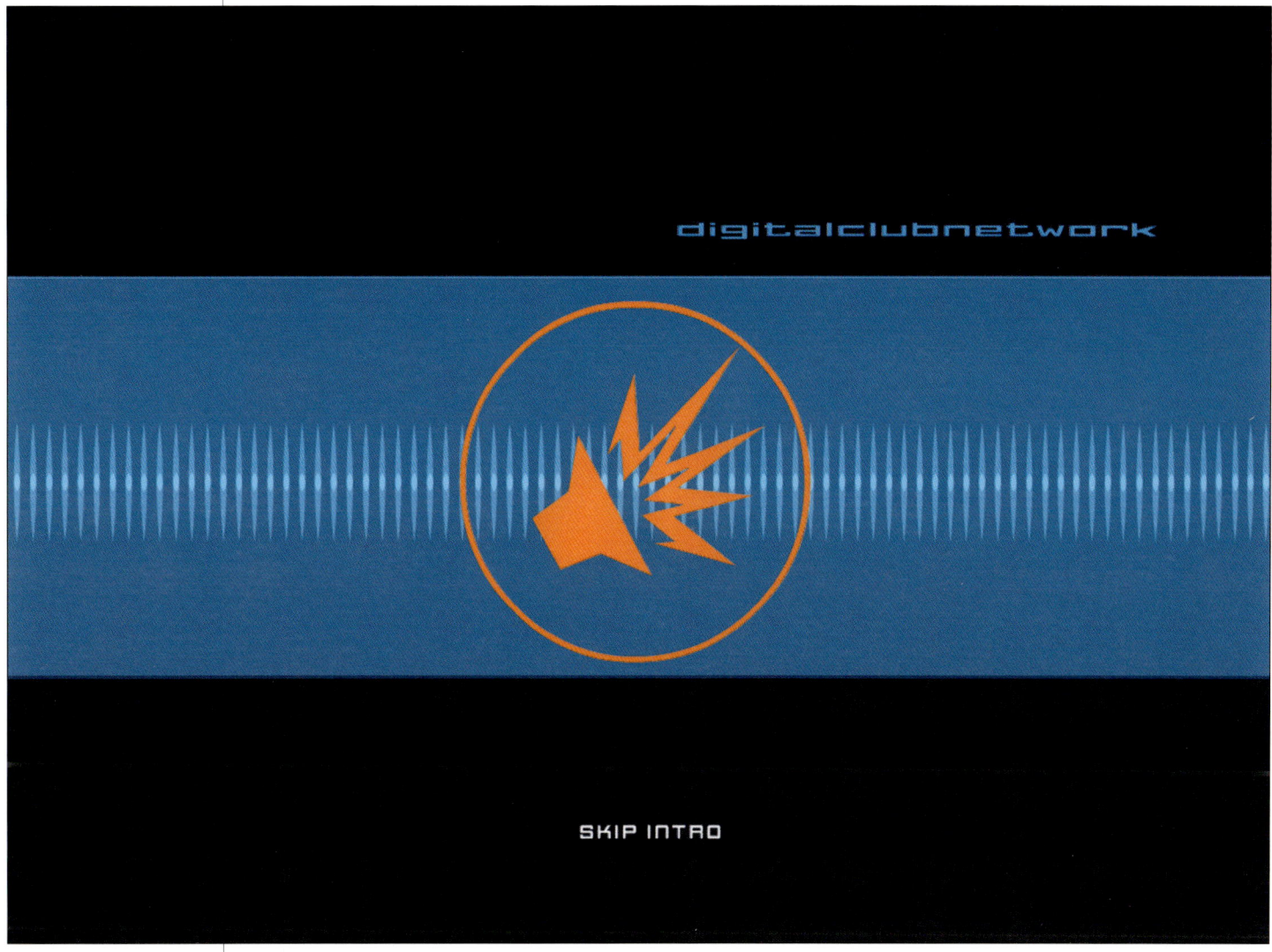

Gold
AGENCY OVEN Digital/New York
CLIENT Digital Club Network "DCN"
ART DIRECTOR Michael Felber
PRODUCERS Jan Thompson, Ari Jacobs
MULTIMEDIA Sean Lyons, Gregory Kennedy, Ming Thompson, David Chin, Michael Kocpsak, Brett Mitchell
PROGRAMMERS Bennett Todd, Jeff Moore, Brian Duggan, Klokie Grossfield, Drew Prochaska
CREATIVE DIRECTOR Ari Jacobs
URL www.digitalclubfest.com
ID 00 0043 N

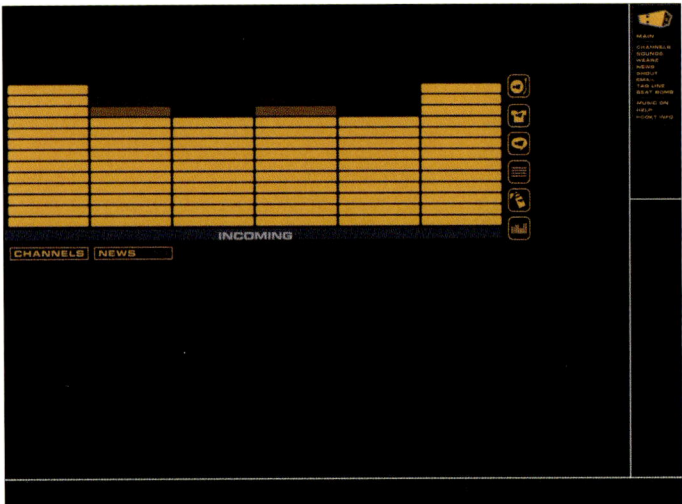

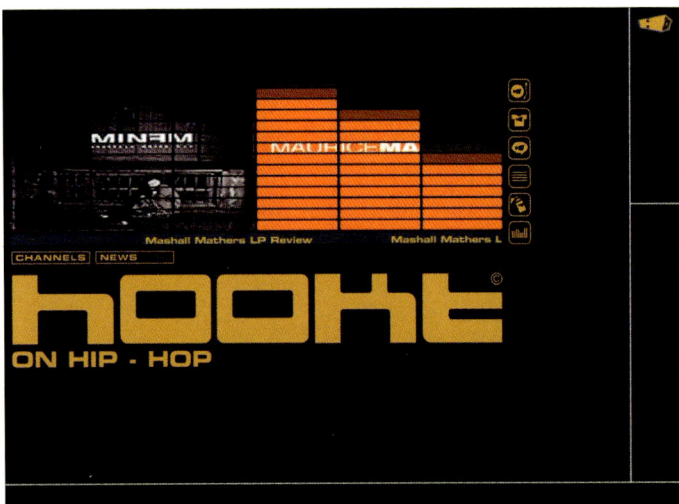

| hip-hop world | The brightest stars of the hip-hop world combine with OVEN Digital's expertise in digital business-building to make Hookt.com the definitive online destination for street culture. As part of a program designed to create a strongly differentiated, fresh online identity, the project team provided comprehensive branding as well as a cutting-edge all-Macromedia Flash interface that engages the visitor with powerful graphics, sound, and animation. To complete the Hookt web package, OVEN Digital engineers provided a complete technological solution, including a complete set of Oracle-based content management tools. This powerful system enables the site owners to easily publish new stories, images, MP3s, background sound loops and RealVideo files on a daily basis. The result is a site which re-engages the user on every repeat visit. |

deep, layered experience

The published content works hand-in-hand with sticky rich-media features such as integrated ichat bulletin boards and chatrooms, as well as custom interactive features like a realistic online graffiti engine. These features, combined with a fast, responsive interface, produce a deep, layered experience which is heavily attractive and rewards user loyalty. In the competitive hip-hop market, strong brands maintain market share by keeping their audience in the crosshairs.

the wired side of street culture

Hookt.com remains a winner because of rock-solid branding, memorable iconography and features attuned to the wired side of street culture. The Beat Bomb programmable online drum machine is just one of many interactive features which capitalize on the interests of a demanding demographic.

{BROADBAND/ web sites}

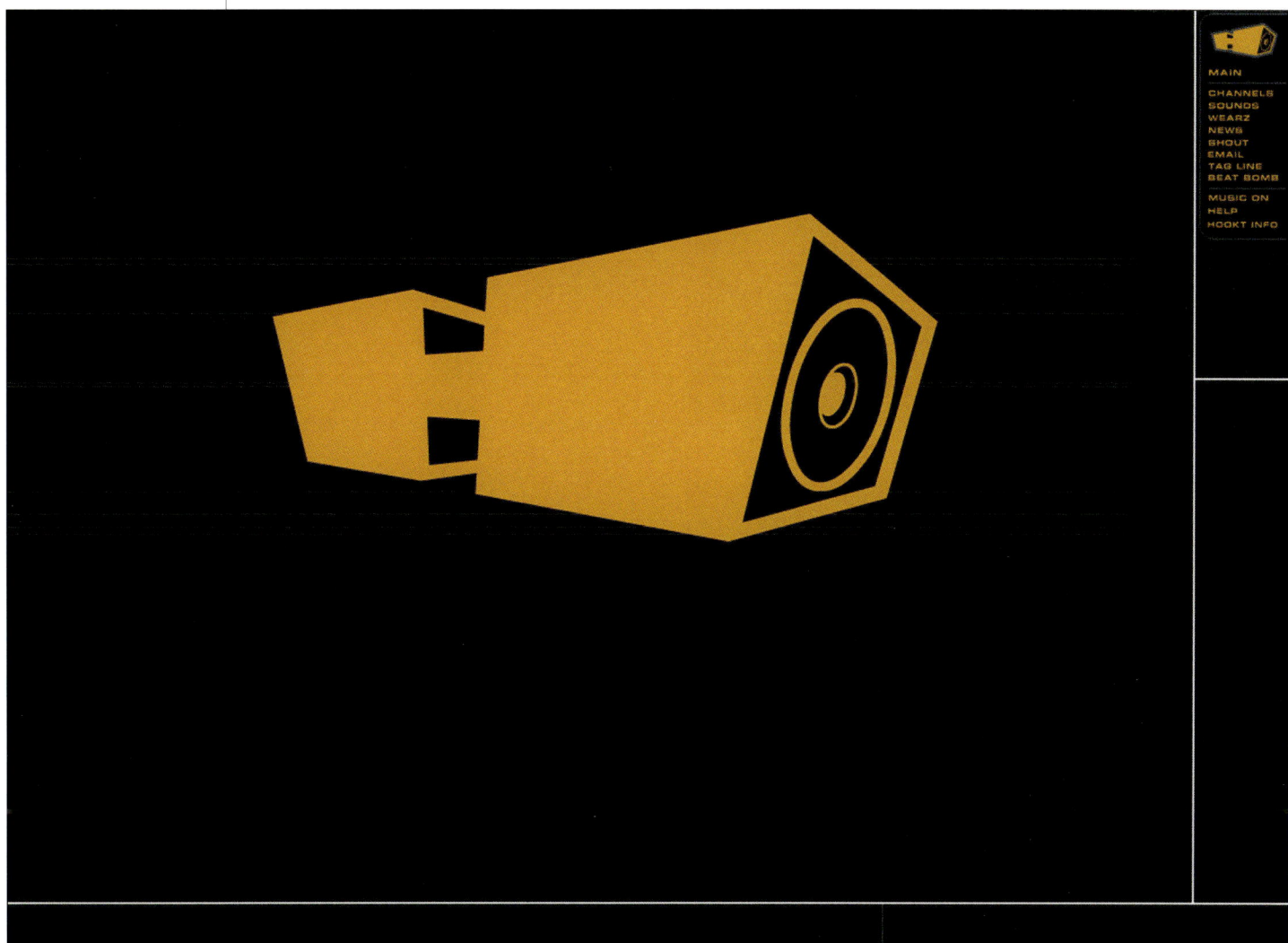

Gold
AGENCY OVEN Digital/New York
CLIENT Hookt
ART DIRECTOR Michael Felber
DIGITAL ARTISTS Gregory Kennedy, Jamie Ferguson
PRODUCERS Brett Mitchell, Jan Thompson, Alex Morse
MULTIMEDIA Andrew Knott, Derek McKenna, Ari Jacobs, Chuck Genco
PROGRAMMERS Matt Jeffries, Ben Moir, Kim Pepper, Ron Teh, Cesar Vega, Bennett Todd, Nathan Lingingstone-Vale
CREATIVE DIRECTOR Ari Jacobs
URL www.hookt.com
ID 00 0042 N

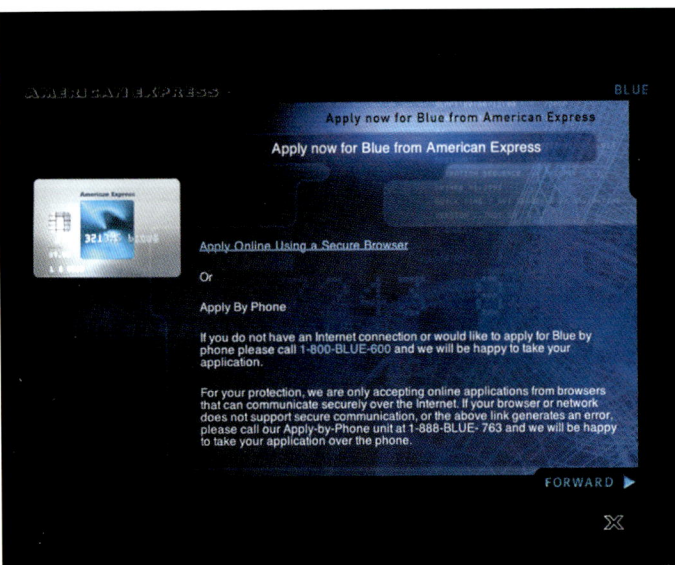

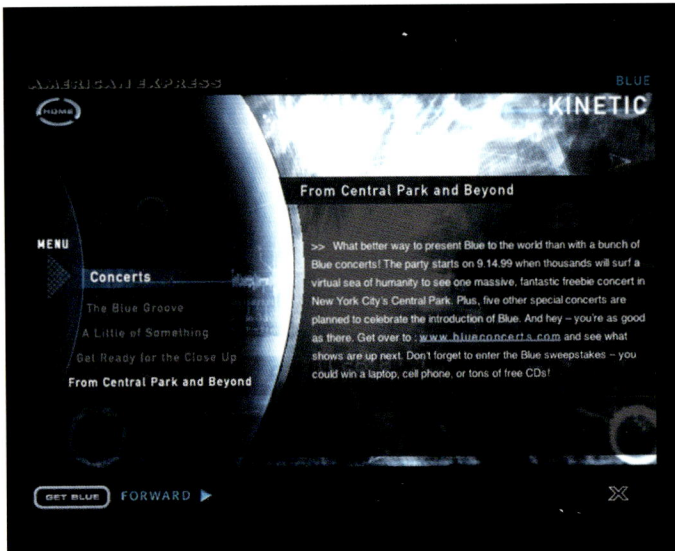

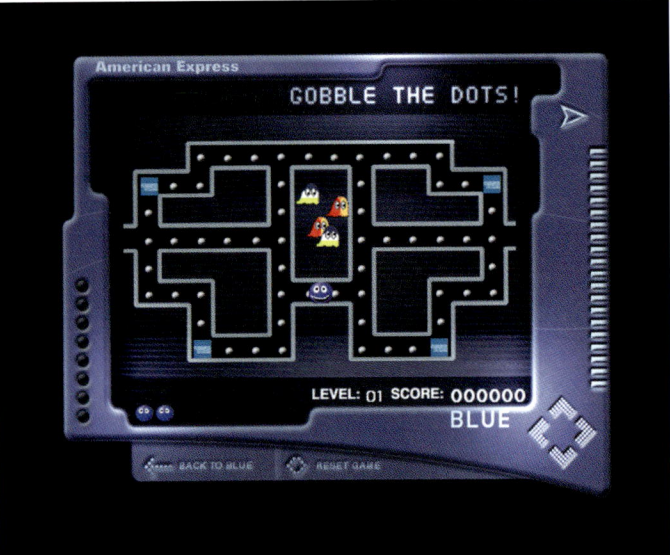

meet blue — The creative brief: Launch the credit card of the future. (And have everyone in America talking about it.)

Thankfully, Blue had a lot going for it. Good benefits. Built-in Smart Chip. And, as everyone said in focus groups, "Man, what a cool looking card…"

the look and feel — So one thing was for sure, the design would be everything. The creative process began by giving Blue a voice. Casual. Witty. Sometimes even cynical. The look and feel? Sleek. Modern. The channels? Well here's how the brainstorming went: "What if we could stage a concert in Central Park… maybe we could even simulcast it on the Blue web site. Wait, what if we could design a CD-ROM…create a virtual Blue experience…it could link to the web site to drive acquisitions. We could even give it out at the concert and insert it in direct mail."

the process was exhilarating — Okay, so the creative solution didn't come that easily. But the process was exhilarating. In the end, Digitas created an exciting, completely integrated campaign, on a scale never before seen in the credit card industry. Who says credit cards can't be sexy?

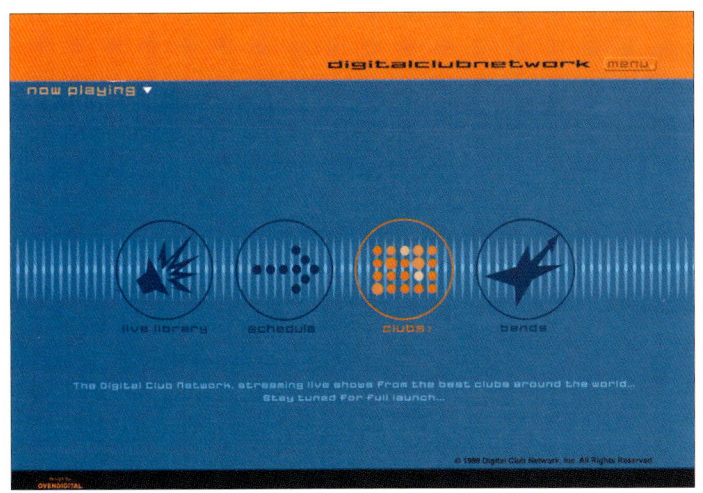

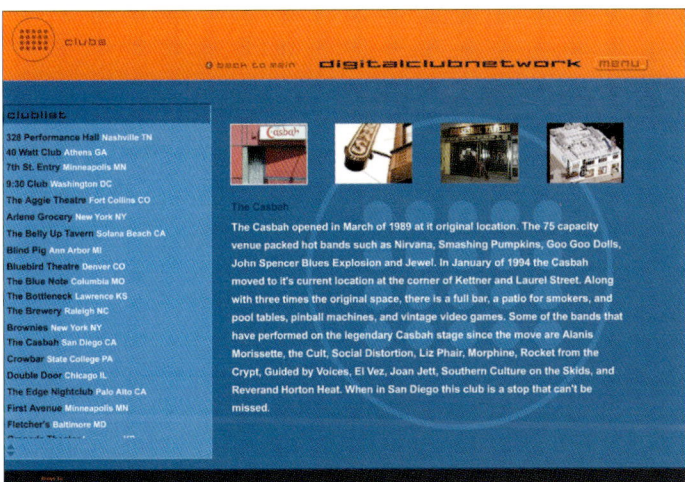

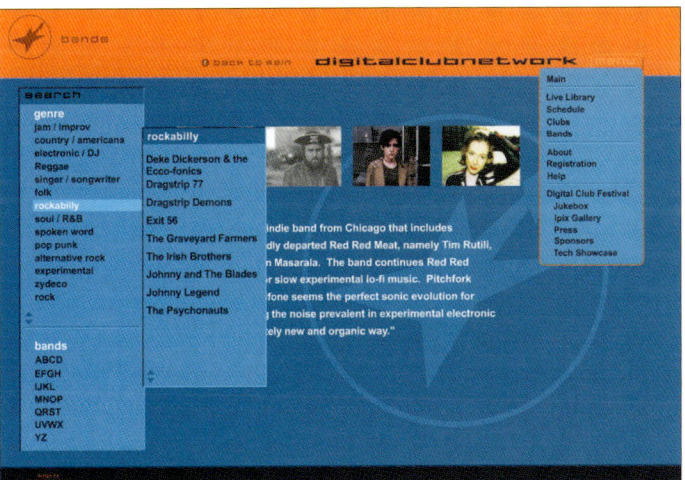

future of the internet has arrived
: Digital Club Network and OVEN Digital prove that the future of the Internet has arrived by delivering a fresh, compelling broadcast experience over existing narrowband networks.

an evolution
: DCN is an evolution of the popular Intel Music Festival. An extremely large-scale site, it delivers audio and video webcasts of live and archived concert performances from a nationwide network of wired clubs. It also serves as a portal for artists and venues from around the world, delivering online interviews with the artists, fan newsletters and pay-per-view "recasts" of archived concert footage and digital music downloads.

truly immersive
: The site interface breaks away from HTML, utilizing Macromedia Flash technology to develop bold but lightweight interactive pages that automatically scale to any screen resolution, leaving the designed page layout intact. The sensory impact of the DCN site is tremendous, from musical loops to active feedback for controls, creating a browsing experience that is truly immersive. The end result is a user experience like no other on a site that differentiates itself from anything else on the web. It is the next generation of the internet, right now.

{BROADBAND/ web sites}

Silver
AGENCY AGENCY.COM/London
CLIENT British Airways
ART DIRECTORS Dave Loder, Asa Medhurst, Joe Zandstra
WRITER James Gartsdale
DIGITAL ARTIST Chris Kilner
PHOTOGRAPHERS Domaine Productions, Agency.com
PRODUCERS Dave Loder, Roger Randall
PROGRAMMER Chris Kilner
ID 00 0044 N

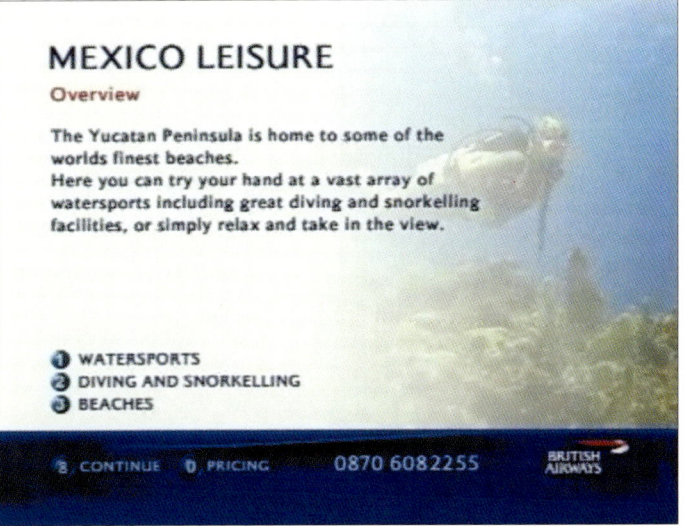

video-on-demand	Between March and June 1999, AGENCY.COM and British Airways piloted a video-on-demand, interactive TV travel experience. After analyzing all the opportunities for e-commerce and online branding to create customer relationships, we realized that the dominant characteristic of this new digital medium was "emotion" rather than "interactivity".
explore deeper narrative levels	Web information architecture is based on turning an infinite amount of interactivity into a coherent whole. But here we had to map out the spine of a linear broadcast story, around which we could structure moments of choice without interrupting the flow of a normal television experience. The audience could then be encouraged to explore deeper narrative levels and, ultimately, more purely interactive services.
based on passive entertainment	The end product successfully combined a TV-like experience, based on passive entertainment and emotion, with more active, web-like utilities. Viewers began the journey by sitting back in their homes to watch travel programming in the conventional "couch potato" fashion. They ended up wandering down many different avenues of video footage, before checking out pricing options and ordering brochures.
emerging technology	We creatively pushed the limits of this emerging technology, transferred our passion for interactivity to a broadcast medium and delivered a happy client and successful trial project. Great work!

{BROADBAND/ web sites}

	Silver
AGENCY	Red Sky Interactive/San Francisco
CLIENT	Nike
ART DIRECTOR	Laura de Young
DIGITAL ARTIST	Alisia Cheuk
PRODUCER	Jon Snydal
PROGRAMMER	Dan Harrington
URL	www.nike.com/moviemaker
	ID 00 0045 N

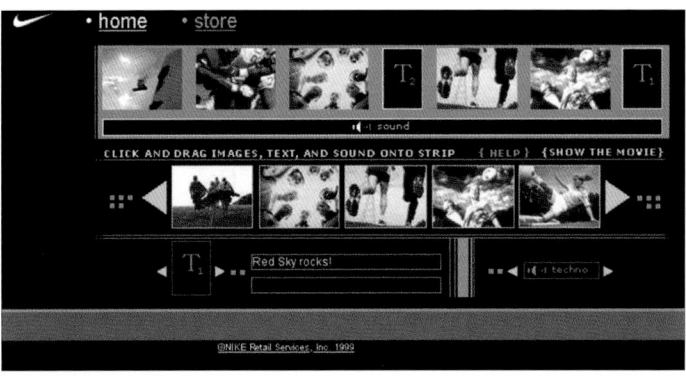

one small request	Years ago, Nike made one small request of us. Build the "best sports site" out there. Charged with this task, we did what any team does when asked to come up with something brilliant, and went across the street to the bar.
when bar tricks go bad	Sometime between the strip Mahjong game and the banana slug races, a written plan emerged, although it was destroyed in an incident that can be seen on FOX's upcoming special "Dangerous Drinking–When Bar Tricks Go Bad."

Still, the seeds of a concept were planted. |
| way cool looking | We knew the site, aside from being highly interactive, easily navigable and, to use an industry term, "way cool looking," would need an added element to make it a true Nike experience.

What emerged was Nike Digital Video. |
| makes an impact, encourages responses | Nike Digital Video embraces the interactive medium to the highest degree, enabling users to participate in their own creative expressions, rather than to just observe someone else's. It's this personal nature that makes an impact, encourages responses, and evokes the now famous Nike sense of inspiration.

We enjoyed making it, and we're glad other folks seem to enjoy using it. |

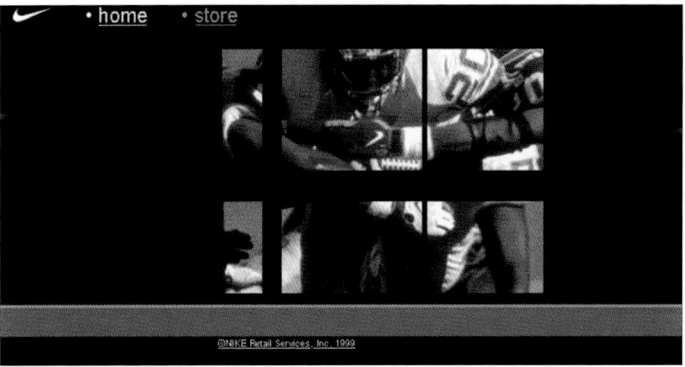

85

{BROADBAND/ web sites}

Bronze
AGENCY | Altrec.com/Bellevue
CLIENT | Altrec.com
ART DIRECTORS | Gabe Kean, Enoch Platas, Kevyn Smith, Dan Riley
WRITER | Gary Fallesen
PHOTOGRAPHERS | Jerry Lessard, Rick Ridgeway, David Keaton, D. Rogers
PRODUCER | Cathryn Buchanan
PROGRAMMERS | Daryn Nakuda, Enoch Platas, Dan Riley
CREATIVE DIRECTOR | Cathryn Buchanan
URL | www.crownofafrica.com
ID 00 0046 N

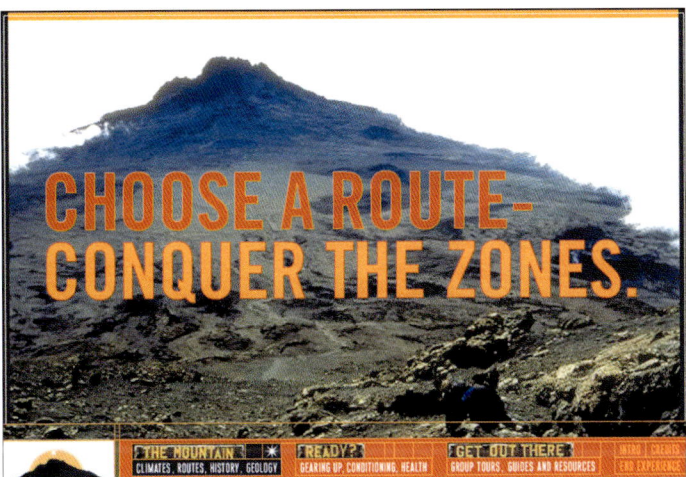

nothing short of amazing	Crown of Africa was accomplished with a new creative group and a 15-day deadline, and the polished, final product belies the chaos, long nights and burritos that drove the process. As one member noted, "The due diligence, long hours and individual expertise of the development team allowed them to pull off a seeming insurmountable task in a very short amount of time, ending with a piece of work that is nothing short of amazing."
a sense of being on Africa's rooftop	Probably the greatest challenge was to give the user a sense of being on Africa's rooftop. Our goal was to take the user away, if only for a moment. By listening to a number of animal screeches, lion roars, and wind audio we came up with a nice selection of effects and ambient sounds to accompany the motion and bring the Kilimanjaro environment to the desktop.
a 3-D view of Kilimanjaro	Another test was the lack of a 3-D map for the mountain. To fill this vacuum our map designer used a variety of formats for the terrain data from MAPROOM 44. The idea was to drape a satellite image over the model and come up with a realistic view of the mountain while adding additional map data. By using Bryce 4, World Construction Set and Photoshop, all parts eventually gave birth to a 3-D view of Kilimanjaro that could be rendered at any angle.
we'll keep our day jobs	Lastly, with no money to pay for professional models, our Crown of Africa experience included doubling as models for the gear, conditioning exercises, and the worsening stages of altitude sickness. It works, but I think we'll keep our day jobs.

{SELF-PROMOTION/ web sites}

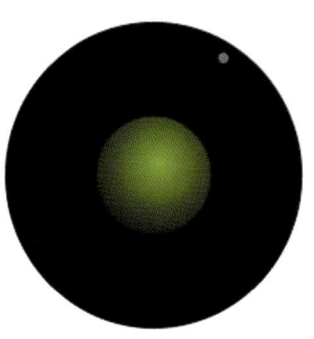

Bronze
AGENCY   DoubleYou/Barcelona
CLIENT   DoubleYou
ART DIRECTOR   Blanca Piera
WRITER   Esther Pino
PROGRAMMERS   Joakim Borgstrom, Xavi Capparos
CREATIVE DIRECTOR   Daniel Solana
URL   www.doubleyou.com
ID   00 0047 N

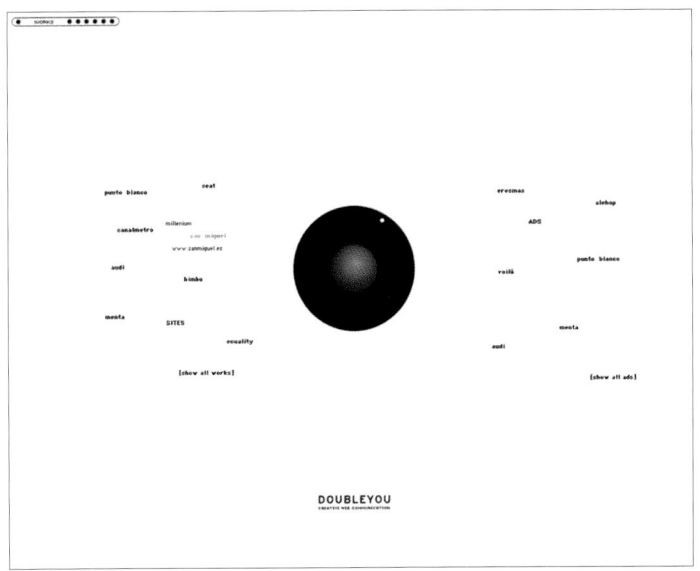

clear and subtle DoubleYou's philosophy is one of developing interactive web sites with a firm and ever-present creative concept behind them. Sites that are clear and subtle, employing user-friendly navigation. Webs that invite the user to get involved, that surprise and innovate and provide instant satisfaction. That's why we've developed a corporate web site whose quick, easy navigation techniques allow the user fluid, interactive access to its contents.

the starting point Doubleyou's mouse icon is the threshold to various characteristics of the company, depending on which side of the sphere is clicked: its philosophy, projects, images from web sites developed, awards, and profiles of its team.

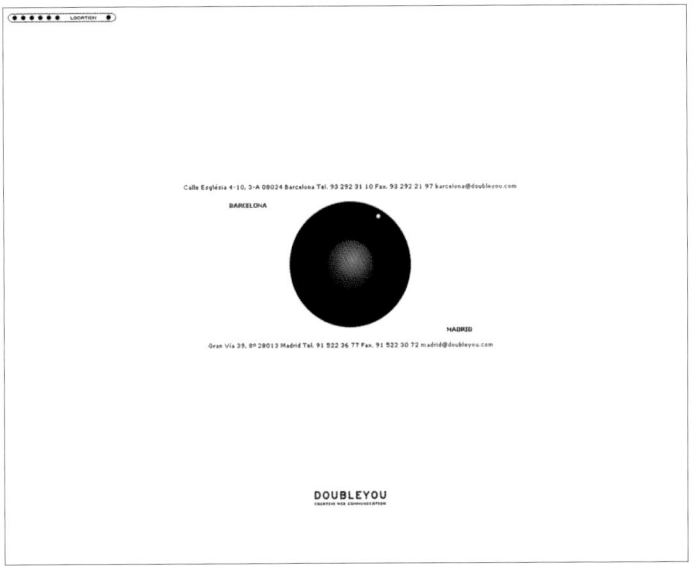

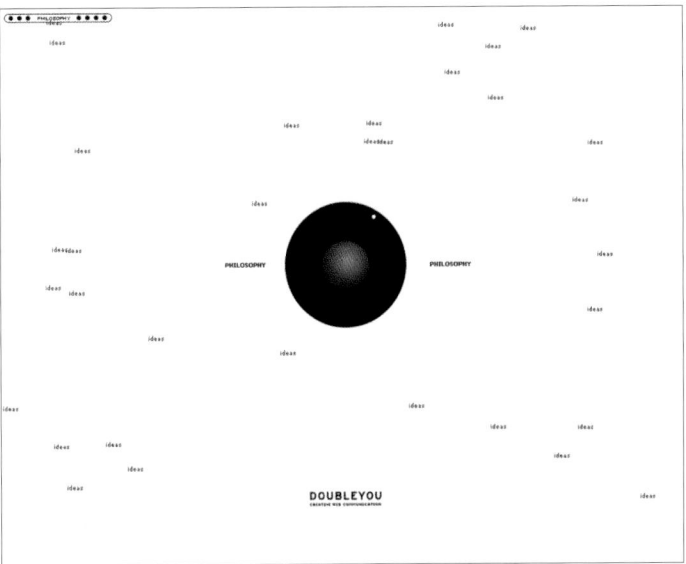

{SELF-PROMOTION/ web sites}

Bronze
AGENCY *Scholz & Volkmer/Wiesbaden*
CLIENT *Scholz & Volkmer*
ART DIRECTOR *Katja Rickert*
WRITERS *Mareike Schmiedt, Chris Kohl*
PROGRAMMER *Thorsten Kraus*
URL *www.scholz-und-volkmer.de*
ID *00 0048 N*

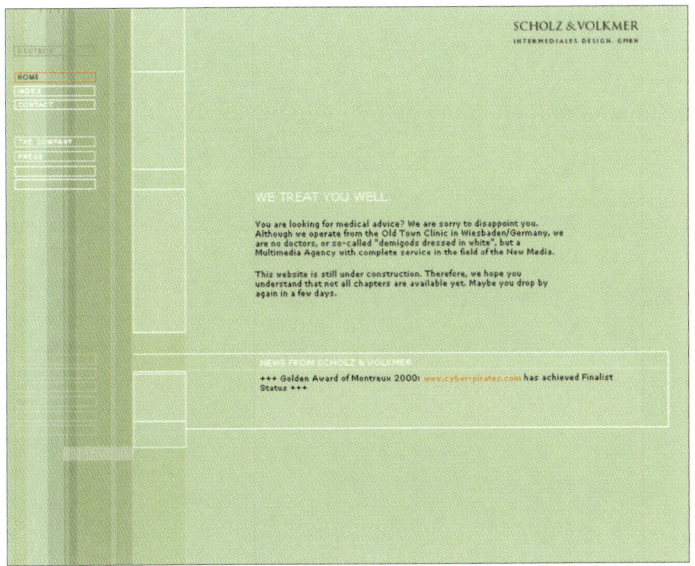

the philosophy of the agency

Web site of the multimedia agency Scholz & Volkmer of Wiesbaden. Due to the fact that the agency is located in the former City Clinics, the "hospital" motif runs through design and texts of the whole web site.

The offer includes information on the philosophy of the agency, its performances, its clients and projects, the awards won, and current job offers (with the possibility to make an online application). In a separate chapter, newspapers and journalists can provide themselves with press releases and photographs for download. Screenshots of the agency's different projects can also be downloaded. It is possible to select one or more chapters at a time for printout.

There is a full version and a text version of the web site. Apart from the German version, there is also an English version.

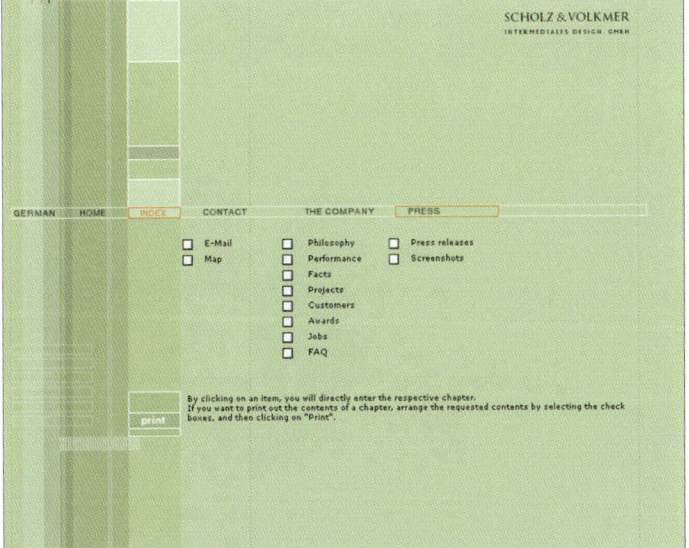

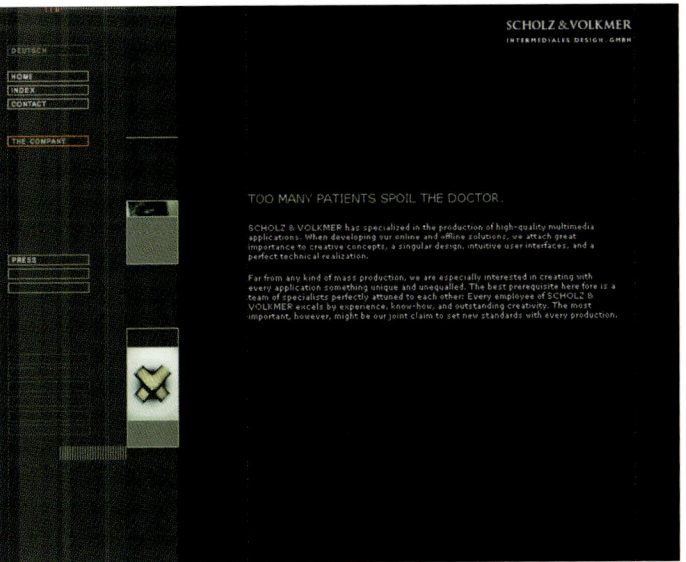

{SELF-PROMOTION/ CD-ROM}

Gold
AGENCY Periscope/Minneapolis
CLIENT Periscope
ART DIRECTORS Chris Cortilet, Lara Wyckoff
WRITER Katerina Martchouk
PRODUCER Susan Ramlet
MULTIMEDIA Justin Bakse
PROGRAMMERS Ron Hodnett, Justin Bakse
ID 00 0049 N

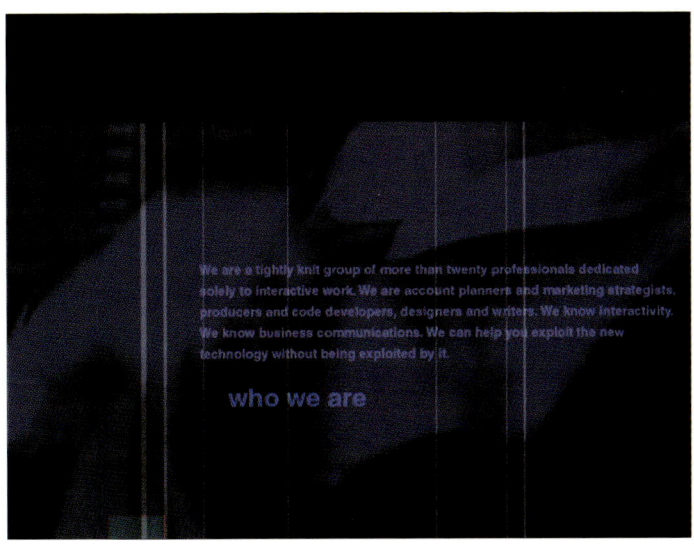

| what? you do interactive? | Periscope is a well-known ad agency, but our interactive work has been in the shadows. "What? You do interactive?" People would raise their eyebrows. We vowed to correct this injustice. |

a strong, collaborative team: In most agencies, chaos rules. Account execs promise clients the world. Creatives bicker and pout. Programmers mock creatives. Producers look heavenward, praying they'll be able to keep everybody in line. The beauty of Periscope Interactive is our ability to blend highly distinct personalities and talents into a strong, collaborative team. The CD-ROM paints an accurate portrait of who we are and what we do, and illustrates how well we do it together.

The printed pamphlet that accompanies the CD introduces prospects to collage characters representing the disciplines that make up Periscope Interactive.

a unique style: On the CD, each is given a unique style of graphics, functionality, copy, and music. The collage characters lead viewers through the CD, explaining the roles they each play in the group. Prospects come to see how Periscope Interactive can help make online media an integral part of their companys', marketing plans.

informational, persuasive and entertaining: The CD is informational, persuasive and entertaining. It showcases our portfolio in a gallery-like environment and effectively demonstrates our interactive design and development capabilities in a highly engaging manner.

{SELF-PROMOTION/ CD-ROM}

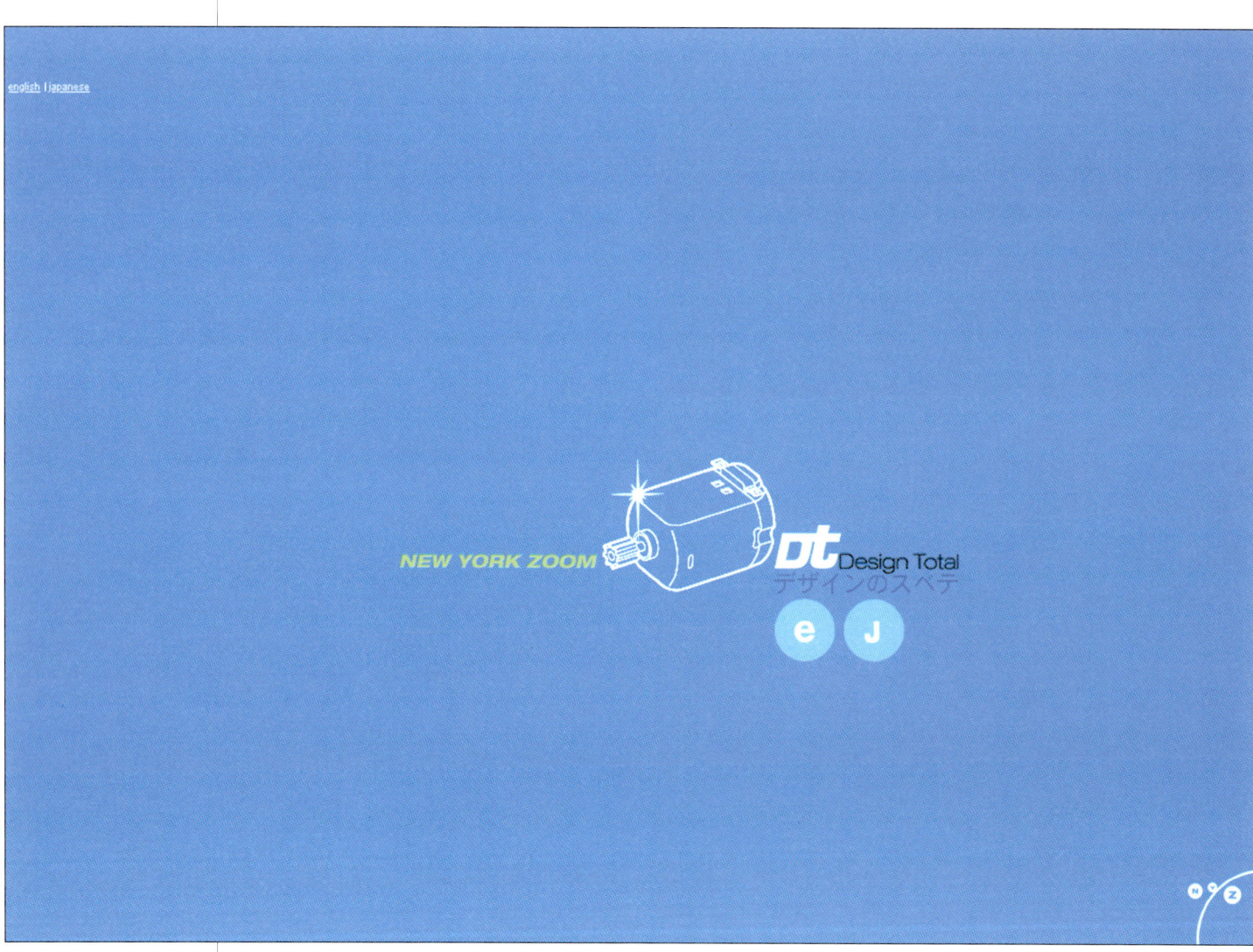

Silver

AGENCY New York Zoom/New York
CLIENT New York Zoom
ART DIRECTORS Matthew Waldman, Alain Grossenbacher
WRITER Matthew Waldman
PRODUCER Anya Block
PROGRAMMER Alan Grossenbacher
URL www.nyzoom.com
ID 00 0051 N

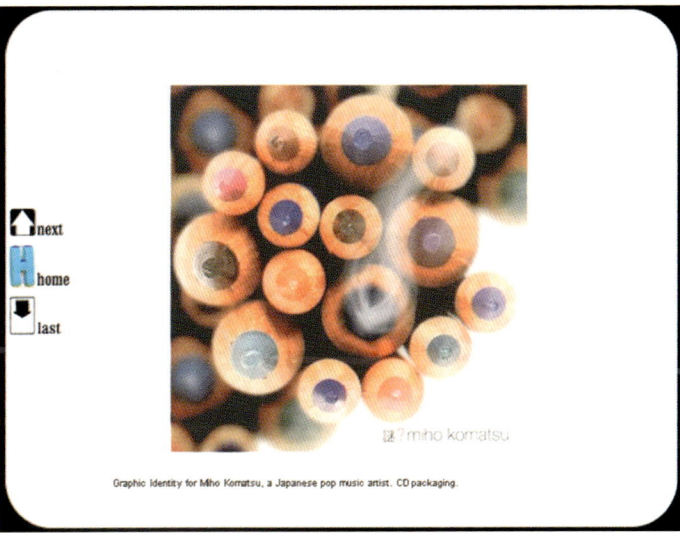

Graphic Identity for Miho Komatsu, a Japanese pop music artist. CD packaging.

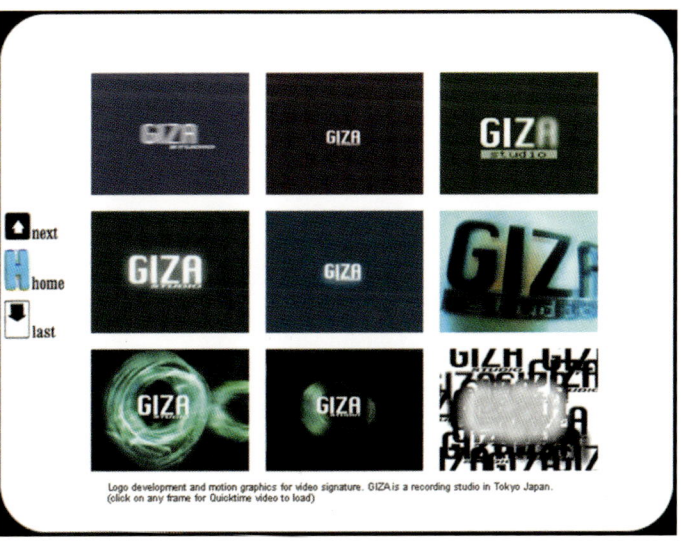

Logo development and motion graphics for video signature. GIZA is a recording studio in Tokyo Japan.
(click on any frame for Quicktime video to load)

tell a story	We at New York Zoom are firm believers in the power of the internet to tell a story.
a visual narrative	The key to good writing is "Write about what you know." We approach design as crafting a visual narrative. We wanted to create a web experience that visually recreated both our physical and philosophical environment without being pedantic.
visual elements	The site is easy to access and our work can be seen with little explanatory text. We chose visual elements from our everyday world. The bank of floor buttons inside the elevators of our building inspired the interface, and a Polaroid photo of the view outside our window set the tone.

{SELF-PROMOTION/ CD-ROM}

Bronze
AGENCY | BBDO Interactive/Duesseldorf
CLIENT | BBDO Interactive
ART DIRECTOR | Nicolaij Kreinjobst
PRODUCERS | Sabine Wagner, Sabine Hirsh
URL | www.bbdo-interactive.de
ID 00 0052 N

integration — Our CD-ROM is a presentation of BBDO INTERACTIVE complete with information about the company, integration into the BBDO network, and the newest projects.

The concept of the CD-ROM is modular. It is possible to make extensions without changing the structure.

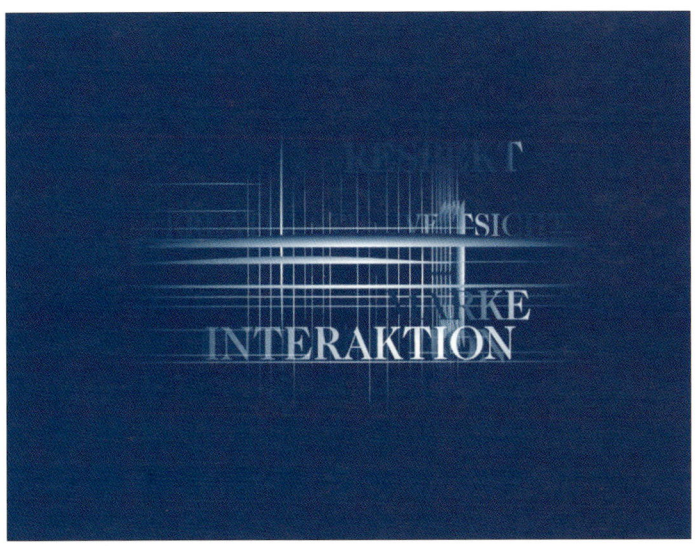

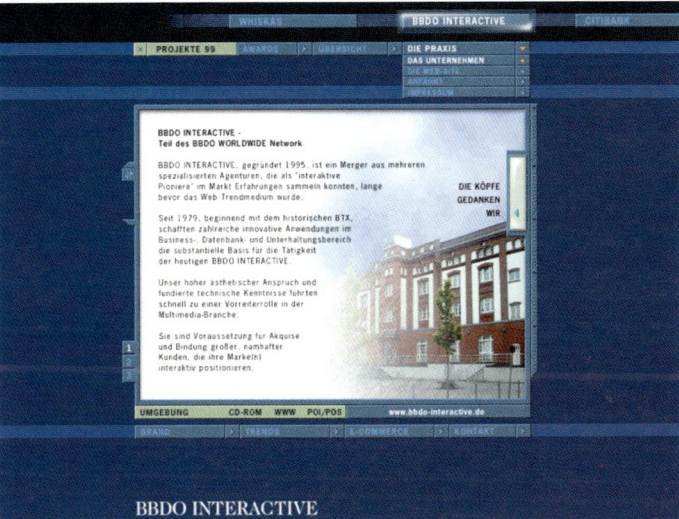

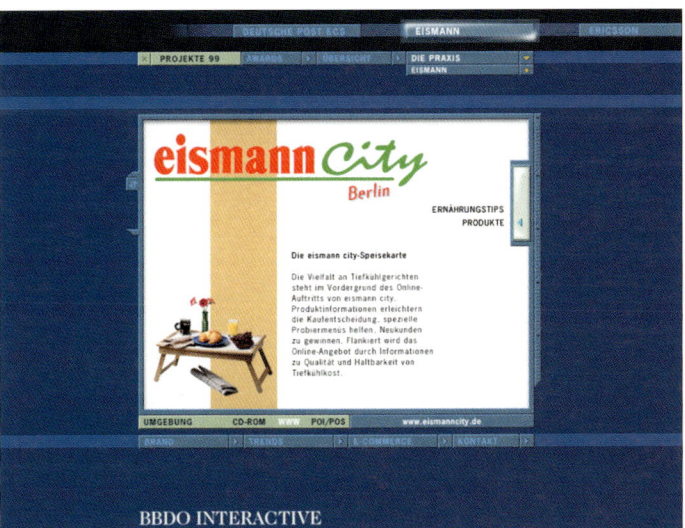

{SELF-PROMOTION/ other digital media}

	Gold
AGENCY	R/GA/New York
CLIENT	R/GA
ART DIRECTOR	Kevin Chiu
DIGITAL ARTIST	David Alcorn
PROGRAMMER	John Jones
URL	www.rga.com/holiday
	ID 00 0053 N

fun winter activity   We wanted to make a holiday card that showed some fun winter activity. Sledding seemed obvious. It started out as one guy sledding, but that wasn't fun enough. We though of a sledding, snowball-throwing, guys-jumping-up, sneak attack, sled-slamming action game. But that became too complicated.

out-of-control element   It was December and the thing needed to get done. So we went with the sledding theme and added some opponents and obstacles to make it a fun, simple racing game. The sled was originally a toboggan, but the spinning disc added a fun, out-of-control element.

the illusion of speed   To make it work, we needed to concentrate on creating the illusion of speed, depth, and descent down a mountain. We tested several different methods of moving the side objects to create speed, but decided on switching successive images on the sides at an increasing rate then blurring them when the racer reached top speed. We did several tests to get the curve of the horizon right and several tests to make an oversized image to pan down for the mountain-range. We were constantly adjusting rates, object positions, scale, and frequency of obstacles to get the right feel. The heads-up display added the finishing touch to heighten the illusion of speed and orientation on the track.

{SELF-PROMOTION/ other digital media}

THIN ICE

Silver
AGENCY	Icon Nicholson/New York
CLIENT	Icon Nicholson
ART DIRECTOR	Sharon Chang
DIGITAL ARTISTS	Sharon Chang, Mayumi Sato, Trevor Van Meter
PROGRAMMER	Wells Packard
CREATIVE DIRECTOR	Sharon Chang, Wells Packard
URL	www.icon-nicholson.com/holiday99/
ID	00 0054 N

engage and entertain — "Thin Ice" was created as Icon Nicholson's 1999 holiday e-greeting – a whimsical distraction designed to engage and entertain.

a refreshing diversion — In this game users are invited to use the mouse to care for a windswept flock of penguins plagued by killer whales swimming just below thin ice. At a time when the holiday media was saturated with millennium bug fears and Doomsday prophesy, Thin Ice presented a refreshing diversion of a winter landscape populated with compelling creatures that interact with each other and the viewer.

the end of the world — The game play is subtle and unexpected. Users are rewarded with a variety of animations depending on their final score along with the millennium message "Happy Holidays" from a cute penguin at the end of the world.

{NONPROFIT ORGANIZATIONS/ web sites}

Gold

AGENCY	OVEN Digital/New York
CLIENT	Shubert Archive
ART DIRECTOR	Alexandra Chan
PRODUCER	Andine Kreisberger
MULTIMEDIA	Ming Thompsen, Robin Snead
PROGRAMMER	Chuck Genco
CREATIVE DIRECTOR	Ari Jacobs
URL	www.shubertarchive.org
ID	00 0055 N

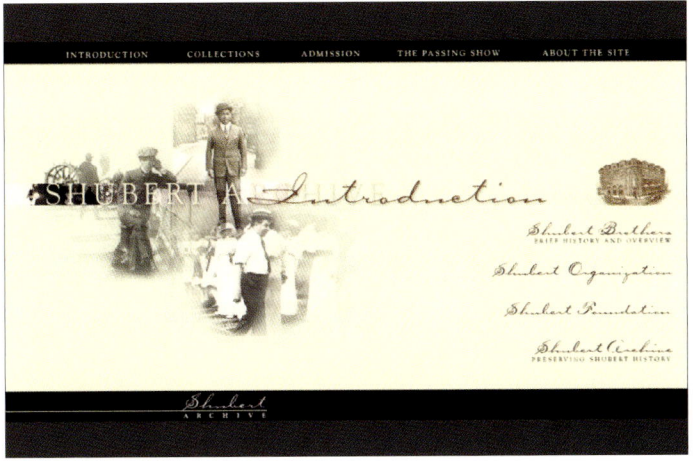

Broadway theater	Established in 1976 by the prestigious Shubert Foundation, the Shubert Archive is charged with preserving the creative and business history of the Broadway theater.
a tool for academic researchers	The Archive focuses on the records of the Shubert Brothers and the Shubert Organization, the leading producers on the Broadway stage. The challenge for OVEN Digital was to build a web site that would serve as a tool for academic researchers, as well as an information destination for Broadway history buffs.
the result	An elegant web site, developed entirely in Macromedia Flash, that includes access to the Archive collections as well as issues of "The Passing Show," the Shubert Archive journal.

{NONPROFIT ORGANIZATIONS/ web sites}

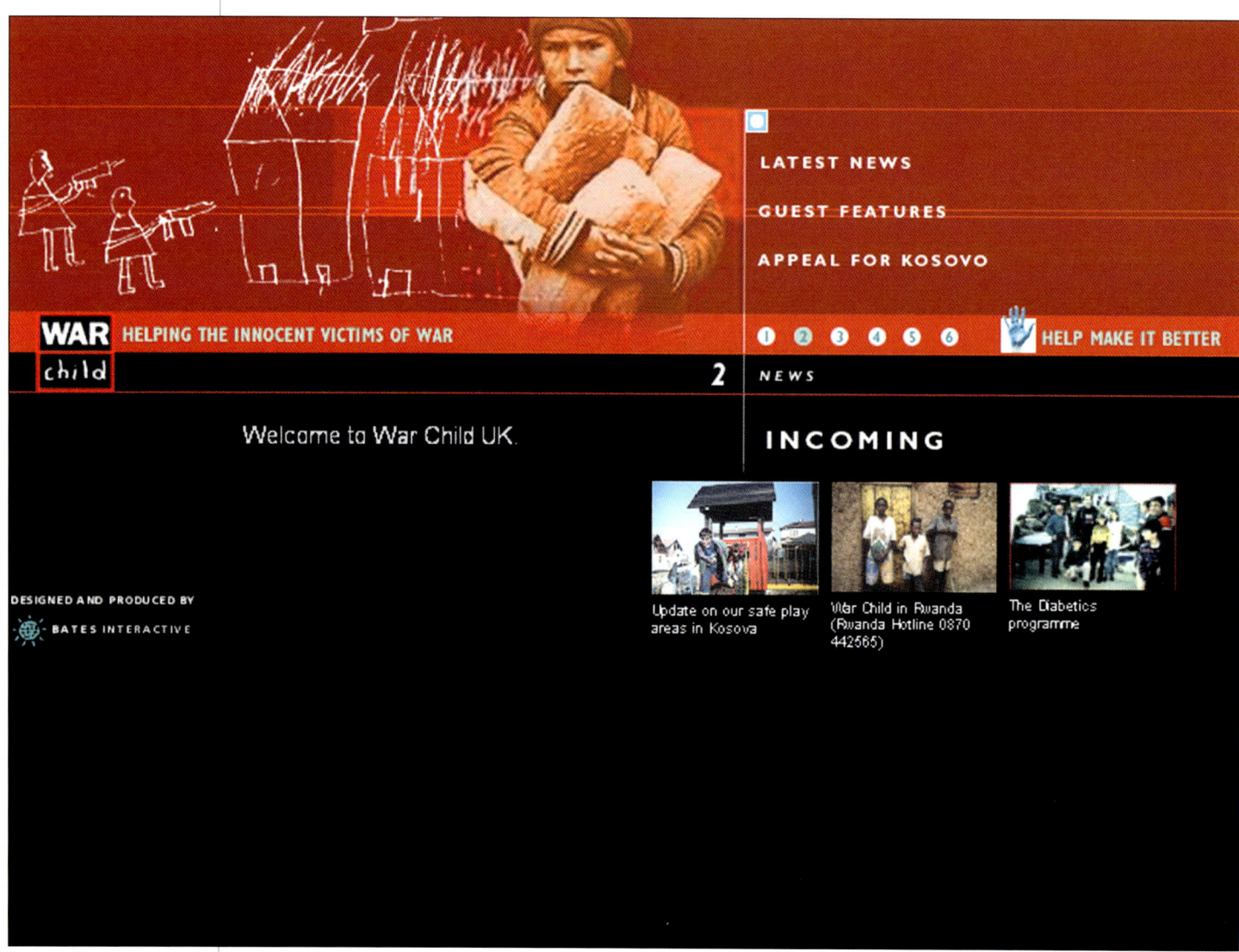

	Silver
AGENCY	Bates Interactive/London
CLIENT	Warchild
ART DIRECTOR	Patrick Semple
DIGITAL ARTISTS	Phil Tarver, Matt Watts
PRODUCERS	Jane Shepherd, Paul Urwin
PROGRAMMER	Iain Catterick
URL	www.warchild.co.uk
	ID 00 0056 N

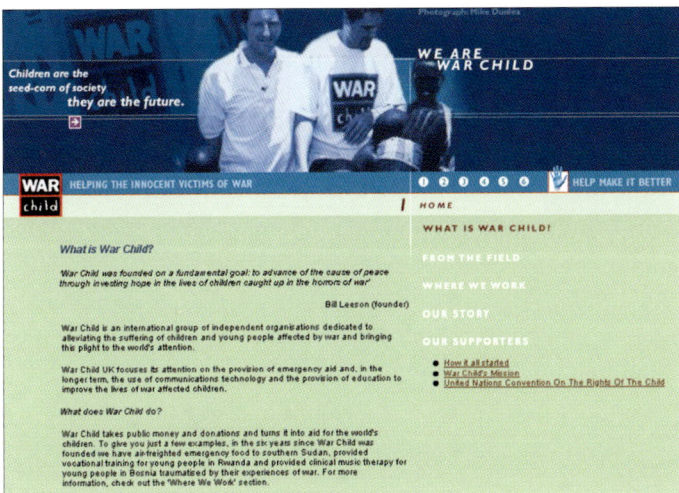

an emotive web site	War Child aims to help children affected by war via emergency relief, long–term rehabilitation and counselling work. The charity wanted an emotive web site to promote and support their global project work, raising awareness of its activities and achievements.
a constant visual theme	The design of the site is based on the War Child logo. The metaphorical distinction between the destructive power of "War" contrasted with the fragility and hope of the "Child" contained in the logo is mirrored in the site via the split-screen treatment. This duality is a constant visual theme.
a quirky touch of humanity	A bespoke content administration system allows War Child to update news information and press releases at all times, maintaining topicality. As a counterpoint to the news and features, animated "attractors" positioned throughout the site reveal "Ad Breaks". These animations illustrate selected personal experiences supplied by members of War Child, and are intended to provide a quirky touch of humanity to what is otherwise a serious subject.
evolve over time	Graphic designers, visual artists, filmmakers, and photographers will produce new ad breaks – allowing the War Child site to evolve over time.

{NONPROFIT ORGANIZATIONS/ web sites}

THE METROPOLITAN MUSEUM OF ART
5,000 YEARS OF ART

- The Collection
- Special Exhibitions
- Explore & Learn
- Calendar

- The Met Store

- Sign Our Guestbook
- Events & Programs
- Educational Resources
- Membership
- News from the Met
- Support the Met
- Visitor Information
- Site Index

Search [   ] Go

THE NEW CYPRIOT GALLERIES

Special Exhibitions

The New Cypriot Galleries
Through December 31, 2001

American Modern, 1925–1940: Design for a New Age
Through January 7, 2001

 Create your own Met Gallery and customize your Met Calendar by signing our guestbook.

 Experience the fine art of shopping at the online Met Store.

 View more than 3,500 works of art in our online collection.

 News from the Met: Met lists European paintings with incomplete Holocaust-era provenance

 Apollo Circle Summer Celebration Benefit tickets are now available online.

Bronze

AGENCY	Icon Nicholson/New York
CLIENT	The Metropolitan Museum of Art
ART DIRECTOR	Matt Berninger
PRODUCER	Marshall Curry
DIGITAL ARTISTS	Mayumi Sato, David Morrow, Maya Kopytman
PROGRAMMER	Jason Wurtzel
CREATIVE DIRECTOR	Lisa Waltuch
URL	www.metmuseum.org

ID 00 0057N

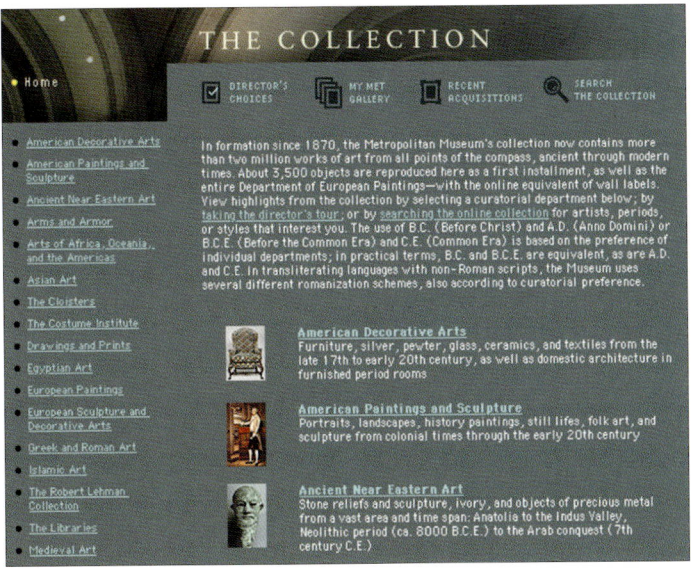

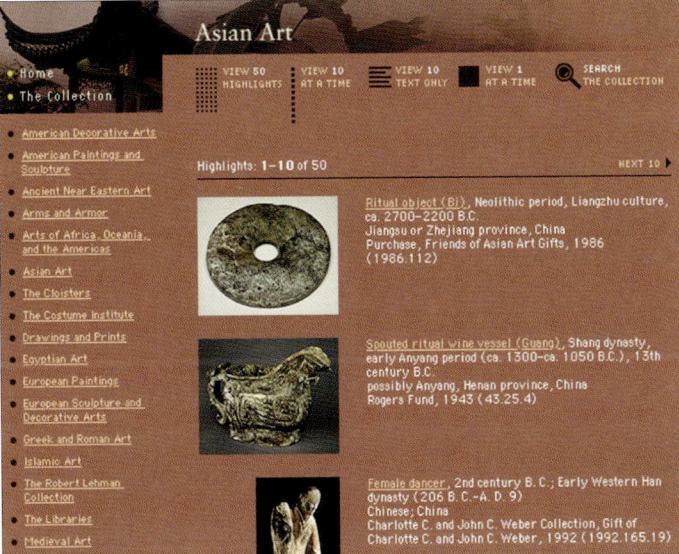

interesting conceptual direction	What makes a web site unique, or "of note" is that it "works" for the user. It does something that is beneficial to us by making our lives easier, more enjoyable, or more efficient. Many times these delights come from new technology, an interesting conceptual direction or even a low-tech idea.
a feat in the redesign	The development team at Icon Nicholson and the Metropolitan Museum of Art worked to achieve such a feat in the redesign of the Metropolitan Museum of Art's web site.
a special place to visit	The Museum itself is a special place to visit – from the grand staircase on Fifth Avenue into the arched great hall to the galleries filled with paintings and sculpture beyond. It is a public experience shared by many.
a personal interaction	The team's task was to transform that public experience into a personal interaction – one person connected through a computer screen 14 inches away. The online visitor is offered a unique experience that maintains the classic, sophisticated feel of the Museum. The visitor to the Museum is treated to the awesome grandeur of the grand entry while the online visitor is treated to a unique piece of art from the collection on the first screen every day, accompanied by an "art fact" or curator observation. Each of these "welcomes" is special, but unique to the approach whether it is virtual or real.

{NONPROFIT ORGANIZATIONS/ CD-ROM}

♥ Vassar Brothers Hospital

zero 2 nine 09
THE PAINLESS GUIDE TO PREGNANCY AND CHILDBIRTH

Silver
AGENCY Smith & Jones/West Sand Lake
CLIENT Vassar Brothers Hospital
ART DIRECTOR Ruth Sadinsky
WRITERS Elisa Gallaro, Mark Shipley
DIGITAL ARTISTS Alan Beberwyck, Michael Neff
PHOTOGRAPHER Gary Gold
PRODUCER Sara Tack
PROGRAMMERS Johnny Dekam, Sara Tack
CREATIVE DIRECTOR Mark Shipley
ID 00 0058 N

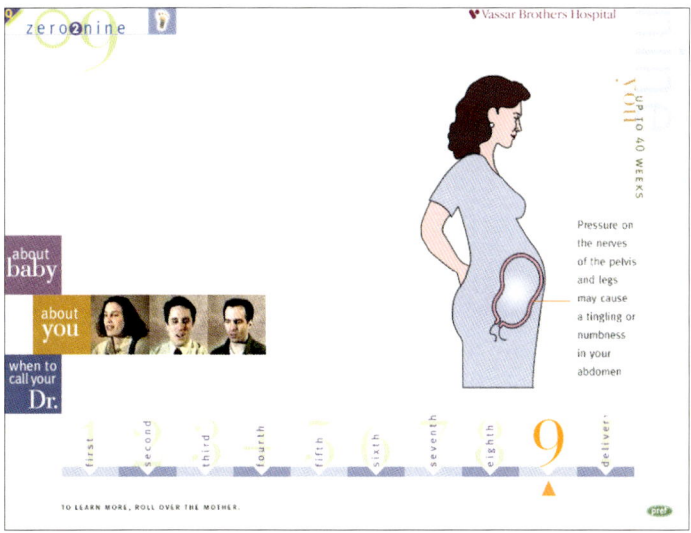

a beautiful 13.25 oz. pencil	Deliver a healthy, bouncing, useful source of information for both the pregnant and the pausing. That was the project. The result: a beautiful 13.25 oz. pencil. We're very proud.
what's normal	Maternity. What's normal? Everyone had opinions and advice, much of it conflicting. Fortunately, we'd done our account planning and had a creative team with relevant experience — some of which indicated the need to change the working title, Going Maternal, to the less inflammatory Zero2Nine.
we listened	To get most of this right, like the title, we listened to the people who'd be using it.
control, comfort, options	Content was based on videotaped interviews: some anecdotal, some highly informed, all contributing to the architecture and attitude. The participants defined what was important during pregnancy and birthing: control, comfort, options, and firm ownership of the decision-making process. We built the CD-ROM with these same attributes.
a bit of false labor	After a bit of false labor — reconciling high-impact graphics with low-memory overhead, generating intuitive navigation and inserting the occasional surprise — Zero2Nine was born. Sure there was some pain, but none of the males involved were quite certain what all the fuss was about.
	While this is our first pencil, we're hoping for a large family.

{NONPROFIT ORGANIZATIONS/ other digital media}

THIS IS A JOKE

	Gold
AGENCY	Leo Burnett/Singapore
CLIENT	Action for Aids Singapore
ART DIRECTORS	Eddie Wong, Yang
WRITERS	Yang, Eddie Wong
PROGRAMMER	D3 Signs
CREATIVE DIRECTORS	Linda Locke, Tay Guan Hin
	ID 00 0059 N

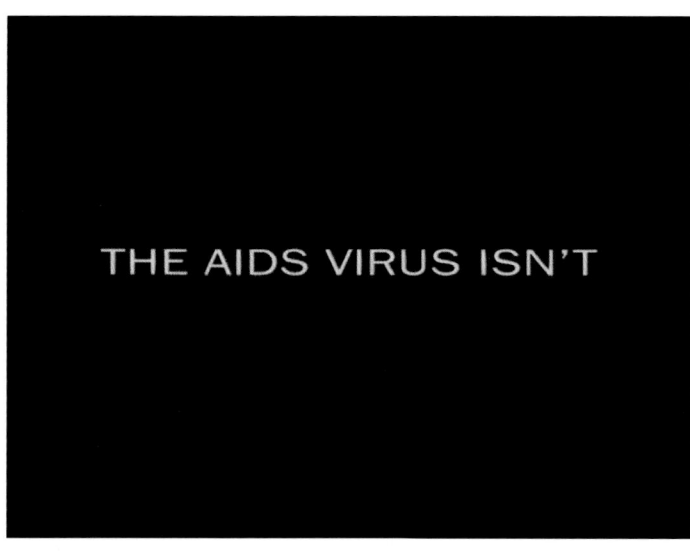

the problem There's still a large number of people who gamble their lives away through promiscuity. It has come to a point where casual sex is treated almost like a game.

The target group also has this aversion to conventional media such as press, posters, radio, and TV. There's a need to ride on a more effective media.

solution We derive our simple insight from observing how computer users get terribly distraught when a virus infects their computers. Imagine how devastating it can be if one's life is "deleted" by the AIDS virus.

Hence, with "Virus," by drawing a parallel between a files-deleting computer virus and the AIDS virus, we demonstrate the deadly consequences of unprotected sex.

"Virus" is e-mailed directly to the target group, which is in turn encouraged to spam out the e-mail to as many friends as possible.

{COLLEGE COMPETITION/ other digital media}

	Silver
COLLEGE	School of Visual Arts/New York
ART DIRECTOR	Steve Chow
WRITER	Steve Chow
DIGITAL ARTIST	Steve Chow
PROGRAMMERS	Steve Chow, Wells Packard
	ID 00 0060 N

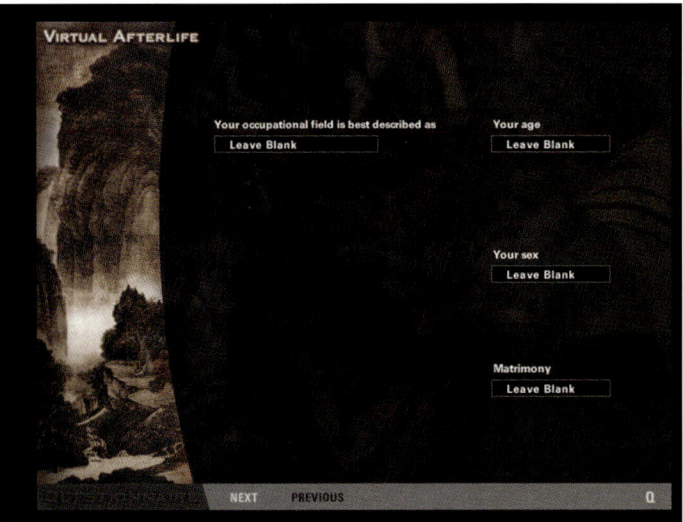

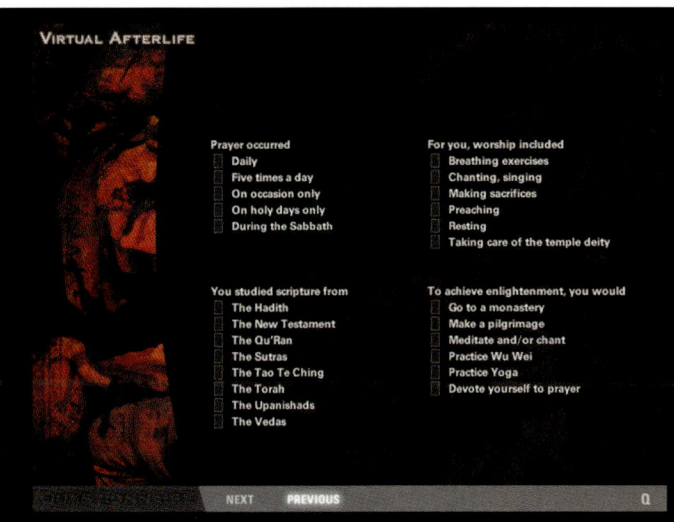

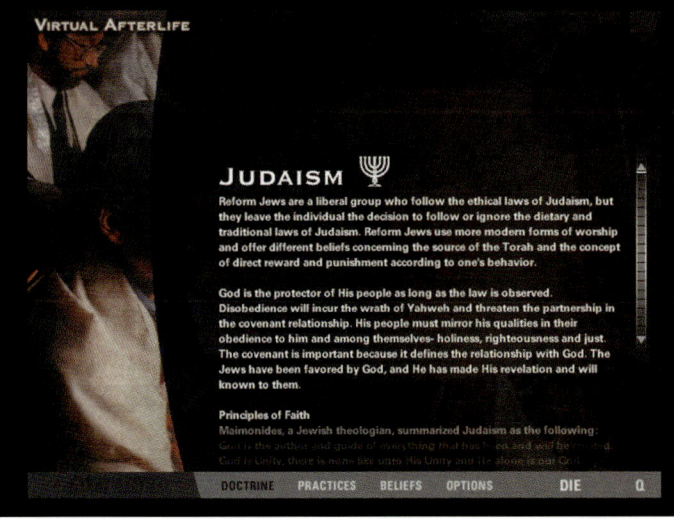

a personalized afterlife
: "Virtual Afterlife" was a challenge in concept, content, and design. To create a multimedia environment in which a person can receive a personalized afterlife, much thought was placed into how to approach the subject.

intertwined
: Research was vital for an attempt to comprehend the sheer amount of relevant information that was intertwined with inconsistent and conflicting data. Focusing on key elements of several religions helped create the necessary structure for a questionnaire and value system that is used for judgment.

proceed to the afterlife
: The questionnaire allows a user to supply basic information necessary to build a profile that would match a corresponding afterlife. After a profile is built, it is the choice of the user to proceed to the afterlife. Options to learn about their chosen religion and to repent or convert to another religion are made available.

simple but imposing
: The transition from life to the afterlife is not a simple or static one. A video was created for each religion that includes images of soul judgment, icons, and funeral rituals. Upon the completion of the process, a simple but imposing illustration was used to show the user's eternal life.

{COLLEGE COMPETITION/ other digital media}

Bronze
COLLEGE | Southern Illinois University/Carbondale
ART DIRECTOR | Aaron Miller
DIGITAL ARTIST | Eric Gehner
PROGRAMMER | Deanna Doelitzsch
CREATIVE DIRECTOR | Travis Alber
ID 00 0061N

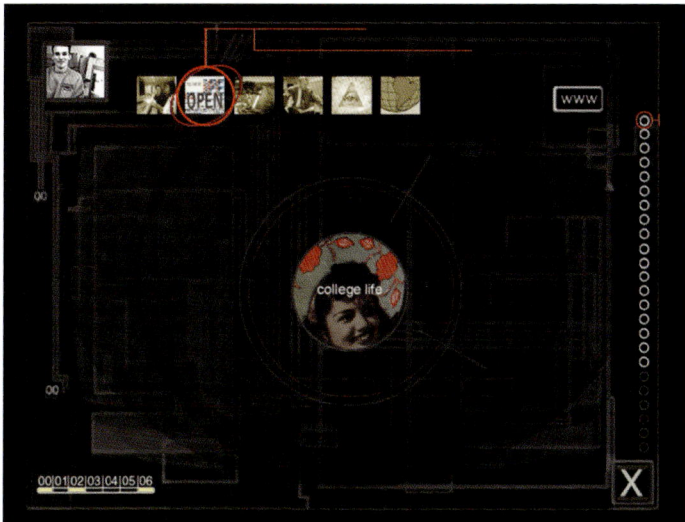

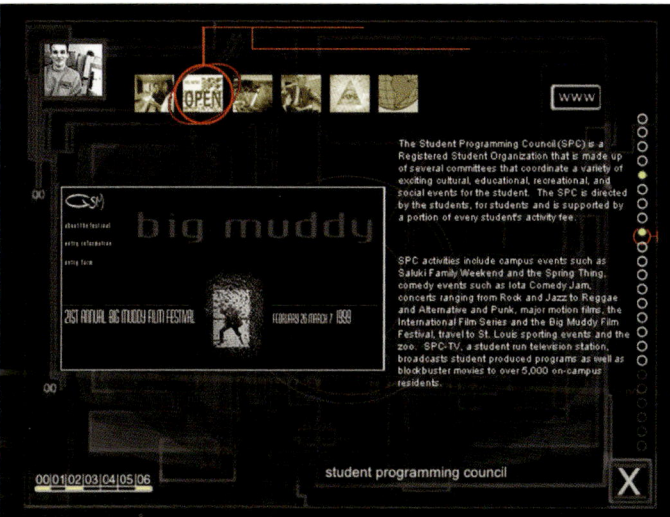

scalable enough

I'm sure I speak for the entire team when I say this was one of the most challenging projects I've ever encountered. Our team was given four weeks to complete the entire interactive CD, from concept to testing. Fortunately, we were able to develop the design shell and navigation before the content was finalized, based on the few demographics available: an 18 to 24-year-old target market composed of Southern Illinois University Carbondale's undergraduate candidates. Also, by working on the project in a number of smaller, staggered phases, we were able to concurrently storyboard and produce, which sped up development. Another big challenge was to create an interface scalable enough to handle three years of updates, which we did with a flexible sidebar navigation and careful commenting of code. In the end it all came together and we found ourselves designing the project packaging just as the master copy of the final project was being burned on CD — the day of the deadline.

a good learning experience

The project's main purpose was recruitment. It was distributed with all of SIUC's undergraduate letters (approximately 10,000 per year) with the intent to encourage those students who were yet undecided. The team consisted of four graduate students from SIUC's Interactive Multimedia Master's Program: Travis Alber, Aaron Miller, Deanna Doelitzsch, and Eric Gehner, and was completed entirely in-house. Not only was it a good production experience, but it was also a good learning experience, teaching us something valuable about working in teams, as well as how to perform with grace under pressure (which is how most things *really* get done in this industry).

13

The Recognition Shoppe – Certificates large, medium, small. We're the best. Work on the premises. Drop off a.m., pick up p.m. Over 30 styles to choose from. All certificates to

merit winners

{BANNERS/ single}

Merit
AGENCY Critical Mass Inc./Calgary
CLIENT Mercedes-Benz USA
ART DIRECTORS Michel Clairo, Jason Delichte
PRODUCERS Ted Hellard, Stepahnie Chamberland
MULTIMEDIA Philippe Clairo
PROGRAMMER Peter Loman
URL www.mbusa.com/ad/category76
ID 00 0062 N

{BANNERS/ single}

Merit

AGENCY	Critical Mass Inc./Calgary
CLIENT	Mercedes-Benz USA
ART DIRECTORS	Jason Delichte, Masanori Benno
PRODUCER	Leah Lacroix
MULTIMEDIA	Philippe Clairo, Gary McKeown
URL	www.mbusa.com/ad/category76

ID 00 0063 N

{BANNERS/ single}

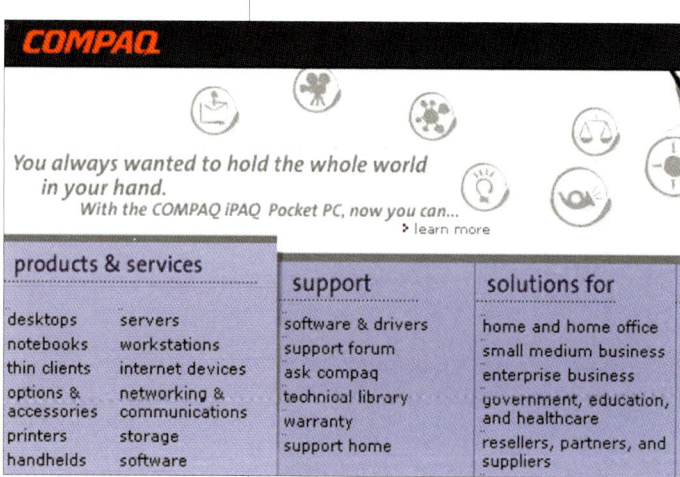
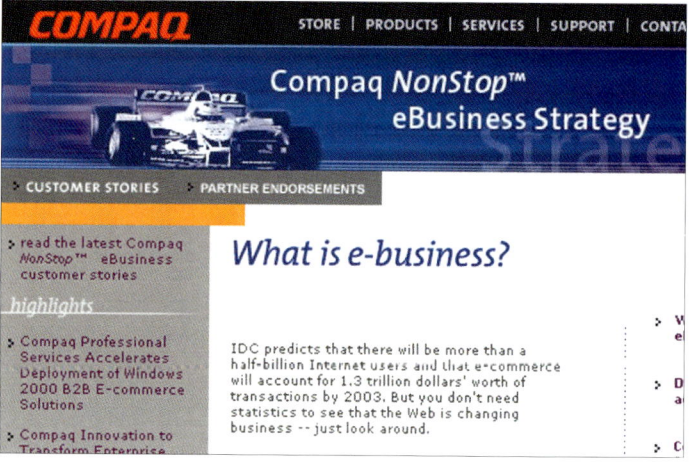

Merit

AGENCY | DDB Digital/New York
CLIENT | Compaq
ART DIRECTOR | Duncan Mitchell
PRODUCER | Gwynne Fitzgerald
CREATIVE DIRECTOR | Steve Hicks
URL | www.awards.ddbdigital.com/compaq_60sec
ID | 00 0064 N

{BANNERS/ single}

	Merit
AGENCY	DDB Digital/Chicago
CLIENT	Universal Pictures
ART DIRECTOR	Chad Bookidis
WRITER	Skip Tramontana
PRODUCERS	Bill Klavon, Scott Moore
CREATIVE DIRECTOR	Robin Kurzer
URL	www.awards.ddbdigital.com/man_on_the_moon
ID	00 0065 N

{BANNERS/ single}

 **TOUCH AND STICK.**

TOUCH AND STICK.

TOUCH AND STICK.

	Merit
AGENCY	DM9 DDB Publicidade/São Paulo
CLIENT	Loctite
ART DIRECTORS	PJ Pereira, Pedro Capeletti
WRITERS	Zeno Millet, Jader Rossetto
PRODUCER	Andrea Evora Cals
URL	www.dm9.com.br/festival/superglue
	ID 00 0066 N

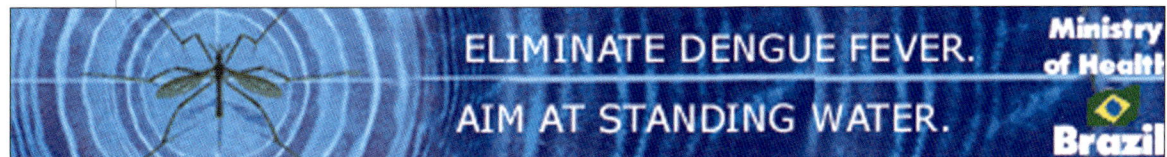

Merit

AGENCY DM9 DDB Publicidade/São Paulo
CLIENT Ministry of Health
ART DIRECTOR Andrea Evora Cals
WRITER PJ Pereira
PRODUCER Zeno Millet
URL www.dm9.com.br/festival/dengue
ID 00 0067 N

{BANNERS/ single}

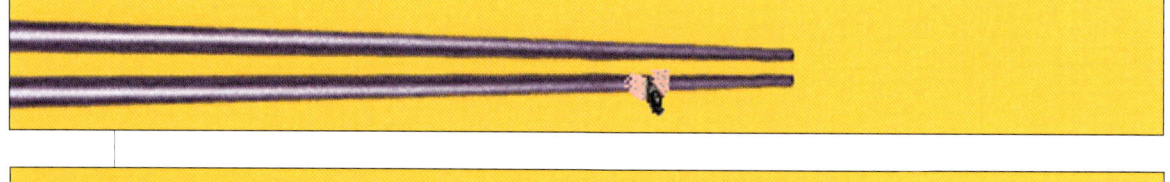
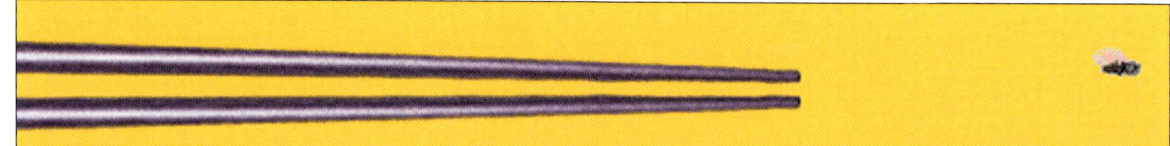

	Merit
AGENCY	EURO RSCG DSW Partners/Salt Lake City
CLIENT	StorageTek
ART DIRECTOR	Craig Marx
WRITER	Ted Tsandes
DIGITAL ARTIST	Scott Durrant
PRODUCERS	Thomas Guthrie, Wayman Hearn
MULTIMEDIA	Scott Durrant
PROGRAMMER	Scott Durrant
CREATIVE DIRECTOR	Bonnie Caldwell
URL	http://awards.dsw.com/sites/stk/index.html
ID	00 0068 N

{BANNERS/ single}

Merit
AGENCY EURO RSCG Partnership/North Sydney
CLIENT Ebet
ART DIRECTOR Scott Ex Rogers
WRITER Scott Mortimer
DIGITAL ARTIST Shmuel Bonkowski
PRODUCERS Chloe Armstrong, Nicole Wright
PROGRAMMER Shmuel Bonkowski
CREATIVE DIRECTOR Scott Ex Rogers
URL http://203.30.131.55/oneshow/banners/goal.html
ID 00 0069 N

{BANNERS/ single}

	Merit
AGENCY	EURO RSCG Partnership/North Sydney
CLIENT	Excite
ART DIRECTOR	Scott Ex Rogers
WRITER	Scott Mortimer
DIGITAL ARTISTS	Aaron Loon, Shmuel Bonkowski
PRODUCERS	Chloe Armstrong, Nicole Wright
PROGRAMMER	Shmuel Bonkowski
CREATIVE DIRECTOR	Scott Ex Rogers
URL	http://viewroom.eurorscg.com.au/oneshow/banners/_lucky.html
ID	00 0070 N

{BANNERS/single}

	Merit
AGENCY	EURO RSCG Partnership/North Sydney
CLIENT	Excite
ART DIRECTOR	Scott Ex Rogers
WRITER	Scott Mortimer
DIGITAL ARTIST	Andrew Lau
PRODUCERS	Chloe Armstrong, Nicole Wright
CREATIVE DIRECTOR	Scott Ex Rogers
URL	http://203.30.131.55/oneshow/banners/skicam.htm
	ID 00 0071 N

{BANNERS/ single}

	Merit
AGENCY	FCB Worldwide/Southfield
CLIENT	Comedy Central
ART DIRECTOR	Anne Bourseleth
WRITER	Dan Sicko
DIGITAL ARTIST	Rootlevel
PRODUCERS	Kathleen Starr, Shawn Vine
MULTIMEDIA	Rootlevel
PROGRAMMER	Rootlevel
CREATIVE DIRECTORS	Peter Arndt, John Gregory, Sam Ajluni
URL	www.webspot.com/pages/slotmachine.html
ID	00.0072.N

{BANNERS/ single}

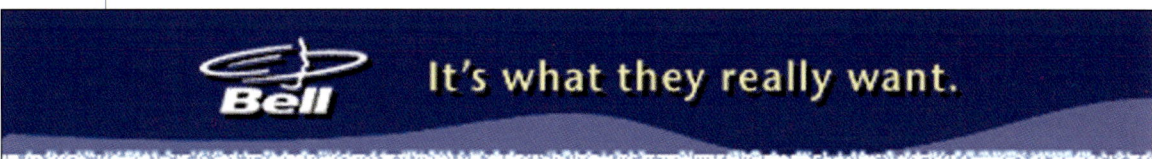

	Merit
AGENCY	Freestyle Interactive/San Francisco
CLIENT	Bell Cossette
PRODUCER	Kim Askew
PROGRAMMERS	Mike Jones, Steve Worley
CREATIVE DIRECTOR	Mike Yapp
URL	www.freestyleinteractive.com/clients/bellca/snow
	ID 00 0073 N

{BANNERS/ single}

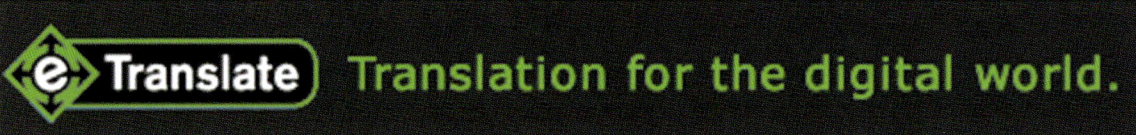

Merit
AGENCY | Freestyle Interactive/San Francisco
CLIENT | Etranslate
PRODUCER | Kim Askew
PROGRAMMERS | Keith Neal, Steve Von Worley
CREATIVE DIRECTOR | Mike Yapp
URL | www.freestyleinteractive.com/clients/etranslate/chaos
ID 00 0074 N

{BANNERS/ _single_ }

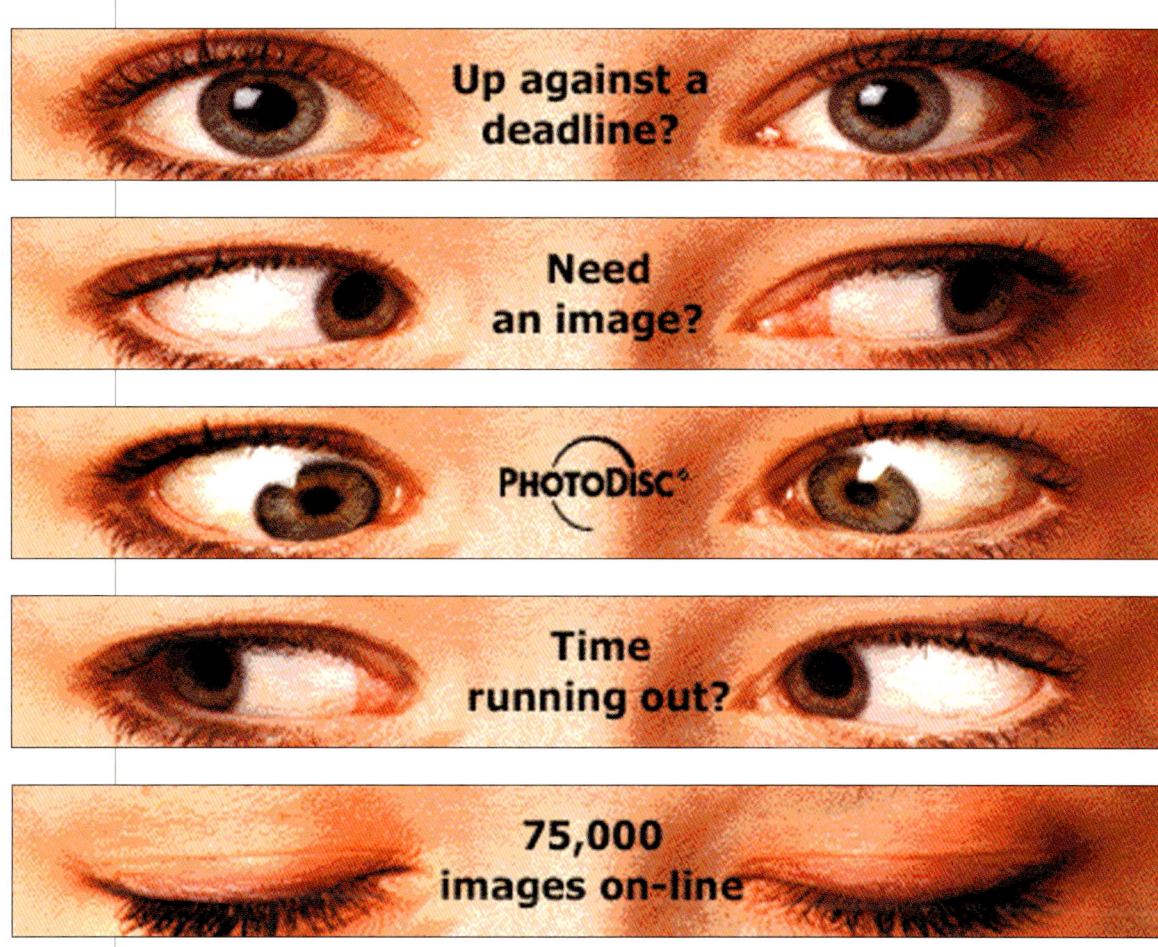

Merit
AGENCY Hyperinteractive/London
CLIENT Photodisc.INC
PROGRAMMERS Richard Mellor, Stephanie Edmonds
CREATIVE DIRECTOR Richard Mellor
URL www.hyperinteractive.com/photodisc/eyes.html
ID 00 0075 N

{BANNERS/ single}

	Merit
AGENCY	Jeff Benjamin/San Francisco
CLIENT	Kay's Flowers
ART DIRECTOR	Jeff Benjamin
WRITER	Jeff Benjamin
PRODUCER	Alberto Escarlate
CREATIVE DIRECTOR	Jeff Benjamin
URL	www.mrbadass.com/oneshow/single
	ID 00 0076 N

{BANNERS/ single}

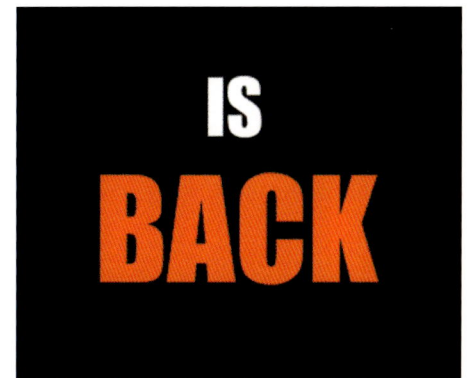
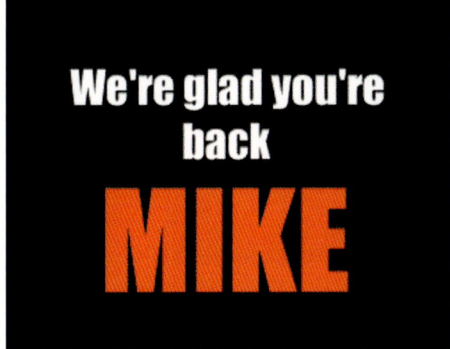

	Merit
AGENCY	Luminant Worldwide/New York
CLIENT	Showtime
ART DIRECTORS	Brandon Griffin, Todd Harrington
WRITER	Todd Harrington
PRODUCER	David Lasday
MULTIMEDIA	Pete Levin
URL	http://i8.interactive8.com/awards/GENERIC_NEW/tyson.html
ID	00 0077 N

{BANNERS/ single}

Merit

AGENCY Modem Media/Chicago
CLIENT 3M
ART DIRECTOR Thomas McCue
WRITER Steve Tullis
PRODUCER Jay Feeley
PROGRAMMER Rob Graham
CREATIVE DIRECTOR Charles Marrelli
URL www.modemmedia.com/oneshow
ID 00 0078 N

{BANNERS/ single}

	Merit
AGENCY	OgilvyInteractive/New York
CLIENT	Sears
ART DIRECTOR	Yolanda Yoh
WRITER	Tim Doherty
DIGITAL ARTIST	Jeff Chuang
PRODUCERS	Kate Kehoe, Elizabeth Gariti
MULTIMEDIA	Valerie Valoueva
PROGRAMMERS	Penny Goodwill, Kelly Fox
CREATIVE DIRECTOR	David Korchin
URL	http://199.229.12.135/awards2000/sears_kitchen2.html
ID	00 0079 N

{BANNERS/ single}

Merit
AGENCY	OgilvyInteractive/New York
CLIENT	Sears
ART DIRECTOR	Jonathon Hudson
WRITER	Tom Elia
DIGITAL ARTISTS	Jeff Chuang, Jose Galvez
PRODUCERS	Kate Kehoe, Elizabeth Gariti
MULTIMEDIA	Kelly Fox, Mark Hofschneider
PROGRAMMERS	Sandy Perez, Josh Dreier, Guy Shahar
CREATIVE DIRECTOR	David Korchin
URL	http://199.229.12.135/awards2000/sears_tugabob.html
ID	00 0080 N

{BANNERS/ single}

Merit
- **AGENCY** Organic/New York
- **CLIENT** Accent Health
- **ART DIRECTOR** Robert Hegeman
- **WRITER** Susan Zucker
- **DIGITAL ARTIST** Robert Hegeman
- **PRODUCER** Brandi Fogel
- **CREATIVE DIRECTORS** Stephen Tortorici, Monique Te Selle
- **URL** http://ads.organic.com/oneshow/accent.html
- **ID** 00 0081 N

{BANNERS/ single}

	Merit
AGENCY	Organic/New York
CLIENT	CDNOW
ART DIRECTOR	John Pompa
WRITER	Dan Ligorner
DIGITAL ARTIST	John Pompa
PRODUCER	Christi Frum
PROGRAMMERS	Aimee Drayer, Sergio Jimenez
CREATIVE DIRECTORS	Stephen Tortorici, Monique Te Selle
URL	http://ads.organic.com/oneshow/cdnowexpando.html
ID	00 0082 N

{BANNERS/ campaign}

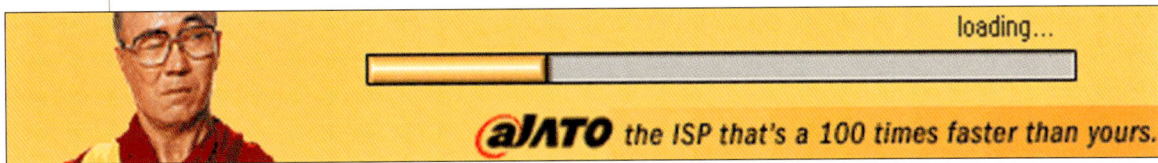

Merit
AGENCY Agenciaclick/São Paulo
CLIENT Ajato Broad Band
ART DIRECTOR Fred Siqueira
WRITER Mauro Alencar
PHOTOGRAPHER Fabio Ribeiro
PRODUCER Jean Boechat
CREATIVE DIRECTOR PJ Pereira
URL www.agenciaclick.com.br/awards/ajato
ID 00 0083 N

{BANNERS/ campaign}

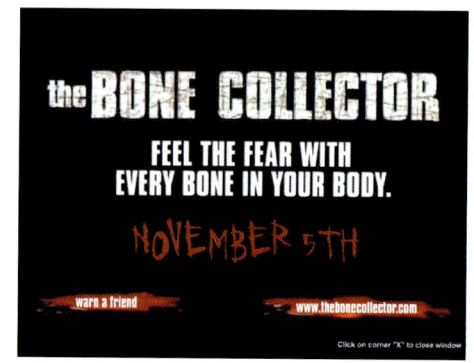

Merit
AGENCY | DDB Digital/Chicago
CLIENT | Universal Pictures
ART DIRECTOR | Chad Bookidis
WRITER | Chad Bookidis, Robin Kurzer
PRODUCER | Bill Klavon
CREATIVE DIRECTOR | Robin Kurzer
URL | www.awards.ddbdigital.com/bone_collector
ID 00 0084 N

{BANNERS/ campaign}

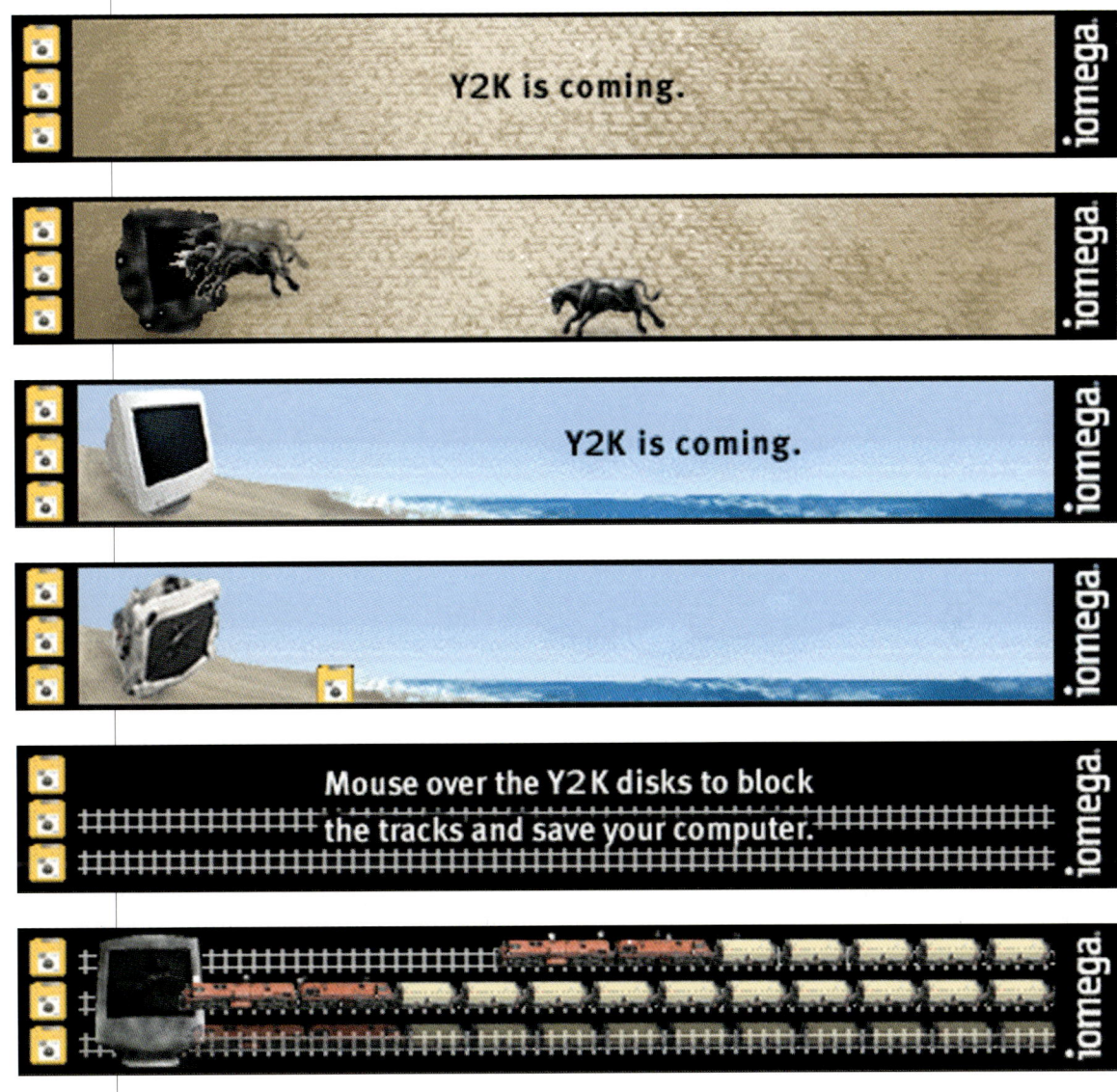

	Merit
AGENCY	EURO RSCG DSW Partners/Salt Lake City
CLIENT	iomega
ART DIRECTOR	Jared Allen
WRITERS	Joe Totten, Tony Hirsch
DIGITAL ARTIST	Nate Baertsch
PHOTOGRAPHER	Paul Wakefield
PRODUCER	John Blodgett
MULTIMEDIA	Freestyle Interactive
PROGRAMMER	Freestyle Interactive
CREATIVE DIRECTORS	Stephen Thompson, Eric Bute
URL	http://awards.dsw.com/sites/iomega/bulls_java/index.html
ID	00 0086 N

{BANNERS/ campaign}

Merit
AGENCY Jeff Benjamin/San Francisco
CLIENT Kay's Flowers
ART DIRECTOR Jeff Benjamin
WRITER Jeff Benjamin
PRODUCER Alberto Escarlate
CREATIVE DIRECTOR Jeff Benjamin
URL www.mrbadass.com/oneshow
ID 00 0087 N

{BANNERS/ campaign}

Merit

AGENCY | OgilvyInteractive/New York
CLIENT | IBM
ART DIRECTOR | Todd Goodale
WRITER | Suzanne Darmory
PHOTOGRAPHER | Nitten Vodukal
PRODUCER | Nick Kady
MULITMEDIA | Neal Lee
PROGRAMMERS | John McGeehan, Matt Webster
CREATIVE DIRECTOR | Audrey Fleisher
URL | http://199.229.12.135/awards2000/placard/implementor/ibm_placard_imp.html
http://199.229.12.135/awards2000/placard/strat468/ibm_placard_strat.html
http://199.229.12.135/awards2000/placard/pspec120/ibm_placard_pspec.html
ID 00 0088 N

{BANNERS/ campaign}

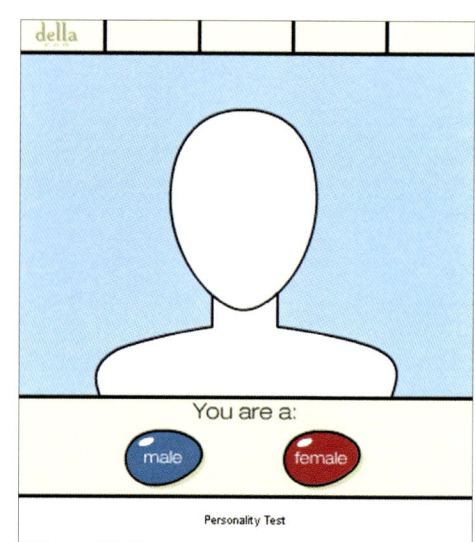

	Merit
AGENCY	SF Interactive/San Francisco
CLIENT	Della
ART DIRECTOR	Emily Seitz
WRITER	Maureen Condron
PROGRAMMERS	Tom Jacobson, Gamelet
CREATIVE DIRECTOR	Betsy Parish
URL	www.staging.sfinteractive.com/oneshow/della/della.html
ID	00 0091 N

{BANNERS/campaign}

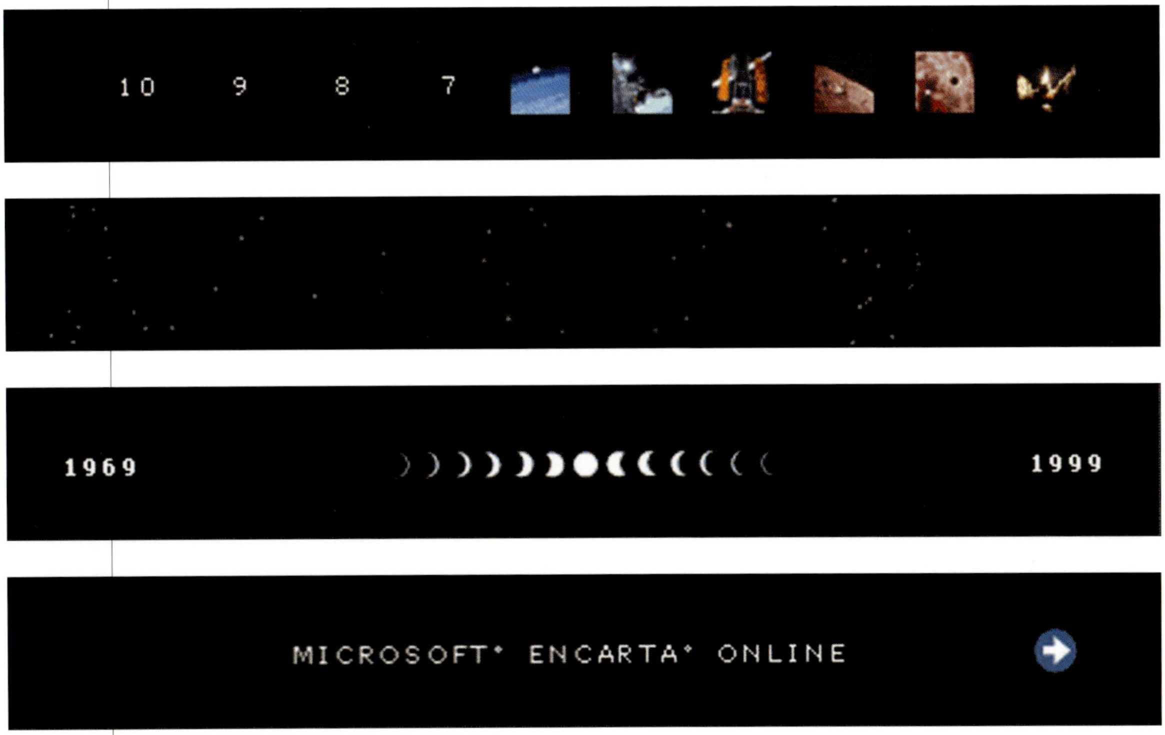

	Merit
AGENCY	Quantum Leap/Chicago
CLIENT	Microsoft Encarta
WRITER	Irene Westcott
DIGITAL ARTIST	Sarah Kretchmer
PRODUCER	Don Adams
CREATIVE DIRECTORS	Margo Johnson, Tom Raith
	ID 00 0089 N

{BANNERS/ campaign}

Merit
AGENCY Quantum Leap/Chicago
CLIENT Microsoft Encarta
WRITER Alice Dobrinsky
DIGITAL ARTIST Jessica Foster
PRODUCER Don Adams
CREATIVE DIRECTORS Margo Johnson, Tom Raith
ID 00 0090 N

{BANNERS/ campaign}

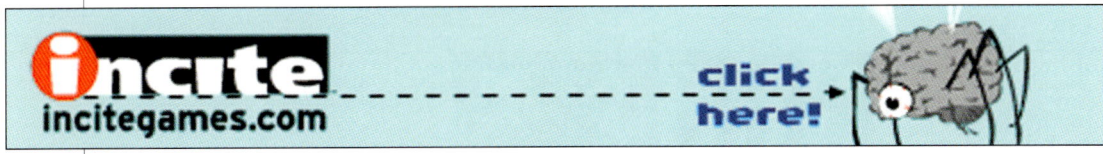
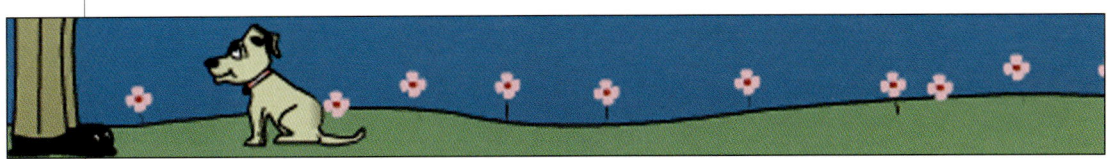
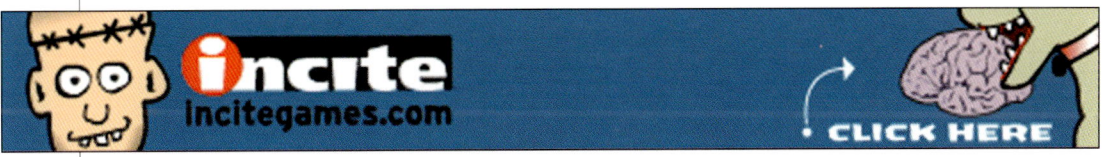

Merit
AGENCY | Zentropy Partners/San Francisco
CLIENT | Computec
ART DIRECTOR | Auryn Zimmer
WRITER | George Chalekian
DIGITAL ARTISTS | Auryn Zimmer, Michael Camara, Allan Aguas
PRODUCER | Kenna Takahashi
URL | http://awards.sf.zentropypartners.com
ID 00 0092 N

{BEYOND/ the banner}

	Merit
AGENCY	Anderson & Lembke/San Francisco
CLIENT	MSN Gaming Zone
ART DIRECTOR	Matthew Schneider
WRITER	Steven B. Nasi
DIGITAL ARTISTS	Tom Ran, @Home
PRODUCER	Jay Bain
MULTIMEDIA	@Home
PROGRAMMER	@Home
CREATIVE DIRECTORS	Doug Green, Jef Loyola, Glen Sheehan
URL	http://stertz.homestead.com/files/brain.html
ID	00 0094 N

{BEYOND/ the banner}

	Merit
AGENCY	AGENCY.COM/New York
CLIENT	Lipton
ART DIRECTORS	Tony Tarr, Joe Zandstra, John Dutton
WRITERS	Michelle Lee, Kathy Rotramel-Stipe
DIGITAL ARTISTS	Dustin Young, John Nack, Tom Simpson
PHOTOGRAPHER	Jodi Lekakos
PRODUCERS	Juliette Leary, Sally Twickler, Jim Droskoski
MULTIMEDIA	Brad Grove, Brian Johnson, Kevin Poor
PROGRAMMERS	Alex Heller, Tom Simpson
CREATIVE DIRECTORS	David Zeigler, Chris Needham, Scott Mager
URL	www.lipton.com
ID	00 0093 N

{BEYOND/ the banner}

 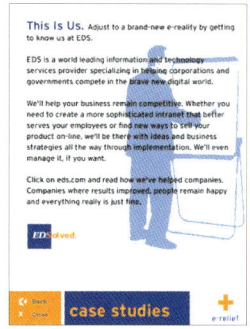

 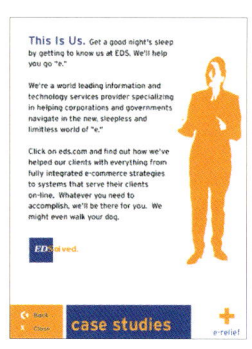

Merit

AGENCY	Duffy Design/Minneapolis
CLIENT	EDS (Electronic Data Systems)
ART DIRECTORS	Paul Malmstrom, Todd Bartz
WRITER	Linus Karlsson
DIGITAL ARTIST	Joel Hermann
PHOTOGRAPHER	Stephanie Rau
PRODUCER	Adam Kmiec
MULTIMEDIA	Todd Bartz
PROGRAMMER	Gwen Williams
CREATIVE DIRECTORS	Joe Duffy, Dan Olsen
URL	http://awards.duffy.com/eds_banners/banners/index.html
ID	00 0095 N

{BEYOND/ the banner}

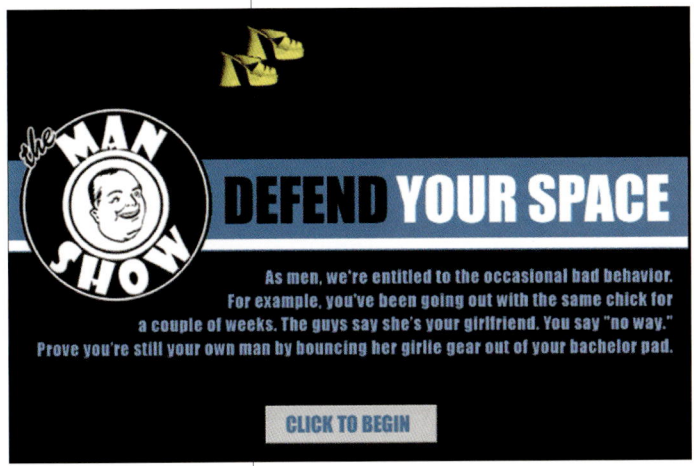
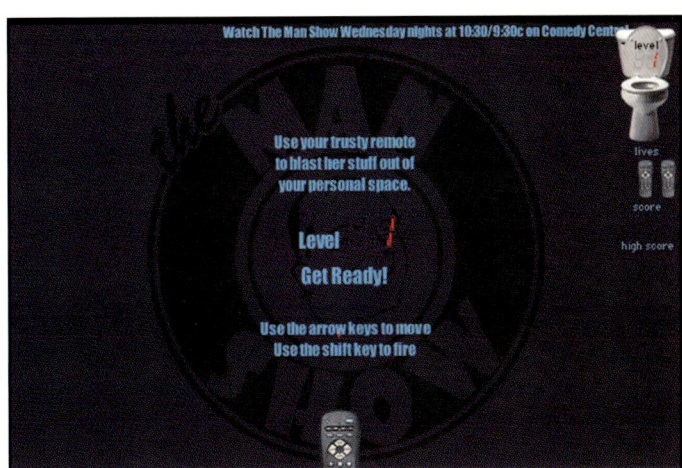

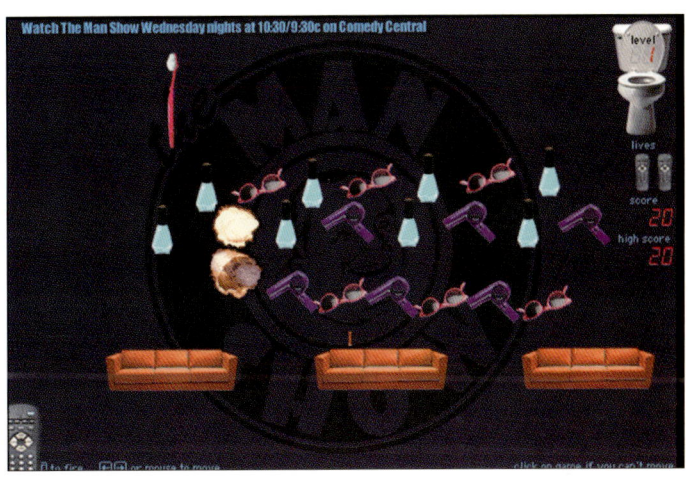

	Merit
AGENCY	FCB Worldwide/Southfield
CLIENT	Comedy Central
ART DIRECTORS	Anne Bourseleth, Peter Arndt
WRITER	Melissa Gessner
DIGITAL ARTIST	Anne Bourseleth
PRODUCERS	Kathleen Starr, Shawn Vine
MULTIMEDIA	Gyro Design
PROGRAMMER	Gyro Design
CREATIVE DIRECTORS	Peter Arndt, John Gregory, Sam Ajluni
URL	www.webspot.com/comedy_central/the_man_show/your_space
ID	00 0096 N

{BEYOND/ the banner}

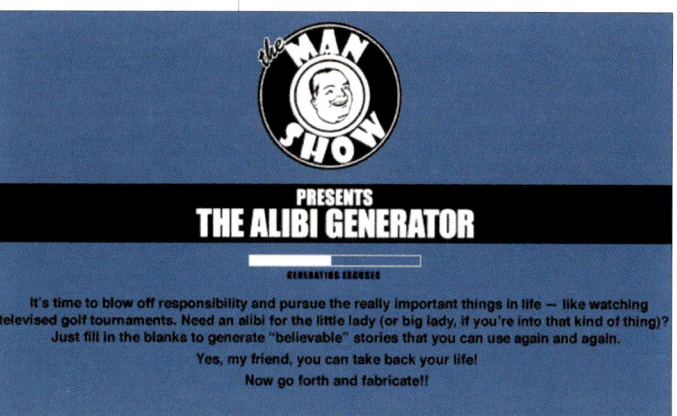
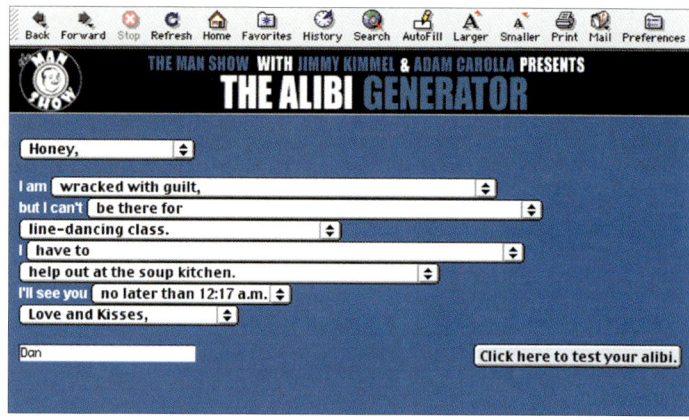
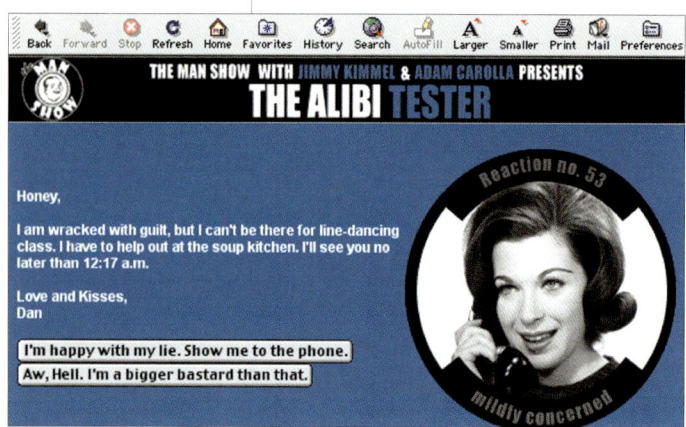

Merit

AGENCY	FCB Worldwide/Southfield
CLIENT	Comedy Central
ART DIRECTOR	Scott Lange
WRITERS	Dan Sicko, John Gregory
PRODUCERS	Kathleen Starr, Shawn Vine
MULTIMEDIA	Gyro Design
PROGRAMMER	Gyro Design
CREATIVE DIRECTORS	Peter Arndt, John Gregory, Sam Ajluni
URL	www.webspot.com/comedy_central/the_man_show/alibi
ID	00 0097 N

{BEYOND/ the banner}

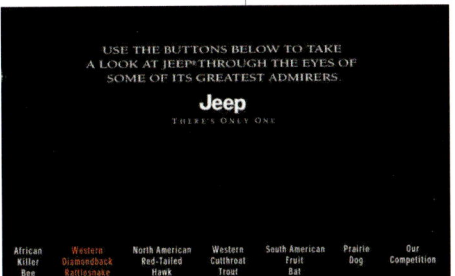
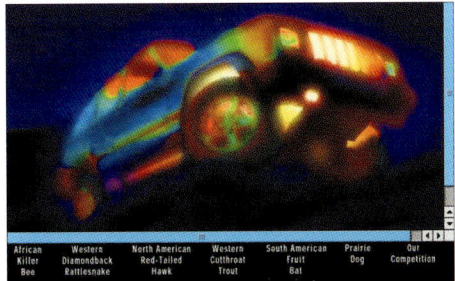
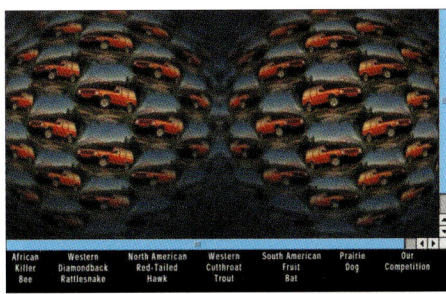

Merit

AGENCY	FCB Worldwide/Southfield
CLIENT	Daimler Chrysler Corp.
ART DIRECTOR	Scott Lange
WRITERS	Dan Sicko, John Gregory
DIGITAL ARTIST	DragonFly Studios
PRODUCERS	Kathleen Starr, Shawn Vine
MULTIMEDIA	Gyro Design
PROGRAMMER	Gyro Design
CREATIVE DIRECTORS	Peter Arndt, John Gregory, Sam Ajluni, Bill Morden
URL	www.webspot.com/jeep/pov
ID	00 0098 N

{BEYOND/ the banner}

Merit

AGENCY	hillmancurtis.com/New York
CLIENT	Intel
ART DIRECTORS	Hillman Curtis, Ian Kovalik
WRITERS	DSW Partners, Kim Bellamy, Jared Allen, Dan Biunchi
DIGITAL ARTISTS	Hillman Curtis, Ian Kovalik
PHOTOGRAPHER	Ian Kovalik
PRODUCER	Homera J. Chaudhry
MULTIMEDIA	Hillman Curtis, Ian Kovalik
CREATIVE DIRECTOR	Hillman Curtis
URL	www.hillmancurtis.com/design/oneshow
ID	00 0099 N

{BEYOND/ the banner}

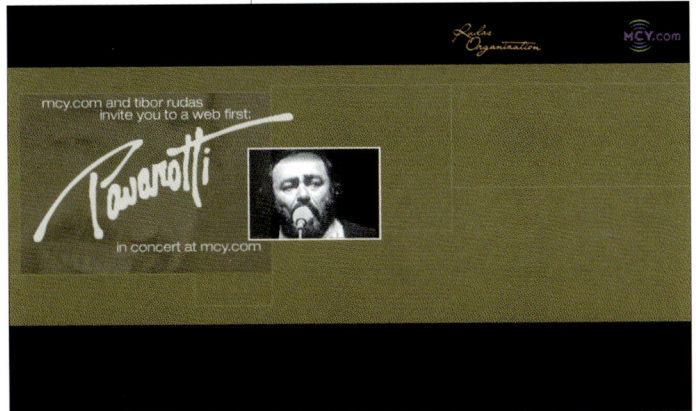
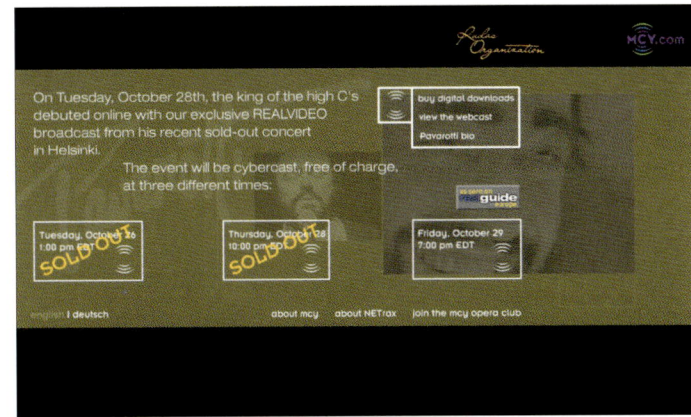
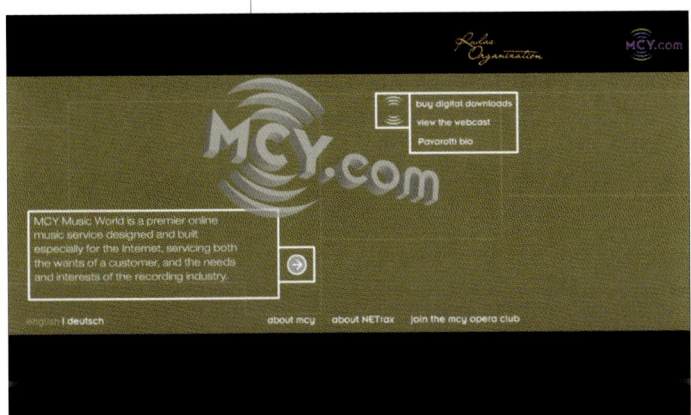
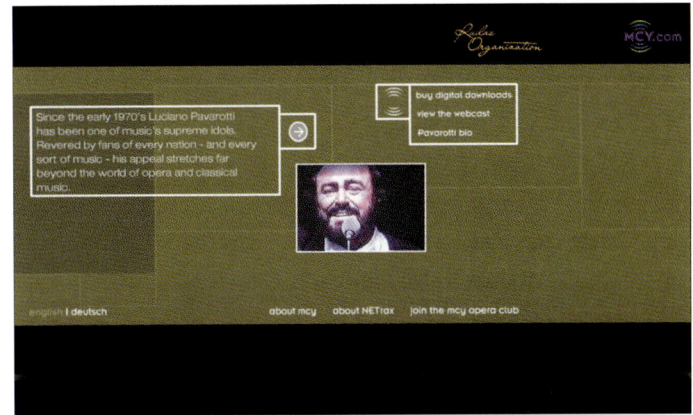

Merit

AGENCY	hillmancurtis.com/New York
CLIENT	MCY Music World, Inc.
ART DIRECTOR	Ian Kovalik
DIGITAL ARTISTS	Hillman Curtis, Ian Kovalik
MULTIMEDIA	Hillman Curtis, Ian Kovalik
PROGRAMMER	Hillman Curtis
CREATIVE DIRECTOR	Hillman Curtis
URL	www.hillmancurtis.com/design/oneshow
ID	00 0100 N

{BEYOND/ the banner}

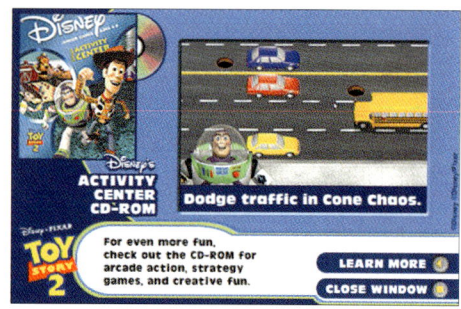

Merit
AGENCY | i-traffic.com/San Francisco
CLIENT | Disney Interactive
ART DIRECTORS | Vina Lam, Doug Miller
WRITER | Jim Ryan
CREATIVE DIRECTOR | Brad Epstein
URL | www.i-traffic.com/awards/award_diaenliven.html
ID 00 0101 N

{BEYOND/ the banner}

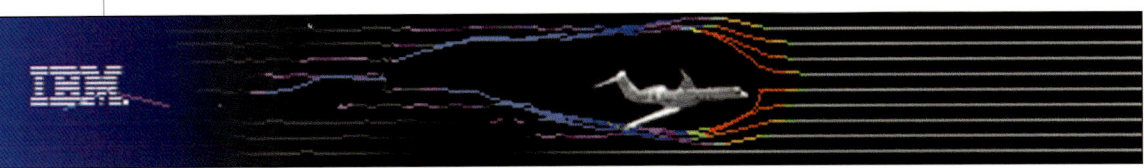

	Merit
AGENCY	OgilvyInteractive/New York
CLIENT	IBM
ART DIRECTORS	Juan Gallardo, Daymon Bruck, Melissa Haworth
WRITERS	David Levy, Tim Doherty
PRODUCERS	Carol Sung, Jude Raymond Fish
MULTIMEDIA	Malvika Mitchell, Scott Huang
PROGRAMMER	Java Banners - Digital Image Design Inc.
CREATIVE DIRECTOR	Audrey Fleisher
URL	http://199.229.12.135/awards2000/airplane/com/didi/simbanners/flow/magicbox_gulf.html
	http://199.229.12.135/awards2000/eseeds/magicbox_seeds.html
	http://199.229.12.135/awards2000/magicbox_best.html
	ID 00 0102 N

{BEYOND/ the banner}

Merit

AGENCY	OgilvyInteractive/New York
CLIENT	IBM
ART DIRECTOR	Daymon Bruck
WRITER	Tim Doherty
PRODUCERS	Angie Ahn, Heavy Industry
MULTIMEDIA	Mark Hofschneider, Neal Lee
CREATIVE DIRECTOR	Audrey Fleisher
URL	http://199.229.12.135/awards2000/ibm_scm/start.htm
	http://199.229.12.135/awards2000/ibmscm1.html
	http://199.229.12.135/awards2000/ibm_scm1.html
	ID 00 0103 N

{BEYOND/ the banner}

	Merit
AGENCY	OgilvyInteractive/New York
CLIENT	Lotus Development Corporation
ART DIRECTORS	Alison Tsoi, Juan Gallardo
WRITERS	Patrick Clarke, David Levy
DIGITAL ARTIST	Nick Barrios
PRODUCERS	Jude Raymond Fish, Carol Sung, Clare Drysdale
MULTIMEDIA	Malvika Mitchell
PROGRAMMERS	Valerie Valoueva, Bob Plotkin, Neal Lee
CREATIVE DIRECTOR	Audrey Fleisher
URL	http://199.229.12.135/awards2000/lotus_coppola.html
	http://199.229.12.135/awards2000/lotus_burson.html
	http://199.229.12.135/awards2000/lotus_shell.html
ID	00 0104 N

{BEYOND/ the banner}

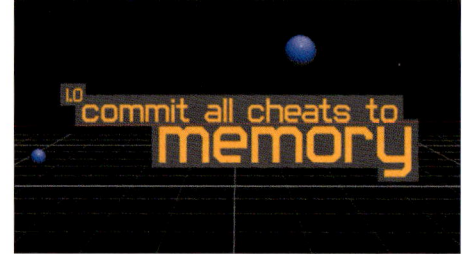

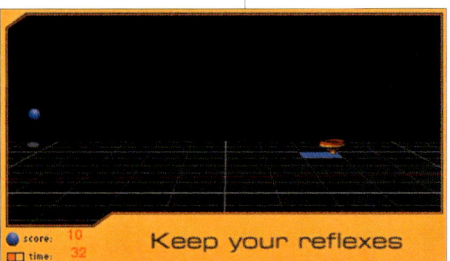
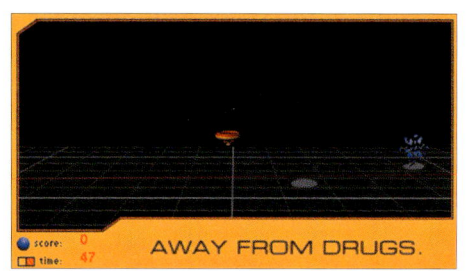
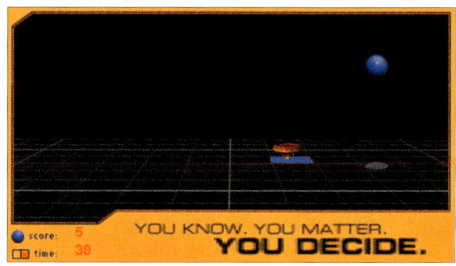

Merit

AGENCY OgilvyInteractive/New York
CLIENT ONDCP (Office of National Drug Control Policy)
ART DIRECTOR Matthew Atkatz
WRITER Ken Grobe
DIGITAL ARTIST Matthew Atkatz
PRODUCER Kate Kehoe
MULTIMEDIA Mark Hofschneider, Valerie Valoueva
CREATIVE DIRECTOR Mach Arom
URL http://199.229.12.135/awards2000/ondcp_dropstopper.html
ID 00 0105 N

{BEYOND/ the banner}

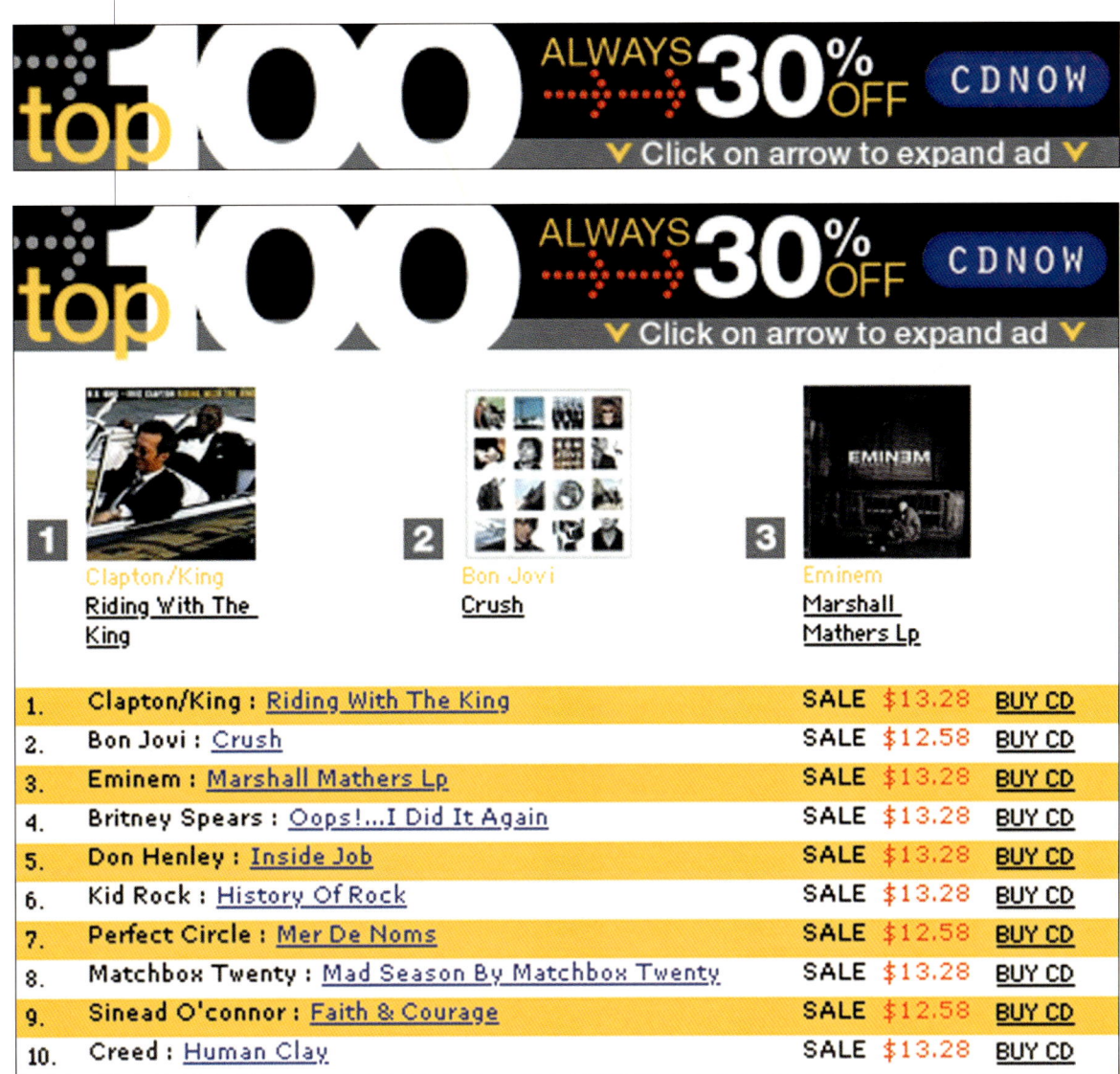

		Merit
AGENCY		Organic/New York
CLIENT		CDNOW
ART DIRECTOR		John Pompa
WRITER		Dan Ligorner
DIGITAL ARTIST		John Pompa
PRODUCER		Christi Frum
PROGRAMMERS		Aimee Drayer, Sergio Jimenez
CREATIVE DIRECTORS		Stephen Tortorici, Monique Te Selle
URL		http://ads.organic.com/oneshow/cdnowexpando.html
		ID 00 0106 N

{BEYOND/ the banner}

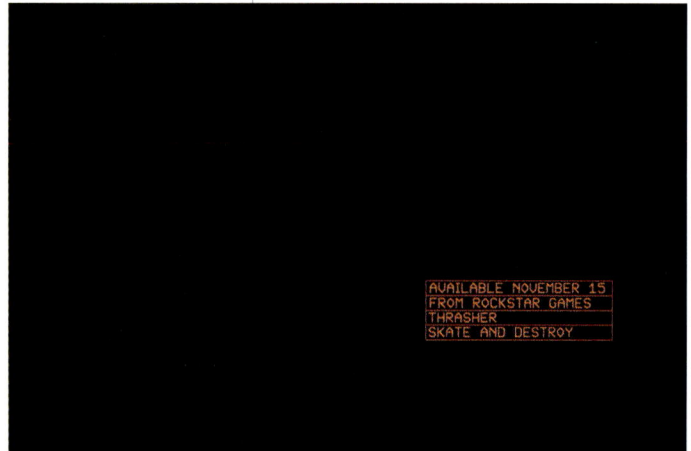

Merit

AGENCY Oyster Partners/London
CLIENT Take Two Interactive
ART DIRECTOR Hugo Manassei
WRITER Dan Houser
DIGITAL ARTIST Jake Portman
PRODUCER Juilian Marsh
CREATIVE DIRECTOR Hugo Manassei
URL www.skateanddestroy.com
ID 00 0107 N

{BEYOND/ the banner}

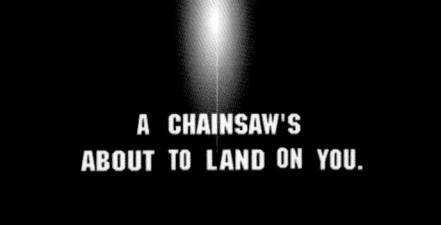
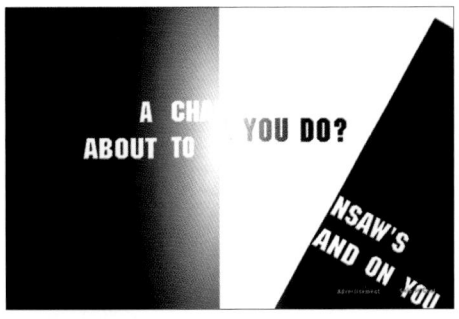

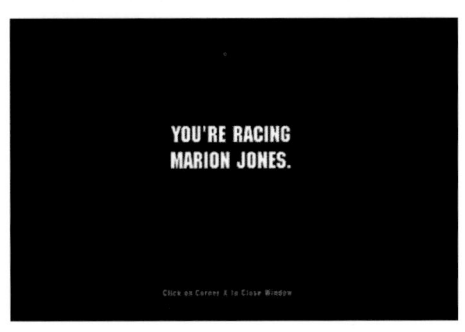

Merit

AGENCY	Wieden + Kennedy/Portland
CLIENT	Nike
ART DIRECTOR	Robert Rasmussen
WRITER	Brian Ford
PRODUCERS	Katie Raye, Elaine Thomas, Katie Shields
MULTIMEDIA	Jeff Keyser
CREATIVE DIRECTOR	Steve Sandoz
URL	www.wk.com/online/whatever/award.htm
USERNAME	online
PASSWORD	7fot92
ID	00 0108 N

{BEYOND/ the banner}

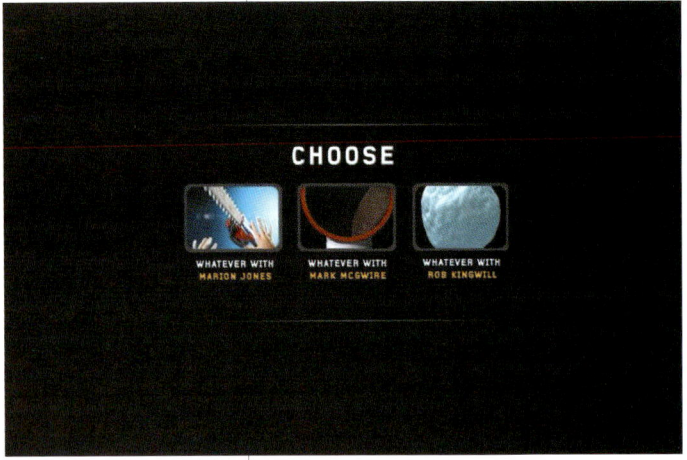
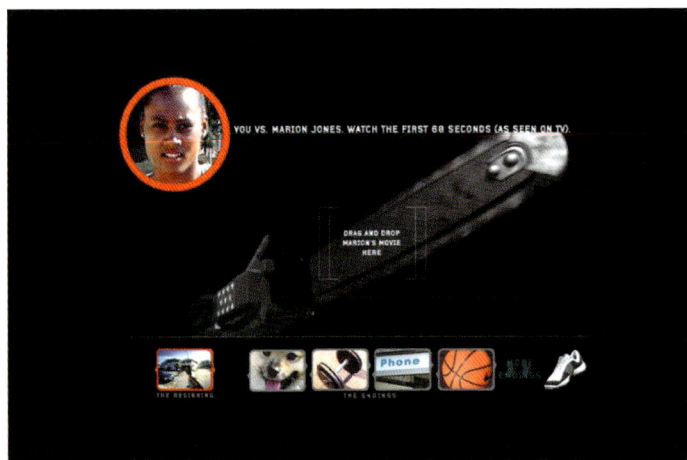
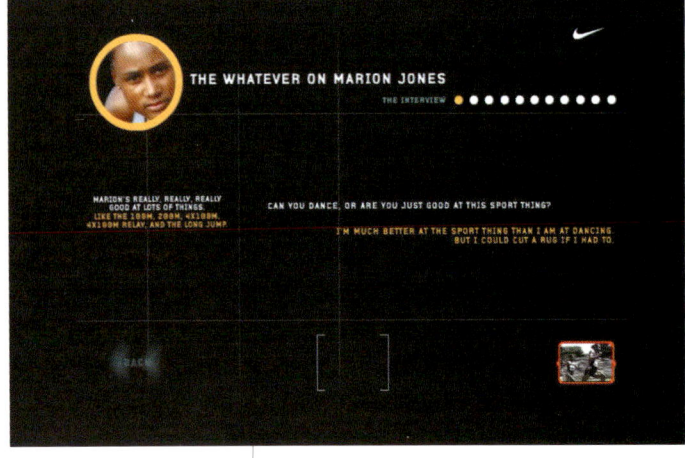

	Merit
AGENCY	Wieden + Kennedy/Portland
CLIENT	Nike
ART DIRECTOR	Andy Fackrell
WRITER	Dylan Lee
DIGITAL ARTIST	Matt Owens
PRODUCERS	Jim Woolfrey, Katie Raye, Katie Shields
MULTIMEDIA	One9ine
PROGRAMMER	One9ine
CREATIVE DIRECTOR	Steve Sandoz
ID	00 0109 N

{PROMOTIONAL ADVERTISING/ web sites}

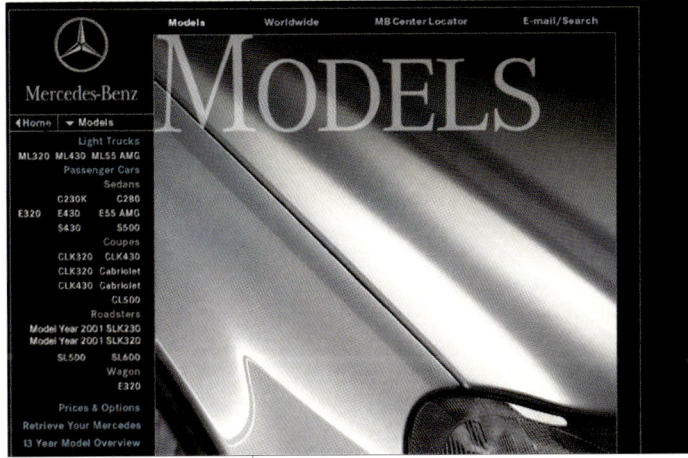

Merit

AGENCY	Critical Mass Inc./Calgary
CLIENT	Mercedes-Benz USA
ART DIRECTORS	Michel Clairo, Jason Delichte
DIGITAL ARTIST	Mark Abernethy
PRODUCERS	Ted Hellard, Stephanie Chamberland
MULTIMEDIA	Philippe Clairo
PROGRAMMER	Peter Loman
URL	http://mclassified.mbusa.com/get_smart/review.html
ID	00 0110 N

{PROMOTIONAL ADVERTISING/ web sites}

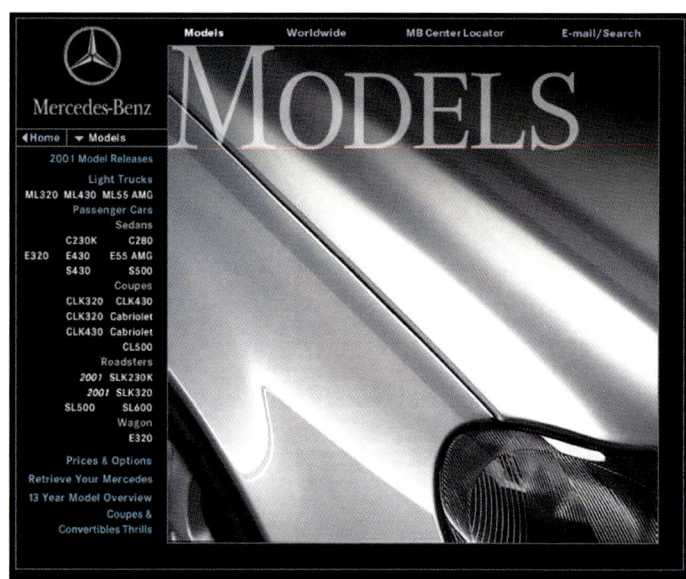

Merit

AGENCY Critical Mass Inc./Calgary
CLIENT Mercedes-Benz USA
ART DIRECTORS Michel Clairo, Jason Delichte
PRODUCERS Ted Hellard, Stepahaine Chamberland
MULTIMEDIA Philippe Clairo
PROGRAMMER Peter Loman
URL www.mbusa.com/ad/slr_concept
ID 00 0111 N

{PROMOTIONAL ADVERTISING/ web sites}

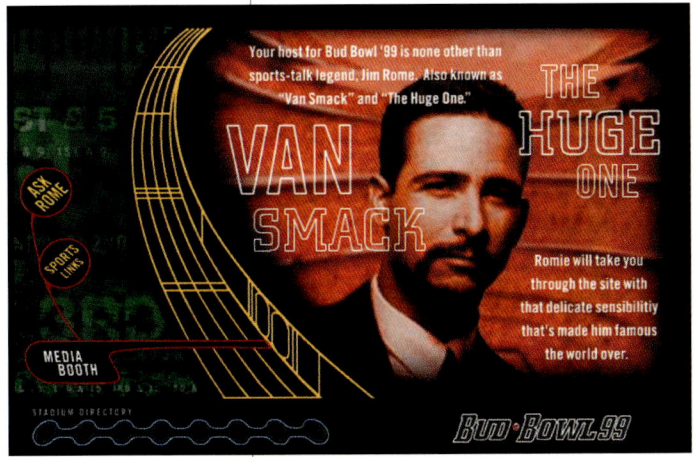
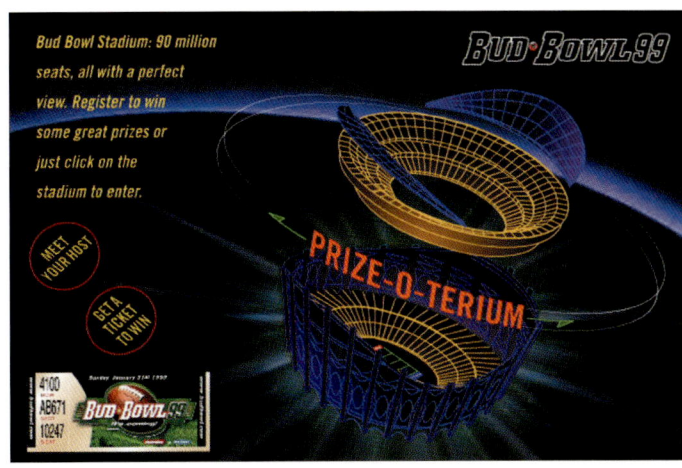

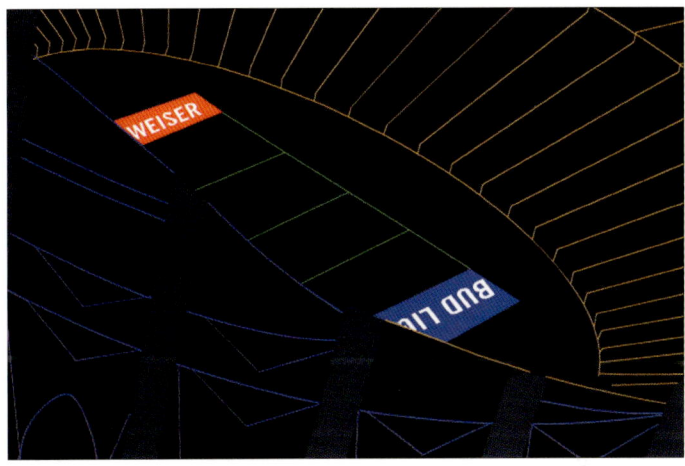

Merit

AGENCY DDB Digital/Chicago
CLIENT Budweiser
ART DIRECTORS Julian Wild, Allen Morgenstern
WRITER Robin Kurzer
PRODUCER Kelly Twohig
CREATIVE DIRECTOR Mark Howell
URL www.awards.ddbdigital.com/bud_bowl99
ID 00 0112 N

{PROMOTIONAL ADVERTISING/ web sites}

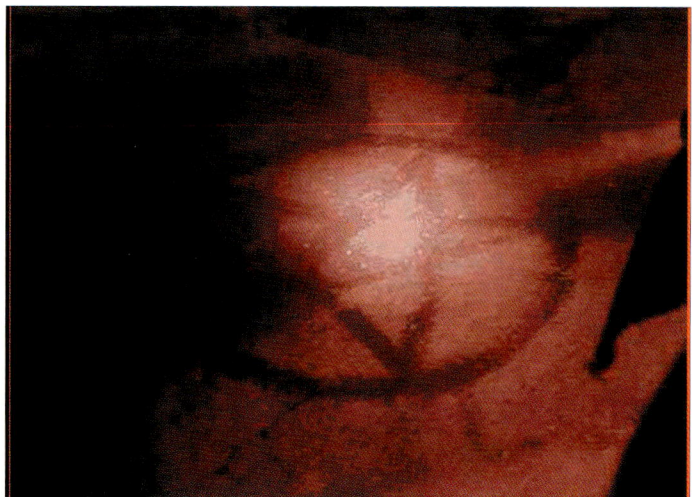

	Merit
AGENCY	DDB Digital/Chicago
CLIENT	Universal Pictures
ART DIRECTOR	Chad Bookidis
PRODUCER	Bill Klavon
CREATIVE DIRECTOR	Robin Kurzer
URL	www.awards.ddbdigital.com/end_of_days

ID 00 0113 N

{PROMOTIONAL ADVERTISING/ web sites}

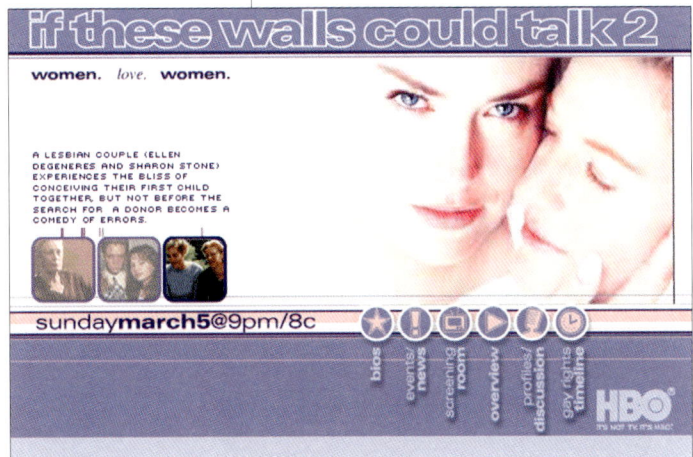
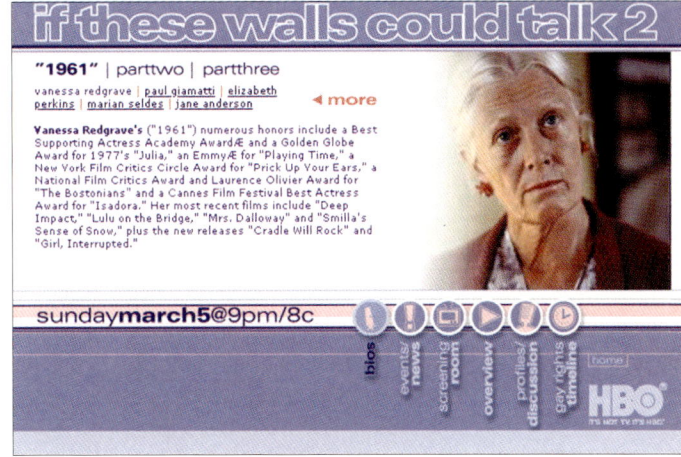
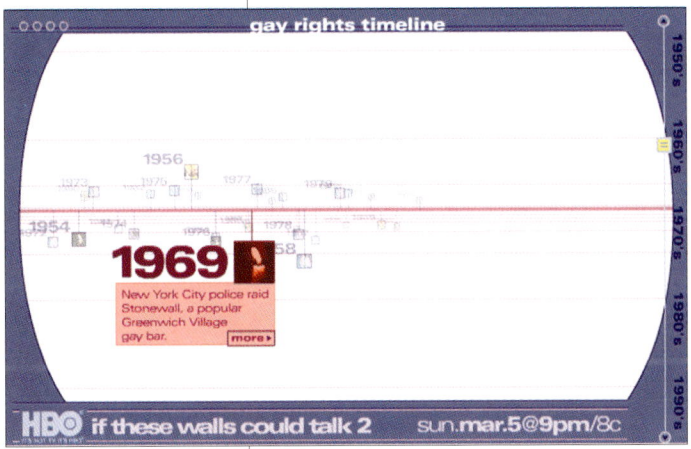
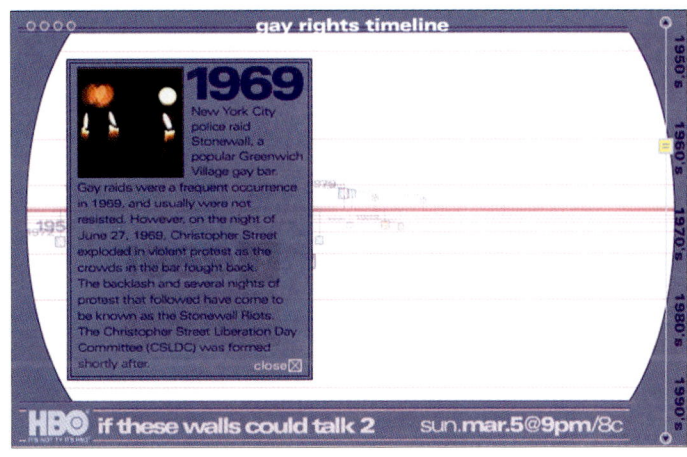

Merit

AGENCY Dennis Interactive/New York
CLIENT HBO
ART DIRECTOR Brandon Bell
DIGITAL ARTIST Jeff Li
PRODUCER Alex Gadd
PROGRAMMERS Chris Phoenix, Wen Sun
CREATIVE DIRECTORS Greg Knoll, Zoe Chan
URL http://dennisinter.com/walls/new
ID 00 0114 N

{PROMOTIONAL ADVERTISING/ web sites}

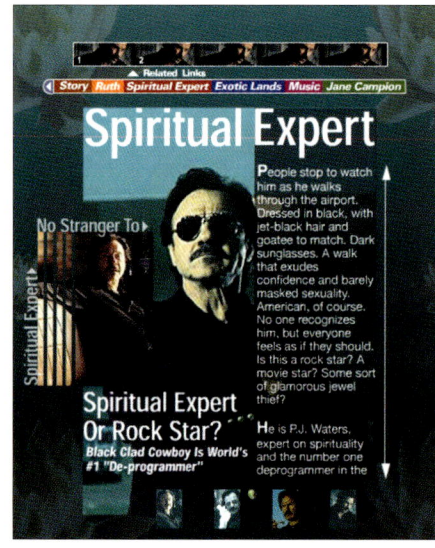

Merit

AGENCY Dennis Interactive/New York
CLIENT Miramax Films
ART DIRECTOR Ze Frank
DIGITAL ARTIST Paul Szypula
PRODUCER Alex Gadd
PROGRAMMER Chris Phoenix
CREATIVE DIRECTOR Greg Knoll
URL www.holysmokethemovie.com
ID 00 0115 N

{PROMOTIONAL ADVERTISING/ web sites}

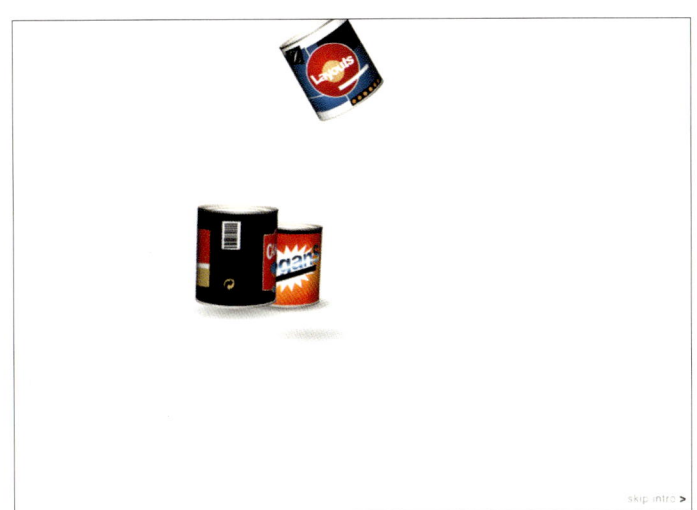

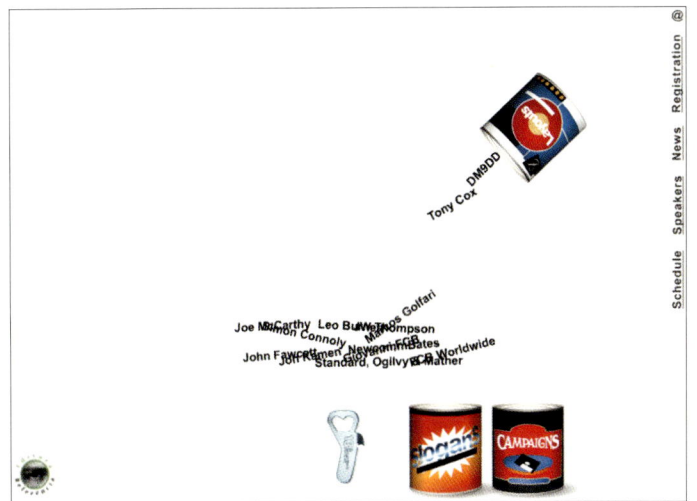

Merit

AGENCY DM9 DDB Publicidade/São Paulo
CLIENT 13th Int'l Ad Creative Week
ART DIRECTOR Andrea Evora Cals
WRITER PJ Pereira
PRODUCER Zeno Millet
URL www.dm9.com.br/festival/cans
ID 00 0116 N

{PROMOTIONAL ADVERTISING/ web sites}

	Merit
AGENCY	Luminant Worldwide/New York
CLIENT	Maybelline
ART DIRECTOR	Peter Loomis
WRITER	Joyce Kauf
DIGITAL ARTIST	Eran Bendheim
PRODUCER	Rebecca Wales-Szyluk
PROGRAMMERS	Roselyn Joshua, Matt Vohr
URL	www.maybelline.com
	ID 00 0117 N

{PROMOTIONAL ADVERTISING/ web sites}

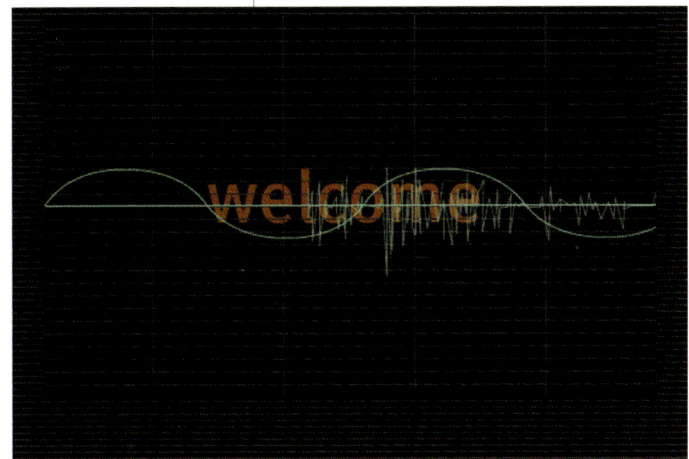

Merit

AGENCY	Saatchi & Saatchi Los Angeles/Torrance
CLIENT	Toyota
ART DIRECTOR	Deanna Rome
WRITERS	Anthony Wells, Heather Reid
PHOTOGRAPHERS	Michael Ruppert, Rick Graves, John Early
PRODUCERS	Carol Swantek, Matt Mayer
PROGRAMMER	IVT Interactive Video Technologies
CREATIVE DIRECTORS	Dean Van Eimeren, Chris Ray
URL	www.isthistoyota.com

ID 00 0118 N

{PROMOTIONAL ADVERTISING/ web sites}

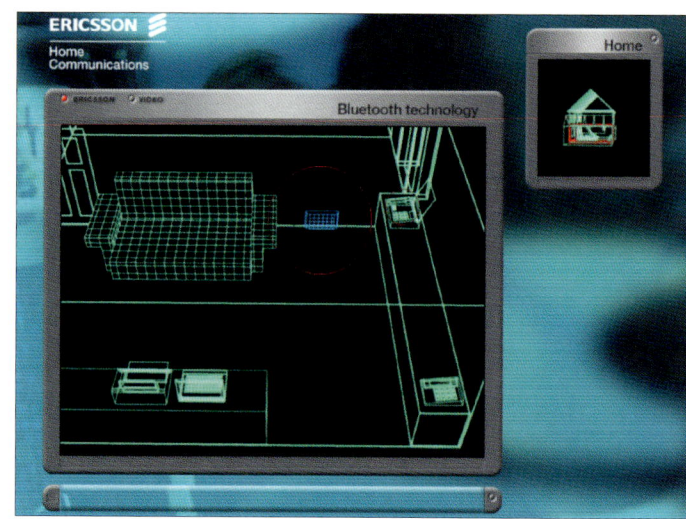
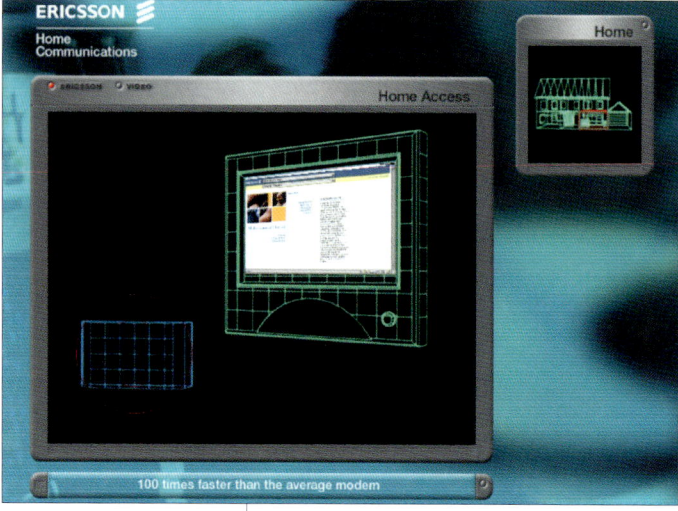
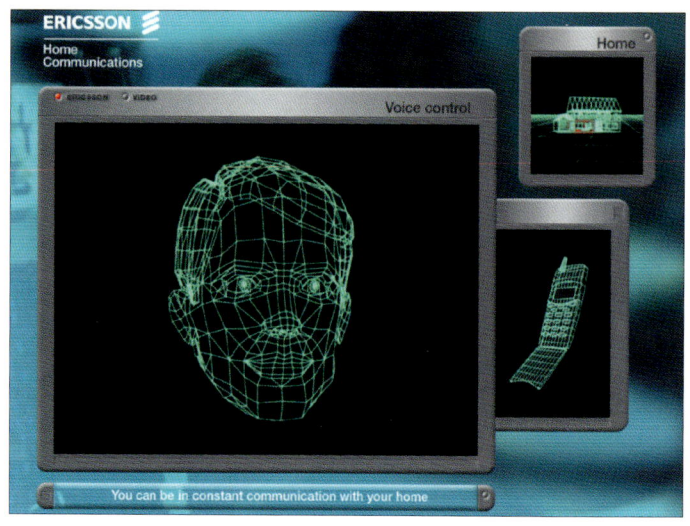

Merit

AGENCY	Wunderman Cato Johnson/London
CLIENT	Home Communications - Ericsson
ART DIRECTORS	Simon Armstrong, Bill Galloway
WRITER	Ross Keenleyside
DIGITAL ARTIST	Anthony Lelliott
PRODUCERS	Rachel Clein, Paul Canty
MULTIMEDIA	Zig
CREATIVE DIRECTORS	Graham Mills, Jack Nolan
	ID 00 0119 N

{PROMOTIONAL ADVERTISING/ CD-ROM}

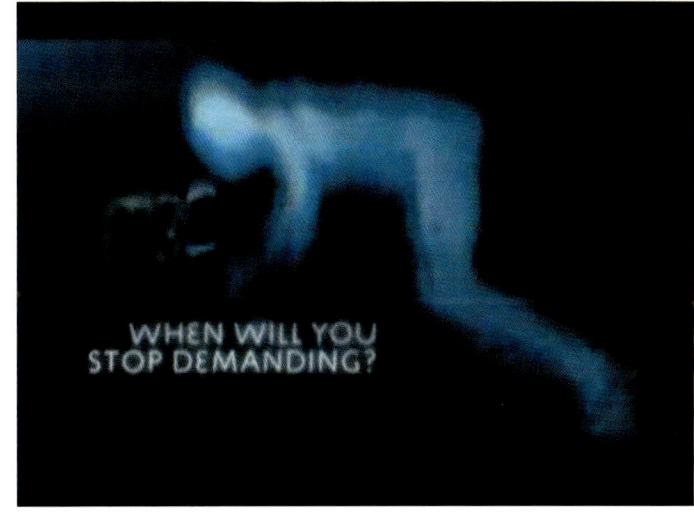

Merit

AGENCY	adidas GMS-Creative/Portland
CLIENT	adidas
ART DIRECTOR	Pam Racs
WRITER	Andrews Jenkins
PROGRAMMER	Lightspeed Studio
ID	00 0120 N

{PROMOTIONAL ADVERTISING/ CD-ROM}

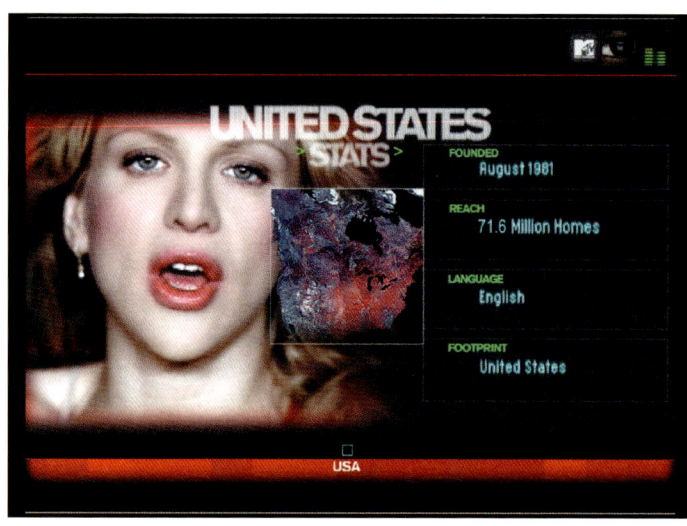

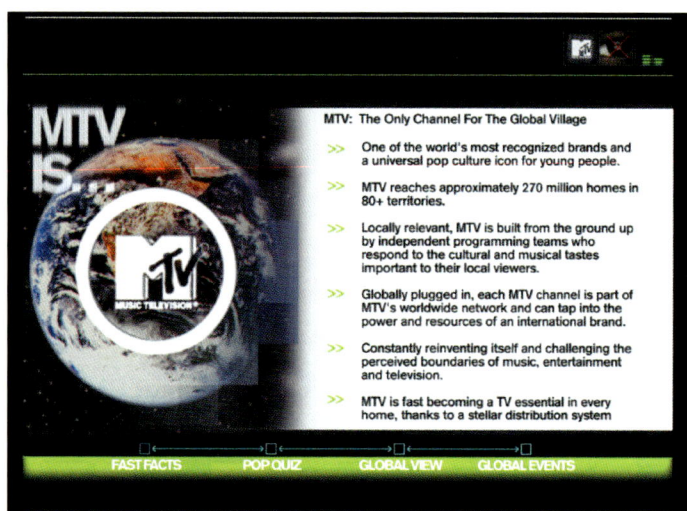

MERIT

- **AGENCY** Digital Ambush/New York
- **CLIENT** MTV Networks
- **ART DIRECTOR** Sarah Beatty
- **WRITER** Melissa Alcruz
- **DIGITAL ARTISTS** Karen Bullis, J.P. Ballas
- **PRODUCER** Lisa Sykes
- **MULTIMEDIA** Jamie Manalio
- **PROGRAMMER** Sean Yeomans
- **CREATIVE DIRECTOR** Lisa Sykes
- **ID** 00 0121 N

{PROMOTIONAL ADVERTISING/ CD-ROM}

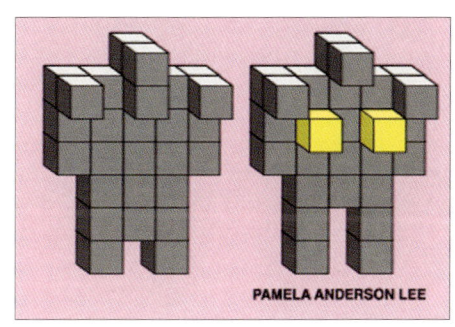

Merit
AGENCY Duffy/New York
CLIENT Art Directors Club
ART DIRECTOR Alan Leusink
WRITER William Gelner
DIGITAL ARTIST Laurie Brown
MULTIMEDIA Alan Leusink
CREATIVE DIRECTOR Neil Powell
ID 00 0122 N

{PROMOTIONAL ADVERTISING/ CD-ROM}

	Merit
AGENCY	Duffy Design/Minneapolis
CLIENT	BMW of North America
ART DIRECTORS	Kevin Flatt, Jason Strong
WRITER	Russ Stark
DIGITAL ARTISTS	Tracey Hogenson, Laurie Brown, Maria Erickson
PHOTOGRAPHERS	Mark LaFavor, various
PRODUCERS	Laura Morris, Louise Dengerud
MULTIMEDIA	Mark Sandau, Christian Erickson
PROGRAMMERS	Christian Erickson, Mark Sandau
CREATIVE DIRECTORS	Joe Duffy, Dan Olson
ID	00 0123 N

{PROMOTIONAL ADVERTISING/ CD-ROM}

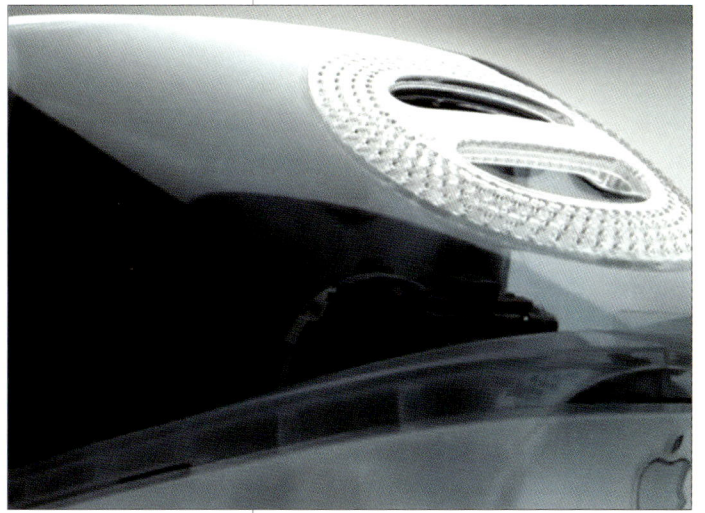

Merit

AGENCY	marchFIRST/Salt Lake City
CLIENT	Apple Computer, Inc.
ART DIRECTORS	Gustaf Fjelstrom, Dave Brinda
WRITER	Nancy Thompson
DIGITAL ARTIST	Dave Skuratowicz
PHOTOGRAPHER	various
PRODUCERS	Carlos Orepezza, Christopher Martin
MULTIMEDIA	Jason Beckwith
PROGRAMMER	Norbert Hendrickse
CREATIVE DIRECTOR	Jim Vandegrift

ID 00 0124 N

{PROMOTIONAL ADVERTISING/ CD-ROM}

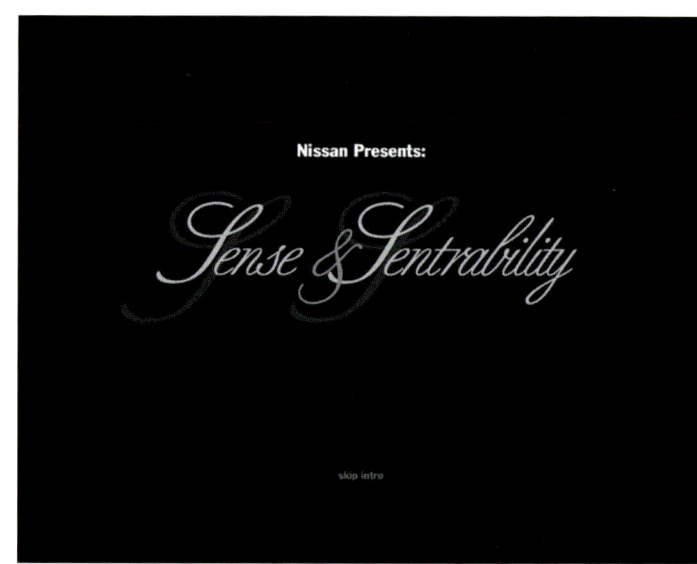

Merit

AGENCY	Media Revolution/Santa Monica
CLIENT	TWBA Chiat/Day
ART DIRECTORS	Stepahnie Uyloan, Jennifer Muranaka
WRITER	Dave Butler
DIGITAL ARTISTS	Ian Burns, Robert Gale
PHOTOGRAPHERS	Charles Hopkins, Rick Rusing, Michael Rausch, Joe Carlson, Brian Garland, Bryan Trela, Michael Rupert
PRODUCER	Emi Mukae
CREATIVE DIRECTOR	Jason Yim

ID 00 0125 N

{PROMOTIONAL ADVERTISING/ CD-ROM}

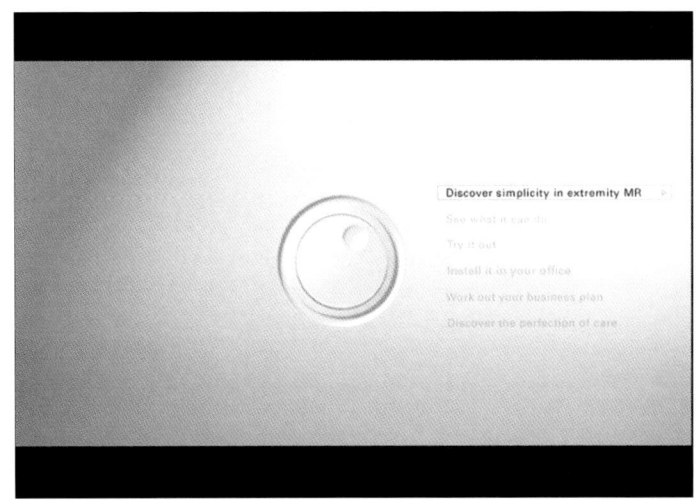
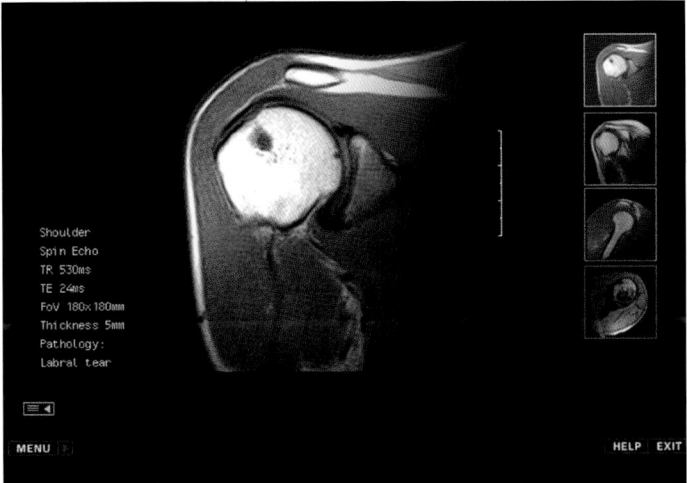

Merit
AGENCY Neue Digitale/Frankfurt
CLIENT Michael Conrad/Leo Burnett for Siemens
MULTIMEDIA Andreas Gahlert
CREATIVE DIRECTOR Olaf Czescher
ID 00 0126 N

{PROMOTIONAL ADVERTISING/ CD-ROM}

Merit
AGENCY New York Zoom/New York
CLIENT Conde Nast Publications
ART DIRECTORS Alain Grossenbacher, Tina Roth
WRITER Warren Dixon
PRODUCER Anya Block
MULTIMEDIA Alain Grossenbacher
PROGRAMMER Federico Gomez
CREATIVE DIRECTOR Matthew Waldman
ID 00 0127 N

{PROMOTIONAL ADVERTISING/ other digital media}

	Merit
AGENCY	EURO RSCG DSW Partners/Salt Lake City
CLIENT	iomega
ART DIRECTORS	Jared Allen, Scott Eggers
WRITERS	Joe Totten, Tony Hirsch
DIGITAL ARTISTS	Steve Warner, Dennis Millard, Brent Evans
PHOTOGRAPHER	Paul Wakefield
PRODUCER	John Blodgett
MULTIMEDIA	Hillman Curtis
PROGRAMMER	Mac Baker
CREATIVE DIRECTORS	Stephen Thompson, Eric Bute
URL	http://awards.dsw.com/sites/iomega/Y2K_Trailers/bull_composite.html
	ID 00 0128 N

{PROMOTIONAL ADVERTISING/ other digital media}

	Merit
AGENCY	Organic/New York
CLIENT	CDNOW
ART DIRECTOR	John Pompa
WRITER	Dan Ligorner
DIGITAL ARTIST	Heidi Herman
PRODUCER	Brandi Fogel
PROGRAMMERS	Alex McCumber, Sergio Jimenez
CREATIVE DIRECTORS	Stephen Tortorici, Monique Te Selle
URL	http://ads.organic.com/oneshow/cdnowwoodstock.html
ID	00 0129 N

{CORPORATE IMAGE - B2C / web sites}

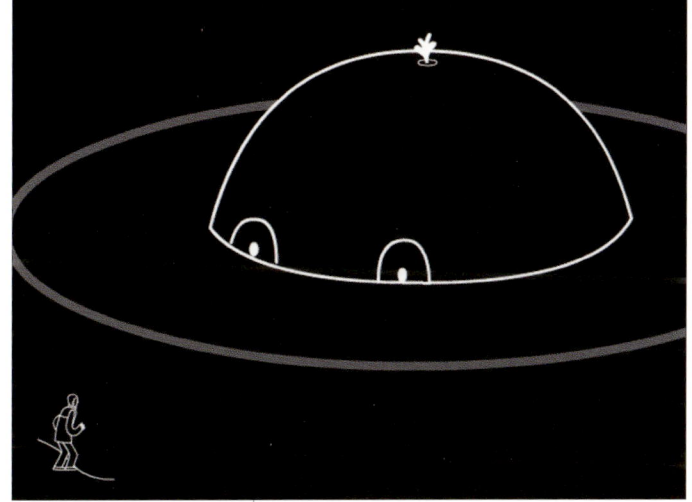
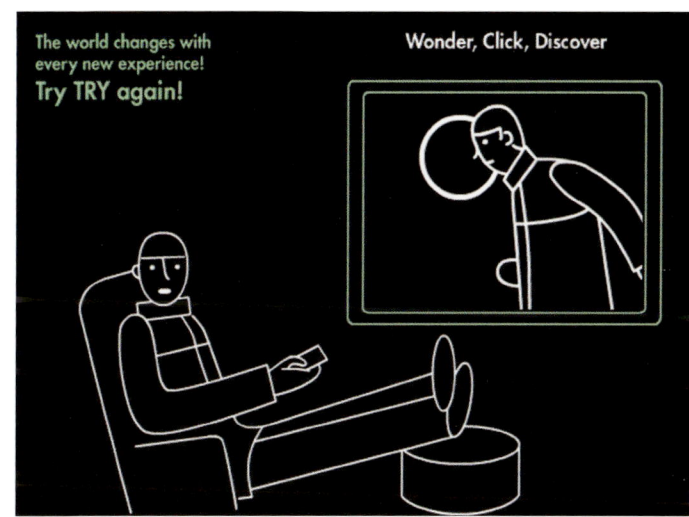

Merit

AGENCY	Aoi Advertising/Tokyo
CLIENT	Try Group
ART DIRECTORS	Peter Girardi, Chris Capuozzo
WRITERS	Natalie Warady, Kaori Murata
DIGITAL ARTIST	Richard McGuire
PRODUCERS	Kumiko Kitamura, Kaori Murata, John Carlin, Natalie Warady
MULTIMEDIA	Iwasaki Katsuhiko, Akira Sano, Colin Holgate
PROGRAMMER	Colin Holgate
CREATIVE DIRECTORS	Hideaki Furukawa, Kotaro Sugiyama, Naoto Oiwa, Peter Girardi
URL	www.willing-to-try.com

ID 00 0130 N

{CORPORATE IMAGE - B2C/ web sites}

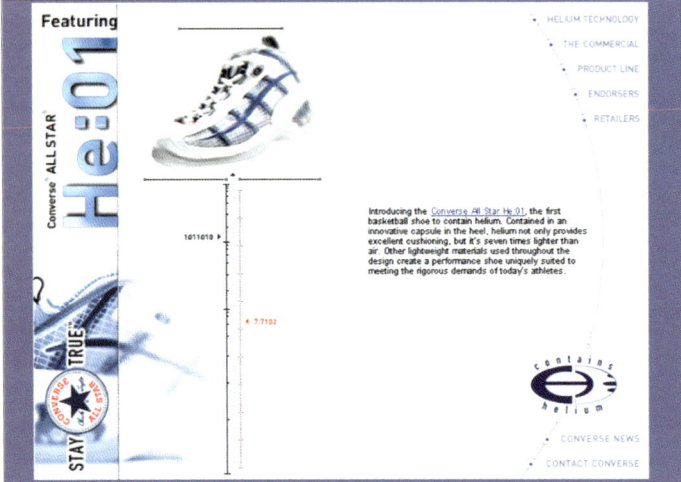
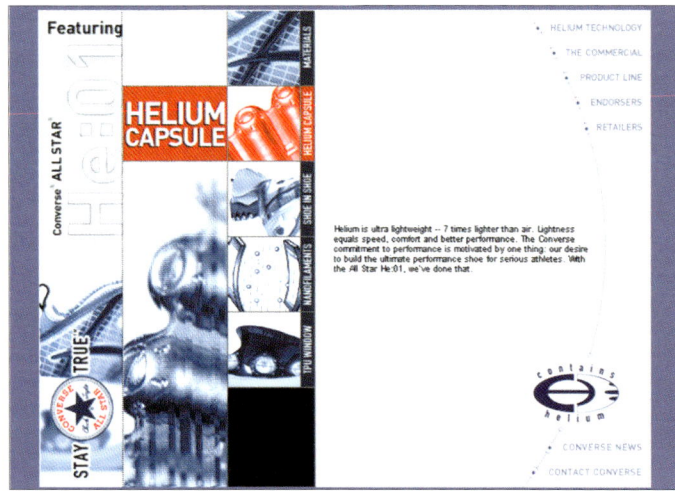
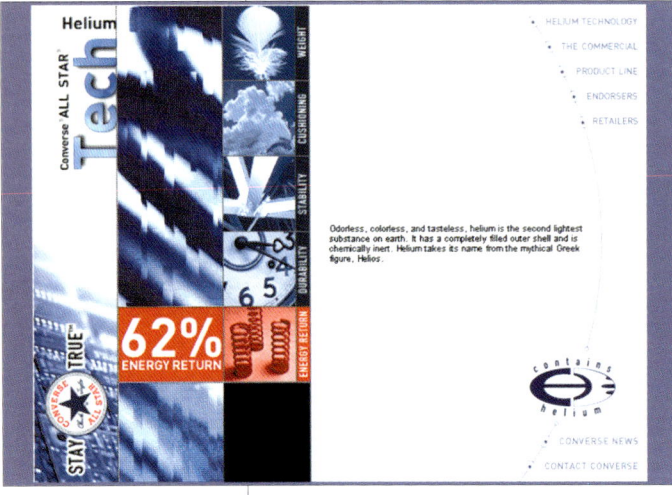

Merit

AGENCY	Arnold Communications/Boston
CLIENT	Converse
ART DIRECTORS	Robert Hodgin, Wade Devers
WRITER	John Simpson
DIGITAL ARTIST	Robert Hodgin
PHOTOGRAPHER	Jonathon Groves
PRODUCER	Azurae Chambers
MULTIMEDIA	Robert Hodgin, Jonathon Groves
CREATIVE DIRECTOR	Robert Hodgin
URL	www.conversehelium.com
ID	00 0131 N

{ CORPORATE IMAGE - B2C / web sites }

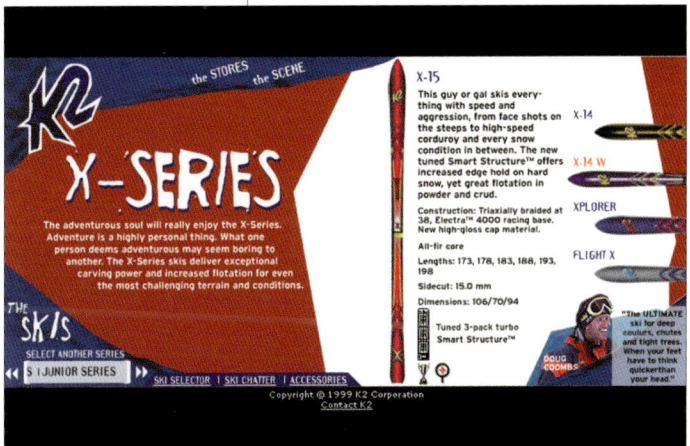

Merit

AGENCY	Cole & Weber/Seattle
CLIENT	K2 Skis
ART DIRECTORS	Todd Derksen, Brent McCoy
WRITERS	Jim Elliott, Marietta Szubski
PRODUCER	Keith Farry
PROGRAMMERS	Todd Derksen, Mark Dreessen, Trina Neilson
CREATIVE DIRECTOR	Ed Lisieski
URL	www.k2skis.com
ID	00 0132 N

{CORPORATE IMAGE - B2C/ web sites}

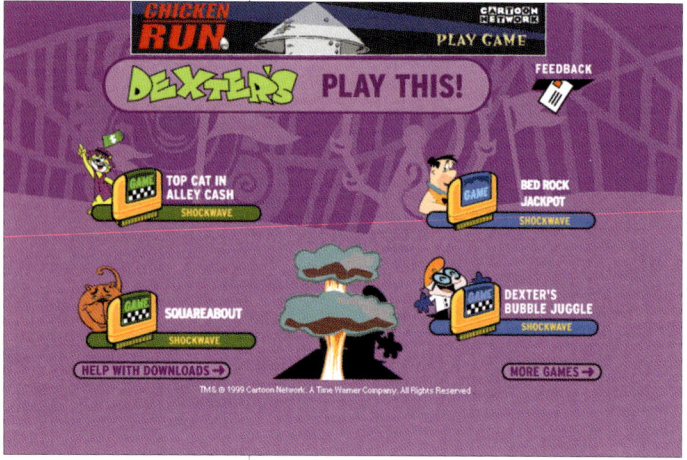
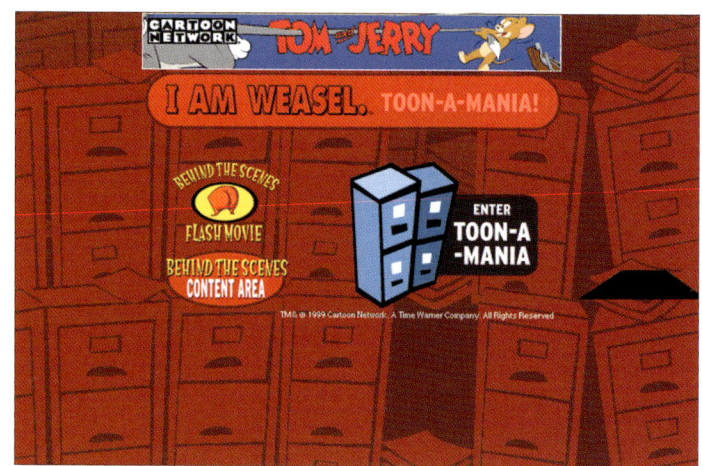

Merit

AGENCY	*Deepend London/London*
CLIENT	*Cartoon Network UK*
ART DIRECTOR	*David Streek*
DIGITAL ARTISTS	*Leon Rosenberg, Foxy*
PRODUCER	*Helen Peacocke*
MULTIMEDIA	*Sue Matthews*
PROGRAMMER	*Guillaume Buat-Menard*
URL	*www.cartoon-network.co.uk*
ID	00 0133 N

{CORPORATE IMAGE - B2C/ web sites}

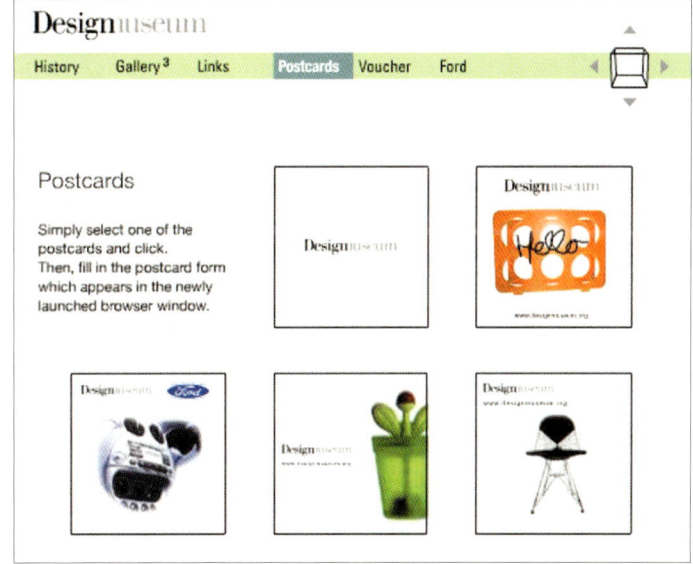

Merit

AGENCY	Deepend London/London
CLIENT	Design Museum
ART DIRECTOR	Fred Flade
WRITER	Naomi Simpson
DIGITAL ARTIST	Fred Flade
PRODUCER	Louise Holben
PROGRAMMER	Gabriel Bucknall
CREATIVE DIRECTOR	Simon Waterfall
URL	www.designmuseum.org
ID	00 0134 N

{CORPORATE IMAGE - B2C/ web sites}

Merit

AGENCY	Doubleyou/Barcelona
CLIENT	Audi
ART DIRECTOR	Blanca Piera
WRITER	Frédéric Sanz
MULTIMEDIA	Joakim Borgström
PROGRAMMERS	Joakim Borgström, Xavi Caparrós
CREATIVE DIRECTOR	Frédéric Sanz
URL	http://audi.vw-audi.es/ttroadster
ID	00 0135 N

{CORPORATE IMAGE - B2C/ web sites}

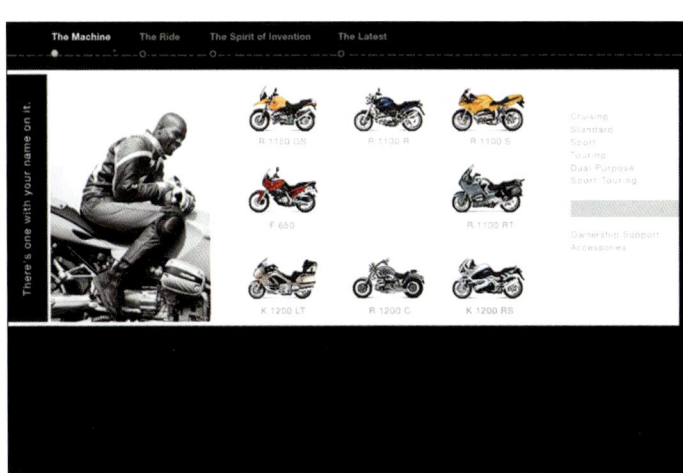
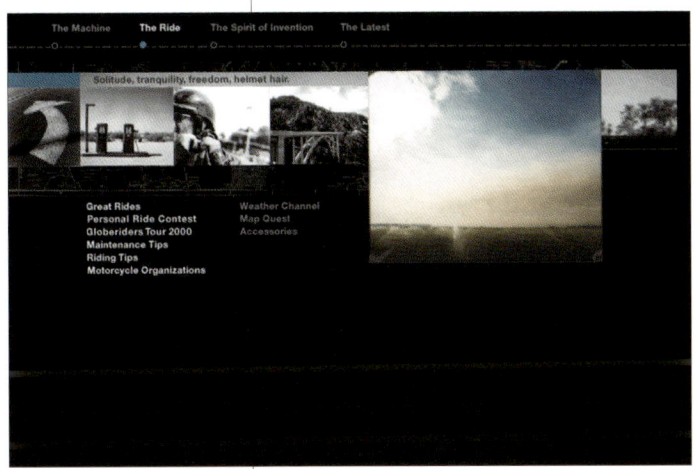
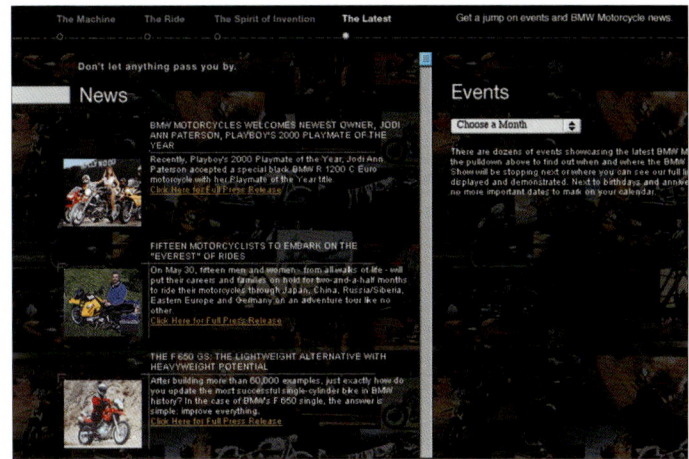

Merit

AGENCY Duffy Design/Minneapolis
CLIENT BMW of North America
ART DIRECTORS Kevin Flatt, Paul Bastyr
WRITERS Russ Stark, Jay Kaskel
DIGITAL ARTISTS Dave Thompson, Joel Hermann
PHOTOGRAPHERS Mark LaFavor, various
PRODUCER Sarah Zanger
MULTIMEDIA Mark Sandau, Christian Erickson, Tom Kunau
PROGRAMMERS Heather Duke, Bob Metcalf, Margaret Bossen, Tom Kunau, Bob Carlson
CREATIVE DIRECTORS Joe Duffy, Dan Olsen
URL www.bmwusacycles.com
ID 00 0136 N

{CORPORATE IMAGE - B2C/ web sites}

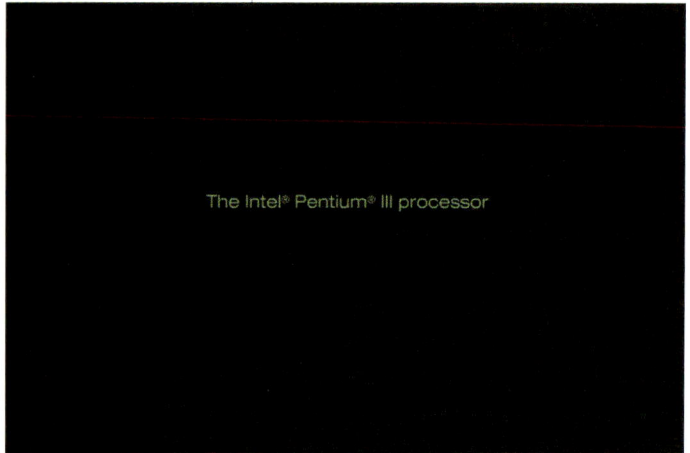
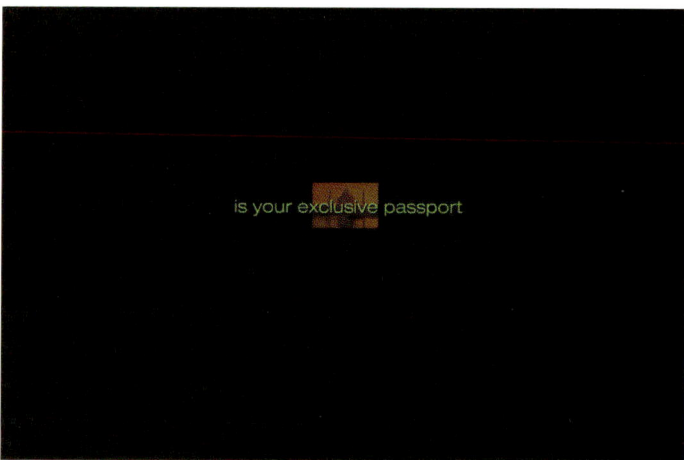
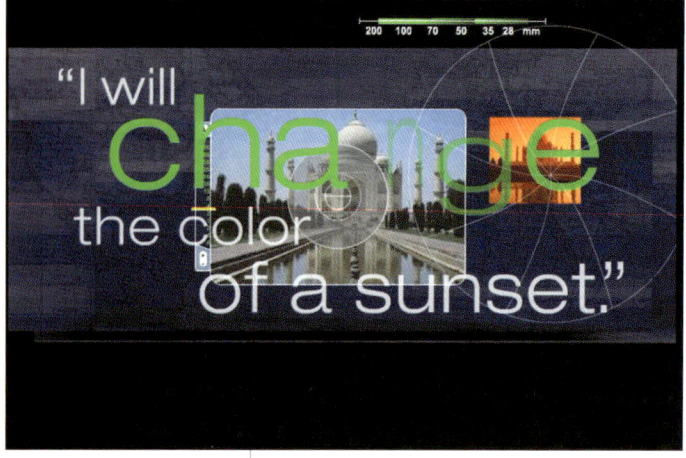

	Merit
AGENCY	EURO RSCG DSW Partners/Salt Lake City
CLIENT	Intel
ART DIRECTORS	Dung Hoang, Gary Brown
WRITERS	Gary Brown, Jennifer Ward, Eric Young
DIGITAL ARTIST	Humaniz
PHOTOGRAPHER	Michael Schoenfeld
PRODUCER	Michael Aaron
MULTIMEDIA	Humaniz
PROGRAMMER	Humaniz
CREATIVE DIRECTORS	Steve Newman, Kimball Carter
URL	http://awards.dsw.com/sites/trek3/trailer/index.htm
ID	00 0137 N

{CORPORATE IMAGE - B2C/ web sites}

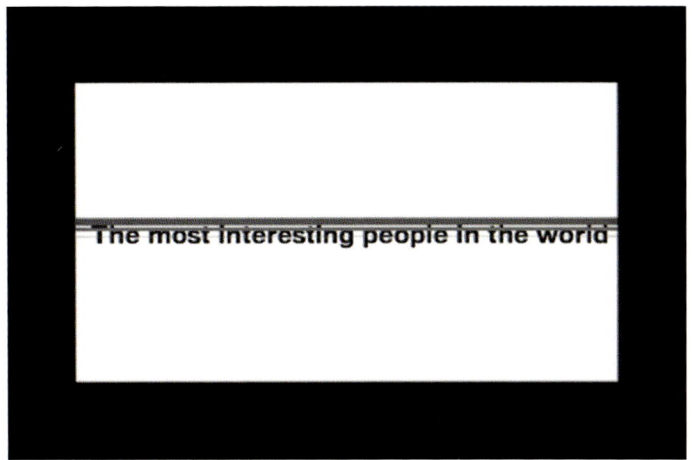

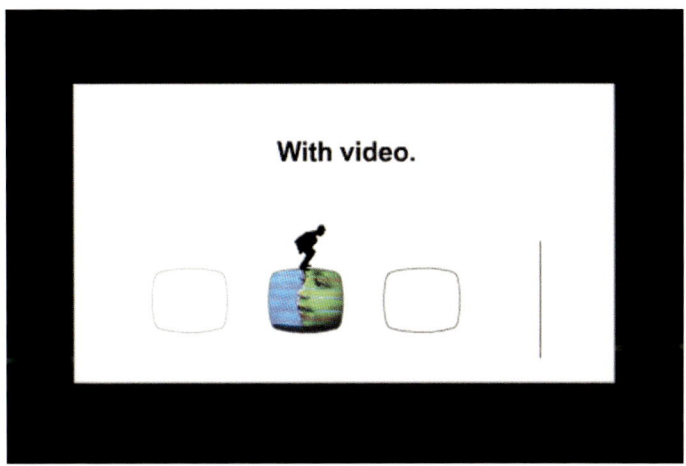

Merit

AGENCY	hillmancurtis.com/New York
CLIENT	The Feed Room
ART DIRECTOR	Ian Kovalik
WRITER	hillmancurtis.com
DIGITAL ARTISTS	Ian Kovalik, Hillman Curtis
PHOTOGRAPHER	Ian Kovalik
PRODUCER	Ian Kovalik
MULTIMEDIA	Ian Kovalik
PROGRAMMERS	Hillman Curtis, Ian Kovalik
CREATIVE DIRECTOR	Hillman Curtis
URL	www.hillmancurtis.com/design/oneshow
ID	00 0138 N

{CORPORATE IMAGE - B2C/ web sites}

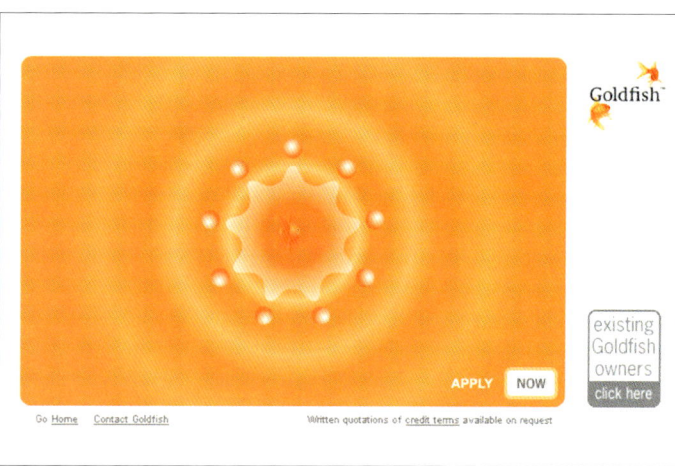

Merit

AGENCY	Hyperlink/London
CLIENT	Goldfish
ART DIRECTOR	Edwin Bradford
DIGITAL ARTIST	Rakesh Mistry
PRODUCER	Cecile Ferre
PROGRAMMER	Steve Webster
CREATIVE DIRECTOR	Yannis Marcou
URL	http://hyperlink.co.uk/goldfish/cards/flash_index.htm
ID	00 0139 N

{CORPORATE IMAGE - B2C/ web sites}

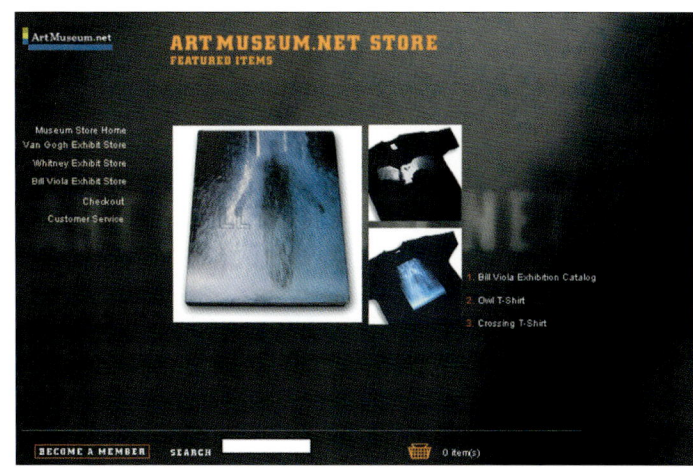
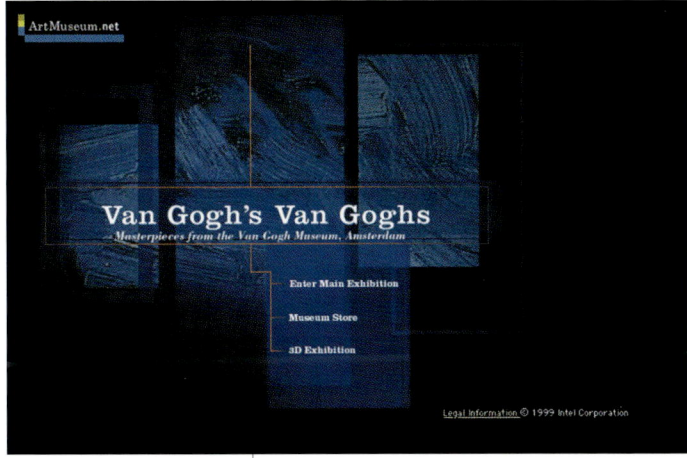
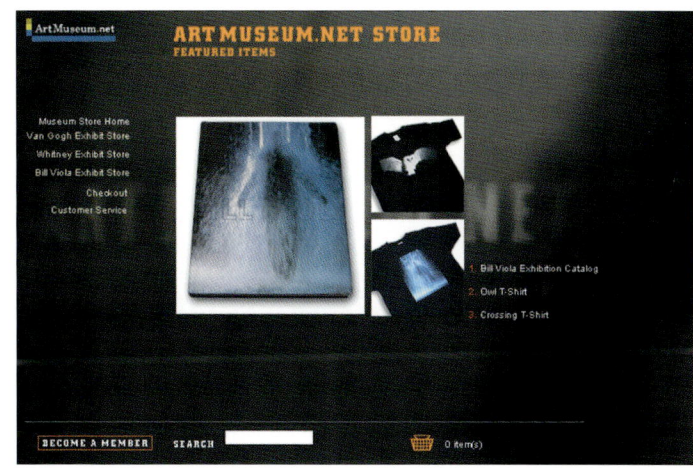

Merit

AGENCY *Intel/Santa Clara*
URL *www.artmuseum.net*
ID *00 0140 N*

{CORPORATE IMAGE - B2C/ web sites}

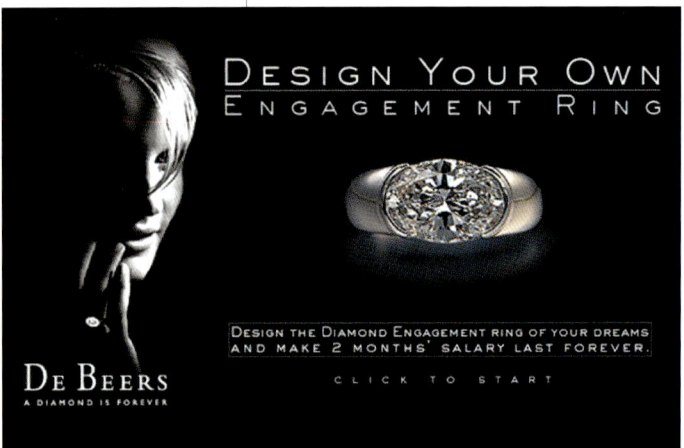

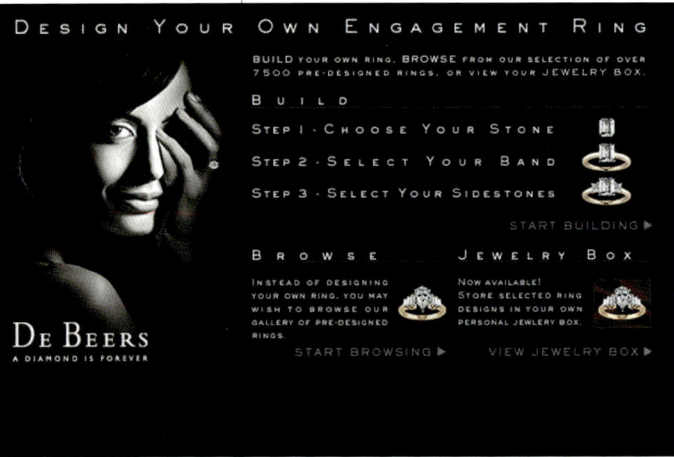

Merit

AGENCY	Luminant Worldwide/New York
CLIENT	The Diamond Information Center
ART DIRECTOR	Howard Coale
DIGITAL ARTIST	Tom Misner
URL	www.adiamondisforever.com/dyoer
ID	00 0141 N

{CORPORATE IMAGE - B2C/ web sites}

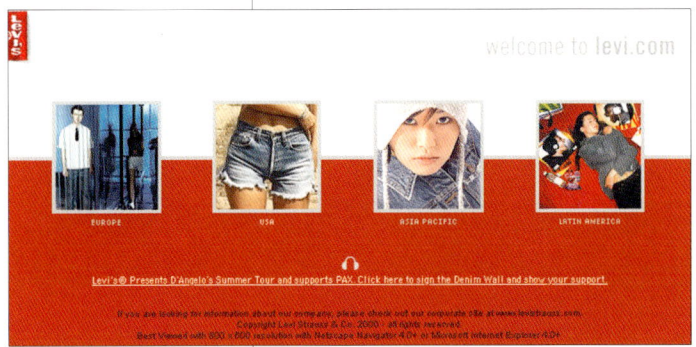
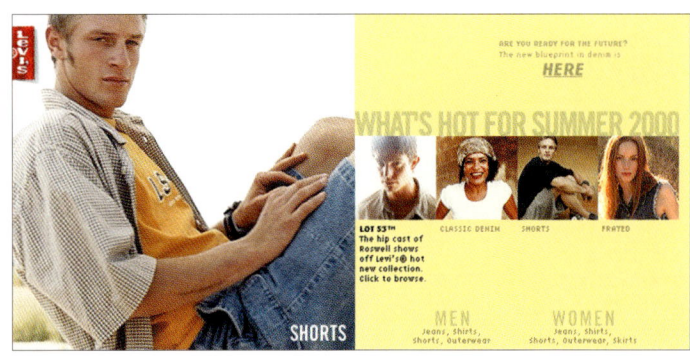

Merit

AGENCY	marchFirst/San Francisco
CLIENT	Levi Strauss & Co.
ART DIRECTOR	Roger Wong
WRITER	Mary Jeanne Deery
DIGITAL ARTIST	Jennifer Kellogg
PHOTOGRAPHER	James Smolka
PRODUCERS	Kristian Schwartz, Gene Hwang
CREATIVE DIRECTOR	Colleen Stokes
URL	www.levi.com
ID	00 0142 N

{CORPORATE IMAGE - B2C/ web sites}

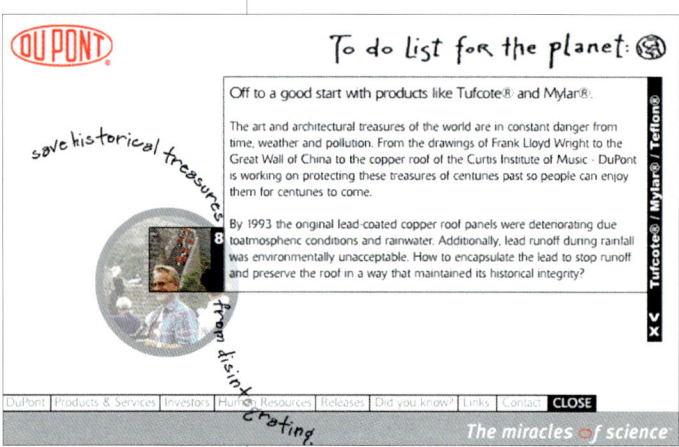

Merit

AGENCY	McCann-Erickson Publicidade Ltda./São Paulo
CLIENT	Dupont of Brazil
ART DIRECTOR	Andre Matarazzo
WRITER	Bob Gebara - Dupont of Brazil
DIGITAL ARTIST	Andre Matarazzo
PHOTOGRAPHER	Romeu Semprini
PRODUCERS	Bob Gebara, Juliano Tosetto, Kropki
MULTIMEDIA	Rico Villas-Boas
PROGRAMMERS	Andre Matarazzo, Thiago Avancine, Kropki
CREATIVE DIRECTORS	Bob Gebara, Andre Matarazzo
URL	www.thunderhouse.com.br/dupont
ID	00 0143 N

{CORPORATE IMAGE - B2C/ web sites}

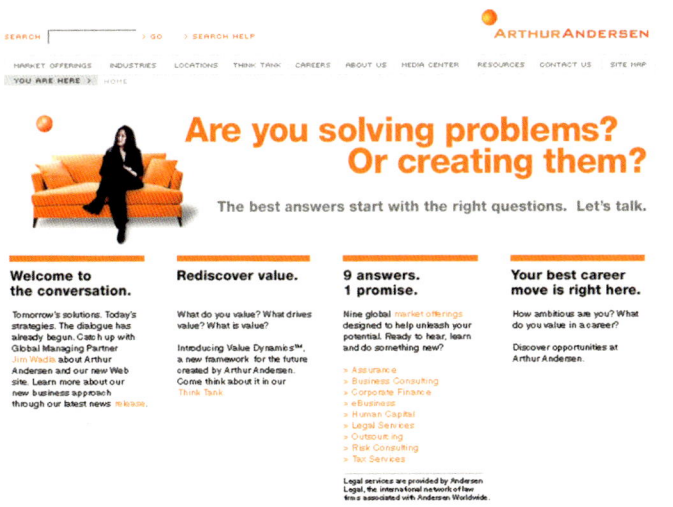
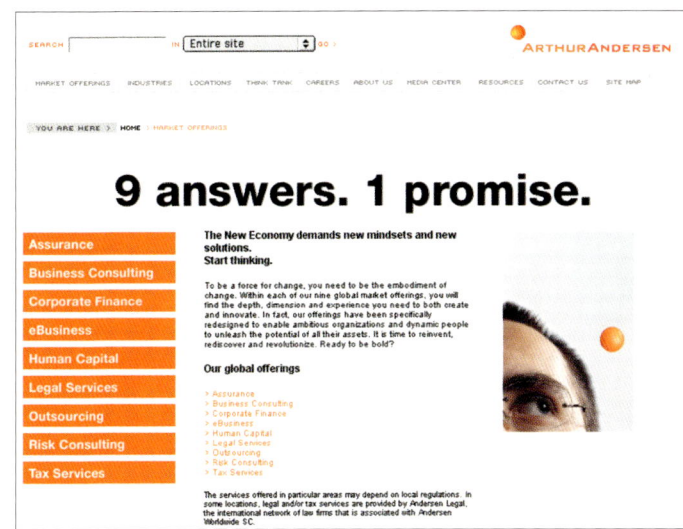
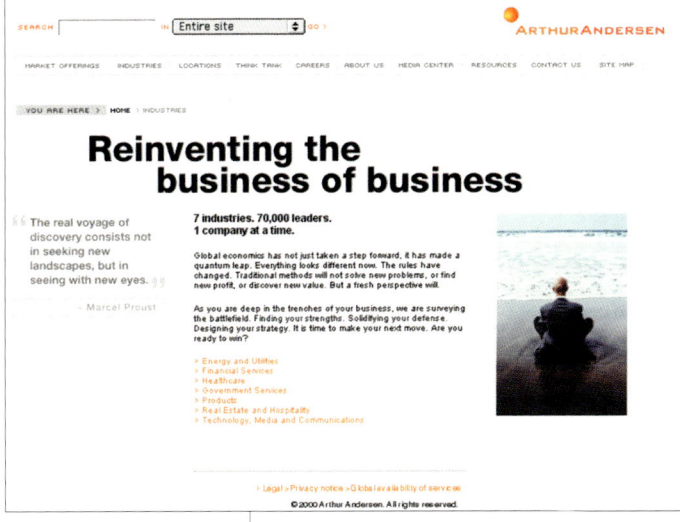
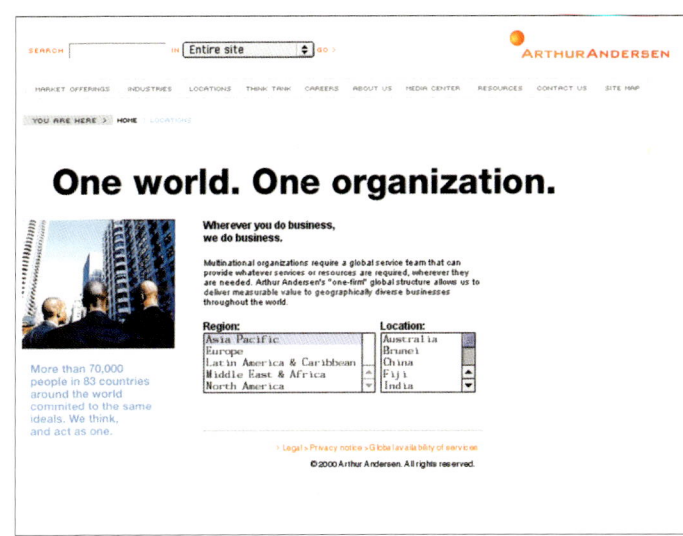

Merit

AGENCY	OgilvyInteractive/New York
CLIENT	Arthur Andersen
ART DIRECTOR	Amanda Gould
WRITERS	Matthew Zucker, Greg Monaco
DIGITAL ARTIST	Jose Galvez
PRODUCER	David Berenbroick
MULTIMEDIA	Malvika Mitchell, Susan Cook
CREATIVE DIRECTORS	Mach Arom
URL	www.arthurandersen.com
ID	00 0144 N

{CORPORATE IMAGE - B2C/ web sites}

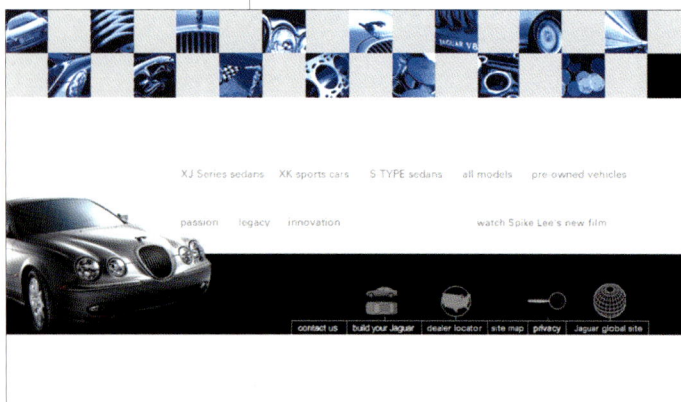
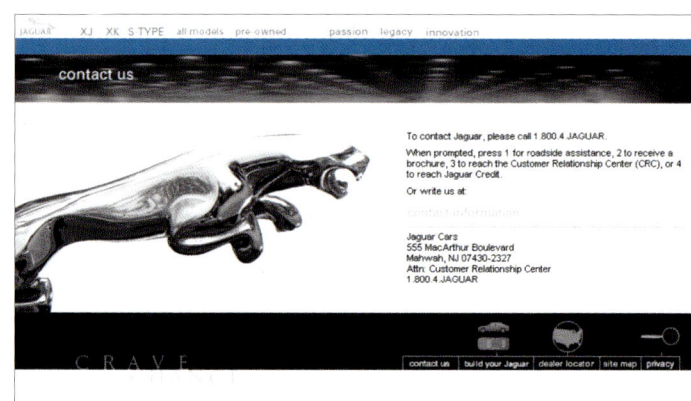
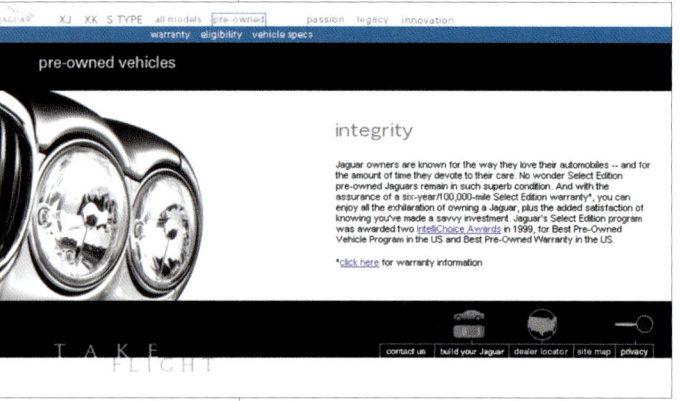
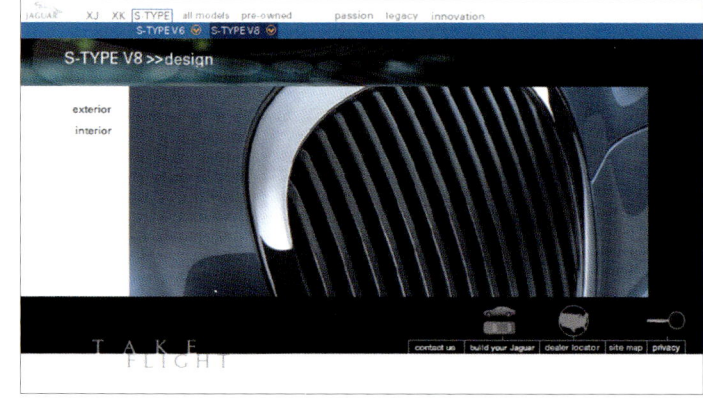

	Merit
AGENCY	OgilvyInteractive/New York
CLIENT	Jaguar North America
ART DIRECTORS	John Mamus, Matthew Atkatz
WRITER	Donna Oetzel
DIGITAL ARTISTS	Rachel Heapps, Jose Galvez
PRODUCER	Janet Heettner
MULTIMEDIA	Malvika Mitchell
PROGRAMMERS	Tommy Chen, Steven Little
CREATIVE DIRECTOR	Mach Arom
URL	www.us.jaguar.com
ID	00 0145 N

{CORPORATE IMAGE - B2C/ web sites}

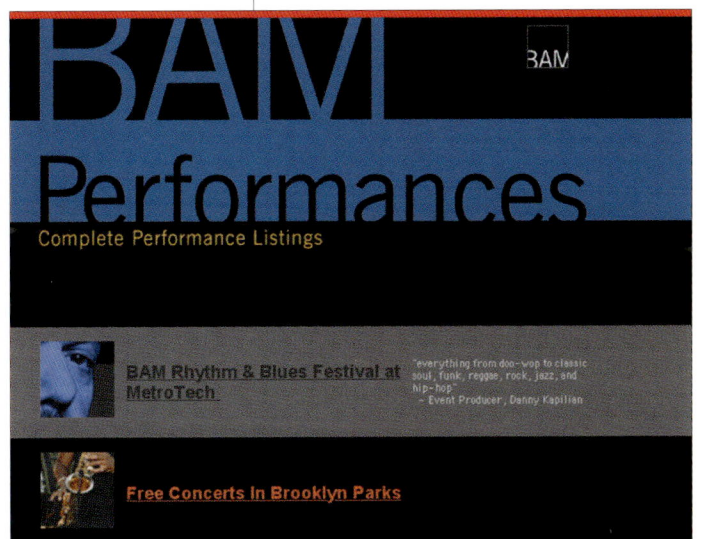

Merit

AGENCY R/GA/New York
CLIENT Brooklyn Academy of Music
ART DIRECTOR Sasha Kurtz
DIGITAL ARTISTS Sasha Kurtz, Lesli Karavil, John Rabasa, Pat Stern
PRODUCERS Scott Schneider, Amy Smith
PROGRAMMER Tom Freudenheim
CREATIVE DIRECTOR Frank Lantz
URL www.bam.org
ID 00 0146 N

{CORPORATE IMAGE - B2C/ web sites}

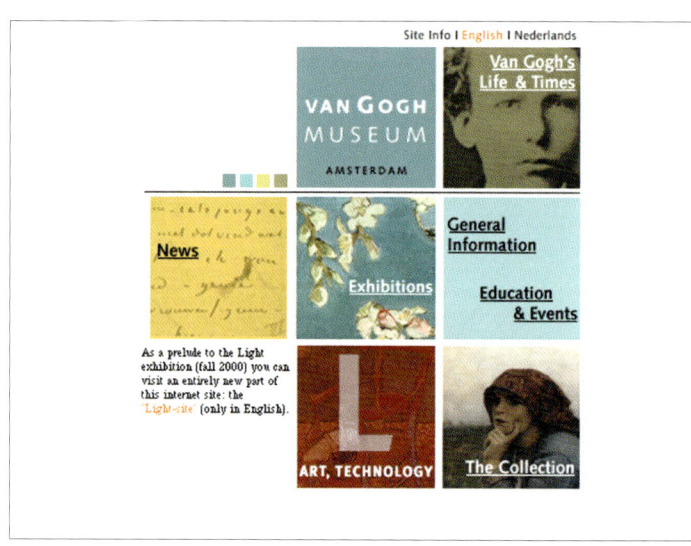
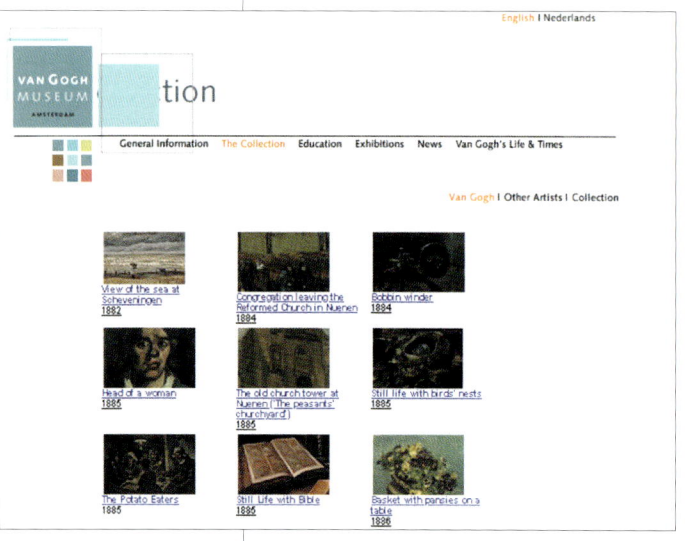
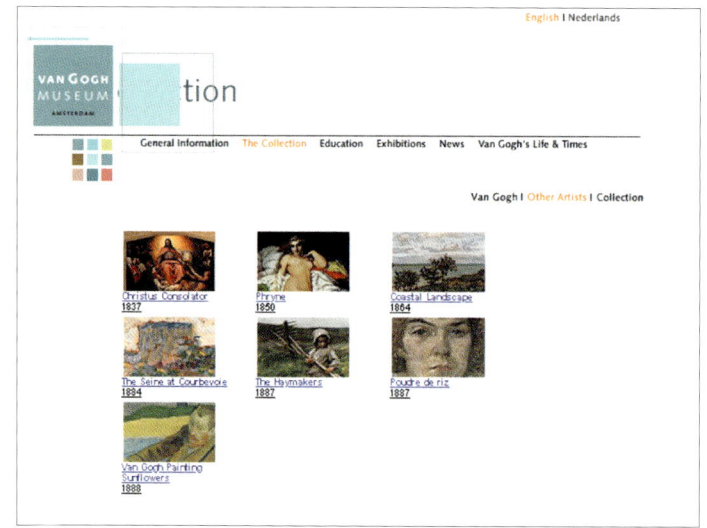

Merit

AGENCY	R/GA/New York
CLIENT	The Van Gogh Museum, Amsterdam
ART DIRECTOR	Jakob Trollback
DIGITAL ARTISTS	Haejin Cho, Nathalie de La Gorce, Yzabelle Munson, Frank Lantz
PRODUCER	Steven Plumlee
PROGRAMMER	Greg Glass
CREATIVE DIRECTOR	Frank Lantz
URL	www.vangoghmuseum.nl
ID	00 0147 N

{CORPORATE IMAGE - B2C/ web sites}

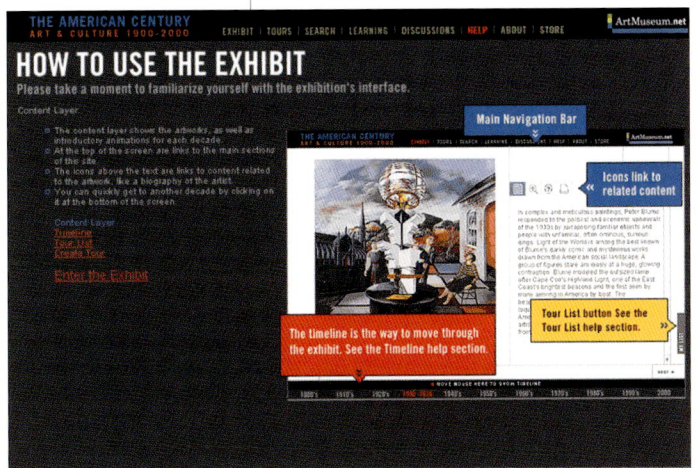

Merit

AGENCY Razorfish/New York
CLIENT Whitney/Intel
ART DIRECTOR Kendall Thomas
DIGITAL ARTISTS Kendall Thomas, Travis Rogers, Ake Brattberg, Stephen Turbek
PRODUCER Jeff Wong
PROGRAMMER Peter Ginsberg
URL http://whitney.artmuseum.net
ID 00 0148 N

{CORPORATE IMAGE - B2C/ web sites}

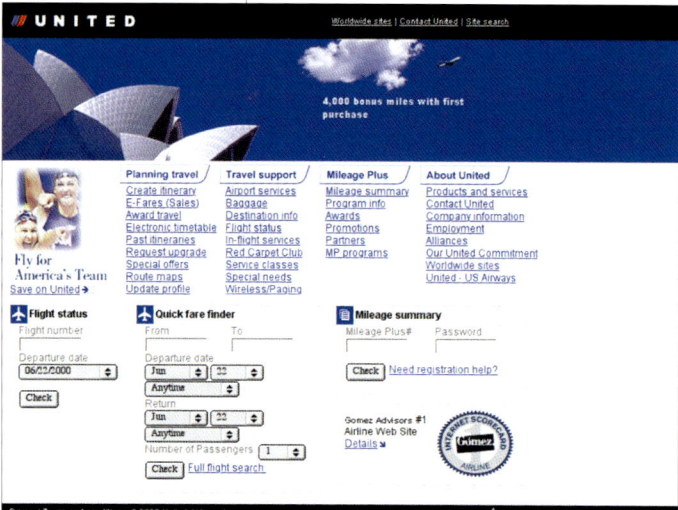
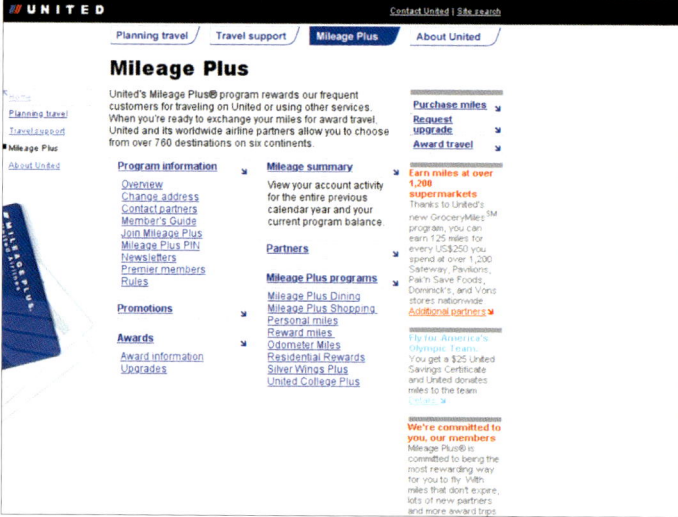
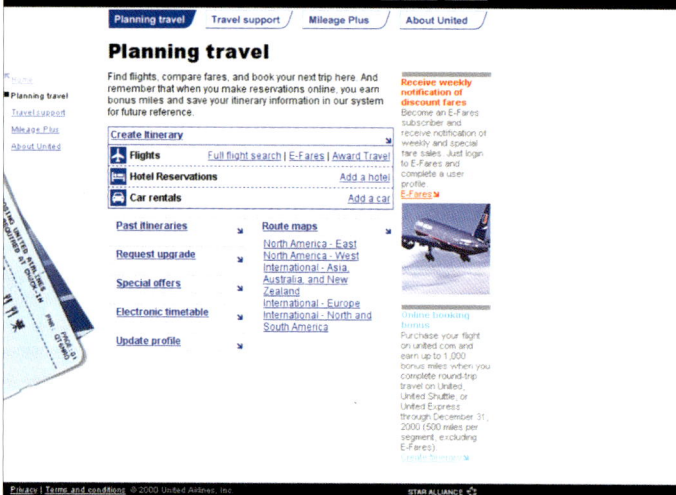
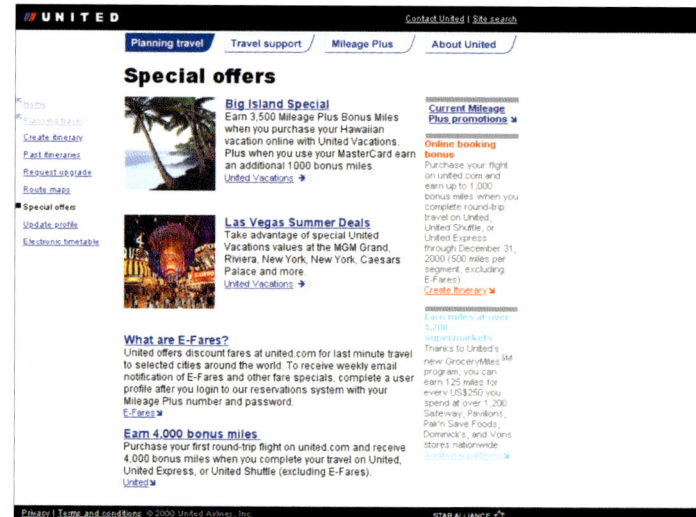

Merit

AGENCY	Sapient/San Francisco
CLIENT	United Airlines
ART DIRECTOR	Philip Kim
WRITER	Dorothy Ivanovich
PROGRAMMERS	Jeremiah Wells, Al Forrestier, Isabel O'Meara, Alejo Jumat, Brian Slutz, Roshan Shankur, Rangarajan Sudharsam, Dejam Vucinic, Suhail Ali, Andy Ockem
URL	www.Ual.com
ID	00 0149 N

{CORPORATE IMAGE - B2C / web sites}

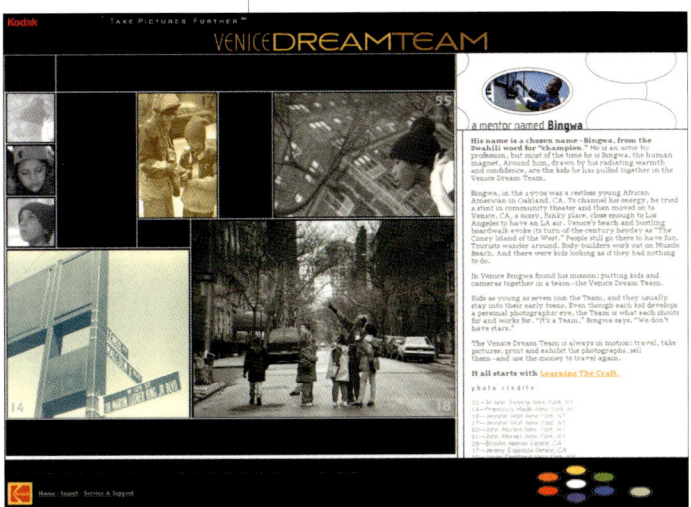
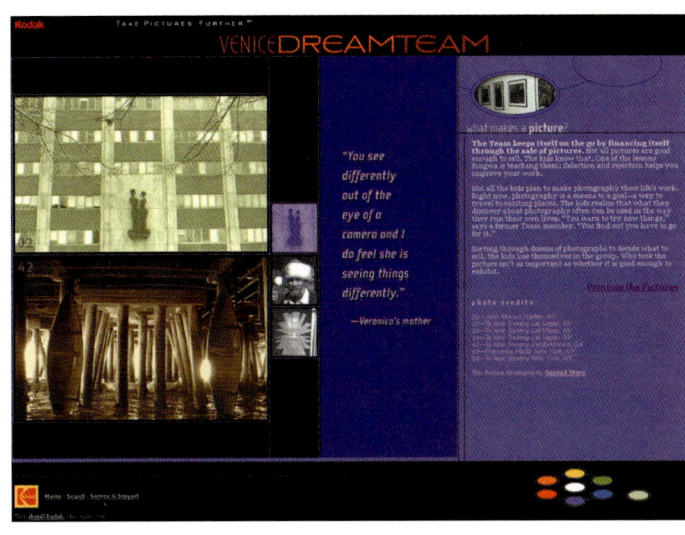
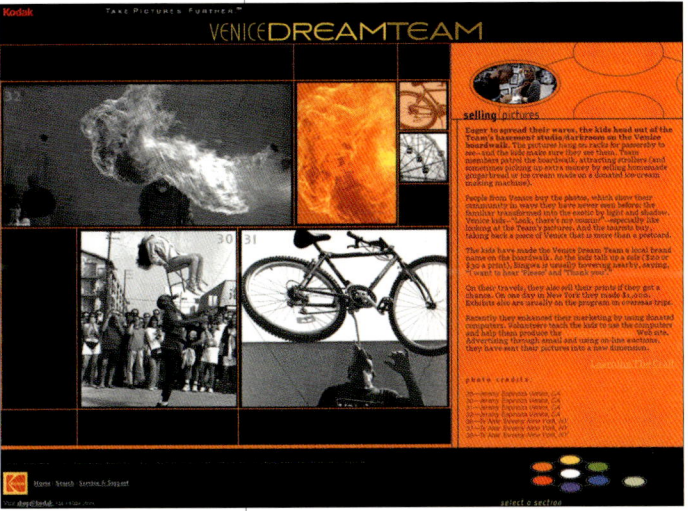

Merit

AGENCY	Second Story/Portland
CLIENT	Kodak
ART DIRECTOR	Brad Johnson
WRITER	Tom Allen
DIGITAL ARTIST	Sam Ward
PHOTOGRAPHER	The Venice Dream Team
PRODUCER	Julie Beeler
PROGRAMMER	Julie Beeler
CREATIVE DIRECTOR	Brad Johnson
URL	www.kodak.com/US/en/corp/features/veniceDreamTeam
ID	00 0150 N

{CORPORATE IMAGE - B2C/ web sites}

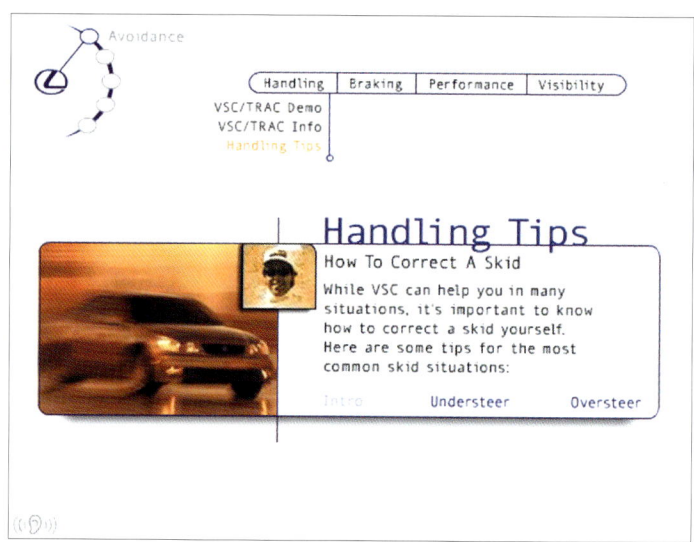

Merit

AGENCY	Team One Advertising/El Segundo
CLIENT	Lexus
ART DIRECTORS	James Kowalski, Brian Doyle
WRITERS	Scott Ivener, Ed Mun
DIGITAL ARTISTS	Lawrence Matthews, Tim Hennessey, Paul Nelson, Skidmore
PHOTOGRAPHER	Sedlick Photography
PRODUCERS	Vincent Tipaldo, Eli Barakat
MULTIMEDIA	Dennis Interactive, 415 Productions
PROGRAMMERS	Dennis Interactive, Matthew Muench, Mike Brannigan
CREATIVE DIRECTORS	Gabrielle Mayeur, Tom Cordner
URL	www.LexusSafety.com
ID	00 0151 N

{ CORPORATE IMAGE - B2C / CD-ROM }

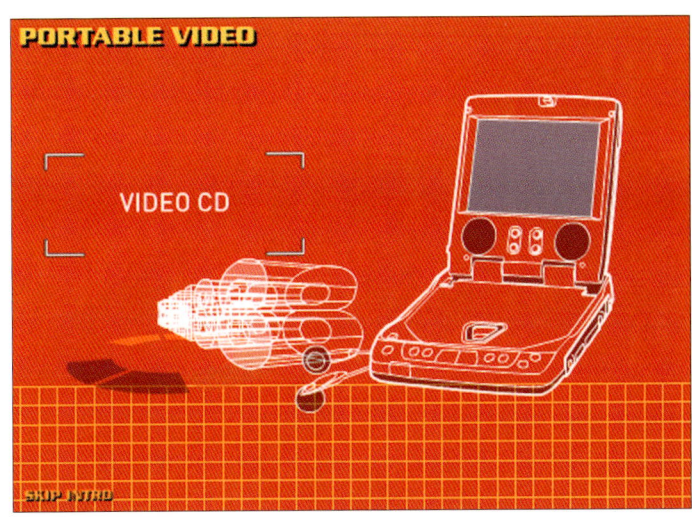
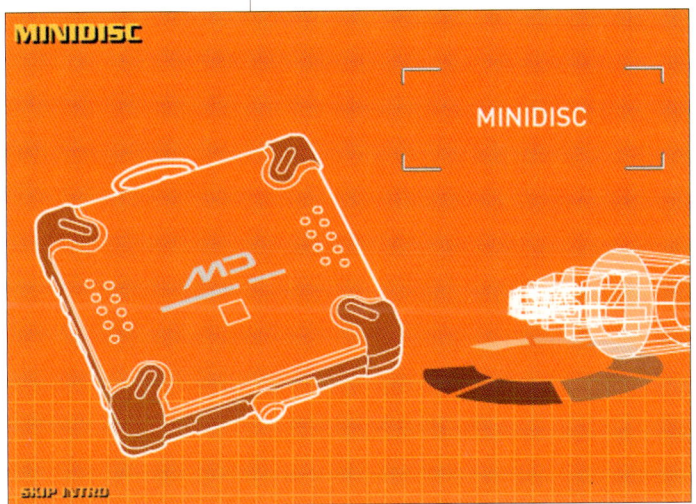

Merit

AGENCY	Ad Planet: Kinetic Interactive Singapore
CLIENT	Aiwa Sales Singapore
ART DIRECTORS	Benjy Choo, Sean Lam
WRITER	Michele Klyne
DIGITAL ARTISTS	Benjy Choo, Sean Lam, Leng Soh, Ivan Hadywibowo
PHOTOGRAPHER	Geoff Studio
PRODUCERS	Benjy Choo, Sean Lam
MULTIMEDIA	Benjy Choo, Sean Lam
PROGRAMMERS	Benjy Choo, Anita Rajagopolan
CREATIVE DIRECTORS	Benjy Choo, Sean Lam
	ID 00 0152 N

{CORPORATE IMAGE - B2C/ CD-ROM}

Merit

AGENCY	Biggs/Gilmore/Kalamazoo
CLIENT	Sea Ray Boats
ART DIRECTORS	Linda Foster, Brad Fleming
WRITERS	Nancy Sturges, Cole Odell, Andy Gould
DIGITAL ARTISTS	Jeff Yonker, Doug Berger
PRODUCERS	Bruce Davis, Kathy Wallace
PROGRAMMERS	Jeff Yonker, Jon Austin
CREATIVE DIRECTOR	Ernie Cox

ID 00 0153 N

{CORPORATE IMAGE - B2C/ CD-ROM}

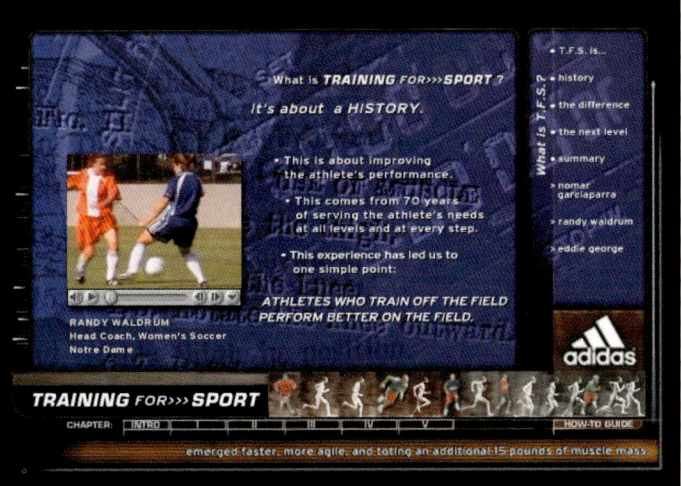

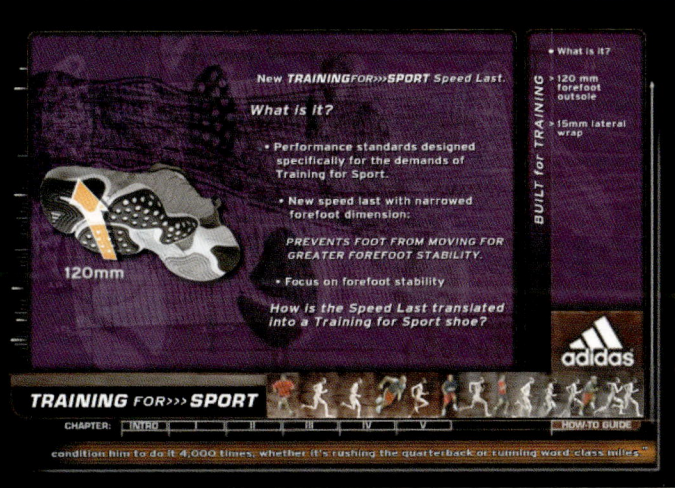
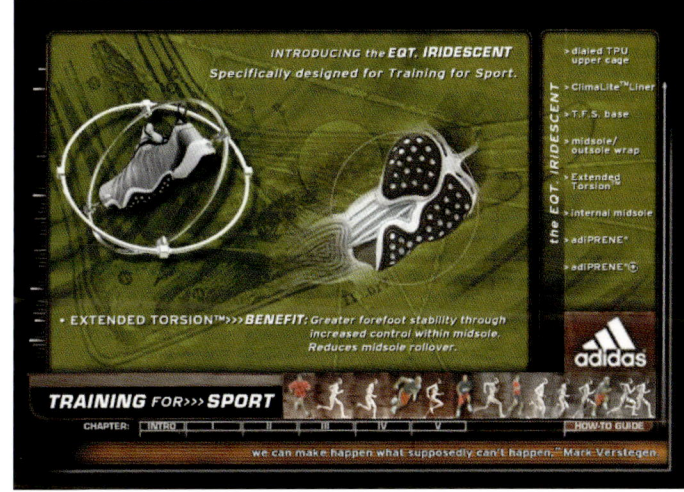

Merit

AGENCY	Lightspeed Studios, Inc./Portland
CLIENT	adidas International
ART DIRECTOR	Toni Smith
WRITER	Andrew Jenkins
DIGITAL ARTIST	Lightspeed Studios
PHOTOGRAPHER	Lightspeed Studios
PRODUCER	Lightspeed Studios
MULTIMEDIA	Lightspeed Studios
PROGRAMMER	Lightspeed Studios
CREATIVE DIRECTOR	Kade Cassey
ID	00 0154 N

{CORPORATE IMAGE - B2C/ other digital media}

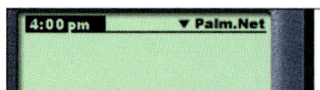
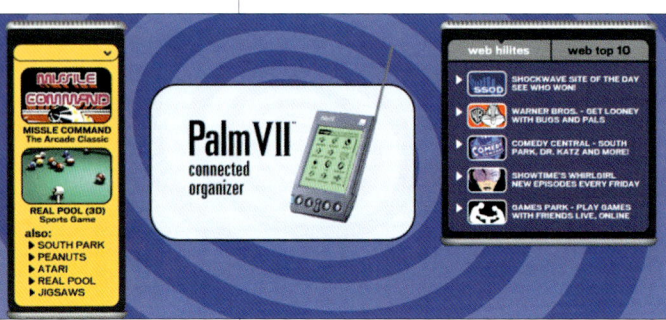

Merit

AGENCY Lot 21 Interactive Advertising/San Francisco
CLIENT Palm Computing
ART DIRECTORS Brian Tsang, Cynthia Schumm
WRITER Dan Tamura
PRODUCER Karen Armstrong
CREATIVE DIRECTOR Paco Vinoly
URL http://restricted.lot21interactive.com/public/oneshow
ID 00 0155 N

{CORPORATE IMAGE - B2B/ web sites}

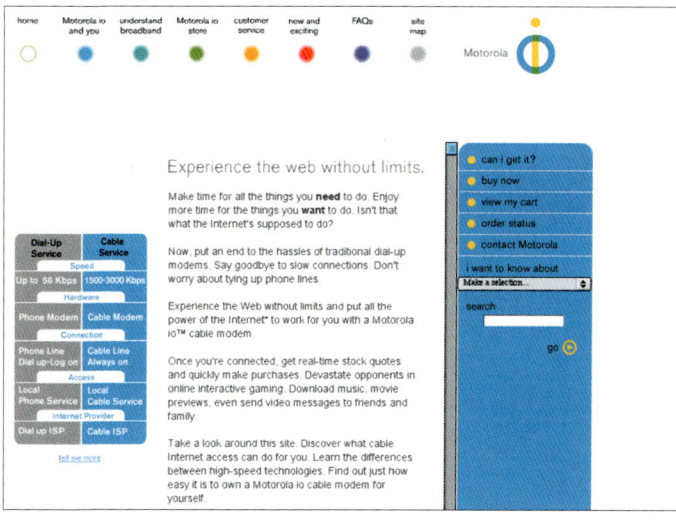
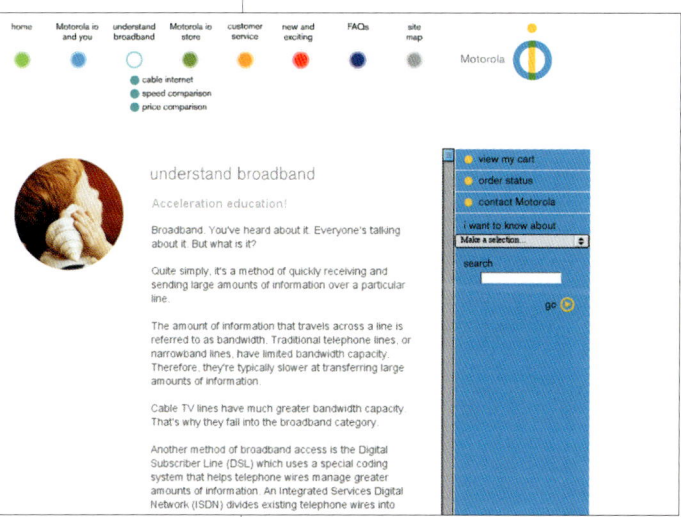
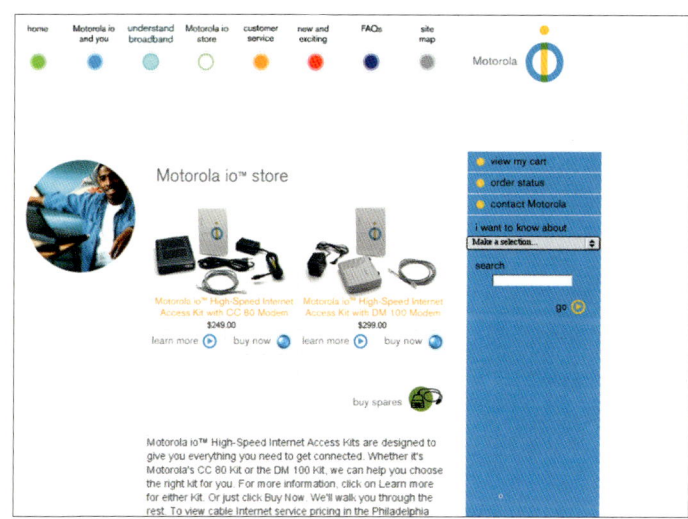

	Merit
AGENCY	AGENCY.COM/New York
CLIENT	Motorola
ART DIRECTORS	Mark Foltz, Nathan Baily
WRITER	Jeff Creel
DIGITAL ARTIST	Andy Allman
PRODUCERS	Kathleen Bur, Jon Goldstein, Colin Kovas
PROGRAMMERS	Don Benish, Jeff Bennet
CREATIVE DIRECTOR	Mark Foltz
URL	http://io.motorola.com
	ID 00 0156 N

{CORPORATE IMAGE - B2B/ web sites}

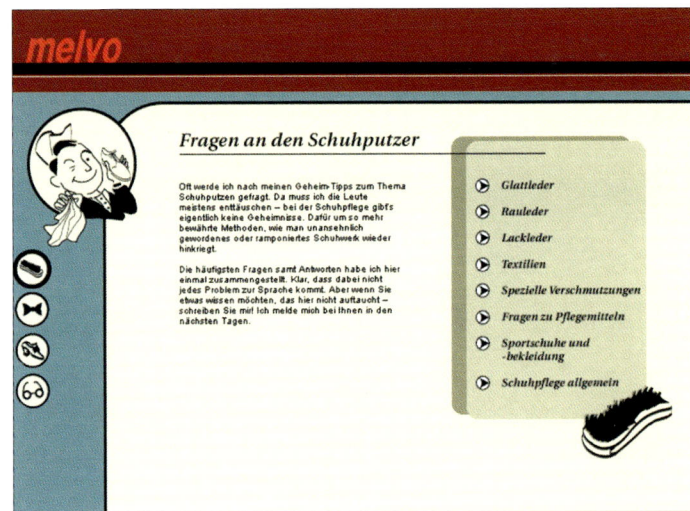

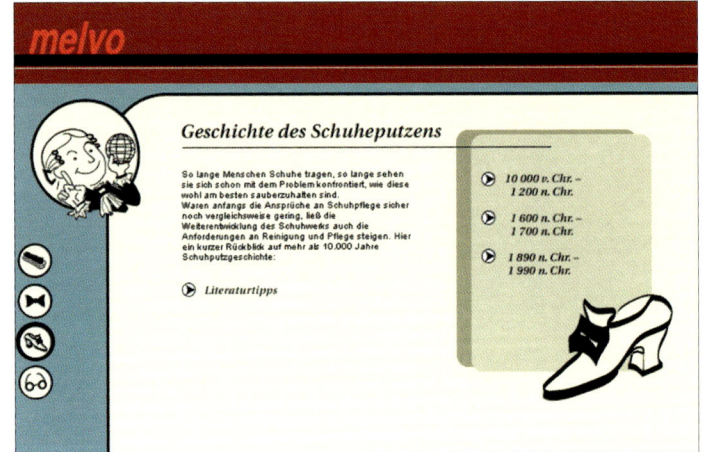

	Merit
AGENCY	agi business media productions GmbH/Stuttgart
CLIENT	Melvo Vertriebsgesellschaft GmbH
ART DIRECTOR	Nathalie Strobl
WRITERS	Rolf Iben, Stefanie Katzschke
DIGITAL ARTISTS	Christa Heinold, Nathalie Strobl
PRODUCER	Gabi Schobess
PROGRAMMERS	Markus Borm, Marco Seiler
CREATIVE DIRECTORS	Christian Schwarm, Gabi Schobess
URL	www.schuhputzer.de
ID	00 0157 N

{CORPORATE IMAGE - B2B/ web sites}

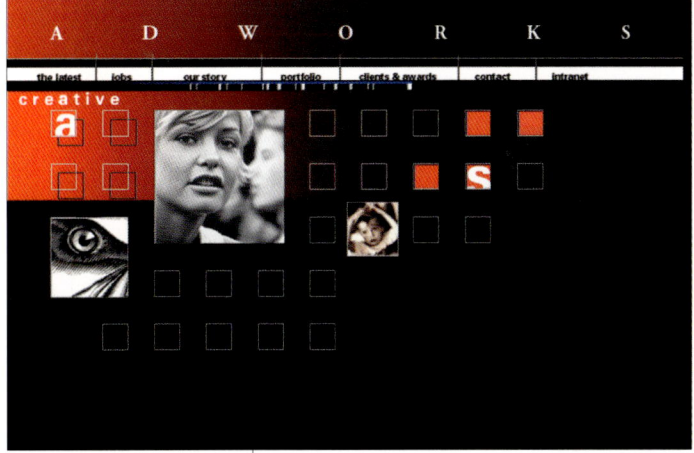
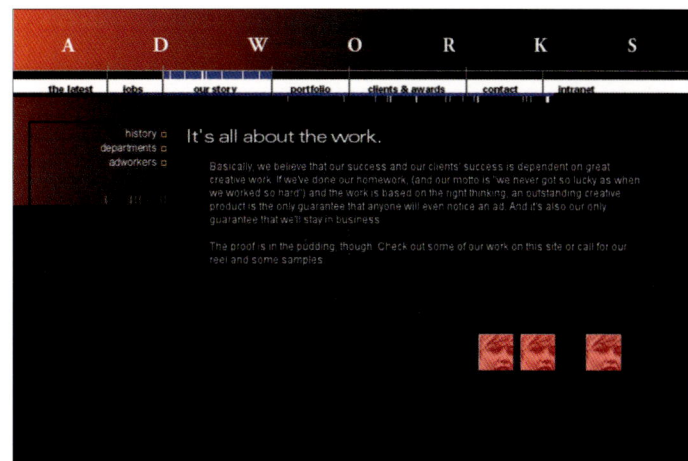
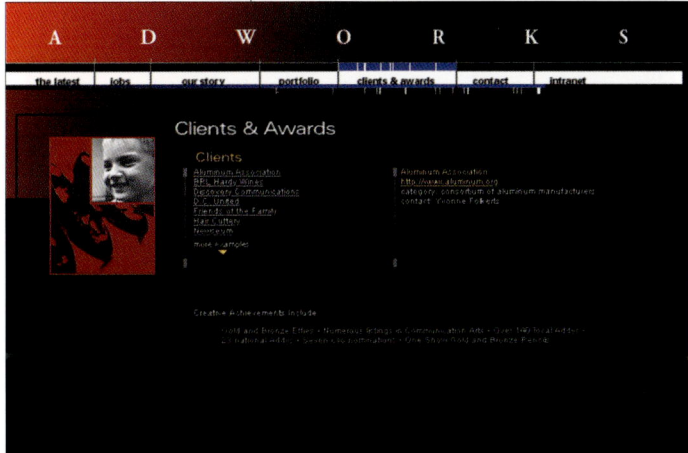
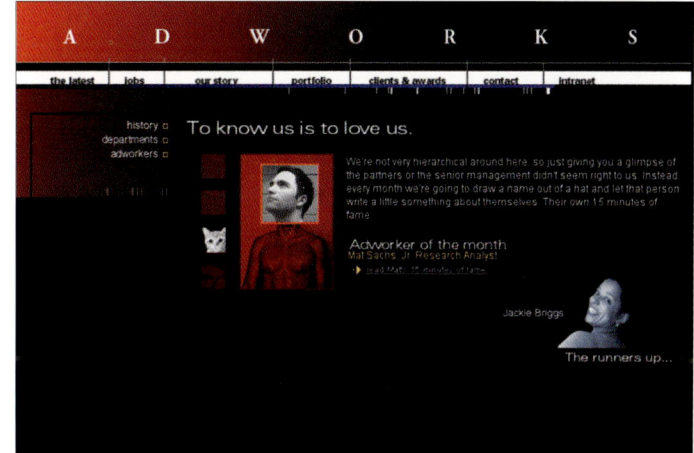

Merit

AGENCY Gr8, LLC/Baltimore
CLIENT Adworks
ART DIRECTORS Lisa Wurfl-Roeca, Glenn Roeca
DIGITAL ARTISTS Andy Spangler
CREATIVE DIRECTOR Morton Jackson
URL www.adworks.com
ID 00 0158 N

{CORPORATE IMAGE - B2B/ web sites}

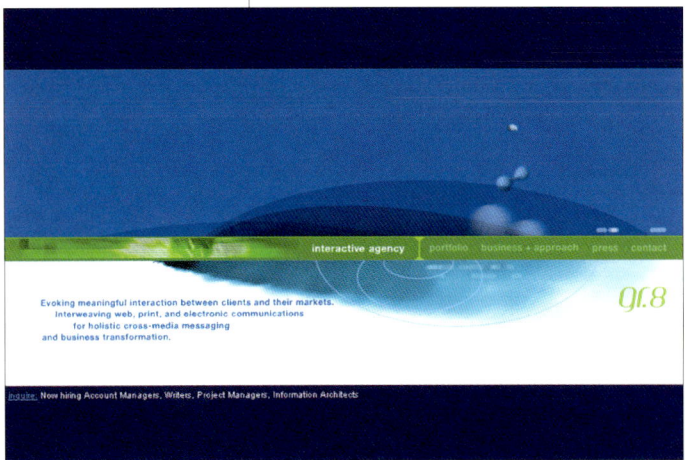
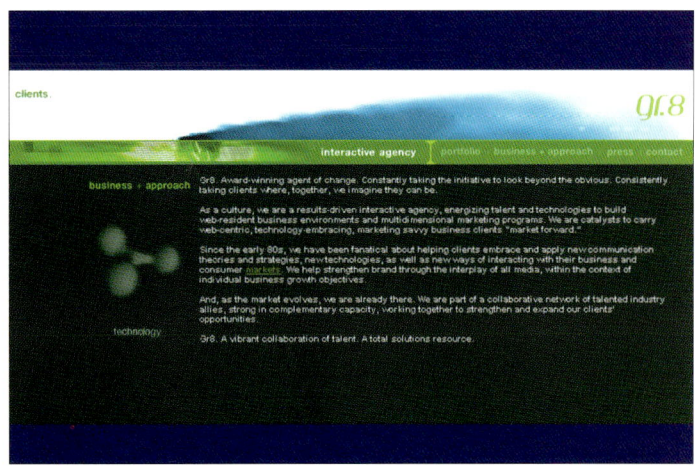
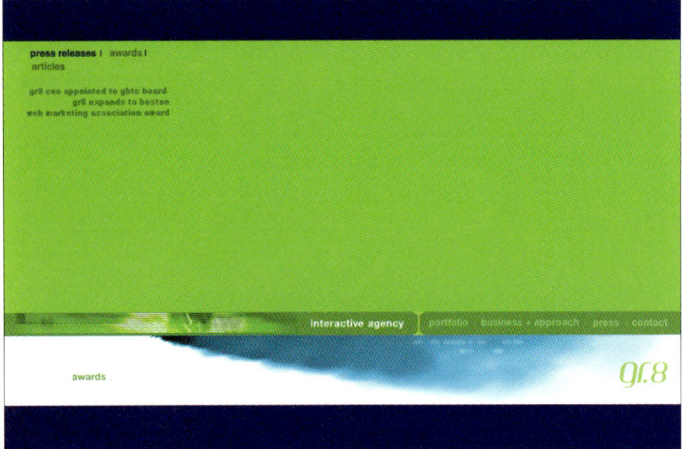
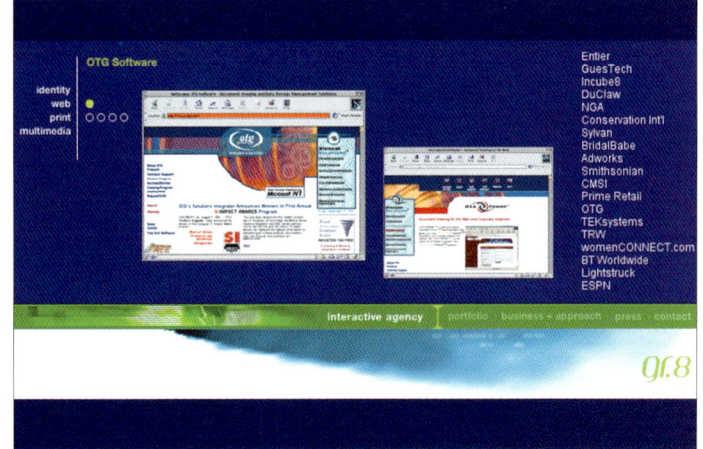

Merit

AGENCY	Gr8, LLC/Baltimore
CLIENT	Gr8
ART DIRECTORS	Morton Jackson, Lisa Wurlf-Roeca, Glenn Roeca
DIGITAL ARTISTS	Andy Spangler, Mark Maloney
MULTIMEDIA	Drew Trujillo
PROGRAMMER	Alex Markson
CREATIVE DIRECTOR	Morton Jackson
URL	www.gr8.com
ID	00 0159 N

{CORPORATE IMAGE - B2B/ web sites}

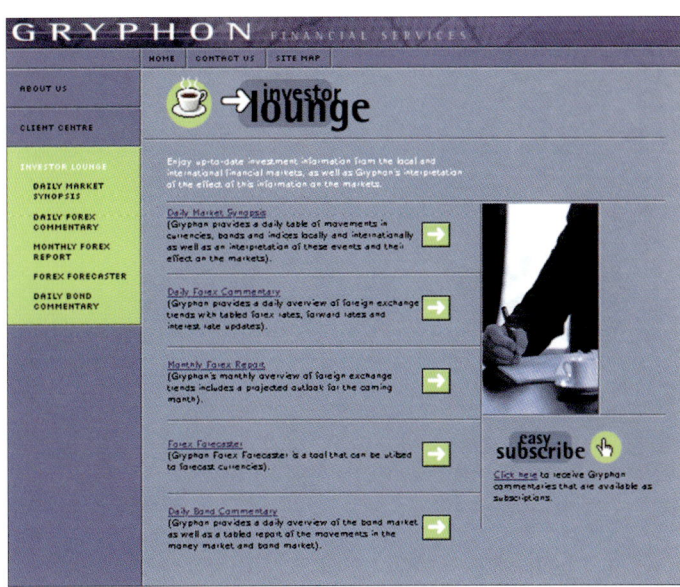
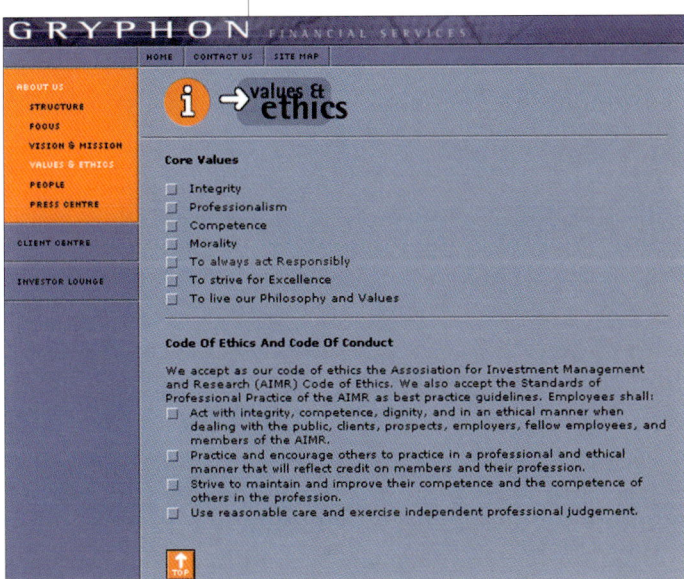
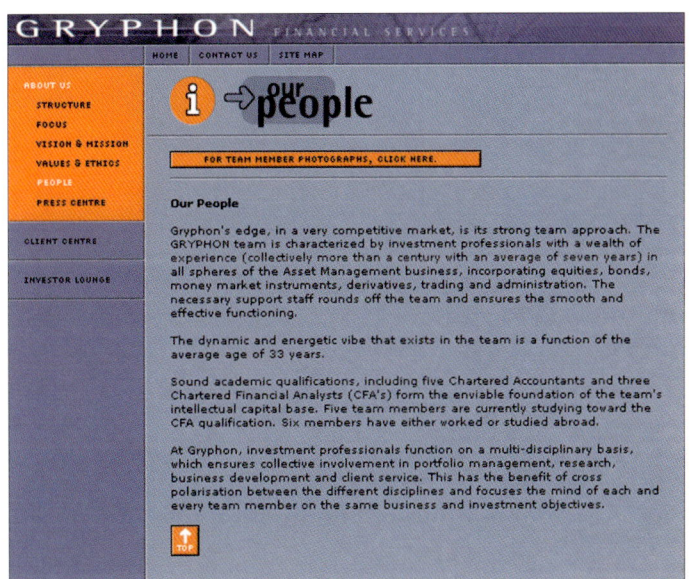

Merit

AGENCY	OgilvyInteractive/Cape Town
CLIENT	Gryphon
ART DIRECTOR	Damian Stephens
WRITER	Davis Hofmeyr
DIGITAL ARTIST	Damian Stephens
PRODUCER	Jack Kluger
PROGRAMMERS	Alan Alst, Duncan Forreston
CREATIVE DIRECTOR	Damian Stephens
	ID 00 0160 N

{CORPORATE IMAGE - B2B/ web sites}

	Merit
AGENCY	Razorfish/London
CLIENT	NatWest
ART DIRECTOR	Olof Schybergson
DIGITAL ARTISTS	Paul Sonley, Panja Gobel, Rick Lippiett, Ali Norris
PRODUCERS	Andy Polaine, Sean Winstanley
MULTIMEDIA	Paul Cleghorn
PROGRAMMERS	Snorre Milde, Martyn Rees
CREATIVE DIRECTOR	Olof Schybergson
URL	www.natwest.com
	ID 00 0161 N

{CORPORATE IMAGE - B2B/ CD-ROM}

Merit

AGENCY	Elephant Seven/Hamburg
CLIENT	Warner Home Video GmbH
ART DIRECTOR	Meibrit Ahrens
WRITER	Louisa Tayman
PRODUCER	Helga Waterkotte
MULTIMEDIA	Ralf-Ingo Koch
PROGRAMMERS	Heiko Kromm, Theiss Klussmeier
CREATIVE DIRECTOR	Meibrit Ahrens
	ID 00 0162 N

{CORPORATE IMAGE - B2B/ CD-ROM}

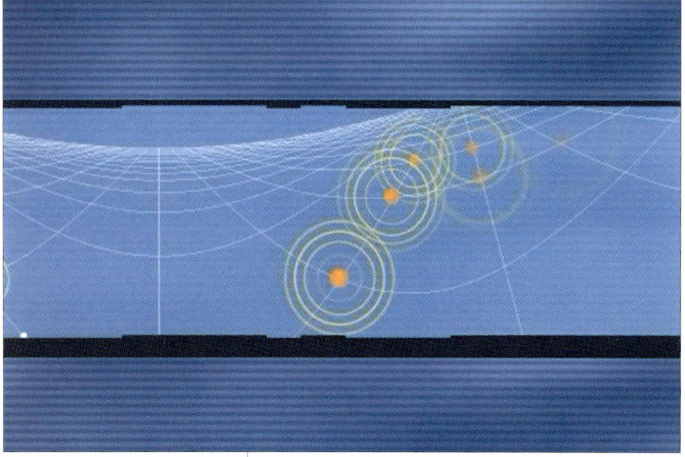
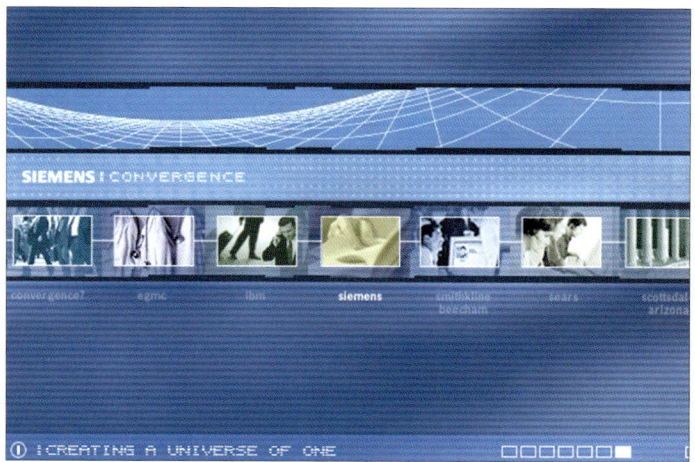

Merit

AGENCY Milligan Design/New York
CLIENT Siemens
ART DIRECTORS Megan Ploska, Michael Milligan
WRITER Peter Yaremko
DIGITAL ARTIST Megan Ploska
PRODUCER Milligan Design
MULTIMEDIA Milligan Design
PROGRAMMER Milligan Design
CREATIVE DIRECTOR Michael Milligan
ID 00 0163 N

{ CORPORATE IMAGE - B2B/ CD-ROM }

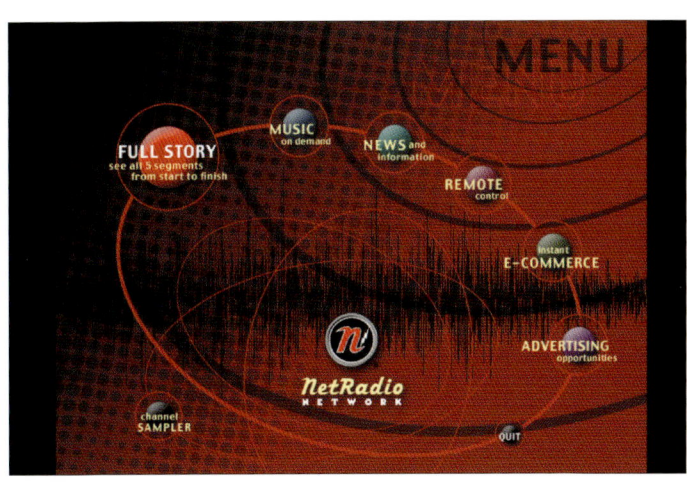
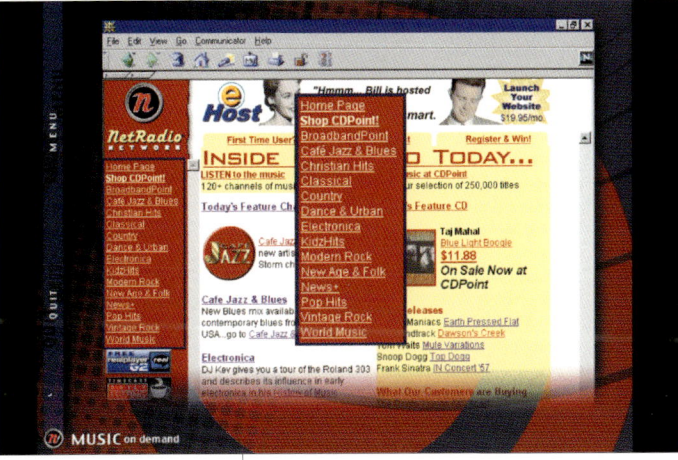
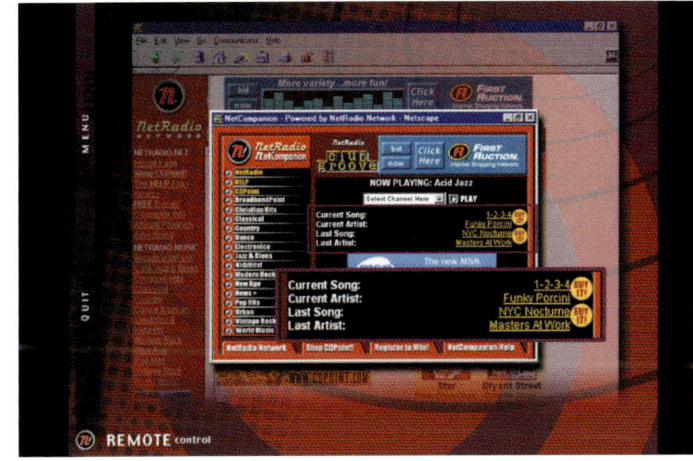

Merit

AGENCY	Periscope/Minneapolis
CLIENT	Net Radio
ART DIRECTOR	Julie DuBois
WRITER	Bruce Hannum
PHOTOGRAPHER	Archive
PRODUCER	Lina Crusan
MULTIMEDIA	Julie DuBois
PROGRAMMERS	Ron Hodnett, Stan Sisneros
CREATIVE DIRECTOR	Chris Cortilet
ID	00 0164 N

{CORPORATE IMAGE - B2B/ other digital media}

Merit	
AGENCY	Pivot Design, Inc./Chicago
CLIENT	Focal Communications Corporation
ART DIRECTOR	Jason Bowman
CREATIVE DIRECTOR	Brock Haldeman
URL	www.pivotdesign.com/tests/dataswap/entry.html
ID	00 0165 N

{E-COMMERCE/ web sites}

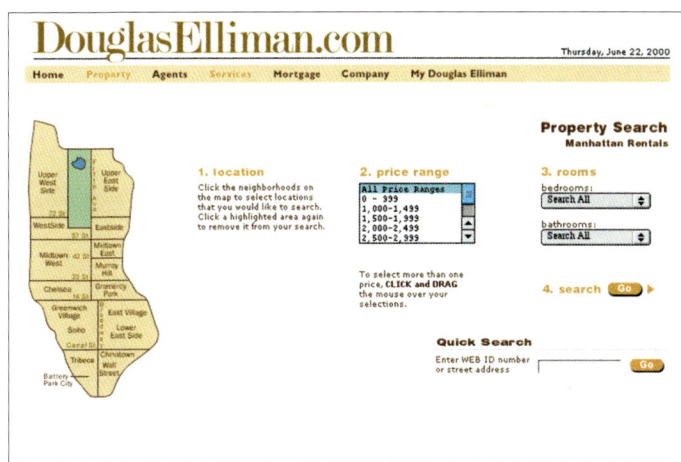
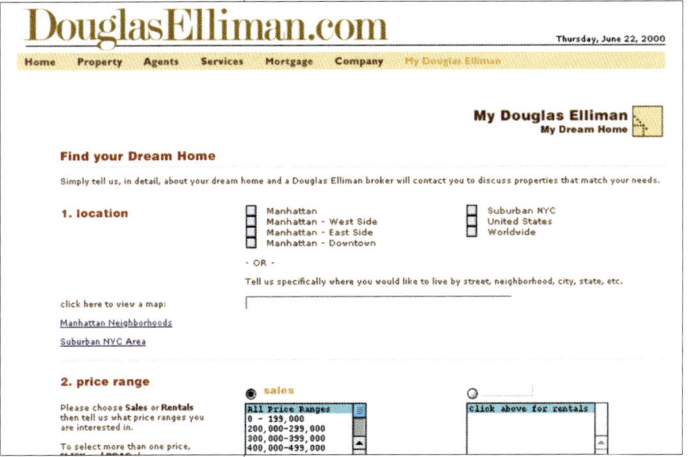
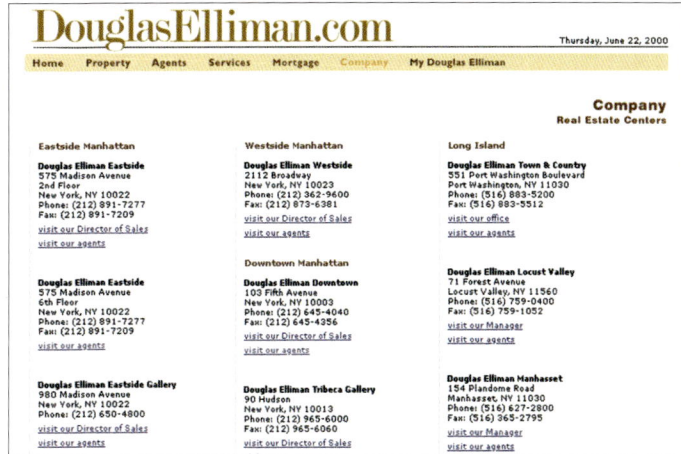

	Merit
AGENCY	Blue Hypermedia/New York
CLIENT	Douglas Elliman
ART DIRECTOR	James Roven
DIGITAL ARTIST	Cara Paul
PROGRAMMER	Crispin Roven
URL	www.douglaselliman.com
ID	00 0166 N

{E-COMMERCE/ web sites}

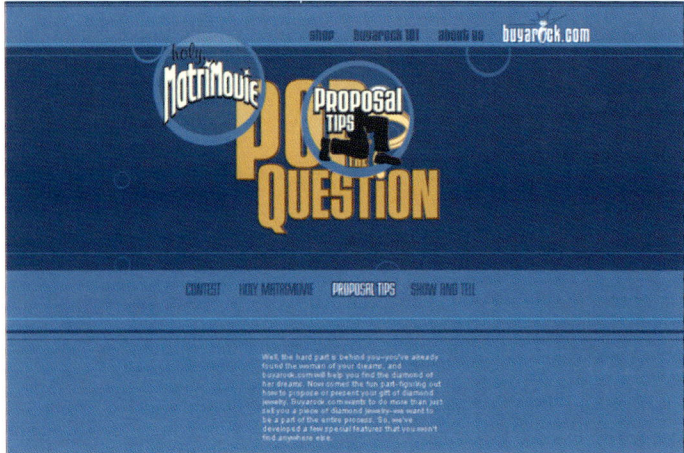
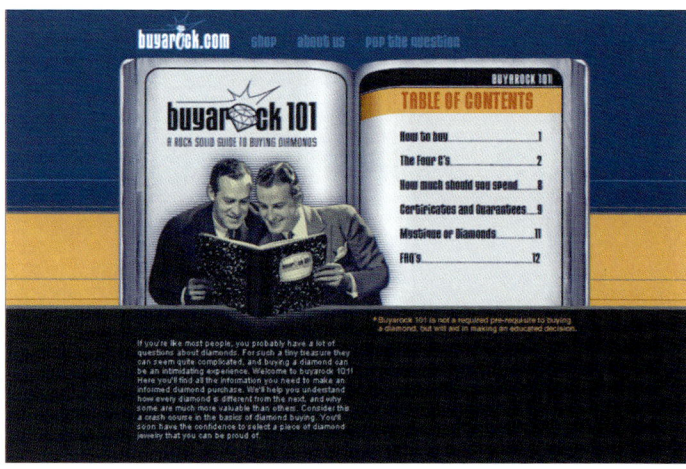

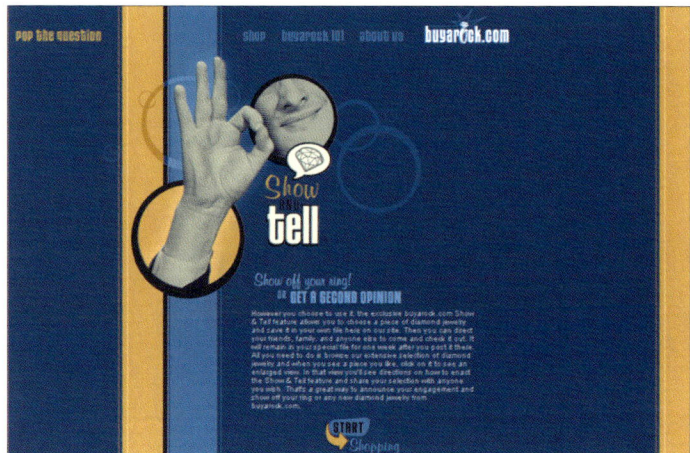

Merit

AGENCY The Chopping Block, Inc./New York
CLIENT buyarock.com
ART DIRECTOR Rob Reed
WRITERS Darleen Scherer, Rob Reed, Walter Ife
DIGITAL ARTIST Rob Reed
PRODUCERS Darleen Scherer, Kym Overton, Harry Groome
PROGRAMMERS Noam Solomon, Andrew Wint
URL www.buyarock.com
ID 00 0167 N

220

{ E-COMMERCE/ web sites }

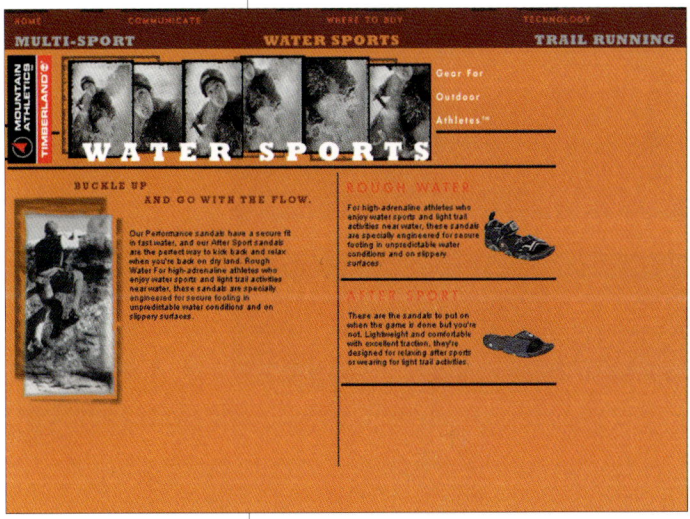

Merit
AGENCY | marchFIRST/Salt Lake City
CLIENT | Timberland
ART DIRECTORS | Agusta Duffey, Dahrong Lee
WRITER | Keith Byrne
DIGITAL ARTISTS | Jose Rivera, Jonathan Hutcheson
PRODUCER | Sun Sun Chung
PROGRAMMERS | Sam Bisbee, Thor Garcia
URL | www.mountainathletics.com
ID 00 0168 N

{E-COMMERCE/ other digital media}

Merit

AGENCY | Modem Media/Norwalk
CLIENT | IBM Personal Systems Group
ART DIRECTOR | Barb Harper
WRITERS | Alexis Schettini, Gabe St. John
DIGITAL ARTISTS | Paul Jasch, Ben Fascitelli
PRODUCERS | Josh Newman, Dave Mozdziak
CREATIVE DIRECTOR | Tom Beeby
URL | www.modemmedia.com/oneshow
ID 00 0169 N

{INTEGRATED BRANDING/ campaign}

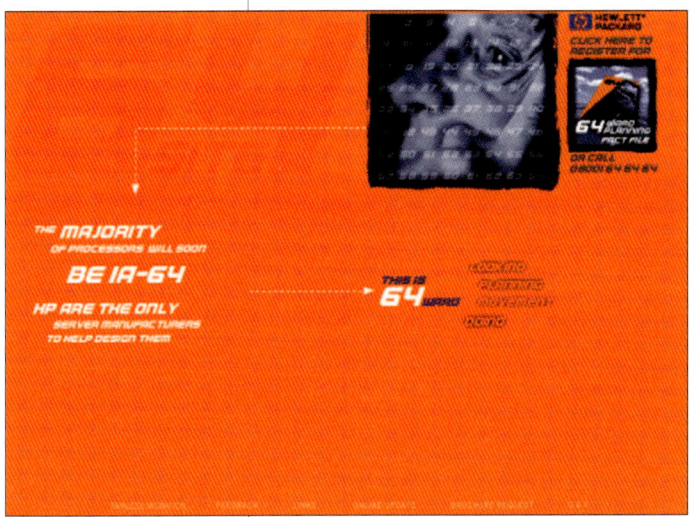

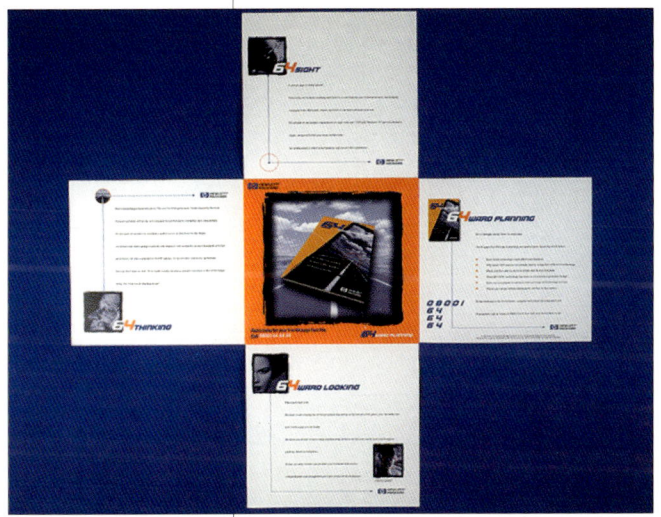
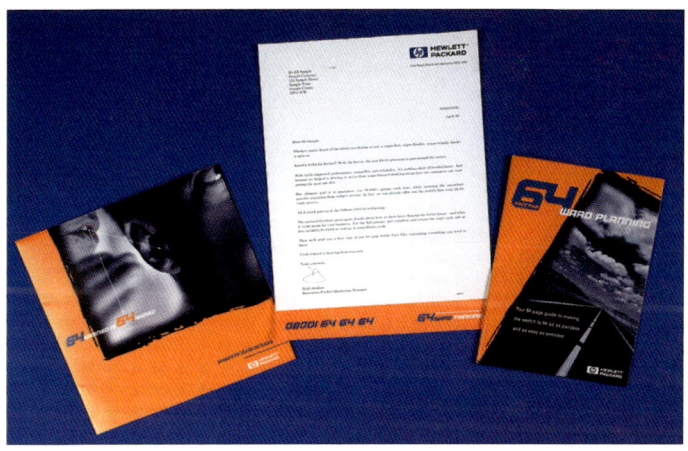

Merit

AGENCY Bates Interactive/London
CLIENT Hewlett Packard
ART DIRECTOR Leora Ucko
DIGITAL ARTIST Leora Ucko
PRODUCER Peter Ahearn
PROGRAMMERS Dan Evans, Steve LLoyd
CREATIVE DIRECTOR Joe Dear
ID 00 0170 N

{INTEGRATED BRANDING/ campaign}

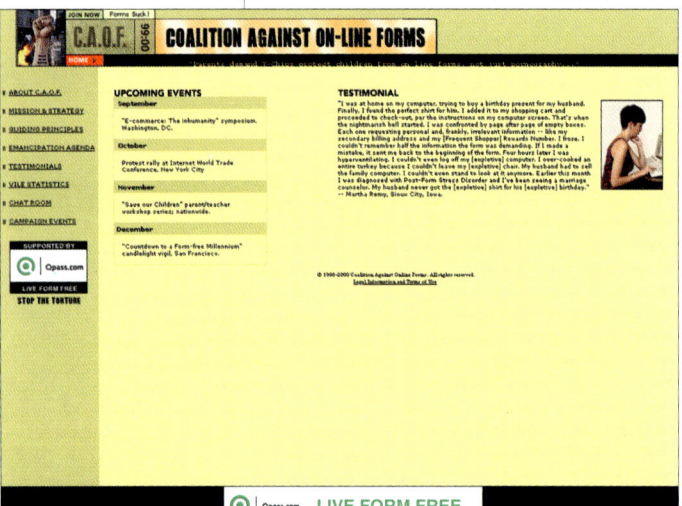
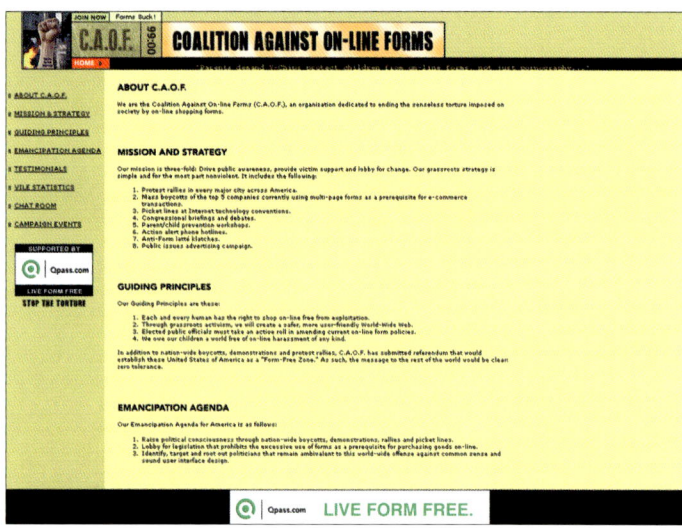
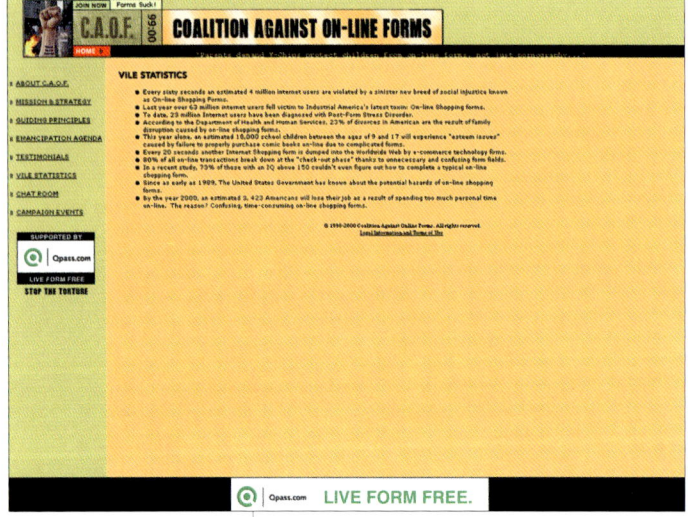
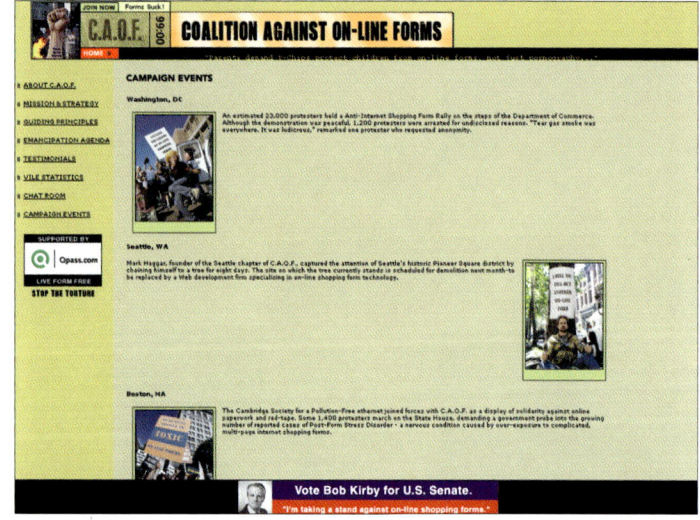

Merit

AGENCY	Cole & Weber/Seattle
CLIENT	Qpass
ART DIRECTORS	Todd Derksen, Brent McCoy, Steve Rudasics
WRITER	Jim Elliott
DIGITAL ARTIST	Sean Onart
PHOTOGRAPHER	Randy Allbritton
PRODUCERS	Wendy Fernandez, Judy Dixon
PROGRAMMERS	Mark Dreessen, Trina Neilson
CREATIVE DIRECTORS	Ed Lisieski, Ron Klein
URL	http://qpass.coleweber.net
ID	00 0171 N

{INTEGRATED BRANDING/ campaign}

	Merit
AGENCY	Duffy Design/Minneapolis
CLIENT	EDS
ART DIRECTORS	Dan Olson, Todd Bartz
WRITERS	Chuck Carlson, Debbie Gold
DIGITAL ARTIST	Joel Herrmann
PHOTOGRAPHER	Gwen Williams
PRODUCER	Kore Peterson
MULTIMEDIA	Todd Bartz
PROGRAMMER	Gwen Williams
CREATIVE DIRECTORS	Joe Duffy, Dan Olson
URL	http://awards.duffy.com/eds_employee/employee_site/index.html
ID	00 0172 N

{INTEGRATED BRANDING/ campaign}

Merit

AGENCY Leo Burnett/Sydney
CLIENT Kellogg Australia
ART DIRECTORS Damian Claassens, Katie Manekshaw
WRITERS Damian Claassens, Kieran Ots, Trent Christie
DIGITAL ARTISTS Cindy Chan, Kieran Ots, Kara Jenkins
PRODUCERS Mark Renshaw, Brenden Johnson
PROGRAMMERS Patrick Kennedy, Spiro Rokos
URL www.cocopops.com.au
ID 00 0173 N

{ INTEGRATED BRANDING/ campaign }

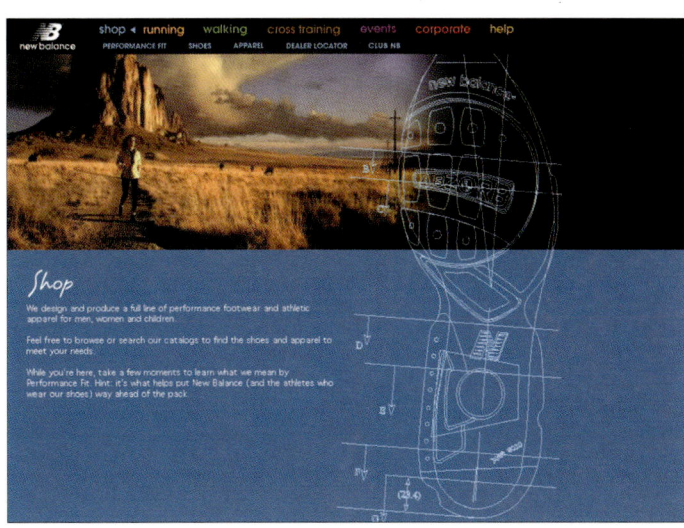
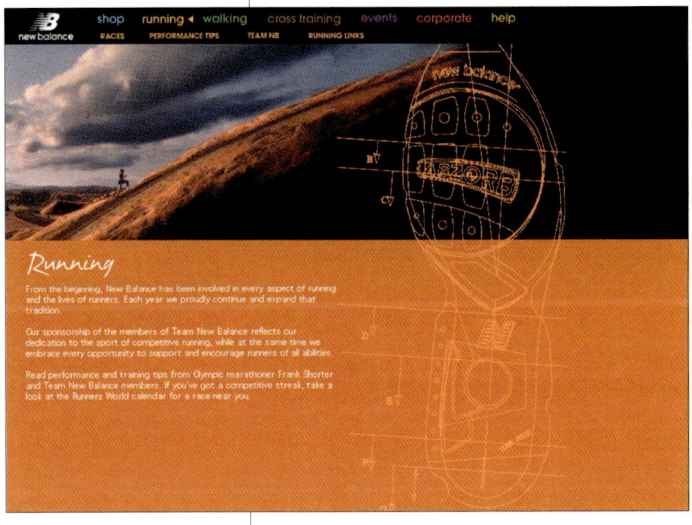
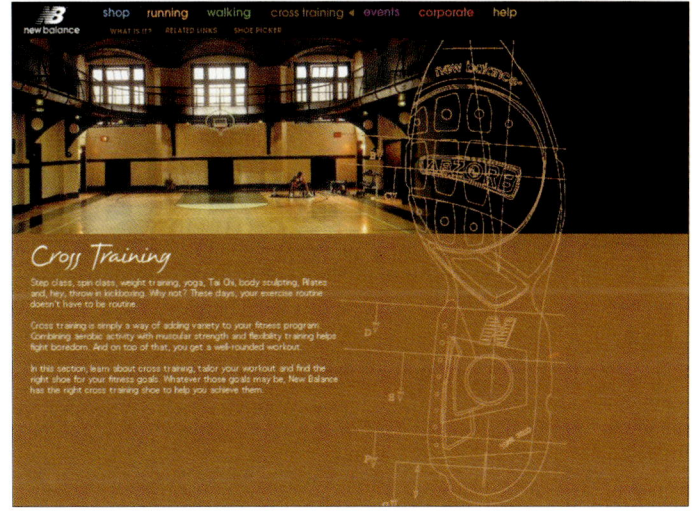

Merit

AGENCY	MVBMS/EURO RSCG/New York
CLIENT	New Balance Athletic Shoe, Inc.
ART DIRECTORS	Vinton Lennon, Lisa Speer, Shanti Marlar
WRITER	Matt Dikdan
DIGITAL ARTIST	Elena Goldstein
PRODUCER	Kim Lewis
PROGRAMMERS	Mans Angantyr, Meg Pullis, Larry Glenn
	Tracy Rudzitis, Aaron Ambrose, Anthony Chou
URL	www.newbalance.com
ID	00 0174 N

{INTEGRATED BRANDING/ campaign}

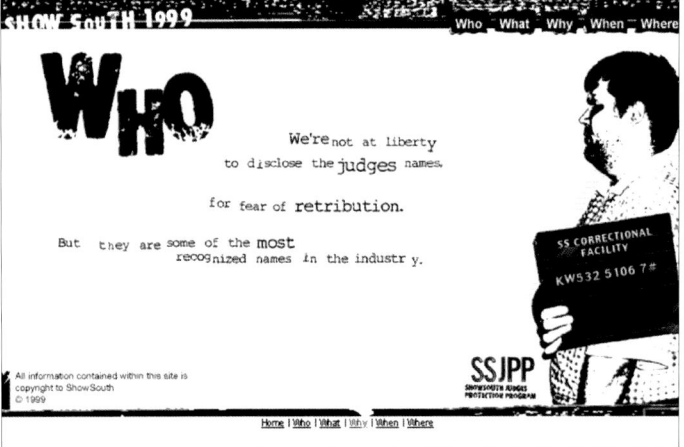
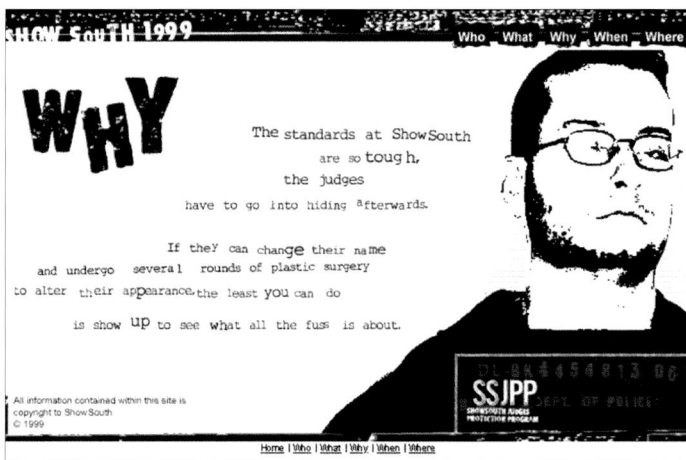

Merit
AGENCY USWeb/CKS/Atlanta
CLIENT Creative Club of Altanta
ART DIRECTOR Paul Brown
WRITER Mike Weidner
DIGITAL ARTIST Armin Vit
PHOTOGRAPHER Paul Abrelat
PRODUCER Halle Griffee-Petrini
MULTIMEDIA Paul Abrelat, Will Weyer
CREATIVE DIRECTOR Minsoo Pak
ID 00 0175 N

{ BROADBAND / web sites }

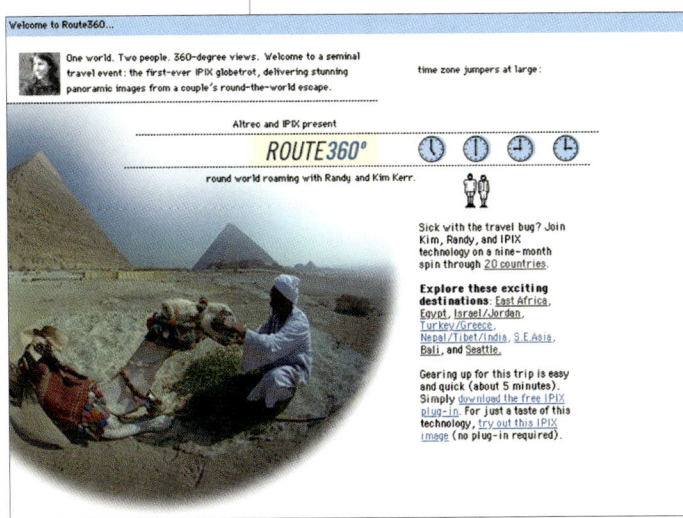

	Merit
AGENCY	Altrec.com/Bellevue
CLIENT	Altrec.com
ART DIRECTORS	Gabe Kean, Enoch Platas, Blaine Donnelson
WRITERS	Randy Kerr, Kim Kerr, Todd Jennings
PHOTOGRAPHER	Randy Kerr
PRODUCER	Cathryn Buchanan
MULTIMEDIA	Randy Kerr
PROGRAMMERS	Enoch Platas, Daryn Nakuda
CREATIVE DIRECTOR	Cathryn Buchanan
URL	www.route360.com
ID	00 0176 N

{BROADBAND/ web sites}

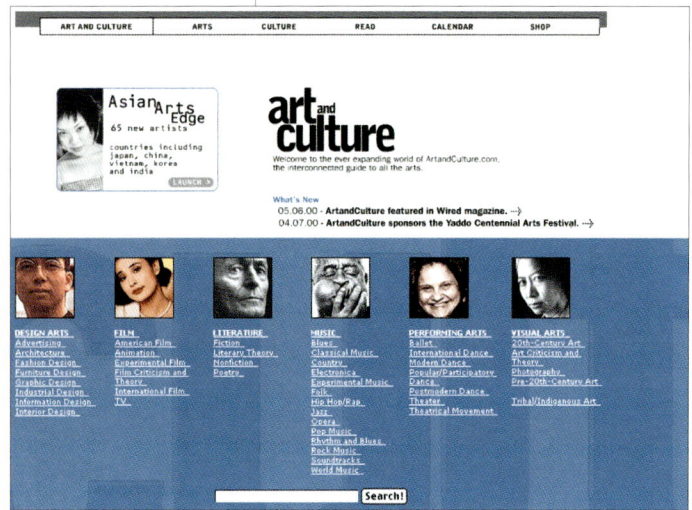
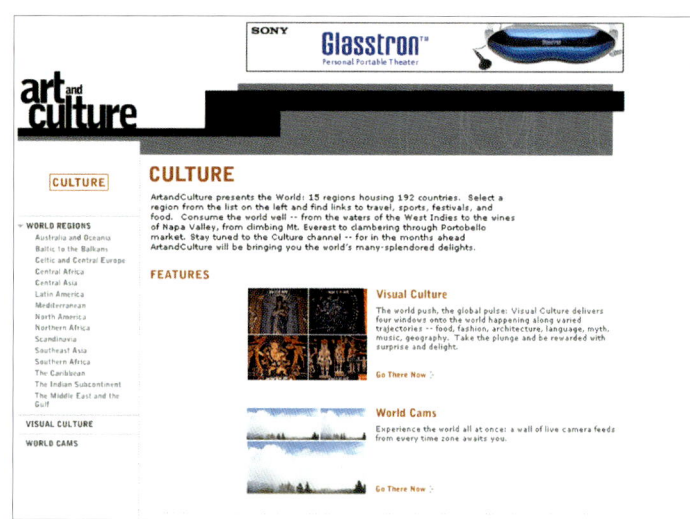
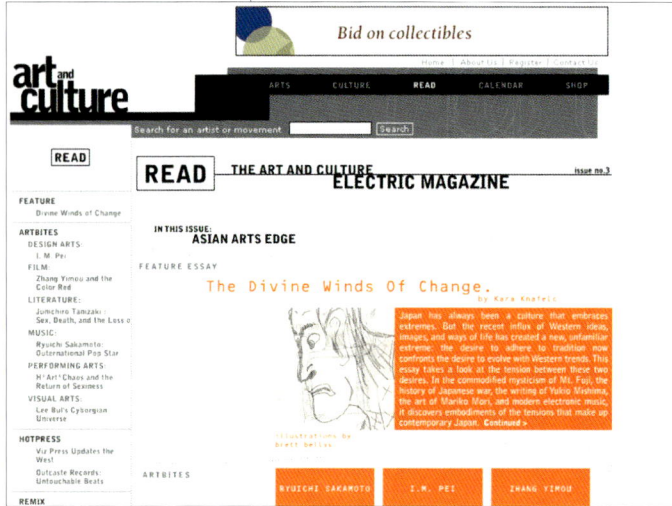
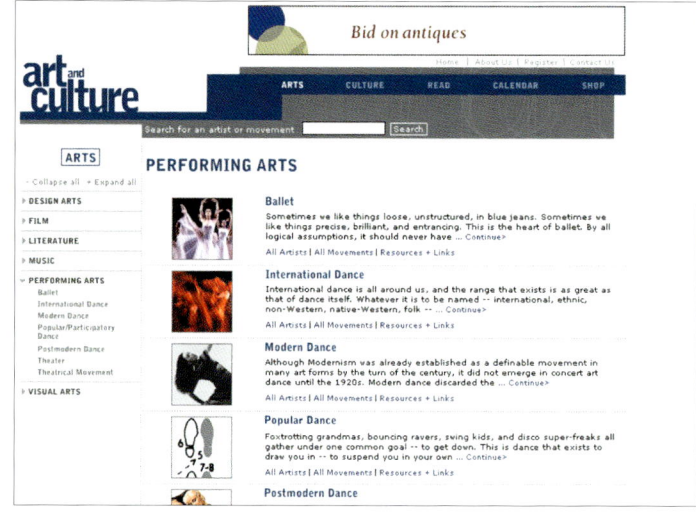

	Merit
AGENCY	Art and Culture/San Francisco
CLIENT	Art and Culture
ART DIRECTOR	Michael Chichi
WRITERS	J.D. Beltran, Daniel Coffeen, Michael Holt, Monique Jenkinson, Lena Katz, Susi May, Joshua Saitz, Jennifer Traig, Robin Ward
DIGITAL ARTIST	Janice Natchek
PRODUCERS	Ed Rivera, Jose Fernandez
MULTIMEDIA	Darin Fong
PROGRAMMERS	Chris Miner, Jim Benster, Marc Adkins
CREATIVE DIRECTOR	Marc Lafia
URL	www.artandculture.com
	ID 00 0177 N

{BROADBAND/ web sites}

Merit

AGENCY	KPE/New York
CLIENT	KPE
ART DIRECTOR	Tracy Long
WRITERS	Tracy Long, Tina Gongsakdi
DIGITAL ARTIST	Tracy Long
PHOTOGRAPHERS	Tracy Long, Shawn Hainsworth
PRODUCERS	Tina Gongsakdi, Tracy Long, Shawn Hainsworth
MULTIMEDIA	Tina Gongsakdi, Tracy Long, Shawn Hainsworth
PROGRAMMERS	Tracy Long, Tina Gongsakdi
ID	00 0178 N

{BROADBAND/ web sites}

Merit

AGENCY OgilvyInteractive/New York
CLIENT IBM
ART DIRECTOR Juan Gallardo
WRITER David Levy
PRODUCER Kate Kehoe
MULTIMEDIA Malvika Mitchell
CREATIVE DIRECTOR Audrey Fleisher
URL http://199.229.12.135/awards2000/ibm@homebroadband/athome1.html
http://199.229.12.135/awards2000/ibm@homebroadband/athome2.html
ID 00 0179 N

{BROADBAND/ web sites}

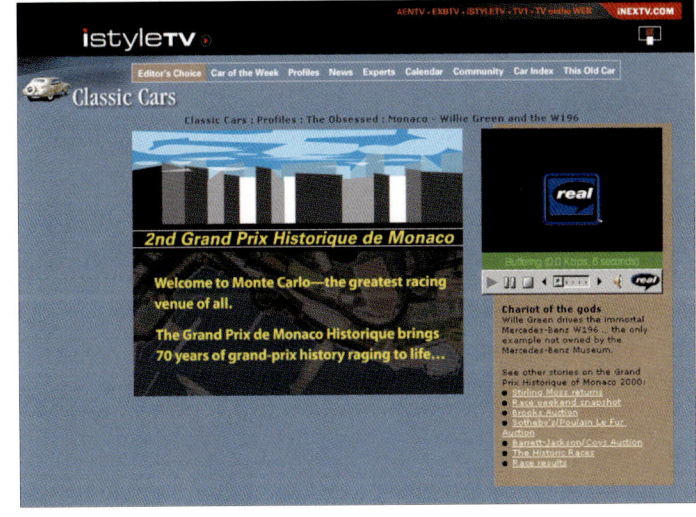

	Merit
AGENCY	OVEN Digital/New York
CLIENT	iNEXTV
ART DIRECTORS	Paulette Bluhm, Kate Stewart
PRODUCERS	Paulina Breytburg, Wendy Krueger
MULTIMEDIA	Paul Madlon
PROGRAMMERS	Andrea Andryshak, Eddie Kucyi, Mike Piccuirro, Eric Sellers, Irina Shuster, Galina Shuster, Chris Mack, Adam Sewell, Simon Tom, Aaron Wald
URL	www.istyle.com/cars
	ID 00 0180 N

{BROADBAND/ web sites}

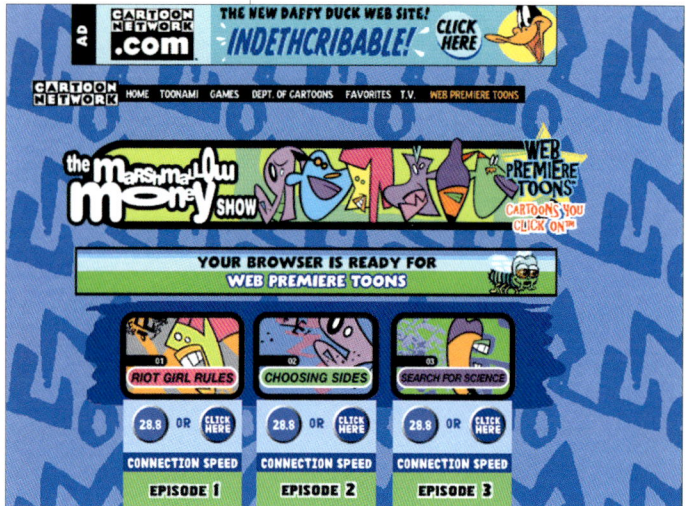

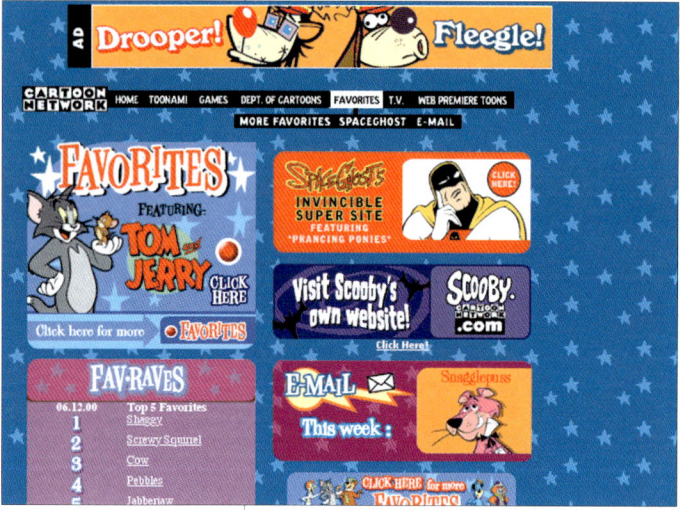

	Merit
AGENCY	Pop Characters/New York
CLIENT	cartoonnetwork.com
ART DIRECTOR	Vincent Lacava
WRITER	Paul Malmont
DIGITAL ARTIST	Vander McClain
PRODUCER	Mark T. Smith
MULTIMEDIA	Michael Sweet, Blister Media
CREATIVE DIRECTOR	Vincent Lacava
URL	www.cartoonnetwork.com/wpt/mmoney
ID	00 0181 N

{BROADBAND / web sites}

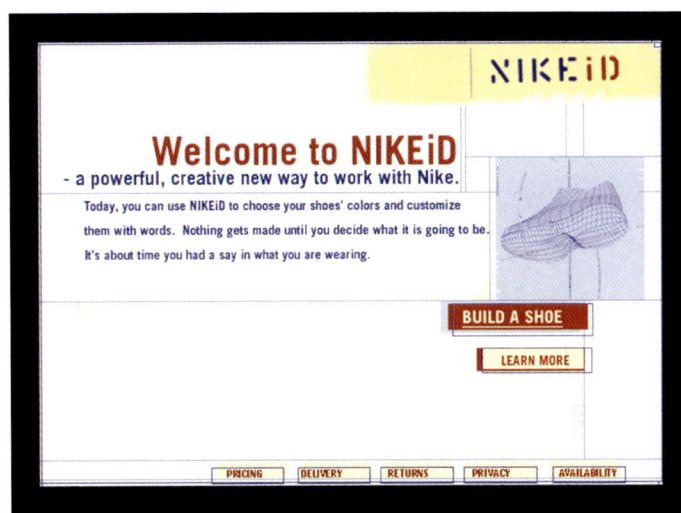

Merit

AGENCY Red Sky Interactive/San Francisco
CLIENT Nike
ART DIRECTOR Laura de Young
WRITER Chris Gatewood
DIGITAL ARTISTS Alisia Cheuk, Amanda Moore
PRODUCERS Stacy Stevenson, Jon Snyda
PROGRAMMER David Gantenbein
CREATIVE DIRECTORS Joel Hladecek, Kirk Gibbons
URL www.nike.com/idstart/index.html
ID 00 0182 N

{SELF-PROMOTION/ web sites}

	Merit
AGENCY	beaufonts/UK
CLIENT	beaufonts
ART DIRECTOR	Ian Mitchell
WRITER	Ian Mitchell
DIGITAL ARTIST	HC
PHOTOGRAPHER	HC
PRODUCER	HC
MULTIMEDIA	Cecilia Garside, David Gibson, David Hand, Jonathon Hitchen, Jon Humphreys, Ian Mitchell, Paul Musgrave, Oliver Payne, Simon Vaughan
PROGRAMMER	Ian Mitchell
CREATIVE DIRECTOR	Beaufonts
URL	www.beaufonts.com
ID	00 0183 N

{SELF-PROMOTION/ web sites}

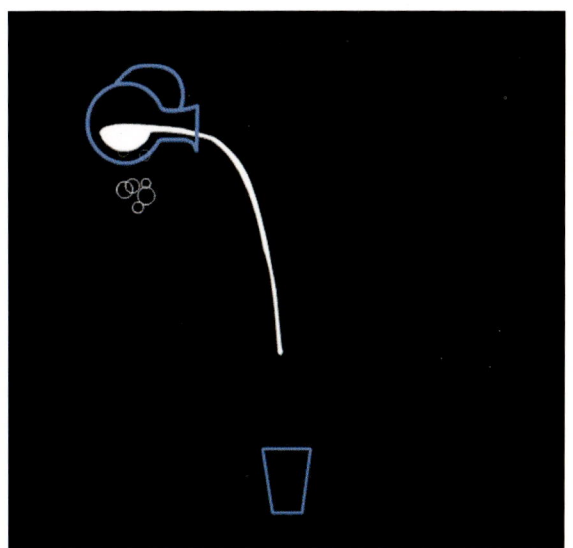

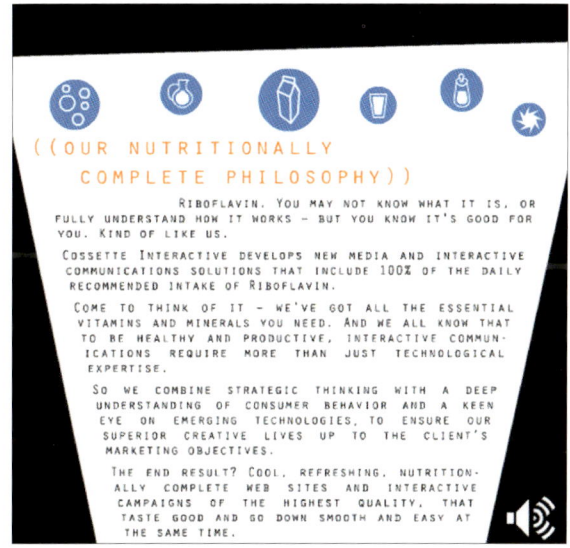

Merit

AGENCY	Cossette Interactive/Toronto
CLIENT	Cossette Interactive
ART DIRECTORS	Nicole Shick, Elizabeth Yanitsky
WRITER	Jon Webber
PRODUCERS	Laura Felstiner, Scott Wassmer
PROGRAMMERS	One Trick Pony, Brent Marshall
CREATIVE DIRECTOR	Michael Convery
URL	www.cossetteinteractive.com
ID	00 0184 N

{SELF-PROMOTION/ web sites}

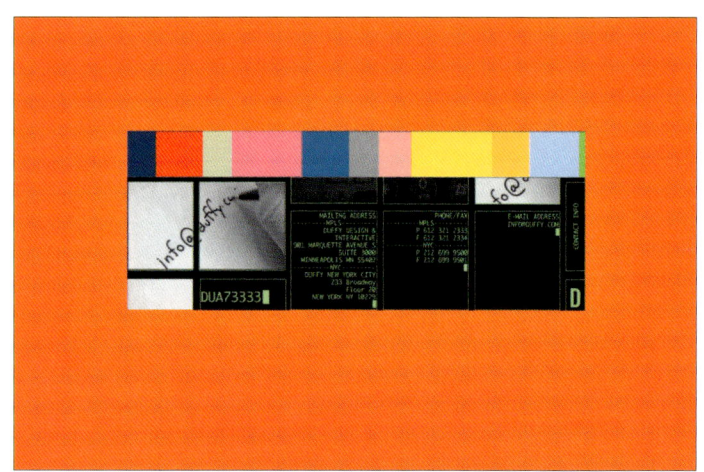

	Merit
AGENCY	Duffy Design/Minneapolis
CLIENT	Duffy
ART DIRECTORS	Dan Olson, Sida Phungjiam, Todd Bartz, Alan Colvin
WRITERS	Debbie Gold, Russ Stark
DIGITAL ARTIST	Laurie Brown
PRODUCER	Jennifer Bremer
MULTIMEDIA	Laurie Brown, Tom Kunau, Mark Sandau, Christian Erickson
PROGRAMMERS	Tom Kunau, Gwen Williams
CREATIVE DIRECTOR	Joe Duffy
URL	www.duffy.com
	ID 00 0185 N

{SELF-PROMOTION/ web sites}

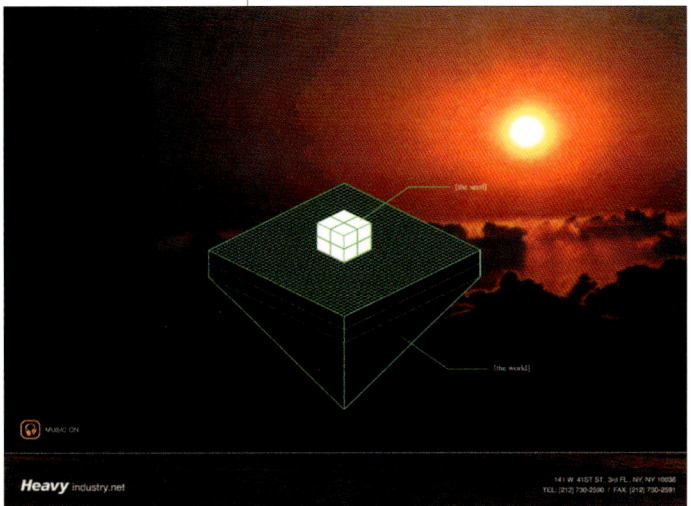

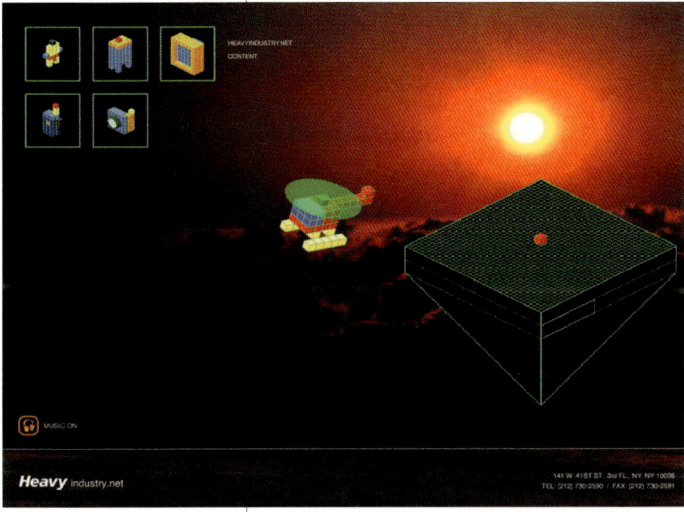
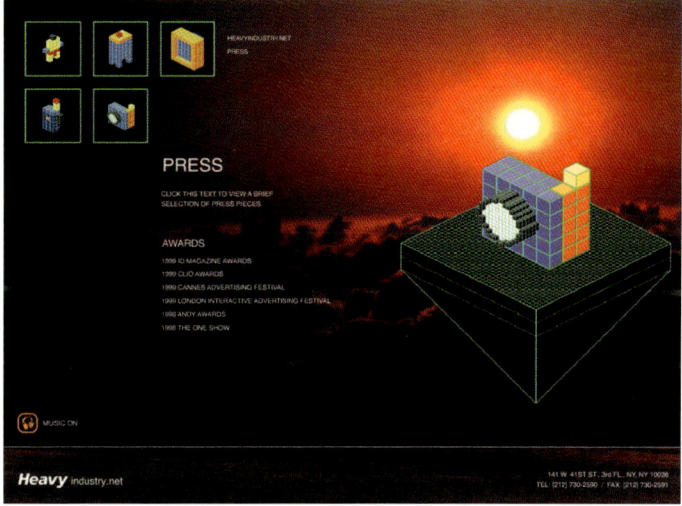

Merit

AGENCY Heavy Industry/New York
CLIENT Heavy Industry
ART DIRECTOR Ryan Honey
PRODUCER Simon Assad
PROGRAMMER Paal Rui
CREATIVE DIRECTOR David Carson
URL www.heavyindustry.net
ID 00 0186 N

{SELF-PROMOTION/ web sites}

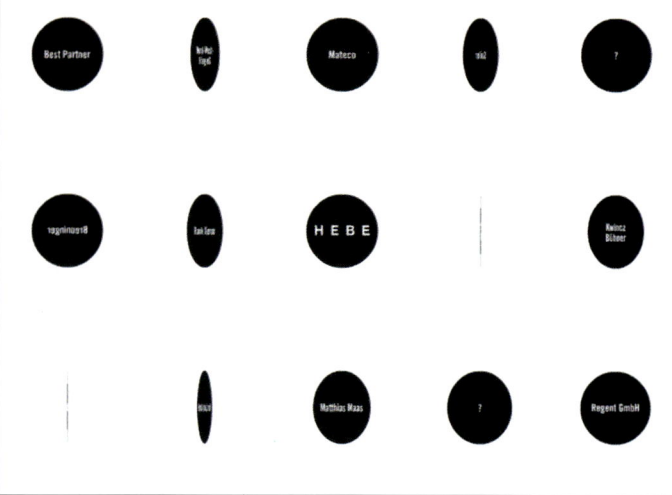

	Merit
AGENCY	HEBE. Werbung & Design/Leonberg
CLIENT	HEBE
ART DIRECTORS	Reiner Hebe, Joerg Bauer
WRITER	Reiner Hebe
DIGITAL ARTISTS	Jan Maier, Joerg Bauer
PHOTOGRAPHERS	Nils Schubert, Werner Pawlok, Francis Koenig, Dominik Hatt
MULTIMEDIA	Joerg Bauer Design
PROGRAMMERS	Joerg Bauer Design, Nullzeit
CREATIVE DIRECTORS	Reiner Hebe, Joerg Bauer
	ID 00 0187 N

{SELF-PROMOTION/ web sites}

THAT'S WHY IT'S NOT ENOUGH TO OFFER GOOD PRODUCTS.

THEY HAVE TO BE TEAMED WITH EFFECTIVE STRATEGIES AND HANDFUL OF GOOD IDEAS THAT WILL MAKE THEM MORE ATTRACTIVE. THAT'S ESSENTIAL.

BUT YOUR COMMUNICATION NEEDS TO BE EXCEPTIONALLY WELL CRAFTED TO MAKE POTENTIAL CLIENTS SIT UP AND TAKE NOTICE.

HERRAIZ SOTO & CO.

HAUTE CUISINE PUBLICITAIRE

Merit

AGENCY	Herraiz Soto & Co./Barcelona
CLIENT	Herraiz Soto
ART DIRECTOR	Angel Herraiz
WRITER	Rafa Soto
PHOTOGRAPHER	Siscu Soler
PRODUCER	Francesca Galera
PROGRAMMER	Francesca Galera
CREATIVE DIRECTORS	Angel Herraiz, Rafa Soto
URL	www.herraizsoto.com
ID	00 0188 N

{SELF-PROMOTION/ web sites}

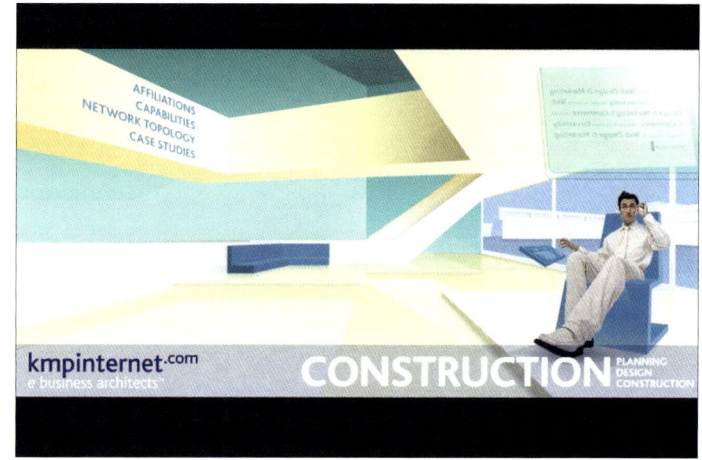

Merit

AGENCY	kmp internet solutions/Stockport
CLIENT	kmpinternet.com
WRITERS	Jeremy Dent, Chris Tomlinson
DIGITAL ARTIST	Rus Jones
PHOTOGRAPHER	Two White Heads
PRODUCER	Nikk Smith
MULTIMEDIA	Rob Shelly
PROGRAMMER	Gaz Jones
CREATIVE DIRECTOR	Mark Daws
URL	www.kmpinternet.com
ID	00 0189 N

{SELF-PROMOTION/ web sites}

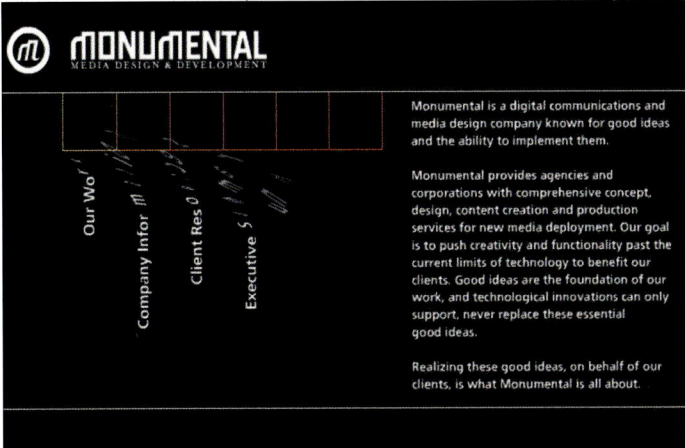
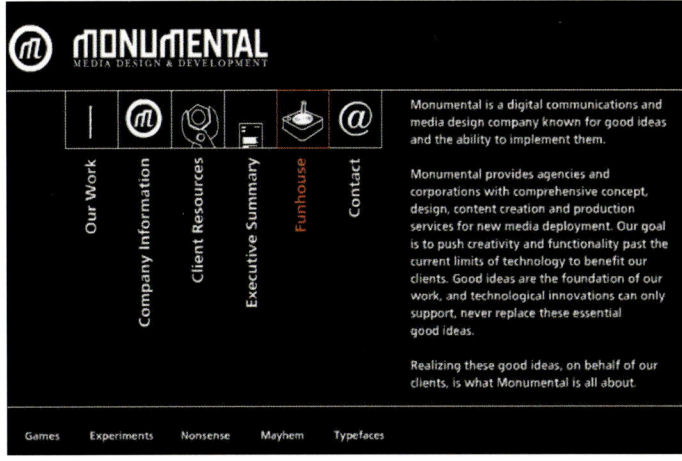
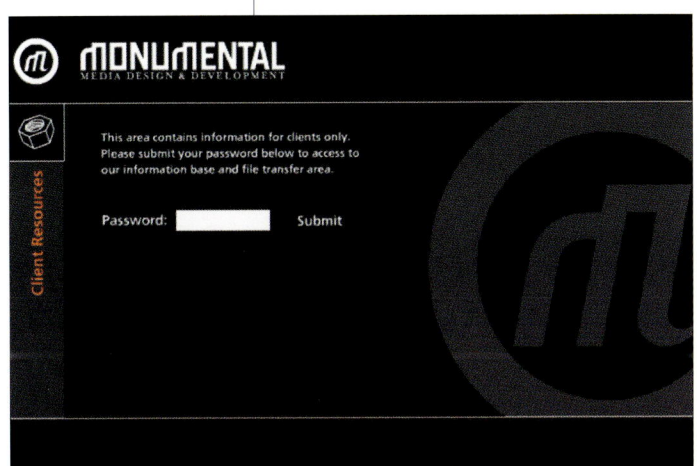
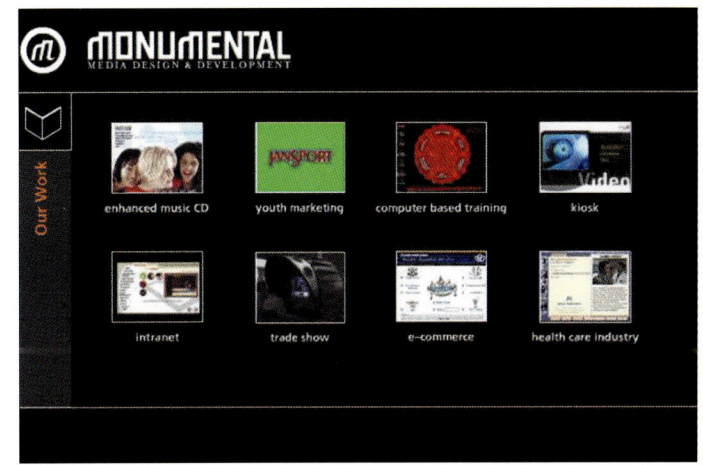

	Merit
AGENCY	Monumental/Atlanta
CLIENT	Monumental
ART DIRECTORS	Oliver Perrin, Bjorn Bosse
WRITER	Oliver Perrin
DIGITAL ARTIST	Bjorn Bosse
MULTIMEDIA	Daniel Crowder
PROGRAMMER	Daniel Crowder
CREATIVE DIRECTOR	Daniel Crowder
URL	www.monumental-i.com
ID	00 0190 N

{SELF-PROMOTION/ web sites}

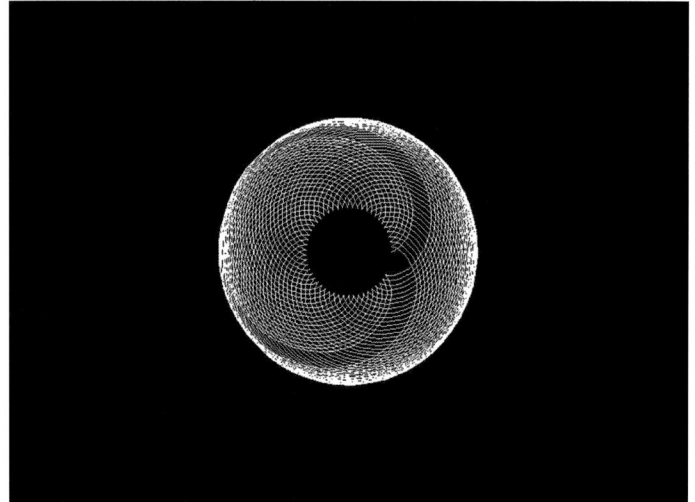
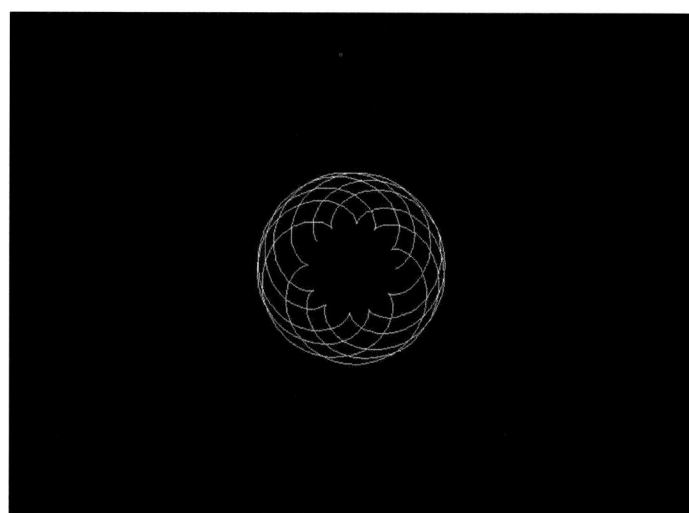

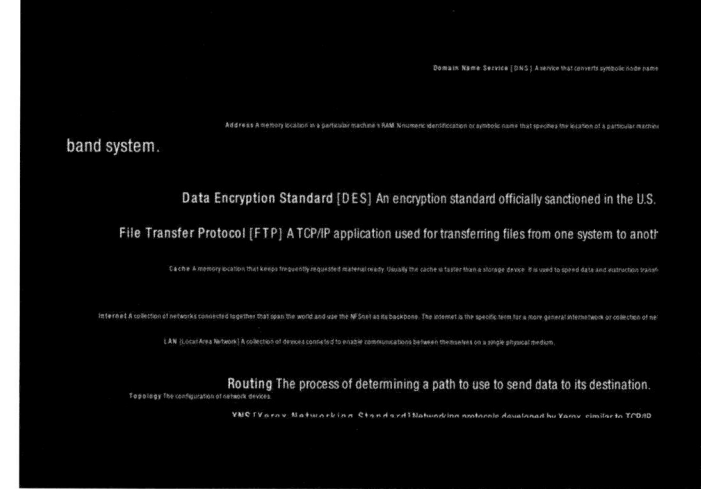

	Merit
AGENCY	Razorfish/San Francisco
CLIENT	Morla Design
ART DIRECTOR	Shane Ginsberg
DIGITAL ARTIST	Ali Norris
PRODUCER	Lissette Fernandez
PROGRAMMER	Dan Spirn
CREATIVE DIRECTOR	Jennifer Morla
URL	www.morladesign.com
	ID 00 0191 N

{SELF-PROMOTION/ CD-ROM}

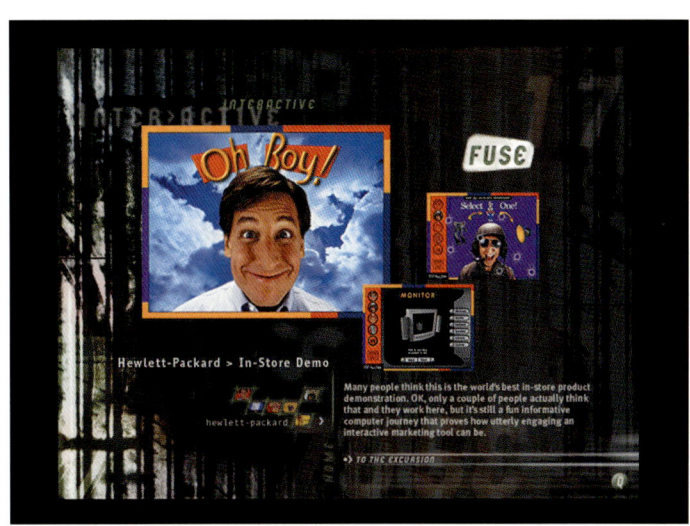

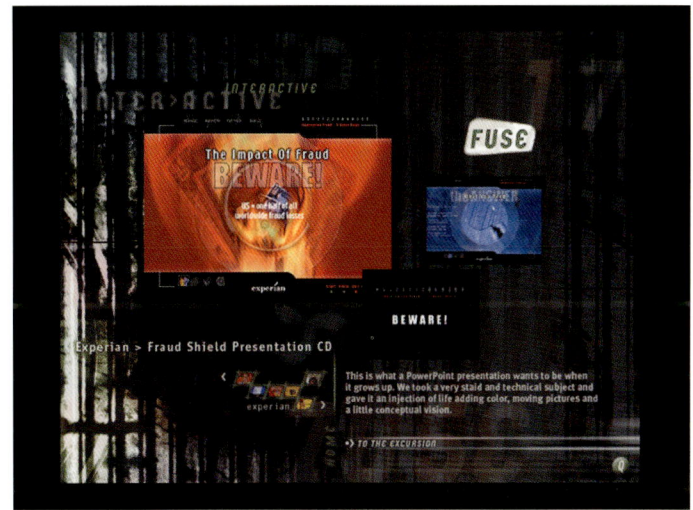

Merit
AGENCY Fuse, Inc./Laguna Beach
CLIENT Fuse, Inc.
ART DIRECTOR Kristi Kamei
WRITER Pat Macke
DIGITAL ARTIST Russell Pierce
PROGRAMMER Mike Bodily
CREATIVE DIRECTOR Stefan Drust
ID 00 0192 N

{SELF-PROMOTION/ CD-ROM}

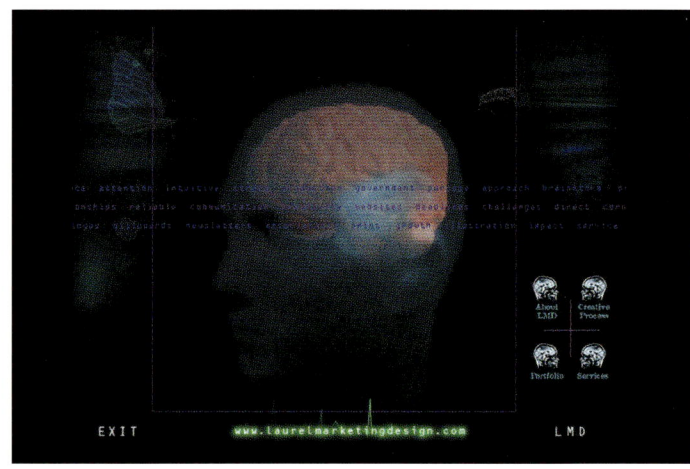
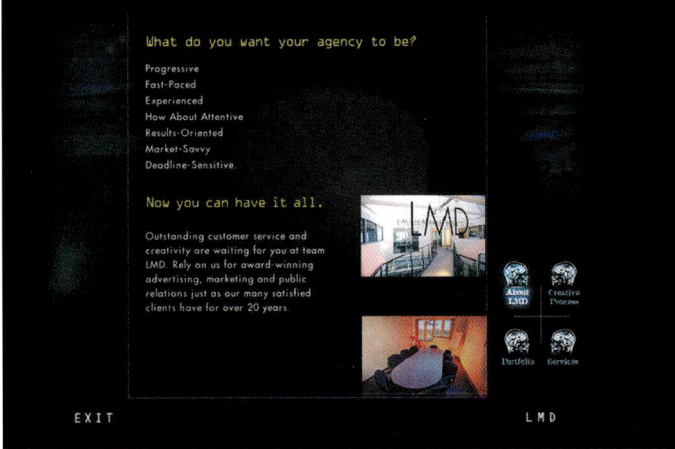
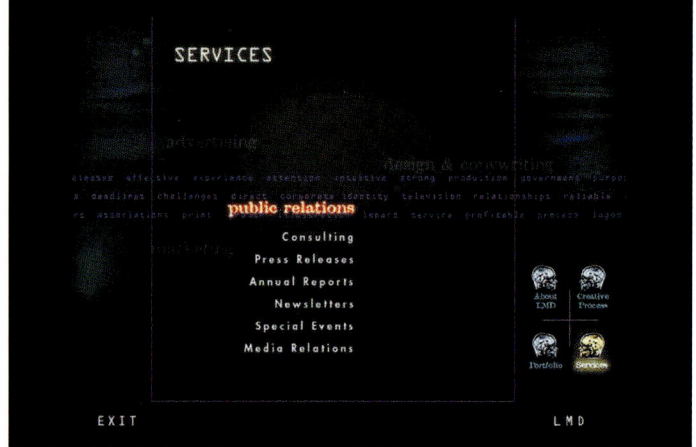

Merit
AGENCY Laurel Marketing and Design/Laurel
CLIENT LMD
ART DIRECTOR Katie Mitchell
WRITER Chrissie Bamber
DIGITAL ARTISTS Dan Croft, Key Owens, Sarah Compton
PHOTOGRAPHER Various
PRODUCER Sarah Pugh
PROGRAMMER Jon Majerick
CREATIVE DIRECTOR Scott Van Der Meid
ID 00 0193 N

{SELF-PROMOTION/ CD-ROM}

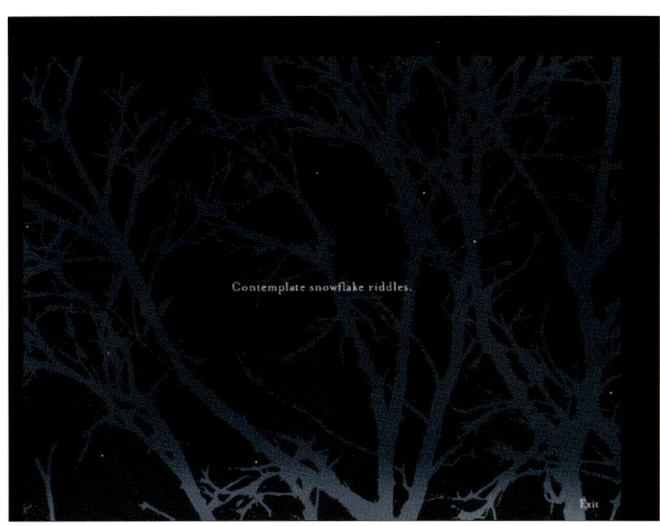

	Merit
AGENCY	Periscope/Minneapolis
CLIENT	Periscope
ART DIRECTORS	Julie DuBois, Chris Cortilet
WRITER	Katerina Martchouk
DIGITAL ARTIST	Mike Schweigert
PRODUCER	Susan Ramlet
MULTIMEDIA	Justin Bakse
PROGRAMMERS	Justin Bakse, Stan Sisneros
CREATIVE DIRECTOR	Chris Cortilet
	ID 00 0194 N

{SELF-PROMOTION/ CD-ROM}

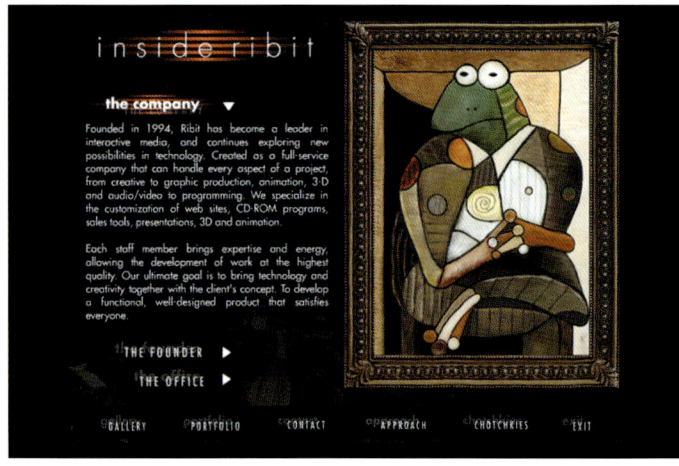

Merit

AGENCY	Ribit Productions, Inc./Dallas
CLIENT	Ribit Productions, Inc.
ART DIRECTORS	Sharon Sham, Royce Butler
WRITER	Robin Moss
DIGITAL ARTIST	Sean Wu
MULTIMEDIA	Len Hewes
PROGRAMMER	Jason Landry
CREATIVE DIRECTOR	Robin Moss

ID 00 0195 N

{SELF-PROMOTION/ other digital media}

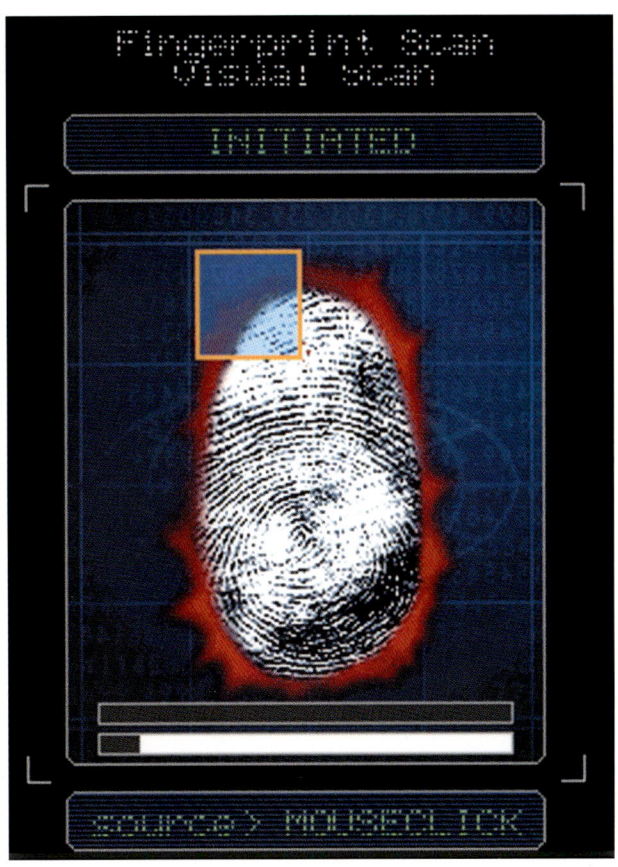

	Merit
AGENCY	OgilvyInteractive/New York
CLIENT	Syndicate
ART DIRECTOR	David Korchin
WRITER	Ken Grobe
DIGITAL ARTIST	Venantius Pinto
PHOTOGRAPHER	Jamie Corl
PRODUCERS	Kate Kehoe, Jamie Corl
PROGRAMMER	Mikhail Goldgaber
CREATIVE DIRECTOR	David Korchin
URL	http://199.229.12.135/awards2000/syndicate.html
ID	00 0196 N

{ NONPROFIT ORGANIZATIONS/ web sites }

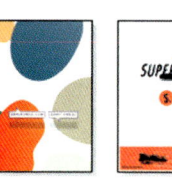
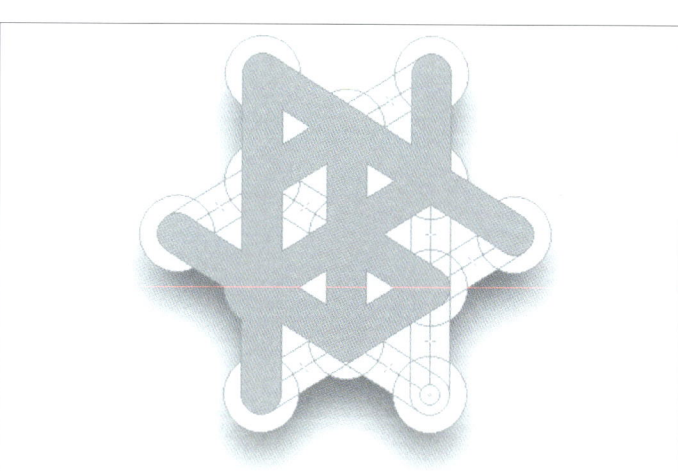

Merit

AGENCY	beaufonts/UK
CLIENT	beaufonts
ART DIRECTOR	Ian Mitchell
WRITER	Ian Mitchell
PHOTOGRAPHER	HC
PRODUCER	HC
MULTIMEDIA	Cecilia Garside, David Hand, Jonathon Hitchen, Jon Humphreys, Ian Mitchell, Paul Musgrave, Oliver Payne, Simon Vaughan
URL	www.beaufonts.com

ID 00 0197 N

{NONPROFIT ORGANIZATIONS/ web sites}

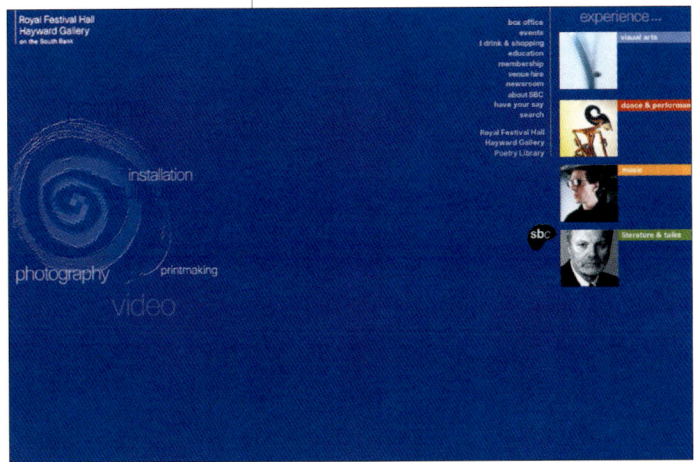

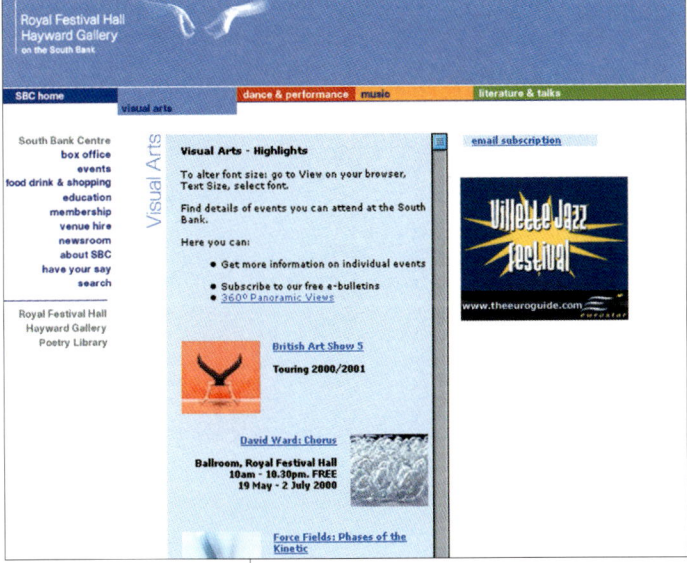
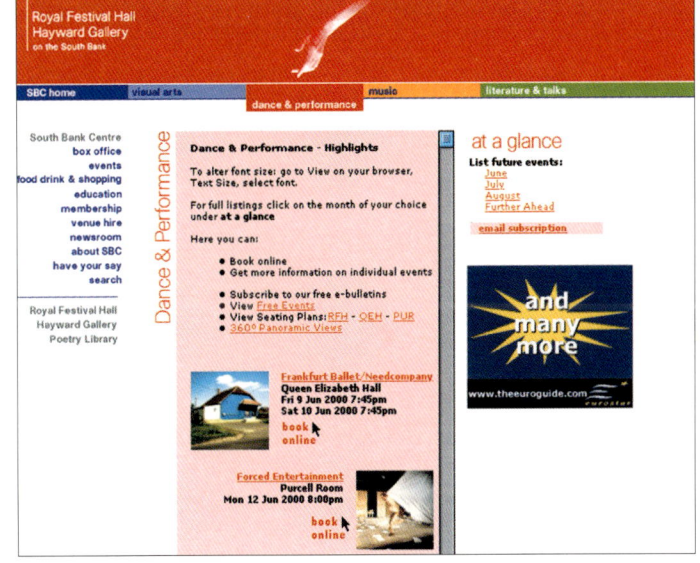

Merit

AGENCY	SYZYGY Ltd/London
CLIENT	South Bank Centre
ART DIRECTOR	Anna-Lisa Schoenecker
WRITER	SBC
DIGITAL ARTISTS	Anna-Lisa Schoenecker, Ali Hutchinson
PHOTOGRAPHER	Richard Haughton
PRODUCER	Marese McGrath
MULTIMEDIA	Dominic Murphy, Richard Guest
PROGRAMMER	John Hunter
CREATIVE DIRECTOR	James Closs
URL	www.sbc.org.uk |// ID 00 0198 N

251

{NONPROFIT ORGANIZATIONS/ web sites}

Merit

AGENCY	Zentropy Partners/Hollywood
CLIENT	Walter Kaitz Foundation
ART DIRECTORS	Dan Benderly, Erik Reponen
DIGITAL ARTIST	Angie Tso
PRODUCERS	Lori Chin, Daniel Hale
PROGRAMMER	Mark Briggs
CREATIVE DIRECTOR	Tiago Soromenho-Ramos
URL	www.walterkaitz.org
ID	00 0199 N

{NONPROFIT ORGANIZATIONS/ CD-ROM}

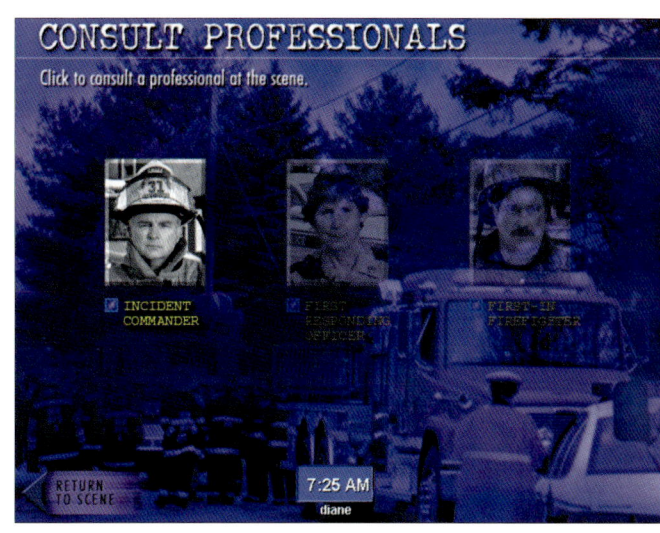
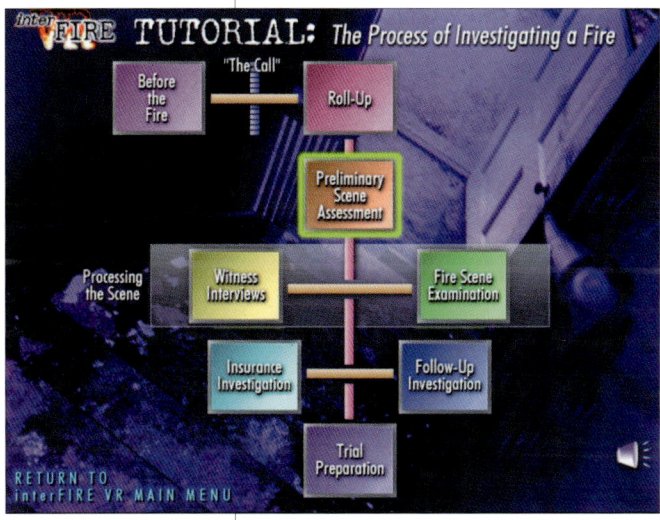
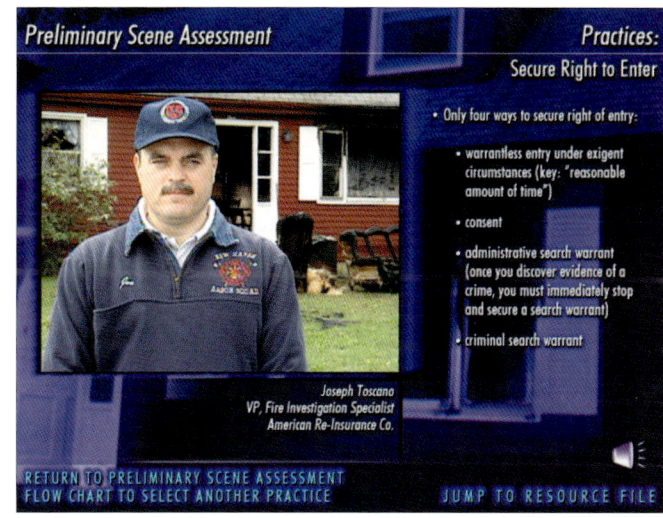

Merit

AGENCY	Stonehouse Media, Incorporated/Princeton
CLIENT	ATF/American Re/NFPA/USFA
ART DIRECTOR	Christine Corbitt
WRITER	Cathy Corbitt
DIGITAL ARTISTS	Christine Corbitt, Brian Dean
PHOTOGRAPHERS	Tony Stewart, Gabe Palacio
PRODUCERS	Rod Ammon, Pat Corbitt
MULTIMEDIA	James Paulus, Debi Hemmerling, Mike Miller
PROGRAMMER	John Mauer
ID	00 0200 N

{COLLEGE COMPETITION/ other digital media}

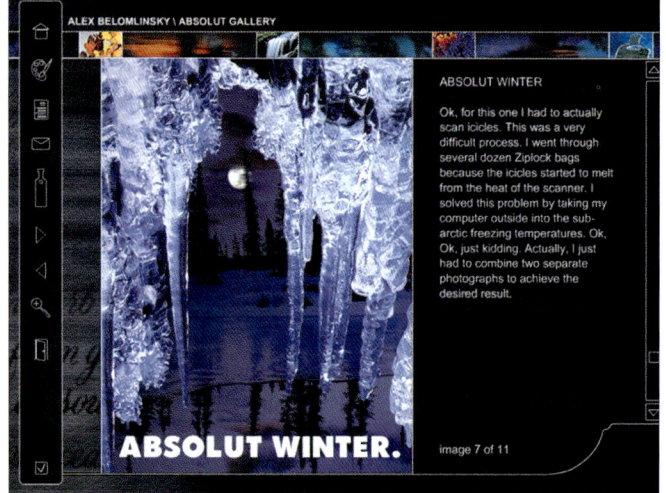
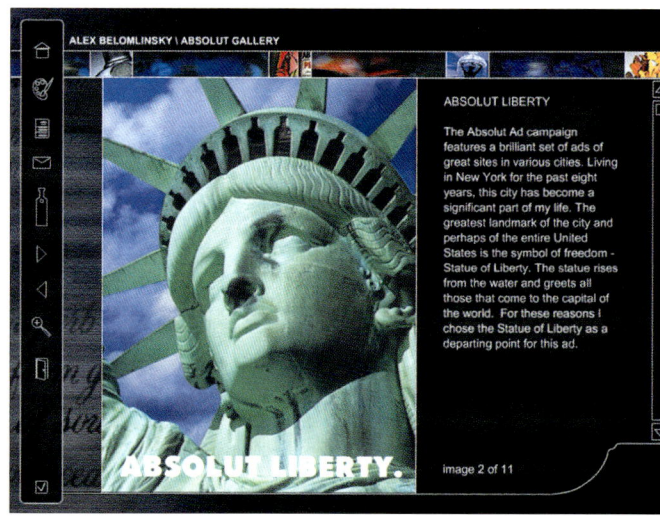
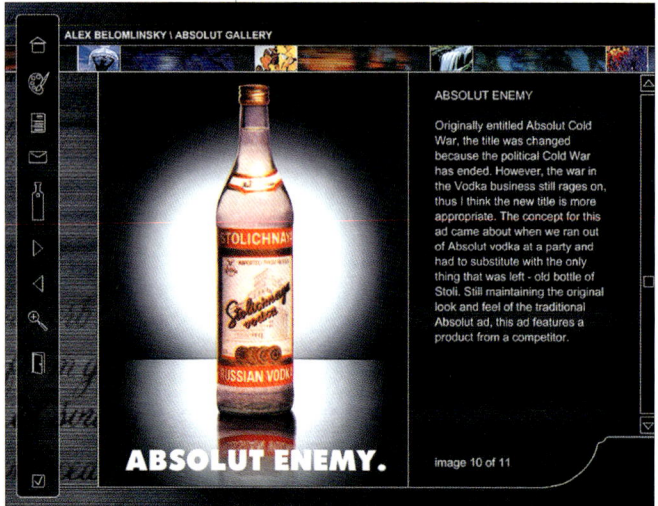
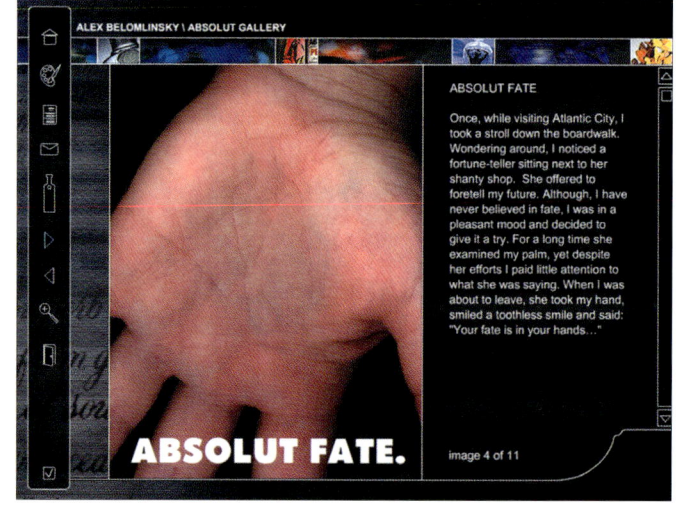

Merit

COLLEGE School of Visual Arts/New York
ART DIRECTOR Alex Belomlinsky
WRITER Paul Katz
DIGITAL ARTISTS Alex Belomlinsky, Eugene Nazarov
PHOTOGRAPHER Alex Belomlinsky
MULTIMEDIA Alex Belomlinsky
PROGRAMMERS Leon Belomlinsky, Larry Ganzman, Alex Belomlinsky
CREATIVE DIRECTOR Alex Belomlinsky
ID 00 0201 N

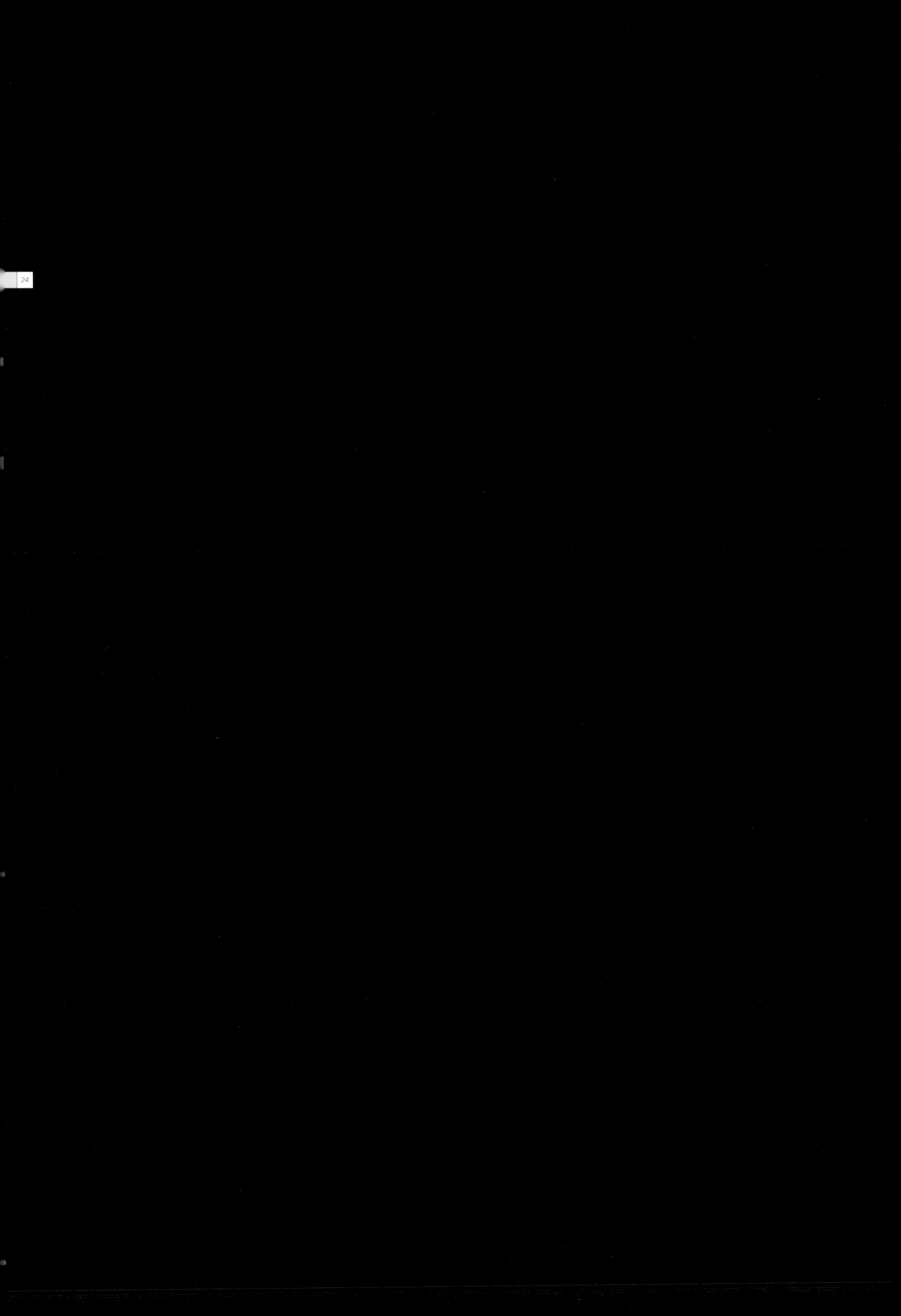

QUIRKY BUT GROUNDED

Want to experience the best in interactive interludes? Ambitious, attractive, open to diversity and excitement. Willing to take risks. Down to earth. Have a raging appetite for adventure.

corporate
profiles

{CORPORATE/ profile}

Cole & Weber | *interactive*

AGENCY Cole & Weber Interactive
address 308 Occidental Avenue South
Seattle, WA 98104
telephone 206-447-9595
fax 206-233-0178
email info@coleweber.net
home page www.coleweber.com

KEY PERSONNEL
Brad Harrington - *Executive Director*
Dave Behn - *Director*
Ed Lisieski - *Associate Creative Director*
Pam Samper - *Client Services*

DELIVERING THE UNEXPECTED
When was the last time an idea or experience bulldozed your preconceived notions? At Cole & Weber we're continually busting out work that leaves an indelible impression. Our integrated approach to planning, advertising, public relations, direct marketing and interactive spawns unexpected ideas that are much bigger than advertising alone. And we've proven the unexpected is effective.

CREATING CHEMISTRY
People intensify their relationships through curiosity, interaction and by fulfilling each other's needs. Cole & Weber Interactive adapts this idea to fuel consumer/brand relationships by providing individuals with personally relevant online experiences that both motivate and intrigue.

DETAILS
year founded 1994
employees 50+

CLIENTS
Nike
betterbricks.com
Outlast Technologies
eVENT Fabrics
Texas Instruments DLP
University of Phoenix Online
Siebel Systems
ImageX
The Bill and Melinda Gates Foundation
Corixa
Intel
Sony

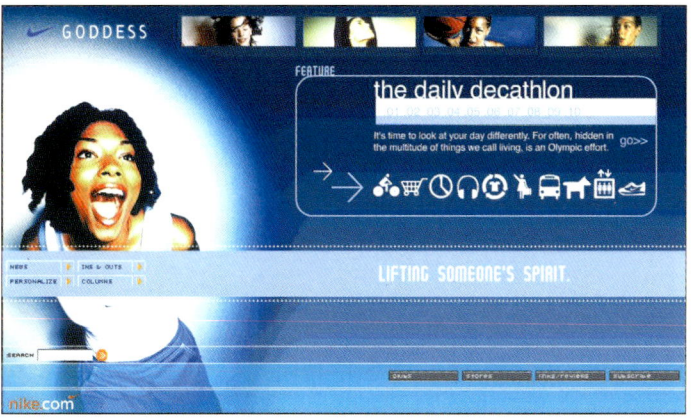

{CORPORATE/ profile}

AGENCY	Tribal DDB Worldwide
address	437 Madison Avenue New York, NY 10022
telephone	212-515-8600
fax	212-515-8660
email	info@tribalddb.com
home page	www.tribalddb.com

KEY PERSONNEL
Matt Freeman - *CEO, North America*
Steven Marrs - *President & Chief Operating Officer, North America*
John Young - *Chief Creative Officer*
Johnny Henricksen - *CEO, Europe*
Jason Goodman - *President & Chief Operating Officer, Europe*

THE VISION
Tribal DDB Worldwide (www.tribalddb.com) was founded on a vision of bringing humanity to the Digital Age with brand and business ideas that stimulate, respect and serve consumers. Born from DDB Worldwide, the most creative advertising agency in the world, Tribal DDB embraces its parent's values of innovation and respect for the individual across all of its consulting, marketing and e-commerce services. Headquartered in New York, Tribal DDB Worldwide includes 21 full service offices spanning 15 countries throughout the Americas, Europe and Asia Pacific. The firm has a worldwide staff of 500.

CLIENTS
Anheuser-Busch
Bristol-Myers Squibb
Clorox
Credit Suisse
ExxonMobil
FTD.com
General Mills
Hasbro
Henkel
Lockheed-Martin
McDonald's
Michelin
Microsoft
PepsiCo
Reuters
Sara Lee
Vodafone
Volkswagen
Universal

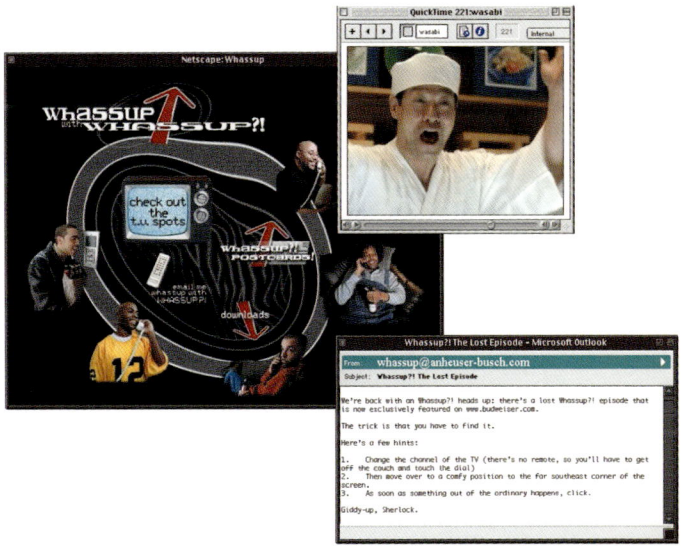

257

{CORPORATE/ profile}

AGENCY	DM9DDB
address	AV. Das Nações Unidas, 12901 35th/36th Floor Torre Norte cep: 04578-000 São Paulo-SP Brazil
telephone	(5511) 5 501-9999
fax	(5511) 5 103-0931
email	mlent@dm9ddb.com.br
home page	www.dm9ddb.com.br
KEY PERSONNEL	Camila Franco, Erh Ray and Sergio Valente - *Chief Executive Officer Creative Directors* Michel Lent Schwartzman - *Head, Interactive Division* Ed Lisieski - *Associate Creative Director*
OVERVIEW	Planning, strategy and creation of integrated, multimedia marketing campaigns.
MISSION	Bring significant results with creative and relevant interactive media work.
SERVICES	Online branding, Media planning, Information architecture and interface design.
AWARDS: 2000	One Show Interactive Gold Pencil - Universo Online
	Elected the 6th most creative new media agency in the world by (IDEA) the International Digital Excellence Association
AWARDS: 1999	Cannes Festival - Cyber Lion
	One Show Interactive Merit Award - Johnson & Johnson
	Art Directors Club - Merit Award
	Advertising Age International Cyberstar
	Cannes Festival - Cyber Lions

DETAILS	
year founded	DM9DDB interactive division established March 1997
clients	Among others: Microsoft AOL Honda Itau Bank Johnson & Johnson Henkel - Loctite Americanas.com Souza Cruz- BAT

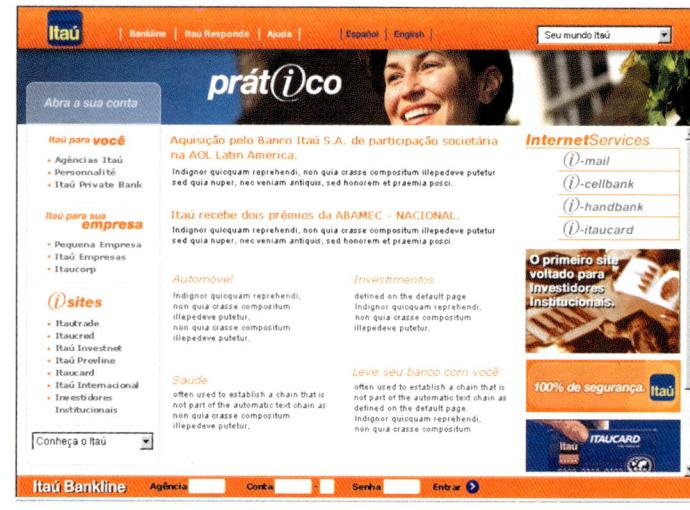

{CORPORATE/ profile}

{CORPORATE/ profile}

EURO RSCG DSW PARTNERS

AGENCY	EURO RSCG DSW Partners
address	4 Triad Center, #400
	Salt Lake City, Utah 84180
telephone	801-364-0919
fax	801-536-7350
home page	www.dsw.com
KEY PERSONNEL	John Dahlin - *Managing Partner*
	Kim Carter - *Partner/Creative Director*
	Peter Klinge - *Parner/Account Services*

PHILOSOPHY — It's true. We're one of the original G2G (Geek-to-Geek) technology agencies. But we recognized early that there was more power in building great brands that rely on technology than simply selling the latest bleeding-edge feature. Because when it comes right down to it, it doesn't matter to us if it's a B2C or a B2B play; if it's not H2H (Human-to-Human), it won't play at all. That's why we try to pry open the human head and heart of the customer in all our work. Whether we're creating the latest multimedia web site for Intel, shooting a TV spot for Ask Jeeves, or launching a new print campaign for Red Hat, we poke and prod and think until we find out what's relevant and real, until we create something that connects in a tangible and visceral way.

CULTURE — DSW. Do Something Wild. It's a mantra for how we think, create and play.

ANCIENT HISTORY — A few G2G success stories: We launched Intel Inside® and made customers care about what microprocessor was inside their PC. We were Netscape's first agency. And we created the "Because It's Your Stuff" campaign for Iomega, which helped average folks to start embracing technology.

DETAILS		
year founded	1986	
employees	230+	
CLIENTS	Alcatel	Knight Ridder
	Ask Jeeves	Minolta-QMS
	CheckFree	Red Hat
	CIDCO	Sales.com
	Commerce One	SUWA
	InFocus	Telocity
	Intel.com	Xigo
	iPIX	Xircom

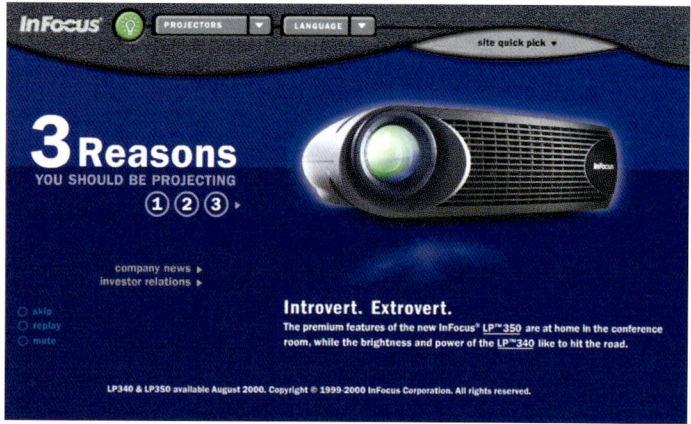

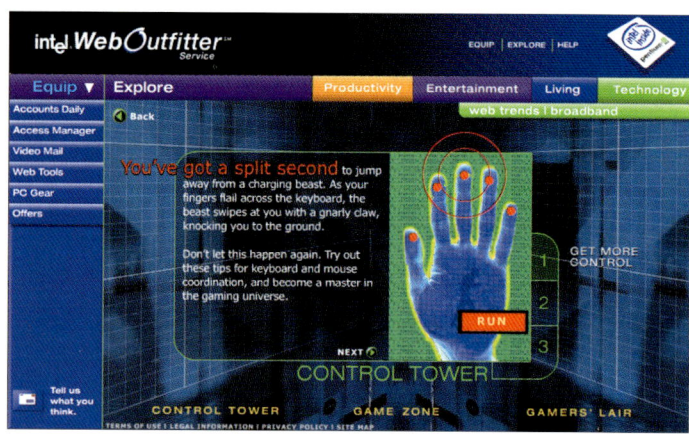

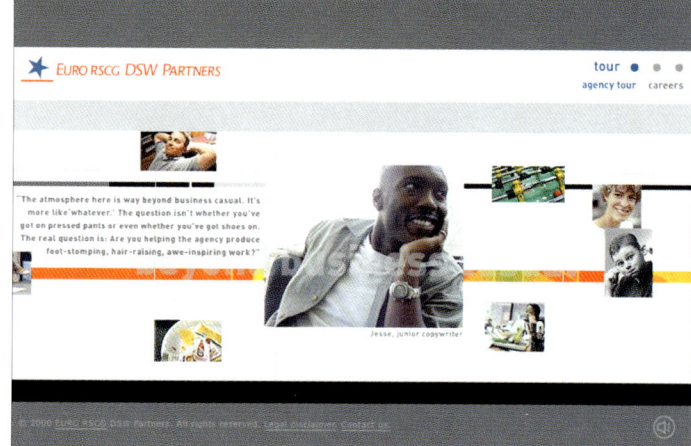

WANT A JOB? We're always looking for talented, driven people who love the web. We need art directors, writers, multimedia designers, account supervisors, technologists, producers, and pretty much anyone else who wants to produce outstanding work for real clients in a great work-and-play environment. Send your samples, URL and/or resume to lynn.kinghorn@dsw.com.

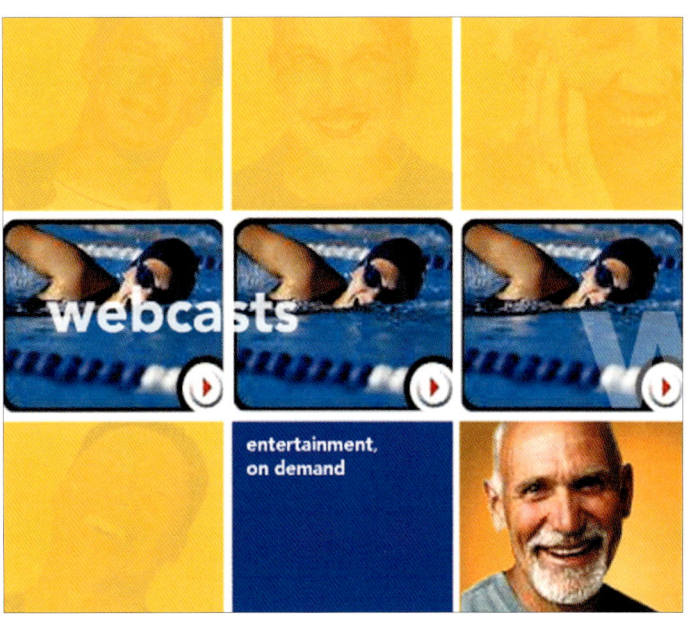

{CORPORATE/ profile}

AGENCY	FCB Worldwide, Inc./Detroit
address	1000 Town Center Drive, Suite 1500
	Southfield, MI 48075
telephone	248-354-5400
fax	248-358-2422
email	bit@detroit.fcb.com
home page	http://webspot.com
KEY PERSONNEL	Mike Vogel - *President*
	Bill Morden - *Chief Creative Officer*
	Sam Ajluni - *Creative Director*
	Peter Arndt - *Interactive Creative Director*
	John Gregory - *Interactive Creative Director*
	Rod Rakic - *Interactive Account Executive*
OVERVIEW	The Detroit office of FCB, formerly Bozell Worldwide, is extraordinarily focused on providing creative solutions to our clients' communication needs, large and small.
PHILOSOPHY	The web is different from all previous mass media in that it facilitates interactivity. We believe that you either use it or lose it.
SERVICES	FCB offers the full range of strategic, brand-focused advertising and media services, including broadcast, print, direct and, of course, award-winning interactive.

CLIENTS	DaimlerChrysler Corporation
	Coleman
	Consumers Energy
	Meritor
	Shop Vac Corporation
	Valassis Communications
INTERACTIVE BRANDS	Chrysler
	Coleman
	Comedy Central
	Jeep®
	Little Caesars
	Shop Vac
	Warner Bros.

{ CORPORATE / profile }

GENEX

AGENCY	Genex
address	10003 Washington Blvd. Los Angeles, CA 90232
telephone	310-736-2000
fax	310-736-2001
email	info@genex.com
home page	www.genex.com
KEY PERSONNEL	Walter Schild - *CEO* David Glaze - *Creative Director* Dalin Clark - *Marketing Director* Kristen Keller - *Human Resources Director*
ENGAGEMENTS	e-business web development & consulting intranet and extranet development networked kiosks broadband wireless online media/advertising
OVERVIEW	Genex is a leading e-business technology firm that helps clients define and build innovative online tools to advance and support their business. Our process combines creative, strategic and engineering expertise in unique ways to deliver measurable, impactful results. Our proven methodology has evolved from years of refinement by our senior staff and clients. As we've grown, this structured process of Discovery, Design, Development and Deployment has helped bring work to market quickly with rock solid reliability and efficiency. Our approach to design is deceptively simple: Focus on the user and brand. This philosophy has led to a wonderfully diverse portfolio and a long and list of prestigious awards. Visit www.genex.com to see the results of our enthusiasm, experience and innovation.

DETAILS	
locations	Atlanta, Denver, Los Angeles
year founded	1995
employees	150
CLIENTS	Acura AlexBlake.com American Honda CitiStreet Dynamic Digital Depth e-Insurance Systems GoldMine Software LifeMasters Supported SelfCare Security First Network Bank Sterling Commerce The Warner Bros. Television Network

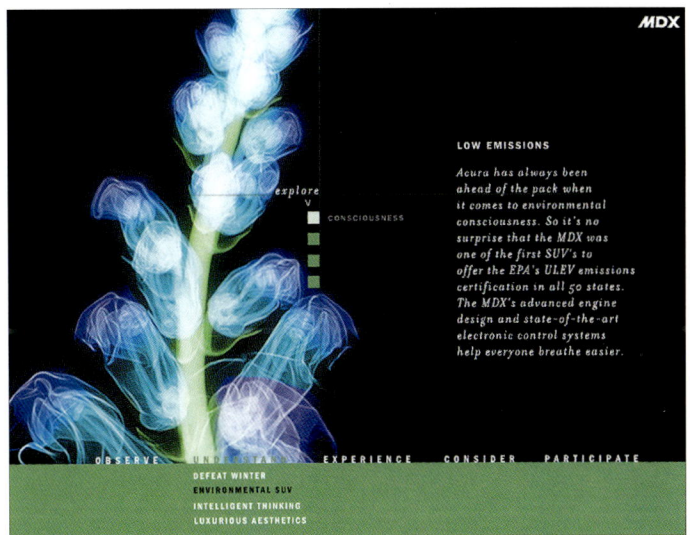

263

{CORPORATE/ profile}

kmpinternet.com
e business architects™

AGENCY Kmpinternet.com
New York City office 245 Park Avenue, 39th Floor
New York, NY 10167
telephone 212-792-4281
fax 212-792-4001
United Kingdom office Regent House, Heaton Lane
Stockport SK4 1BS
England, United Kingdom
telephone + 44 (0)161 429 6590
fax + 44 (0)161 476 0370
email info@kmpinternet.com
home page www.kmpinternet.com

KEY PERSONNEL Bill Daring - *Chairman*
Jon Keefe - *MD*
Jeremy Dent - *Business Development Director*
Nikk Smith - *Technical Director*

SOLUTIONS Kmpinternet.com offers its corporate clients complete e-business solutions, from creative concepts to technical design and online applications. Established in 1994, the company continues to build on its reputation of being at the cutting edge of technological developments in the world of e-business, making web sites and intranets more effective and interactive for clients.

A HOLISTIC APPROACH With offices in London, Manchester, New York and Perth, the company currently employs over 35, working in creative, technical and strategic management disciplines. This combination of creative flair with a strong technical ability and strategic management capabilities enables kmpinternet.com to offer a holistic professional approach to e-business.

CATEGORIES Kmpinternet.com's work can be categorized into four main areas:
1. E-business (commerce, intranets and extranets)
2. E-marketing (adware, multimedia and netmarketing)
3. Portal and community site development
4. Specialist online applications (online learning, telemedicine, telegovernance)

AWARDS The company has developed an online community for the biotechnology industry, www.biofind.com, which receives 5-7 million hits a month, and its multi-award winning spin-off site Patents Place (www.patentplace.com). Another web community created by KMP is the environmental portal Envirospace (www.envirospace.com), which allows the environmental sector to communicate in a magazine format.

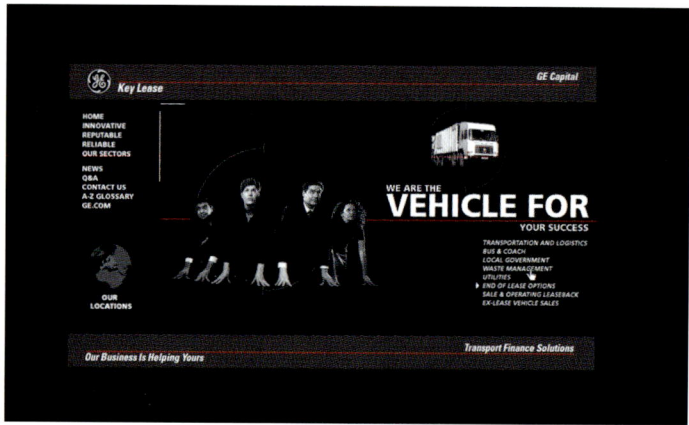

STRATEGIC ALLIANCES	Kmpinternet.com has strategic alliances with Microsoft, Oracle, Macromedia, Blue stone, IBM/Lotus, Infobank and Teamware Group (Fujitsu) and offer a wide range of specialist internet technologies from application server configuration/ development, WAP technology and programming skills for sophisticated internet database integration. For an overview of kmpinternet.com's work visit: www.gekeylease.com and www.manchesterairport.co.uk.
DETAILS	
year founded	1994
employees	30
CLIENTS	GE Capital (US)
	Macromedia (US)
	Manchester Airport
	Ticketline
	Ministry of Sound
	David Halsall International
	Biofind
	Make Headway
	Patents Place
	BankWest (Australia)

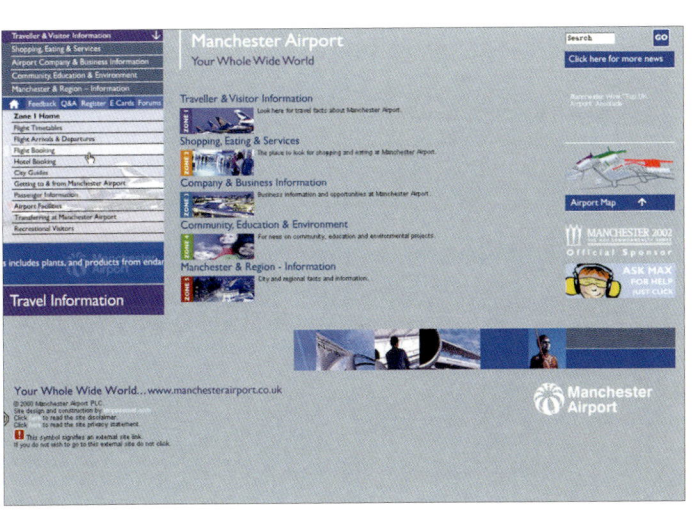

{CORPORATE/ profile}

AGENCY	i-traffic
New York City office	20 Exchange Place, 9th and 10th Floors New York, NY 10005
telephone	212-651-1850
fax	212-651-1851
San Francisco office	China Basin Landing 185 Berry Street, #4807 San Francisco, CA 94107
telephone	415-348-8800
fax	415-348-8812
Chicago office	opening fall 2000
home page	www.i-traffic.com
POSITION	i-traffic is the leading full service advertising agency dedicated to maximizing clients' ROI through interactive channels.
OWNERSHIP	i-traffic, a subsidiary of AGENCY.COM was founded in 1995. i-traffic, referred to as "i-traffic," was acquired by AGENCY.COM in October 1999.
MISSION	We are dedicated to helping our clients maximize customer acquisition, retention, profitable revenue and core brand equities – at optimum ROI.
SERVICES	i-traffic customizes its services around the unique interactive marketing needs of each client, and we measure our performance on quantifiable results, not effort. Services that we provide include:

- Account Management
- Strategic Planning
- Creative (banners, buttons, rich media, e-mail)
- Media planning and buying
- Affiliate Marketing Services
- Strategic alliance negotiations and management
- Campaign performance tracking, reporting and analysis
- Test coordination and optimization of ROI

JOB OPPORTUNITIES	Check out www.i-traffic.com To apply e-mail team@i-traffic.com
CLIENTS	Answer Financial — IMotors British Airways — Incyte Genomics Discover — Nokia Discovery — Sprint First Auction — Staples

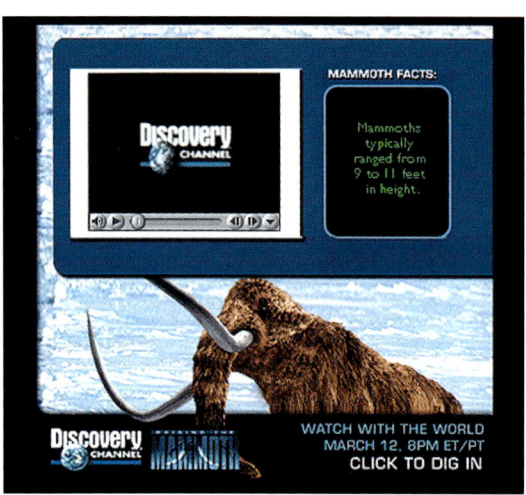
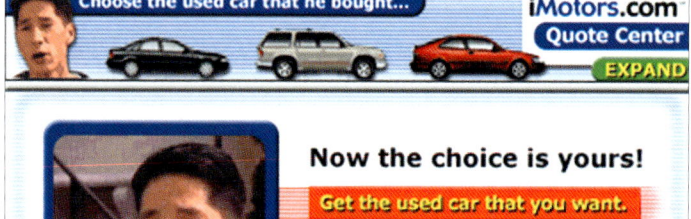

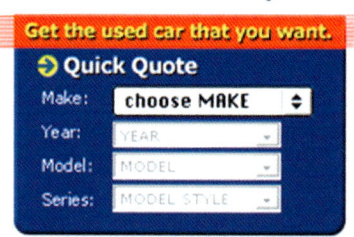

{CORPORATE/ profile}

LEAPNET

AGENCY	Leapnet, Inc.
address	420 W. Huron Chicago, IL 60610
telephone	312-528-2400
fax	312-528-2601
email	info@leapnet.com
home page	www.leapnet.com

KEY PERSONNEL
Frederick A. Smith - *Chairman*
Robert M. Figliulo - *Vice Chairman & CEO*
Stephen J. Tober - *President and COO*
Richard Giuliani - *Chief Creative Officer*
David Hernandez - *Executive Creative Officer*
Matthew Hanson - *Chief Technology Officer*

OVERVIEW
Leapnet, Inc. (Nasdaq: LEAP) is an internet professional services company with a unique balance of creative, strategic e-business consulting, accelerated solution delivery and globalization expertise. Leapnet subsidiaries include Quantum Leap Communications, an internet development and marketing company, and Planet Leap, a globalization company.

SERVICES
Leapnet offers a full spectrum of internet services, from large-scale e-commerce systems to customer loyalty programs and global marketing strategies to dynamic, user-oriented web sites and back-end integration to custom software development. Leapnet goes beyond the traditional offerings of creative, strategy and technology to include a dedicated globalization practice, enabling companies to compete effectively across the divides of language and culture.

DETAILS	
year founded	1993
employees	600
CLIENTS	Adobe
	American Airlines
	Anheuser-Busch
	Apple Computer
	Ernst & Young
	Lincoln National
	Microsoft
	Morningstar
	MSNBC.com
	SAM'S Club
	Starwood Hotels and Resorts
	Sunoco
	Unisys
	Wal-Mart Stores, Inc.
	Williams

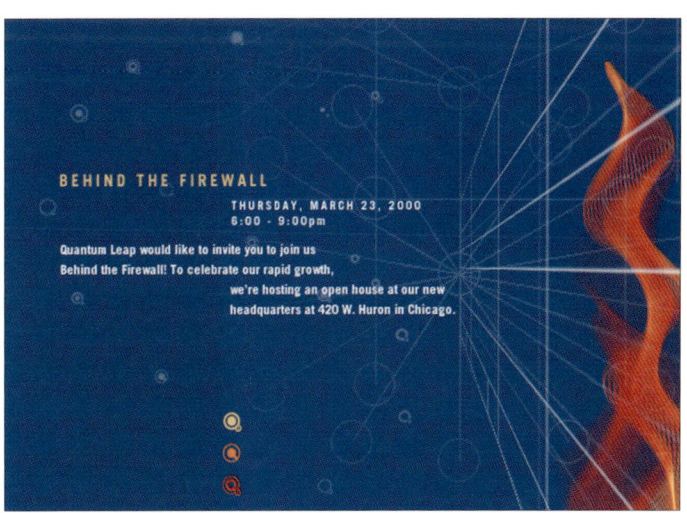

{CORPORATE/ profile}

 MARTIN INTERACTIVE

AGENCY Martin Interactive
the interactive division of The Martin Agency
address One Shockoe Plaza
Richmond, VA 23219
telephone 804-698-8000
fax 804-698-8521
email interact@martininteractive.com
home page www.martininteractive.com
year founded 1994

KEY PERSONNEL Barbara Thornhill Joynes - *Partner*
Christine Branin - *VP, Management Director*
Dave Parrish - *VP, Creative Director*

WHAT WE'RE NOT Interactive companies often strive to be "all things to all people." While end-to-end services are a necessity if an aggressive digital vision is to become reality, Martin Interactive believes that certain parts of the spectrum are more commoditized than others. Namely, implementation. Sure, we've got the internal capabilities and external partnerships to get the work done. But we don't want to be known for having the most programmers, having the largest server configuration or placing technical implementation above the idea.

WHAT WE ARE Our emphasis – as a daily operating philosophy and by reputation – is on innovation. We channel our technical knowledge into determining those business-building ideas that will result in the most added value for our clients. We are a marketing-oriented interactive agency that can take your brand – its essence, values, personality and strengths – and effectively translate that into the digital world. We look at your business goals, and design the web strategy that will bring you the best results. Our commitment to innovation, combined with the creative and technological talent, make the ideas a reality.

WHO WE ARE Each client team is led by an ownership team representing the four cornerstone disciplines of a digital program: strategy, creative, project management and engineering. This ownership team works with the rest of our interactive-dedicated professional staff – account strategists, account managers, media planners and buyers, researchers, analysts, writers, art directors, interactive architects, designers, project managers, web developers and engineers. These in-house resources allow us to provide turn-key digital services, from site development to online marketing programs to e-commerce solutions.

CLIENTS BB&T
Careerbuilder
Charles Schwab
Cityspree
Coca-Cola
Dasani
FMC Agricultural
Gerber
Marriott
Network Solutions
Novartis Consumer Health
Pulsar
Reynolds Metals
Seiko
TV Land
Vertex
Yellow Pages Publishers Association

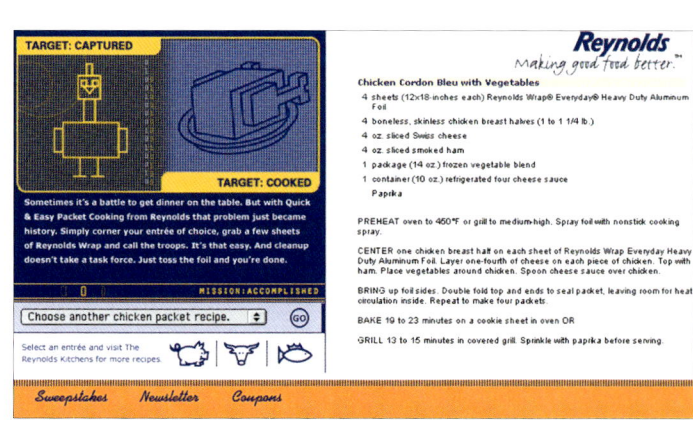

{ CORPORATE/ profile }

NEW YORK ZOOM

AGENCY	New York Zoom, Inc.
address	55 Broad Street, Suite 20A
	New York, NY 10004
telephone	212-968-8908
fax	212-968-8175

KEY PERSONNEL Matthew Waldman - *President and Chief Creative Officer*
Anya Block - *Everything Manager*
Max Baltimore - *Dream Interpreter*
Alain Grossenbacher - *Senior Designer*
Tina Roth - *Designer*

OVERVIEW New York Zoom is a design studio that collaborates with clients to produce award-winning solutions to their creative and strategic challenges.

SERVICES New York Zoom provides creative thinking that both respects and transcends media and platform. Our interactive, print, broadcast and direct mail work has consistently added value to our clients' web sites, identities, videos, print collateral, offline marketing, as well to the brands themselves.

MISSION Our mission is harnessing creative thinking and problem solving to enhance our clients' businesses, through strategy, design and production, in any combination that suits their needs.

DESIGN PHILOSOPHY New York Zoom's design philosophy focuses on education, method and solution. Our award-winning design team rigorously hones in to the most precise expressions of a company's identity, product or message, and we welcome client input in all aspects of our design.

VALUES Like our design philosophy, our values reflect our commitment to focused client collaboration. We work with clients to quickly understand their product and message, and ensure that our process is understood by the client as well. This honesty is critical to our success, since listening to client needs is our business, and educating clients about the solution we're helping them produce is critical to theirs.

DETAILS	
year founded	1997
employees	6
CLIENTS	Condé Nast Publications
	ANA (All Nippon Airlines)
	Ladies' Home Journal Magazine
	SwissAir/Sabena
	Panasonic
	New York Blood Center
	Dentsu
	Seiko Japan

269

{CORPORATE/ profile}

OVENDIGITAL

AGENCY OVEN Digital
address 10 Crosby Street
New York, NY 10013
telephone 212-253-2100
email newbiz@oven.com
homepage www.oven.com

KEY PERSONNEL Henry Bar-Levav - *Founder and CEO*

Leon Stiel - *Chief Strategy Officer*

Steve Cannon - *Chief Technology Officer*

Suzanne Porta - *Director of Market Development*

Mike Quigley - *Director of Business Development*

OVERVIEW OVEN is a leading internet consulting and development company headquartered in New York City. Its mission is to provide both established corporations and aggressive start-ups with a complete, integrated array of strategic consulting, design, and technology services. A privately held company founded in 1996, OVEN employs over 250 internet professionals at its offices in New York, San Francisco, Boston, Pittsburgh, Toronto, London, Paris, Sydney, Hong Kong and Tokyo.

STRATEGY OVEN offers clients concrete strategic solutions for the rapidly changing online environment. Whether by crafting successful revenue models and effective branding strategies or producing thorough market analyses and identifying optimal partners, OVEN provides the wide-ranging expertise its clients need to thrive.

DESIGN OVEN's award-winning creative talent has crafted the most original, stylish and elegant interactive sites on the internet. Cutting through the clutter on the web today, OVEN's designers have crafted sites which are at once useful tools, ergonomic workspaces and compelling, memorable experiences.

TECHNOLOGY The technology experts at OVEN are pioneers in swiftly delivering "end-to-end" solutions. Using the latest back-end tools, they develop the most advanced e-commerce, content management and streaming media systems in the industry on a custom basis. Instead of foisting predefined models onto clients, OVEN addresses current needs while creating extensible platforms for future growth.

AWARDS Ranked number 7 interactive agency in the world and fourth in the US by awards won (*Advertising Age Int'l*, June 2000).

ALLIANCES IBM Corporation
BEA Systems
Sun Microsystems
Cisco Systems
Macromedia
Art Technology Group
RealNetworks
TogetherSoft
Akamai Technologies
Idiom

CLIENTS Tiffany & Co.
Itochu International
SkySports
eCountries
Quixi
Shubert Archive
iNEXTV
Digital Club Network
Hookt
Sullivan & Cromwell
Silicon Alley Reporter
MoMA
HarperCollins

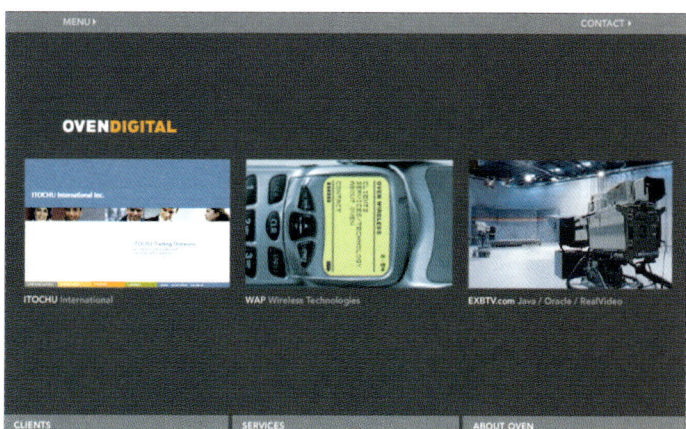

{CORPORATE/ profile}

Architects for the
New Economy

AGENCY	Sapient
address	One Memorial Drive Cambridge, MA 02142
telephone	617-621-0200
fax	617-621-1300
email	info@sapient.com
home page	www.sapient.com

KEY PERSONNEL

Jerry A. Greenberg -
*Co-Chairman of the Board of Directors,
Co-Chief Executive Officer*

J. Stuart Moore -
*Co-Chairman of the Board of Directors,
Co-Chief Executive Officer*

Edward G. Goldfinger -
Chief Financial Officer

Clement Mok -
Chief Creative Officer

Rick E. Robinson -
Chief Experience Officer

Merle Sprinzen -
Chief Marketing Officer

OVERVIEW Sapient is a leading e-services consultancy that helps its clients discover and harness the competitive advantages that are possible in an increasingly digital, networked world.

SERVICES Sapient's approach is team-based; teams begin with the client, and include our industry and subject matter experts, along with leaders in integrated strategy, integrated engagement leadership, technology, creative, and experience modeling disciplines. Team in place, we then follow through with an approach honed over years and projects: Our One Team Approach — a unified methodology that melds the expertise of our subject matter experts with the experience of our industry leaders and disciplines to deliver unparalleled strategy and implementation.

DETAILS Founded in 1991, Sapient now employs 3,200 people in offices in Atlanta, Austin, Cambridge (US), Chicago, Dallas, Denver, Dusseldorf, Houston, London, Los Angeles, Milan, Minneapolis, Munich, New Delhi, New York, San Francisco, Sydney, Tokyo and Washington, D.C.

Sapient is included in the Standard & Poor's (S&P) 500 Index.

CLIENTS
Adobe
United
Hewlett-Packard
Hallmark
Nordstrom

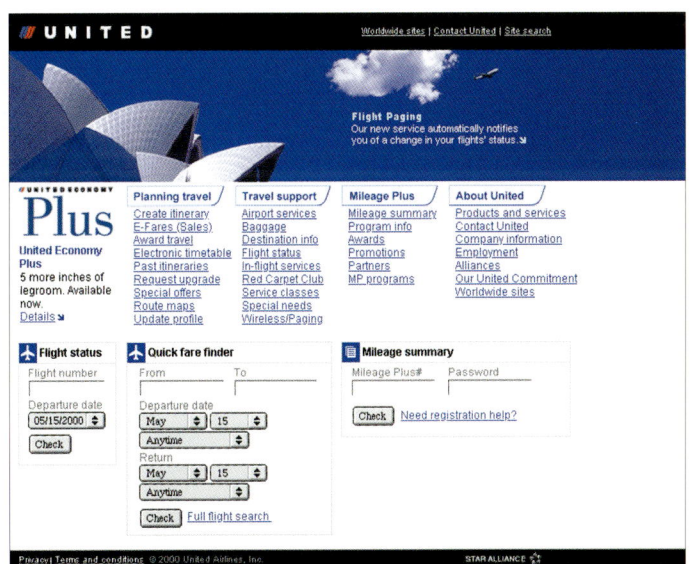

{CORPORATE/ profile}

(zentropy : partners)

AGENCY	Zentropy Partners
address	6600 Lexington Avenue Hollywood, CA 90038
telephone	323-993-9800
fax	323-993-9818
e-Mail	info@zentropypartners.com
URL	www.zentropypartners.com

KEY PERSONNEL

John Connors - *CEO*

Ryan Magnussen - *President*

Michael Tey - *President US*

Tiago Soromenho Ramos & John Wolfarth - *Regional Creative Directors*

CREATIVE DIRECTORS

North America — Art Bradshaw, Bob Powers, Katie Rogin, Carlos Garavito

Europe — Mathew Mayes, Mark Sargent, Helene Varchavsky

South America — Mauricio Pommella

New Business Directors — Eric Bragg, Steven Voci, Matt Azar

OUR COMPANY

Headquartered in Cambridge, Massachusetts, with an additional 14 offices in North America, South America, and Europe, Zentropy Partners works with national and global Fortune1000 and dot-com companies to conceive, build and market digital businesses.

OUR SERVICES

Our services include digital business consulting, customer relationship management, emerging technology research & development, Web site development, and online marketing.

OUR CLIENTS

Some of our notable clients include General Motors, Microsoft, Nautica Brands, Unilever, Brooks Brothers, The Coca-Cola Company, PricewaterhouseCoopers and Reebok International.

OUR PEOPLE

Our people are our most valued asset. From the Director of Technology with a Masters degree in English literature to the Engagement Manager with a curatorial background in photography to the Project Manager who edited children's books, our people are as diverse as the clients and varied disciplines that make up our world.

CREATIVITY

How We Think:

A design philosophy cannot easily be expressed in words, especially in light of the paradigmatic shifts in the new media space. But it is possible to illustrate some of the principles we believe in. We call these principles the ZP Manifesto. These beliefs inform our thinking, our designs, our ideas. Of course, as with all principles or rules, they are meant to be broken.

ZP MANIFESTO | 10 Principles

I. Be functional, yet original.
II. Deconstruct, but instruct.
III. Destroy work; strive for something better.
IV. Merge with the flow. Add something. Assume nothing.
V. When you walk, things move toward you.
VI. Wow. Wow. Wow.
VII. If you make mistakes, make big mistakes.
VIII. When pressure is applied, breathe first. Think second. React third.
IX. There is absolute beauty in experiment.
X. Trust your instincts. Believe. Try. Focus.

A FEW GOOD MEN AND WOMEN

Our eyes and ears are attuned to the marketplace for the most vital resource a creative company needs for survival: the human resource. Exceptional talent is hard to find. And even harder to hire. If Zentropy Partners seems like the kind of place for you, then visit our Web site at www.zentropypartners.com or e-Mail our Director of Recruitment, Mark Hoinacki, at mhoinacki@zentropypartners.com, for employment opportunities.

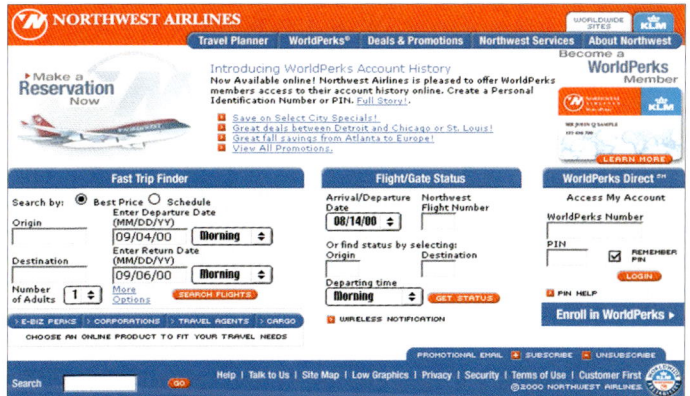

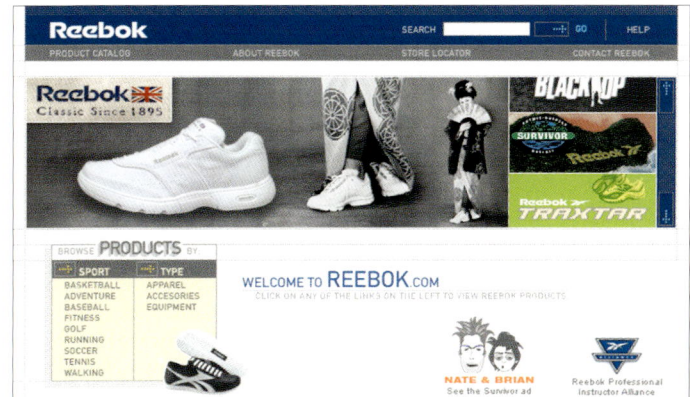

WEB HEADS

Creative-minded people needed to be inspired by the world's greatest new-media advertising. Applicants must be willing to sift through 200 superbly designed and executed Web sites, banners, and CD-ROMS as chosen by 29 top creative directors. Acute appreciation of exquisitely crafted copy and cutting-edge graphic design a must. Familiarity with a pencil a plus but not required. Inquire within.

index

{INDEX/ agency}

Ad Planet Kinetic Interactive/Singapore 30, 38, 205
adidas GMS-Creative/Portland 173
Agenciaclick/São Paulo 5, 137
AGENCY.COM/London 82
AGENCY.COM/New York 147, 209
agi business media productions GmbH/Stuttgart 210
Altrec.com/Bellevue 86, 229
Anderson & Lembke/San Francisco 146
Aoi Advertising/Tokyo 183
Arnold Communications/Boston 14, 70, 184
Art and Culture/San Francisco 230
Bates Interactive/London 104, 223
BBDO Interactive/Duesseldorf 96
Beaufonts/UK 236, 250
Biggs/Gilmore/Kalamazoo 58, 206
Blue Hypermedia/New York 219
Cole & Weber/Seattle 185, 224
Cossette Interactive/Toronto 237
Critical Mass Inc./Calgary 116, 117, 163, 164
DDB Digital/Chicago 119, 138, 165, 166
DDB Digital/New York 118
Deepend/London 32, 44, 62, 186, 187
Dennis Interactive/New York 48, 167, 168
Digital Ambush/New York 174
Digitas/Boston 76
DM9 DDB Publicidade/São Paulo 6, 120, 121, 169
DoubleYou/Barcelona 88, 188
Duffy Design/Minneapolis 74, 148, 176, 189, 225, 238
Duffy/New York 175
Elephant Seven/Hamburg 42, 54, 56, 215
EURO RSCG DSW Partners/Salt Lake City 24, 26, 28, 122, 139, 181, 190
EURO RSCG Partnership/North Sydney 7, 123, 124, 125
FCB Worldwide/Southfield 2, 4, 126, 149, 150, 151
Fork Unstable Media/Hamburg 50
Freestyle Interactive/San Francisco 3, 127, 128
Fuse Inc./Laguna Beach 245
Genex/Los Angeles 18
Gr8, LLC/Baltimore 211, 212
Heavy Industry/New York 239
HEBE. Werbung & Design/Leonberg 240
Herraiz Soto & Co./Barcelona 241
hillmancurtis.com/New York 152, 153, 191
Hyperinteractive/London 129
Hyperlink/London 192
i-traffic.com/San Francisco 154
Icon Nicholson/New York 100, 106
Intel/Santa Clara 193
Jeff Benjamin/San Francisco 130, 140
kmp internet solutions/Stockport 242
KPE/New York 231
Laurel Marketing and Design/Laurel 246
Leo Burnett/Singapore 110
Leo Burnett/Sydney 226
Lightspeed Studios, Inc./Portland 207

Lot 21 Interactive Advertising/San Francisco 208
Luminant Worldwide/New York 131, 170, 194
marchFIRST/Salt Lake City 177, 221
marchFirst/San Francisco 195
Margeotes Fertitta + Partners/New York 48
Martin Interactive/Richmond 8
McCann-Erickson Publicidade/São Paulo 196
Media Revolution/Santa Monica 178
Milligan Design/New York 216
Modem Media/Chicago 132
Modem Media/Norwalk 222
Monumental/Atlanta 243
MVBMS/EURO RSCG/New York 227
Neue Digitale/Frankfurt 179
New York Zoom/New York 94, 180
OgilvyInteractive/Cape Town 213
OgilvyInteractive/New York 60, 133, 134, 141, 155, 156, 157, 158, 197, 198, 232, 249
Organic/New York 68, 135, 136, 159, 182
OVEN Digital/New York 78, 80, 102
Oyster Partners/London 12, 160
Periscope/Minneapolis 92, 217, 247
Pivot Design, Inc./Chicago 218
Pop Characters/New York 234
Quantum Leap/Chicago 143, 144
R/GA/New York 46, 98, 199, 200
RAW Interactive/New York 20
Razorfish/London 214
Razorfish/New York 201
Razorfish/San Francisco 244
Red Sky Interactive/San Francisco 84, 235
Renaissance Multimedia/New York 52
Resource/Columbus 34, 40
Ribit Productions, Inc./Dallas 248
Saatchi & Saatchi Los Angeles/Torrance 171
Sapient/San Francisco 36, 64, 66, 102
Scholz & Volkmer/Wiesbaden 16, 90
Second Story/Portland 203
SF Interactive/San Francisco 142
Smith & Jones/West Sand Lake 108
Stonehouse Media, Inc./Princeton 253
SYZYGY Ltd./London 251
Team One Advertising/El Segundo 204
The Chopping Block, Inc./New York 220
tinderbox interactive/Capeto 22
USWeb/CKS/Atlanta 228
Wieden + Kennedy/New York 10
Wieden + Kennedy/Portland 72, 161, 162
Wunderman Cato Johnson/London 172
Zentropy Partners/Hollywood 252
Zentropy Partners/San Francisco 145

{INDEX / art directors}

Acoca, Natalie 14
Ahrens, Meibrit 215
Allen, Jared 26, 28, 139, 181
Armstrong, Simon 172
Arndt, Peter 2, 149
Atkatz, Matthew 158, 198
Baily, Nathan 209
Bartz, Todd 148, 225, 238
Bastyr, Paul 189
Bauer, Joerg 240
Beatty, Sarah 174
Bell, Brandon 167
Belomlinsky, Alex 254
Benderly, Dan 252
Bendheim, Eran 170
Benjamin, Jeff 130, 140
Benno, Masanori 117
Berninger, Matt 106
Bluhm, Paulette 233
Bookidis, Chad 119, 138, 166
Bosse, Bjorn 243
Bourseleth, Anne 4, 126, 149
Bowman, Jason 218
Bradford, Edwin 192
Brinda, Dave 177
Brown, Paul 228
Brown, Gary 190
Bruck, Daymon 155, 156
Bryce, Clint 22
Butler, Royce 248
Cals, Andrea Evora 6, 121, 169
Capeletti, Pedro 120
Capuozzo, Chris 183
Carter, Kimball 24
Chan, Alexandra 102
Chan, Zoe 48
Chang, Sharon 100
Chaytor, James 12
Chichi, Michael 230
Chiu, Kevin 98
Choo, Benjy 38, 205
Chow, Steve 112
Chun, Matthew 20
Claassens, Damian 226
Clairo, Michel 116, 163, 164
Coale, Howard 194
Coe, Dan 34
Colvin, Alan 238
Corbitt, Christine 253
Cortilet, Chris 92, 247
Crawford, Justin 48
Curtis, Hillman 152
de Young, Laura 84, 235

DeChant, Bernie 36, 64
Delichte, Jason 116, 117, 163, 164
Derksen, Todd 185, 224
Devers, Wade 184
Donnelson, Blaine 229
Doyle, Brian 204
Drew Davis, Kevin 10
DuBois, Julie 217, 247
Duffey, Agusta 221
Dutton, John 147
Eggers, Scott 26, 28, 181
Fackrell, Andy 72, 162
Felber, Michael 78, 80
Fjelstrom, Gustaf 177
Flade, Fred 187
Flatt, Kevin 74, 176, 189
Fleming, Brad 206
Foltz, Mark 209
Foster, Linda 58, 206
Frank, Ze 48, 168
Gallardo, Juan 11, 155, 157, 232
Galloway, Bill 172
Gates, Geoffrey 2
Gibson, Nicky 62
Ginsberg, Shane 244
Girardi, Peter 183
Goodale, Todd 141
Gould, Amanda 197
Griffin, Alex 32
Griffin, Brandon 131
Grossenbacher, Alain 94, 180
Habib, Nadim 42
Harper, Barb 222
Harrington, Todd 131
Haworth, Melissa 155
Hebe, Reiner 240
Hegeman, Robert 135
Henkel, Andi 56
Herraiz, Angel 241
Hoang, Dung 24, 190
Hodgin, Robert 14, 70, 184
Honey, Ryan 239
Hudson, Jonathon 134
Jackson, Morton 212
Johnson, Brad 203
Kamei, Kristi 245
Karavil, Lesli 46
Kean, Gabe 86, 229
Kim, Philip 66, 202
Korchin, David 249
Kovalik, Ian 152, 153, 191
Kowalski, James 204
Kreinjobst, Nicolaij 96

{INDEX / art directors}

Kurtz, Sasha 199
Lacava, Vincent 46, 234
Lam, Sean 30, 38, 205
Lam, Vina 154
Lange, Scott 150, 151
Le, Dave 36, 64
Lee, Dahrong 221
Lennon, Vinton 227
Leung, Vivian 48
Leusink, Alan 175
Loder, Dave 82
Long, Tracy 231
Malmstrom, Paul 148
Mamus, John 198
Manassei, Hugo 160
Manekshaw, Katie 226
Marlar, Shanti 227
Marx, Craig 122
Matarazzo, Andre 196
McCarthy, Chip 18
McCoy, Brent 185, 224
McCue, Thomas 132
McGrath, Holly 76
Medhurst, Asa 82
Miller, Aaron 114
Miller, Doug 154
Milligan, Michael 216
Mitchell, Duncan 118
Mitchell, Ian 236, 250
Mitchell, Katie 246
Morgenstern, Allen 165
Muranaka, Jennifer 178
Murray, Elaine 40
Newman, Steve 24
Odendaal, Andries 22
Olson, Dan 225, 238
Pereira, PJ 120
Perrin, Oliver 243
Phillips, Dower 70
Phungjiam, Sida 238
Piera, Blanca 88, 188
Platas, Enoch 86, 229
Ploska, Megan 216
Pompa, John 68, 136, 159, 182
Prieve, Michael 10
Racs, Pam 173
Rasmussen, Robert 72, 161
Reed, Rob 220
Reichard, Peter 16
Reischman, Garrick 34
Reponen, Erik 252
Rickert, Katja 90
Riley, Dan 86

Roeca, Glenn 211, 212
Rogers, Scott Ex 7, 123, 124, 125
Rome, Deanna 171
Roth, Tina 180
Rotkopf, Renee 60
Roven, James 219
Rudasics, Steve 224
Sadinsky, Ruth 108
Schatzberger, Richard 44
Schneider, Matthew 146
Schoenecker, Anna-Lisa 251
Schumm, Cynthia 208
Schybergson, Olof 214
Seitz, Emily 142
Semple, Patrick 104
Sham, Sharon 248
Shick, Nicole 237
Siqueira, Fred 137
Smith, Toni 207
Smith, Kevyn 86
Speer, Lisa 227
Spektor, Jenya 52
Stephens, Damian 213
Stewart, Kate 233
Streek, David 186
Strobl, Nathalie 210
Strong, Jason 176
Tarr, Tony 147
Thomas, Kendall 201
Torres, Martin 170
Trollback, Jakob 200
Tsang, Brian 208
Tsoi, Alison 157
Ucko, Leora 223
Uyloan, Stepahnie 178
Veelo, Edwin 5
Viets, Oliver 54
Vist, Terje 20
Vogt, Michael 56
Wagner, Robbie 8
Waldman, Matthew 94
Whelan, Bill 70
Wild, Julian 165
Wong, Roger 195
Wong, Eddie 110
Wurlf-Roeca, Lisa 211, 212
Wyckoff, Lara 92
Yang 110
Yanitsky, Elizabeth 237
Yoh, Yolanda 133
Zandstra, Joe 82, 147
Zimmer, Auryn 145

{INDEX/ clients}

13th Int'l Ad Creative Week 169
3M 132
Accent Health 135
Action for Aids Singapore 110
adidas 173
adidas International 207
Adobe 36, 64
Adworks 211
Aiwa Sales Singapore 205
Ajato Broad Band 137
Altrec.com 86, 229
American Express 20, 76
Apple Computer 44, 177
Art and Culture 230
Art Directors Club 175
Arthur Andersen 197
ATF/American Re/NFPA/USFA 253
Audi 188
BBDO Interactive 96
beaufonts 236, 250
Bell Cossette 127
BMW 3 Series Coupe 74
BMW of North America 176, 189
British Airways 82
Brooklyn Academy of Music 199
Budweiser 165
Burton Snowboards 34
buyarock.com 220
Calvin Klein 10
Cartoon Network/UK 186
cartoonnetwork.com 234
CDNOW 68, 136, 159, 182
Comedy Central 4, 126, 149, 150
Compaq 118
Computec 145
Concave Scream 30
Conde Nast Publications 180
Converse 184
Cossette Interactive 237
Creative Club of Altanta 228
Daimler Chrysler Corp. 151
DaimlerChrysler AG/Stuttgart 54
Della 142
Design Museum 187
Digital Club Network "DCN" 80
Discovery Communications Inc. 46
Disney Interactive 154
DoubleYou 88
Douglas Elliman 219
Drug Free America 8
Duffy 238
Dupont of Brazil 196
Ebet 123
EDS (Electronic Data Systems) 148, 225

Etranslate 128
Excite 124, 125
Express 40
Focal Communications Corporation 218
FT.com 62
Fuse, Inc. 245
General Motors of Brazil 5
Goldfish 192
Gr8 212
Gryphon 213
HBO 167
Heavy Industry 239
HEBE 240
Herman Miller 18
Herraiz Soto 241
Hewlett Packard 223
Home Communications - Ericsson 172
Hookt 78
IBM 11, 60, 141, 155, 156, 232
IBM Personal Systems Group 222
Icon Nicholson 100
iNEXTV 233
Intel 24, 152, 190
iomega 26, 28, 139, 181
Jaguar North America 198
K2 Skis 185
Kay's Flowers 130, 140
Kellogg Australia 226
kmpinternet.com 242
Kodak 203
KPE 231
Levi Strauss & Co. 195
Levi Strauss Germany 42
Lexus 204
Lipton 147
Little Caesars Enterprise, Inc. 2
LMD 246
Loctite 120
Lotus Development Corporation 157
Lufthansa Systems Network 50
Margeotes Fertitta + Partners 48
Maybelline/Maybelline 5 Contest 170
MCY Music World, Inc. 153
Melvo Vertriebsgesellschaft GmbH 210
Mercedes-Benz USA 116, 117, 163, 164
Michael Conrad/Leo Burnett for Siemens 179
Michigan Fresh Vegetable Council 58
Microsoft Encarta 143, 144
Ministry of Health 121
Miramax Films 168
Monumental 243
Morla Design 244
Motorola 209
MSN Gaming Zone 146

{INDEX/ clients}

MTV Networks 174
NatWest 214
Net Radio 217
New Balance Athletic Shoe, Inc. 227
New York Zoom 94
Nike 72, 84, 161, 162, 235
ONDCP (Office of National Drug Control Policy) 158
Orange 7
Palm Computing 208
Periscope 92, 247
Pestbusters 38
PhotoDisc Inc. 129
Qpass 224
Quba Werbeagentur, Thomas Querfurth 56
R/GA 98
Renaissance Multimedia 52
Ribit Productions, Inc. 248
Rockstar Games 12
Scholz & Volkmer 90
Sea Ray Boats 206
Sears 133, 134
Showtime 131
Shubert Archive 102
Siemens 216
Sonic Net 3
South Bank Centre 251
StorageTek 122
Syndicate 249
Take Two Interactive 160
The Association of Marketers 22
The Diamond Information Center 194
The Feed Room 191
The Metropolitan Museum of Art 106
The Van Gogh Museum/Amsterdam 200
Timberland 221
Toyota 171
Try Group 183
TWBA Chiat/Day 178
United Airlines 66, 202
Universal Pictures 119, 138, 166
Uol-Universo Online 6
USM U. Schaerer Söhne AG 16
Vassar Brothers Hospital 108
Viaduct 32
Volkswagen of America, Inc. 14, 70
Walter Kaitz Foundation 252
Warchild 104
Warner Home Video GmbH 215
Whitney/Intel 201

{INDEX/ colleges}

School of Visual Arts/New York 112, 254
Southern Illinois University/Carbondale 114

{INDEX/ creative directors}

Abbett, Jeremy 50
Ahrens, Meibrit 215
Ajluni, Sam 2, 4, 126, 149, 150,151
Alber, Travis 114
Apostolou, Paul 42, 54, 56
Arndt, Peter 2, 4, 126, 149, 150, 151
Arom, Mach 158, 197, 198
Bajec, Dennis 34
Barcelona, Christopher 40
Bauer, Joerg 240
Beaufonts 236
Beeby, Tom 222
Belomlinsky, Alex 254
Benjamin, Jeff 130, 140
Brunelle, Tim 14
Bryce, Clint 22
Buchanan, Cathryn 86, 229
Bute, Eric 26, 28, 139, 181
Caldwell, Bonnie 122
Carson, David 239
Carter, Kimball 24, 190
Cassey, Kade 207
Chan, Zoe 167
Chang, Sharon 100
Chase, Oonie 76
Choo, Benjy 38, 205
Clos, James 251
Convery, Michael 237
Cordner, Tom 204
Cortilet, Chris 217, 247
Cox, Ernie 58, 206
Crowder, Daniel 243
Curtis, Hillman 152, 153, 191
Czescher, Olaf 179
Daws, Mark 242
Dear, Joe 223
Drust, Stefan 245
Duffy, Joe 148, 176, 189, 225, 238
Epstein, Brad 154
Fleisher, Audrey 11, 60, 141, 155, 156, 157, 232
Foltz, Mark 209
Furukawa, Hideaki 183
Gebara, Bob 196
Gibbons, Kirk 235
Girardi, Peter 183
Glaze, David 18
Goldstein, Bill 20
Gragnano, Alison 48
Green, Doug 146
Gregory, John 2, 4, 126, 149, 150, 151
Haldeman, Brock 218
Heard, Bill 76
Hebe, Reiner 240

Herraiz, Angel 241
Hicks, Steve 118
Hin, Tay Guan 110
Hladecek, Joel 235
Hodgin, Robert 184
Howell, Mark 165
Jackson, Morton 211, 212
Jacobs, Ari 78, 80, 102
Jensen, Lance 70
Johnson, Brad 203
Johnson, Margo 143, 144
Klein, Ron 224
Knoll, Greg 48, 167, 168
Korchin, David 133, 134, 249
Kurzer, Robin 119, 138, 166
Lacava, Vincent 234
Lafia, Marc 230
Lam, Sean 30, 38, 205
Lantz, Frank 46, 199, 200
Lawner, Ron 14, 70
Lisieski, Ed 185, 224
Locke, Linda 110
Loyola, Jef 146
Mager, Scott 147
Manassei, Hugo 12, 160
Marcou, Yannis 192
Marrelli, Charles 132
Matarazzo, Andre 196
Mayeur, Gabrielle 204
Mellor, Richard 129
Milligan, Michael 216
Mills, Graham 172
Morden, Bill 151
Morla, Jennifer 244
Moss, Robin 248
Needham, Chris 147
Newman, Steve 24, 190
Nolan, Jack 172
Oiwa, Naoto 183
Olsen, Dan 148, 176, 189, 225
Packard, Wells 100
Pafenbach, Alan 14, 70
Pak, Minsoo 228
Parish, David 8
Parish, Betsy 142
Pereira, PJ 5, 137
Powell, Neil 175
Raith, Tom 143, 144
Ray, Chris 171
Rodgers, Scott Ex 7, 123, 124, 125
Rodriguez, Alexis 20
Sandoz, Steve 72, 161, 162
Sanz, Frédéric 188

{INDEX / creative directors}

Schmidt, Barbara 42, 54, 56
Schobess, Gabi 210
Schwarm, Christian 210
Schybergson, Olof 214
Sheehan, Glen 146
Shipley, Mark 108
Solana, Daniel 88
Soromenho-Ramo, Tiago 252
Soto, Rafa 241
Stephens, Damian
Stokes, Colleen 195
Sugiyama, Kotaro 183
Sykes, Lisa 174
Te Selle, Monique 68, 135, 136, 159, 182
Thompson, Stephen 26, 28, 139, 181
Tortorici, Stephen 68, 135, 136, 159, 182
Van Der Meid, Scott 246
Van Eimeren, Dean 171
Vandegrift, Jim 177
Vennerholm, Greg 34
Vinoly, Paco 208
Waldman, Matthew 180
Waltuch, Lisa 106
Waterfall, Simon 32, 187
Whelan, Bill 14
Yapp, Mike 3, 127, 128
Yim, Jason 178
Zeigler, David 147

{INDEX / digital artists}

@Home 146
Abernethy, Mark 163
Acoca, Natalie 14
Aguas, Allan 145
Alcorn, David 98
Allman, Andy 209
Atkatz, Matthew 158
Austin, Jon 58
Baertsch, Nate 139
Ballas, J.P. 174
Barrios, Nick 157
Bauer, Joerg 240
Beberwyck, Alan 108
Belluardo, Randy 20
Belomlinsky, Alex 254
Berger, Doug 206
Bonkowski, Shmuel 123, 124
Bosse, Bjorn 243
Bourseleth, Anne 149
Brown, Laurie 74, 175, 176, 238
Bullis, Karen 174
Burns, Damian 24
Burns, Ian 178
Camara, Michael 145
Capshaw, Stan 58
Chan, Cindy 226
Chang, Sharon 100
Cheuk, Alisia 84, 235
Cho, Haejin 200
Choo, Benjy 205
Chow, Steve 112
Chuang, Jeff 133, 134
Compton, Sarah 246
Corbitt, Christine 253
Croft, Dan 246
Curtis, Hillman 152, 153, 191
de La Gorce, Nathalie 200
Dean, Brian 253
Delhaut, Michael 10
DragonFly Studios 151
Dulkinys, Amanda 18
Durrant, Scott 122
Erickson, Maria 176
Evans, Brent 26, 28, 181
Fascitelli, Ben 222
Ferguson, Jamie 78
Flade, Fred 187
Foster, Jessica 144
Foxy 186
Freestyle Interactive 4
Gale, Robert 178
Galvez, Jose 60, 134, 197, 198
Garcia, Eliseo 20
Gates, Geoffrey 2
Gehner, Eric 114

{INDEX/ digital artists}

Gibson, Nicky 62
Gobel, Panja 214
Goldstein, Elena 227
Griffin, Alex 32
Hadywibowo, Ivan 205
HC 236
Heapps, Rachel 11, 198
Hegeman, Robert 135
Heinold, Christa 210
Hennessey, Tim 204
Herman, Heidi 182
Hermann, Joel 148, 189, 225
Hodgin, Robert 14, 70, 184
Hogenson, Tracey 74, 176
Humaniz 190
Hutcheson, Jonathan 221
Hutchinson, Ali 251
Jasch, Paul 222
Jenkins, Kara 226
Jensen, Kate 14
Jones, Rus 242
Karavil, Lesli 199
Kellogg, Jennifer 195
Kennedy, Gregory 78
Kilner, Chris 82
Kopytman, Maya 106
Kovalik, Ian 152, 153, 191
Kraus, Mark 14
Kretchmer, Sarah 143
Kurtz, Sasha 199
Lam, Sean 30, 205
Lau, Andrew 125
Lelliott, Anthony 172
Li, Jeff 167
Lightspeed Studios 207
Lippiett, Rick 214
Long, Tracy 231
Loon, Aaron 124
Maier, Jan 240
Maloney, Mark 212
Matarazzo, Andre 196
Matthews, Lawrence 204
McClain, Vander 234
McGuire, Richard 183
Millard, Dennis 26, 28, 181
Misner, Tom 194
Mistry, Rakesh 192
Mittmann, Andrea 50
Moore, Amanda 235
Morrow, David 106
Nack, John 147
Natchek, Janice 230
Nazarov, Eugene 254
Neff, Michael 108
Nelson, Paul 204

Norris, Ali 214, 244
Odendaal, Andries 22
Oleszczul, Jason 40
Onart, Sean 224
One9ine, 72
Ots, Kieran 226
Owens, Matt 162
Owens, Key 246
Paul, Cara 219
Pierce, Russell 245
Pinto, Venantius 249
Ploska, Megan 216
Pompa, John 68, 136, 159
Portman, Jake 12, 160
Rabasa, John 199
Ran, Tom 146
Reed, Rob 220
Rivera, Jose 221
Rogers, Travis 201
Rootlevel 126
Rosenberg, Leon 186
Sato, Mayumi 100, 106
Schatzberger, Richard 44
Schoenecker, Anna-Lisa 251
Schweigert, Mike 247
Simpson, Tom 147
Skidmore 204
Skuratowicz, Dave 177
Soh, Leng 205
Sonley, Paul 214
Spangler, Andy 211, 212
Stephens, Damian 213
Stern, Pat 199
Strobl, Nathalie 210
Szypula, Paul 168
Tarver, Phil 104
Thomas, Kendall 201
Thompson, Dave 189
Tso, Angie 252
Ucko, Leora 223
Van Meter, Trevor 100
Van Norden, Marc 14
Veelo, Edwin 5
Velez, Victor 60
Vit, Armin 228
Wagner, Robbie 8
Ward, Sam 203
Warner, Steve 26, 28, 181
Watts, Matt 104
Wu, Sean 248
Yin, Wilson 18
Yonker, Jeff 206
Young, Dustin 147
Zimmer, Auryn 145

{INDEX/ multimedia}

415 Productions, 204
@Home 146
Abrelat, Paul 228
Bakse, Justin 92, 247
Barasch, Mark 20
Bartz, Todd 148, 225
Beckwith, Jason 177
Belomlinsky, Alex 254
Blister Media 234
Borgström, Joakim 188
Brand, Stephen 18
Brown, Laurie 238
Bruchhaeuser, Florian 56
Chin, David 80
Choo, Benjy 205
Clairo, Philippe 116, 117, 163, 164
Cleghorn, Paul 214
Cook, Susan 197
Crowder, Daniel 243
Curtis, Hillman 26, 28, 152, 153, 181
Dennis Interactive 204
DragonFly Studios 2, 4
DuBois, Julie 217
DuCharme, Peter 14, 70
Durrant, Scott 122
Erikson, Christian 74, 176, 189, 238
Fein, Steve 20
Fong, Darin 230
Fox, Kelly 134
Freestyle Interactive 139
Gahlert, Andreas 179
Garside, Cecilia 236, 250
Genco, Chuck 78
Gibson, David 236
Gongsakdi, Tina 231
Grossenbacher, Alain 180
Grove, Brad 147
Groves, Jonathon 184
Guest, Richard 251
Gyro Design 149, 150, 151
Hainsworth, Shawn 231
Hand, David 236, 250
Hemmerling, Debi 253
Hewes, Len 248
Hitchen, Jonathon 236, 250
Hodgin, Robert 14, 70, 184
Hofschneider, Mark 134, 156, 158
Holgate, Colin 183
Huang, Scott 155
Humaniz, 190
Humphreys, Jon 250

Jacobs, Ari 78
Joerg Bauer Design 240
Johnson, Brian 147
Katsuhiko, Iwasaki 183
Kennedy, Gregory 80
Kerr, Randy 229
Keyser, Jeff 161
Knott, Andrew 78
Koch, Ralf-Ingo 215
Kocpsak, Michael 80
Kovalik, Ian 152, 153, 191
Kunau, Tom 189, 238
Kunder, Tom 74
Lam, Sean 205
Lee, Neal 141, 156
Leusink, Alan 175
Levin, Pete 131
Lightspeed Studios 207
Long, Tracy 231
Lyons, Sean 80
Madlon, Paul 233
Manalio, Jamie 174
Matthews, Sue 186
McKenna, Derek 78
McKeown, Gary 117
Miller, Mike 253
Milligan Design 216
Mitchell, Brett 80
Mitchell, Malvika 60, 155, 157, 197, 198, 232
Murphy, Dominic 251
Neill, Ben 70
One9ine 72
One9ine 162
Paulus, James 253
Pittmen, Jackie 8
Poor, Kevin 147
Rootlevel, 126
Sandau, Mark 74, 176, 189, 238
Sano, Akira 183
Shelly, Rob 242
Siqueira, Marcelo 5
Snead, Robin 102
Sweet, Michael 234
Thompsen, Ming 80, 102
Tooze, Paul 22
Trujillo, Drew 212
Valoueva, Valerie 133, 158
Villas-Boas, Rico 196
Weyer, Will 228
Zig 172

{INDEX/ photographers}

Abrelat, Paul 228
AGENCY.COM 82
Allbritton, Randy 224
Archive 217
Barry, David 60
Belomlinsky, Alex 254
Bruchhaeuser, Florian 56
Burbridge, Richard 10
Carlson, Joe 178
Cash, Bill 14, 70
Corl, Jamie 249
Crosby, Celeste 48
Domaine Productions 82
Early, John 171
Gold, Gary 108
Graves, Rick 171
Groves, Jonathon 184
Hainsworth, Shawn 231
Hatt, Dominik 240
Haughton, Richard 251
HC 236, 250
Henkel, Andi 56
Hopkins, Charles 178
Keaton, David 86
Kerr, Randy 229
Koenig, Francis 240
Kovalik, Ian 152, 191
LaFavor, Mark 74, 176, 189
Lekakos, Jodi 147
Lessard, Jerry 86
Lightspeed Studios 207
Lim, Claire 30
Long, Tracy 231
Mullen, Ed 52
Palacio, Gabe 253
Parry, Keith 32
Pawlok, Werner 240
Rau, Stephanie 148
Rausch, Michael 178
Ribeiro, Fabio 137
Ridgeway, Rick 86
Rogers, D. 86
Ruppert, Michael 171
Rusing, Rick 178
Schoenfeld, Michael 24, 190
Schubert, Nils 240
Sedlick Photography 204
Semprini, Romeu 196
Smolka, James 195
Soler, Siscu 241

Stewart, Tony 253
Studio, Geoff 205
The Venice Dream Team 203
Two White Heads 242
Vodukal, Nitten 141
Wakefield, Paul 26, 28, 139, 181
Williams, Gwen 225

{INDEX/ producers}

Aaron, Michael 24, 190
Adams, Don 143, 144
Ahearn, Peter 223
Ahn, Angie 11, 156
Albright, Leslie 60
Ammon, Rod 253
Armstrong, Karen 208
Armstrong, Chloe 123, 124, 125
Askew, Kim 3, 127, 128
Assad, Simon 239
Bain, Jay 146
Barakat, Eli 204
Beeler, Julie 203
Berenbroick, David 197
Block, Anya 94, 180
Blodgett, John 26, 28, 139, 181
Boechat, Jean 5, 137
Bremer, Jennifer 74, 238
Breytburg, Paulina 233
Buchanan, Cathryn 86, 229
Bur, Kathleen 209
Burger, Christia 22
Burhans, Sara 58
Canty, Paul 172
Chamberland, Stepahnie 116, 163, 164
Chambers, Azurae 184
Chaudhry, Homera 152
Chiappa, Jonathon 36, 64
Chin, Lori 252
Choo, Benjy 38, 205
Chung, Sun Sun 221
Clein, Rachel 172
Corbitt, Pat 253
Corl, Jamie 249
Crusan, Lina 217
Curry, Marshall 106
Davis, Bruce 206
Dengerud, Louise 176
Dixon, Judy 224
Droskoski, Jim 147
Drysdale, Clare 157
Dwyer, Pat 60
Escarlate, Alberto 130, 140
Evora Cals, Andrea 120
Farry, Keith 185
Feeley, Jay 132
Felstiner, Laura 237
Fernandez, Lissette 244
Fernandez, Wendy 224
Fernandez, Jose 230
Ferre, Cecile 192

Fish, Jude Raymond 11, 155, 157
Fitzgerald, Gwynne 118
Fogel, Brandi 135, 182
Frum, Christi 68, 136, 159
Gadd, Alex 167, 168
Galera, Francesca 241
Gariti, Elizabeth 133, 134
Gebara, Bob 196
Goldstein, Jon 209
Gongsakdi, Tina 231
Griffee-Petrini, Halle 228
Groome, Harry 220
Groves, Jon 14, 70
Guthrie, Thomas 122
Hainsworth, Shawn 231
Hale, Daniel 252
Hamann, Heidi 56
HC 236, 250
Hearn, Wayman 24, 122
Heettner, Janet 198
Hellard, Ted 116, 163, 164
Helweg, Karen 18
Hirsh, Sabine 96
Holben, Louise 32, 187
Hostler, Tom 44, 62
Hwang, Gene 195
Heavy Industry 11, 60, 156
Jacobs, Ari 80
Jensen, Chris 14
Johnson, Brenden 226
Kady, Nick 141
Kanipe, Darrell 8
Kedrowitsch, Dirk 42, 54
Kehoe, Kate 133, 134, 158, 232, 249
Kitamura, Kumiko 183
Klavon, Bill 138, 119, 166
Kluger, Jack 213
Kmiec, Adam 148
Kovalik, Ian 191
Kovas, Colin 209
Kreisberger, Andine 102
Kropki 196
Krueger, Wendy 233
Lacroix, Leah 117
Lam, Sean 30, 38, 205
Lasday, David 131
Leary, Juliette 147
Lewis, Kim 227
Lightspeed Studios 207
Loder, Dave 82

{INDEX/ producers}

Long, Tracy 231
Lopez, Mailet 52
Marsh, Juilian 160
Martin, Christopher 177
Mayer, Matt 171
McGrath, Marese 251
Meves, Diane 34
Millet, Zeno 6, 121, 169
Milligan Design 216
Mitchell, Brett 78
Moore, Scott 119
Morris, Laura 176
Morse, Alex 78
Mozdziak, Dave 222
Mukae, Emi 178
Murata, Kaori 183
Newman, Josh 222
Norman, Shelly 8
Odell, Ray 18
Orepezza, Carlos 177
Overton, Kym 220
Pascal 36, 64
Peacocke, Helen 186
Peterson, Kore 225
Pezzulo, Jessica 76
Plumlee, Steven 200
Polaine, Andy 214
Pugh, Sarah 246
Ramlet, Susan 92, 247
Randall, Roger 82
Raye, Katie 10, 72, 161, 162
Reichert, Nicole 42
Renshaw, Mark 226
Rivera, Ed 230
Roland, Mindy 48
Rosenberg, Jeremy 60
Scherer, Darleen 220
Schneider, Scott 46, 199
Schobess, Gabi 210
Schwartz, Kristian 195
Shepherd, Jane 104
Shields, Katie 72, 161, 162
Smith, Mark T. 234
Smith, Nikk 242
Smith, Amy 199
Snydal, Jon 84, 235
Starr, Kathleen 2, 4, 126, 149, 150, 151
Stevenson, Stacy 235
Sung, Carol 155, 157
Swantek, Carol 171

Sykes, Lisa 174
Tack, Sara 108
Takahashi, Kenna 145
Thomas, Elaine 10, 72, 161
Thompson, Jan 78, 80
Tipaldo, Vincent 204
Tosetto, Juliano 196
Treichel, Marc 54
Twickler, Sally 147
Twohig, Kelly 165
Urwin, Paul 104
Vine, Shawn 4, 126, 149, 150, 151
Wagner, Sabine 96
Wallace, Kathy 206
Wassmer, Scott 237
Waterkotte, Helga 215
Whelan, Bill 70
Winstanley, Sean 214
Wong, Jeff 201
Woolfrey, Jim 72, 162
Wright, Nicole 123, 124, 125
Zanger, Sarah 189

{INDEX/ programmers}

@Home 146
Adkins, Marc 230
Ali, Suhail 66
Alst, Alan 213
Andryshak, Andrea 233
Angantyr, Mans 227
Austin, Jon 58, 206
Avancine, Thiago 196
Baker, Mac 26, 28,181
Bakse, Justin 92, 247
Baut-Menard, Guillaume 32
Beeler, Julie 203
Belomlinsky, Alex 254
Belomlinsky, Leon 254
Benish, Don 209
Bennet, Jeff 209
Benster, Jim 230
Bisbee, Sam 221
Blankenberg, Jeff 40
Bodily, Mike 245
Bonate, Vitor 5
Bonkowski, Shmuel 7, 123, 124
Borgström, Joakim 88, 188
Borm, Markus 210
Bornand, Andrew 34
Bossen, Margaret 189
Brannigan, Mike 204
Briggs, Mark 252
Bruchhaeuser, Florian 56
Buat-Menard, Guillaume 186
Bucknall, Gabriel 187
Bylinski, Sebastian 48
Caparrós, Xavi 88, 188
Carlson, Bob 74
Catterick, Iain 104
Chen, Tommy 198
Choo, Benjy 38, 205
Chow, Steve 112
Collins, Shawn 36, 64
Crowder, Daniel 243
Curtis, Hillman 153, 191
D3 Signs 110
Dekam, Johnny 108
Dennis Interactive 204
Derksen, Todd 185
Digital Image Design 155
Doelitzsch, Deanna 114
DragonFly Studios 2
Drayer, Aimee 68, 136, 159
Dreessen, Mark 185, 224
Dreier, Josh 134
Duggan, Brian 80

Duke, Heather 74, 189
Durrant, Scott 122
Edmonds, Stephanie 129
Erickson, Christian 176
Evans, Dan 223
Forrestier, Al 66, 202
Forreston, Duncan 213
Fox, Kelly 133
Freestyle Interactive 4, 139
Freudenheim, Tom 199
Futrelle, Genevieve 76
Galera, Francesca 241
Gamelet 142
Gantenbein, David 235
Ganzman, Larry 254
Garcia, Thor 221
Genco, Chuck 102
Gibson, Nicky 62
Ginsberg, Peter 201
Glass, Greg 200
Glenn, Larry 227
Goldgaber, Mikhail 249
Gomez, Federico 180
Gongsakdi, Tina 231
Goodwill, Penny 133
Graham, Rob 132
Grossenbacher, Alan 94
Grossfield, Klokie 80
Groves, Jon 14, 70
Gyro Design 149, 150,151
Hall, Randy 34
Harrington, Dan 84
Hasselblad, Marcus 36, 64
Heinen, Klemens 42
Heller, Alex 147
Hendrickse, Norbert 177
Hodnett, Ron 92, 217
Holgate, Colin 183
Humaniz 190
Hunter, John 251
IVT Interactive Video Technologies 171
Jacobson, Tom 142
Jarry, Jeff 40
Jeffries, Matt 78
Jimenez, Sergio 68, 136, 159,182
Joerg Bauer Design 240
Jones, John 46, 98
Jones, Gaz 242
Jones, Mike 127
Jumat, Alejo 66
Keller, John 74
Kennedy, Patrick 226

{INDEX/ programmers}

Kilner, Chris 82
Klussmeier, Theiss 215
Koch, Ralf-Ingo 54
Kovalik, Ian 191
Kraft, Manfred 16
Kraus, Thorsten 90
Kromm, Heiko 215
Kropki, 196
Kucyi, Eddie 233
Kunau, Tom 238
Lam, Sean 30, 38
Landry, Jason 248
Lee, Gene 36, 64
Lee, Neal 157
Lightspeed Studios 173, 207
Lingingstone-Vale, Nathan 78
Little, Steven 198
LLoyd, Steve 223
Loman, Peter 116, 163, 164
Long, Tracy 231
Macrone, Michael 10
Majerick, Jon 246
Malmquist, Shelly 74
Markson, Alex 212
Marshall, Brent 237
Matarazzo, Andre 196
Mauer, John 253
McCumber, Alex 182
McGeehan, John 141
Mellor, Richard 129
Metcalf, Bob 189
Mhaskar, Mandar 40
Milde, Snorre 214
Milligan Design 216
Miner, Chris 230
Mitchell, Ian 236
Moir, Ben 78
Moore, Jeff 80
Muench, Matthew 204
Murphy, Brendan 18
Nakuda, Daryn 86, 229
Neal, Keith 3, 128
Neilson, Trina 185, 224
Nullzeit 240
O'Meara, Isabel 66, 202
Ocken, Andy 66
One Trick Pony 237
One9ine 72, 162
Packard, Wells 100, 112
Pascal 36, 64
Pepper, Kim 78
Perez, Sandy 134

Phoenix, Chris 48, 167, 168
Piccuirro, Mike 233
Platas, Enoch 86, 229
Plotkin, Bob 157
Prochaska, Drew 80
Pullis, Meg 227
Rajagopolan, Anita 205
Rees, Martyn 214
Riley, Dan 86
Rodriguez, Jose 20
Rokos, Spiro 226
Rootlevel 126
Roven, Crispin 219
Rui, Paal 239
Sandau, Mark 176
Schatzberger, Richard 44
Seiler, Marco 210
Sellers, Eric 233
Shahar, Guy 134
Shankur, Roshan 66
Simonson, Alec 76
Simpson, Tom 147
Sisneros, Stan 217, 247
Slutz, Brian 66
Solomon, Noam 220
Spektor, Jenya 52
Spirn, Dan 244
Stanley, Joel 40
Studt, Jan-Michael 50
Sudharsan, Rangarajan 66
Sun, Wen 167
Tack, Sara 108
Teh, Ron 78
Thompson, Dave 74
Todd, Bennett 78, 80
Tooze, Paul 22
Troiano, Jonathon 36, 64
Valoueva, Valerie 157
Vega, Cesar 78
von Raven, Andreas 42
Von Worley, Steve 3, 128
Vucinic, Dejan 66
Wagner, Robbie 8
Watrous, Tim 24
Webster, Steve 192
Webster, Matt 141
Wells, Jeremiah 66, 202
Williams, Gwen 148, 225, 238
Wint, Andrew 220
Worley, Steve 127
Wurtzel, Jason 106
Yeomans, Sean 174
Yonkers, Jeff 58, 206

{INDEX/ writers}

Alcruz, Melissa 174
Alencar, Mauro 137
Allen, Tom 203
Allen, Jared 152
Bamber, Chrissie 246
Bellamy, Kim 152
Beltran, J.D. 230
Benjamin, Jeff 130, 140
Biunchi, Dan 152
Bookidis, Chad 138
Brown, Gary 190
Brunelle, Tim 14, 70
Butler, Dave 178
Byrne, Keith 221
Carlson, Chuck 74, 225
Chalekian, George 145
Chow, Steve 112
Christie, Trent 226
Claassens, Damian 226
Clarke, Patrick 157
Coffeen, Daniel 230
Condron, Maureen 142
Corbitt, Cathy 253
Creel, Jeff 209
Darmory, Suzanne 141
Deery, Mary Jeane 195
Dent, Jeremy 242
Dikdan, Matt 227
Dixon, Warren 180
Dobrinsky, Alice 144
Doherty, Tim 133, 155, 156
DSW Partners 152
Edelstein, Betsy 170
Edwards, Andrew 52
Egan, Bob 20
Elia, Tom 134
Elliot, R. 18
Elliott, Jim 185, 224
Fallesen, Gary 86
Ford, Brian 72, 161
Gallaro, Elisa 108
Gartsdale, James 82
Gatewood, Chris 235
Gebara, Bob 196
Gelner, William 175
Gessner, Melissa 149
Gold, Debbie 225, 238
Gongsakdi, Tina 231
Gould, Andy 206
Gragnano, Alison 48
Gregory, John 150, 151

Grobe, Ken 158, 249
Hannum, Bruce 217
Harrington, Todd 131
Hebe, Reiner 240
hillmancurtis.com 191
Hirsch, Tony 26, 28, 139, 181
Hofmeyr, Davis 213
Holt, Michael 230
Houser, Dan 12, 160
Iben, Rolf 210
Ife, Walter 220
Ivanovich, Dorothy 66, 202
Ivener, Scott 204
Jenkins, Andrew 173, 207
Jennings, Todd 229
Jensen, Lance 70
Kanipe, Darrell 8
Karlsson, Linus 148
Kaskel, Jay 189
Katz, Paul 254
Katzschke, Stefanie 210
Keenleyside, Ross 172
Kerr, Kim 229
Kerr, Randy 229
Klyne, Michele 38, 205
Koerfers, Nina 54
Kohl, Chris 90
Kurzer, Robin 138, 165
Lam, Sean 30
Lee, Dylan 72, 162
Lee, Michelle 147
Levy, David 11, 232, 155, 157
Ligorner, Dan 68, 136, 159, 182
Long, Tracy 231
Macke, Pat 245
Mair, James 32
Malmont, Paul 234
Martchouk, Katerina 92, 247
Mau, Brant 10
Millet, Zeno 120
Mitchell, Ian 236, 250
Monaco, Greg 197
Mortimer, Scott 7, 123, 124, 125,
Moss, Robin 248
Mun, Ed 204
Murata, Kaori 183
Nasi, Steven B. 146
Odell, Cole 206
Oetzel, Donna 198
Ots, Kieran 226
Pereira, PJ 5, 6, 121, 169

{INDEX/writers}

Perrin, Oliver 243
Pino, Esther 88
Probe, Kathy 20, 76
Reed, Rob 220
Reid, Heather 171
Reisiger, Marcus 56
Richau, Daniel 42
Rossetto, Jader 120
Rotramel-Stipe, Kathy 147
Ryan, Jim 154
Sanz, Frédéric 188
SBC 251
Schade, Paisley 14
Scherer, Darleen 220
Schettini, Alexis 222
Schmiedt, Mareike 16, 90
Shipley, Mark 108
Sicko, Dan 2, 4, 126, 150, 151
Simpson, John 184
Simpson, Naomi 187
Soto, Rafa 241
St. John, Gabe 222
Stark, Russ 74, 176, 189, 238
Stuever, Beth 58
Sturges, Nancy 206
Szubski, Marietta 185
Tamura, Dan 208
Tayman, Louisa 215
Thompson, Nancy 177
Tomlinson, Chris 242
Totten, Joe 26, 28, 139, 181
Tramontana, Skip 119
Tsandes, Ted 122
Tullis, Steve 132
Waldman, Matthew 94
Wall, Stacy 10
Warady, Natalie 183
Ward, Jennifer 24, 190
Webber, Jon 237
Weidner, Mike 228
Wells, Anthony 171
Westcott, Irene 143
Widner, Kathleen 58
Williams, Hal 48
Wong, Eddie 110
Yang, 110
Yaremko, Peter 216
Young, Eric 24, 190
Zasa, Jay 60
Zucker, Susan 135
Zucker, Matthew 197